The Art of Dining

The Art of Dining
A HISTORY OF COOKING & EATING

Sara Paston-Williams

THE NATIONAL TRUST

Distributed by Harry N. Abrams, Inc., Publishers

First published in Great Britain in 1993 by
National Trust Enterprises Limited,
36 Queen Anne's Gate, London SW1H 9AS

Reprinted in 1995

Acknowledgements
The author and publishers would like to thank the following for their kind
permission to use material:

The Dovecote Press Ltd for the excerpt from *A Kingston Lacy Childhood*
by Viola Bankes, Dundalgan Press (W. Tempest) Ltd for the excerpt from
An Old Ulster House by Mina Lenox-Conyngham, Eric Glass Ltd for the
excerpt from *Down the Kitchen Sink* by Beverley Nichols (W.H. Allen
1974), copyright © Beverley Nichols 1974, Victor Gollancz for the
excerpt from *Mistress of Charlecote; The Memoirs of Mary Elizabeth Lucy* by
Alice Fairfax-Lucy, David Higham Associates and Random House UK Ltd
for the excerpt from *Ancestral Voices* by James Lees-Milne published by
Chatto and Windus.

British Library Cataloguing in Publication Data
A catalogue record for this book is available from the British Library.

ISBN 0 7078 0173 7 (The National Trust)

ISBN 0-8109-1940-0 (Abrams)

Distributed in North America by Harry N. Abrams, Incorporated,
New York. A Times Mirror Company

Picture research by Samantha Wyndham

Designed by Newton Engert Partnership

Production management by Bob Towell

Phototypeset in Monotype Lasercomp Plantin 110
by Southern Positives and Negatives (SPAN), Lingfield, Surrey

Produced by Mandarin Offset

Printed in China

Frontispiece: The dining-room at Kedleston, Derbyshire, designed by
Robert Adam in the 1760s. Bacchus, the tutelary deity of the 18th-century
dining-room, is carved on the marble chimney-piece, while the pictures
round the wall celebrate the pleasures of the table. On the sideboards
in the apse are wooden knife-boxes and a magnificent ormulu perfume
burner. A plate-warmer in the form of a Greek vase stands by the
fireplace, and two chestnut roasters, also in the form of Greek vases,
stand on the dining-table.

CONTENTS

Introduction

We may live without poetry, music and art;
We may live without conscience, and live without heart;
We may live without friends; we may live without books;
But civilized man cannot live without cooks.

He may live without books, – what is knowledge but grieving?
He may live without hope, – what is hope but deceiving?
He may live without love, – what is passion but pining?
But where is the man that can live without dining?

Edward Robert Bulwer, Earl of Lytton, *Lucile*, 1860

The late 19th-century kitchen at Cragside, Northumberland. A massive 'Eagle' range by H. Walker & Son and a roasting range and ovens by Dinning & Cooke of Newcastle stand side by side. Meat was roasted by means of a hydraulic jack, operated by the cook from a hole in the floor. A hydraulic dumb-waiter lift links the kitchen with the basement scullery so that heavy cast-iron pots and pans did not have to be carried downstairs by hand.

When I was asked to write this book, the commission seemed perfectly straightforward: provide a history of cooking and eating, tapping into the rich seam of information and examples in the care of the National Trust. But as my publisher and I began to get down to the nitty gritty, so the enormity of the task unfolded.

If the realms of the kitchen and the dining-room are to be examined, it cannot be assumed that the food and drink arrived ready packaged, as if purchased that day from the supermarket. Thus the history of food has to be investigated too, bringing with it diet, nutrition, religious attitudes, agricultural and economic history, and even specific historical events, like Columbus' voyage to the Americas, the marriage of Charles II to a princess from Portugal, and the Boston Tea Party. Beyond the realms of the kitchen and the dining-room must be considered the market and the shop, the deer park and the rabbit warren, the dairy and the ice-house, the game larder and the still-room, the confectionery and the buttery, the breakfast-room and the banqueting-house. As Rudyard Kipling said to his daughter Elsie, when he heard she had bought the huge Cambridgeshire mansion of Wimpole Hall, 'Bird, I hope you have not bitten off more than you can chew!'

To try to bring some order into this vast area, we have organised the book into five chapters, arranged chronologically. Although the Trust has in its care Roman buildings like Chedworth Villa in Gloucestershire, it would be impractical and misleading to cover this period. Therefore I have begun the book with the late medieval, early Tudor period and finished it with the Victorian-Edwardian era, seen by many as the swansong of the English country house before the devastation of the First World War.

Each chapter is divided into three. The first part tackles the diffuse subject of the food available. In the medieval and early Tudor chapter, this section is lengthy, to introduce the various parts of the diet – bread, meat, fish, exotic foodstuffs, etc. To avoid tedious repetition, in some chapters I have looked in depth at one topic: for instance, the arrival in Britain of the three beverages, tea, chocolate and coffee finds prominence in the Stuart chapter.

In this first part, I have tried, wherever possible, to describe the diet of all levels of society; in the words of the 19th-century French gastronome Brillat-Savarin 'Tell me what you eat and I will tell you what you are.' This is not always easy, as accounts of the poor man's table are perforce neglected, except when illuminated by the concern of the more fortunate. This has a knock-on effect on the remaining sections of each chapter, where I tend to concentrate on the cooking and eating habits of the wealthier levels of society. The National Trust's records and houses mostly derive from the gentry and the aristocracy, so this is inevitable. I have also used more modest examples like the Tudor Welsh farmhouse of Tŷ Mawr at Wybrant in Gwynedd, the 17th-century yeoman farmer's house at Townend in Cumbria, the 19th-century Apprentice's House at Styal Mill in Cheshire and the modest Edwardian household of the Straw family in Worksop in Nottinghamshire.

In the second section of each chapter, I have concentrated on the kitchen and its companion service rooms. In 1973, when Erddig in North Wales passed to the National Trust, a new departure in the visitor route was introduced at the suggestion of the Architectural Adviser, Gervase Jackson-Stops. Instead of starting the tour of the house by entering the front door and the rooms of state, the visitor was ushered through a series of workyards and service areas that are such a feature of Erddig. This backdoor approach has clearly found favour with visitors, for kitchens, dairies and servants' quarters have proved enduringly popular. Many of the most interesting are featured here, from the medieval kitchens of Bodiam Castle in Sussex and Fountains Abbey in Yorkshire to the 'high-tech' service areas of Cragside in Northumberland and Castle Drogo in Devon. At the end of each 'kitchen' section, I have included historical recipes, first in their original, then modern adaptations so you can try them for yourself.

In the third part of each chapter, I have looked at the eating areas of houses. This section has evolved very much into a history of social manners, from the elaborate ritual of the medieval feast to the almost equally elaborate arrangement of the Victorian formal dinner, not forgetting breakfast, luncheon or nuncheon, teas and suppers. Again, National Trust houses have proved a rich seam: the impressive High Great Chamber of Hardwick Hall and the great Adam dining-room with its 18th-century buffet at Kedleston Hall, both in Derbyshire; the Breakfast Room of the Robartes at Lanhydrock in Cornwall; the Speakers' Parlour at Clandon Park in Surrey, with its detailed Victorian dining book. But there are unexpected surprises, too, like the banqueting houses much beloved by the Tudors and Stuarts, which can be seen at houses like Lacock Abbey in Wiltshire and Hardwick.

A book of this kind cannot be written without the help and support of many people. At the National Trust, I have been given information and advice by a whole host of administrators and other house staff, historic buildings representatives and other individuals; they are sadly too numerous to name, but they know that I am very grateful for their help. I should also like to thank the many archivists in public record offices and librarians all over the country who have provided information, but particularly those from my own local library in Liskeard whose help has been beyond the call of duty. Also, grateful thanks to Mary Mauchline for her information on life in a medieval monastery; to Pam Sambrook for sharing her wide knowledge of the history of

The presentation of fish, from Mrs Beeton's *Book of Household Management*.

The dining-table at Charlecote Park, Warwickshire, set for dessert. The centrepiece is an early Victorian silver palm tree with a serpent and native Indian figures.

brewing; to the food historian Maggie Black for her advice; and to Jacinth Rogers and Sarah Jackson for help with research in Norfolk and Northern Ireland respectively. Thanks also to the economic historian Malcolm Thick and Gervase Jackson-Stops, Architectural Adviser to the National Trust and Oliver Garnett, the guidebook editor, for reading the manuscript and contributing many constructive comments, and to Samantha Wyndham and Pat Eaton who have added so much to the book with their picture research. The 'office' help I have had from Sheila Mortimer, Barbara Cupid and Caroline Worlledge has been tremendous and I shall forever be in Caroline's debt for her understanding and support, as well as her typing – her eyesight will never be the same! The editorial assistance from Marilyn Inglis and Anthony Lambert was invaluable. My two local typists, Berenice Pilcher and Bernadette Yeatman also have my gratitude. But above all, I should like to say a big 'thank you' to my publisher, Margaret Willes, who gave me the opportunity to write the book in the first place, and whose endless patience and encouragement have helped turn it into a reality.

On a more personal note, special thanks must go to my parents, both of whom love cooking and eating, for helping me experiment with some strange ingredients and combinations and last, but certainly not least, to Alan and Peter whose love and unwavering belief in me have spurred me on.

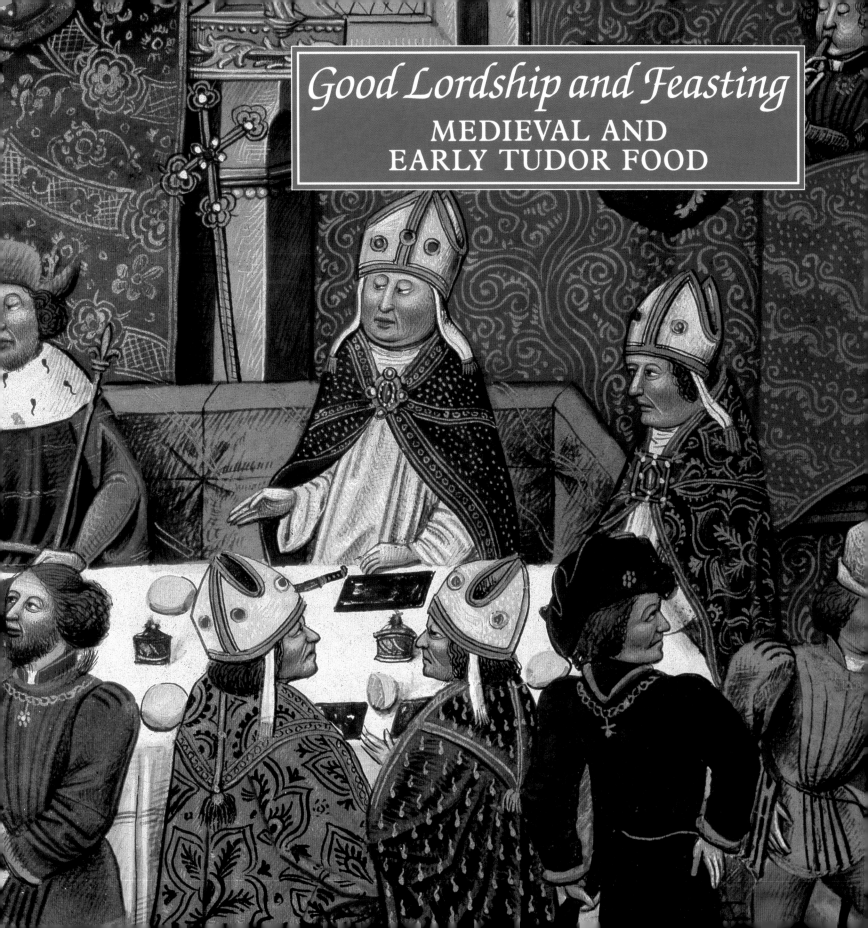

Good Lordship and Feasting

MEDIEVAL AND EARLY TUDOR FOOD

Good Lordship and Feasting

His bread, his ale were finest of the fine
And no one had a better stock of wine
His house was never short of bake-meat pies
Of fish and flesh, and these in such supplies
It positively snowed with meat and drink

The Franklin in Chaucer's *Canterbury Tales*

I

Looking at the daily life and preoccupations of medieval man from the modern perspective is rather like peering down the wrong end of a telescope. A wholesome, reliable food supply, which we in the West now take for granted, was for them always a precarious part of life, so precarious that any breakdown could cause famine and death.

Although England, Wales, Scotland and Ireland are all comparatively small in area, transport was rudimentary and consequently many communities relied very much on their own food supplies. Food was moved around the coast and up rivers by barge and boat, but medieval roads were so deplorable that land-locked areas were more or less left to their own resources. The roads that were heavily used, like those approaching London, were such that in the mid-14th century: 'all the folks who bring victuals and wares by cart and horses to the City do make grievous complaint that they inset great damage, and are often times in peril of losing what they bring, and sometimes do lose it, because the roads without the City gates are so torn up and the pavement so broken, as may be seen by all persons on view thereof.'

Small food markets existed in towns throughout the land, but most people lived in the countryside, so organised that they had little chance of acquiring money to buy food. Instead, they produced what they needed on small farms, owned by the lord of the manor, and in return worked a set number of days each week on his own farm, or gave him a share of the produce. They also gave a tenth of their produce, a tithe, to the Church. Huge barns like that at Coggeshall in Essex, Buckland Abbey in Devon, and Great Coxwell in Oxfordshire, were built to collect this ecclesiastical tax.

Many peasants were serfs: they could not move from their land and much of their lives was ruled by the lord of their particular manor. Early in the period, the expanding population forced some peasants to extend cultivation on to more marginal land causing the spectre of famine to become reality when harvests failed. Roots and herbs gathered from the hedgerows were often the only food. The Black Death in 1348–9, which may have halved the population of England, was a turning point in the fortunes of the poor

Previous pages: An illustration from Jean de Wavrin's late 15th-century *Chronique d'Angleterre*, depicting the King of Portugal seated under his canopy of state with John of Gaunt, Duke of Lancaster, on his right hand. The high table is laid with dagger-shaped knives, elaborate salts, fine manchet bread and pewter trenchers. Servers present dishes of poultry and small, whole animals, which have been dressed with the correct sauce by the clerk of the kitchen at the serving hatch.

The Great Barn at Buckland Abbey, Devon, built by the Cistercian monks *c.*1300 for storage of crops, wool and hides from the abbey's estates, with a winnowing area in the centre.

medieval farmer. Land was no longer in short supply. In the confusion and turmoil following the epidemic, many serfs fled and rented land elsewhere. Landowners, acquiescing at the freedom gained by their peasants, usually preferred to rent out their own farms to gain an assured income without the worry and expense of managing an estate under increasingly difficult conditions.

The unpredictablility of Britain's weather has always been with us. But during this period, this uncertainty was particularly pronounced. After a bout of unstable weather around 1300, the next 150 years saw a period of cool, wet summers, becoming warmer and drier around 1500, before the onset of 'the Little Ice Age'.

From the late 14th until the early 16th century the ordinary rural inhabitant of England usually had enough food and occasionally could afford to eat and drink to excess. However, the memory of the famine year of 1371 as the 'grete dere yere' lasted to the 16th century because nothing as bad had been experienced in the intervening years. Towards the end of the 15th century, things began to change. Population was on the rise, and small farmers were being forced off the land by landlords who could make more money by amalgamating farms into larger units to raise sheep for wool. Sir Thomas More satirised this trend in 1517: 'Your sheep, that were wont to be so meek and tame and so small eaters, now, as I hear say, be become so great devourers, and so wild, that they eat up and swallow down the very men themselves.'

The aristocracy had the resources to insulate itself from temporary shortages, and continued to buy some foodstuffs even when prices were high: wheat bread was eaten whether wheat cost 3s 4d or 13s 4d a quarter. Only a series of extremely bad harvests could disrupt the established routines. The largest single item in household budgets was food and drink, which accounted for rather less than half the expenditure of a knight like Sir Hugh Luttrell of Dunster Castle in Somerset in the 1420s. Most estates provided part of the needs of the household, but supplies were also bought from the surrounding countryside or from markets in towns if more convenient. Some lords also retained rights of pre-emption from their tenants, enabling the Luttrells, for instance, to buy fish 'at the Lord's price': in 1422–3 salt conger, which fetched 6d each on the market, were being acquired for 4d by the household at Dunster. The wealthy would have less regional variations in diet; wheat bread, fresh beef, herring, spices from the Orient and Gascon wine were all available to those prepared to pay the price. On the other hand, small landowners, who held a single manor for instance, were more likely to remain self-sufficient.

Despite the poor state of the roads, traders flocked to market towns, travelling slowly but surely with their carrier carts and packhorse trains. According to records, food traders made up a high proportion of the occupations in medieval towns, and townspeople apparently enjoyed a better diet than their country cousins. Nevertheless measures had to be taken to protect the purchaser against dishonest tradesmen, and dependence on outside supplies made them vulnerable to scarcity. Indeed, much of our information about the contents of the medieval table comes from the laws promulgated to prevent dishonesty and corrupt practices.

Bread

Bread was truly the staff of life in medieval times, eaten by all levels. Quality and type were determined by the flour. Wheat made the finest, whitest bread but was not grown

Left: September from the late 15th-century Benninck Book of Hours. This scene shows wheat being harvested, probably destined to make fine white manchet bread for the lord's table. Two peasants are taking a meal of coarse brown bread with ale, beer or cider, and possibly hard cheese.

Below: The 16th-century watermill at Nether Alderley, Cheshire. In the Middle Ages and Tudor times, corn-mills powered by wind or water were the property of the landlord, who could compel his tenants to bring their corn and hand over part of it as a toll. Corn was ground at Nether Alderley right up to 1939.

easily throughout Britain, as it needed good soil. As a result the best quality wheaten bread called *pandemain* (*panis dominis*, or lord's bread), made from the finest flour was consider to be a luxury. Other breads of similar quality were *wastel* from the Norman-French *gastel* for cake and *manchet*, which has a whole series of possible derivations: perhaps from *mayne*, thought to be the name for the best quality flour in medieval times; from *manger*, French for to eat; or from *main*, French for hand, because manchet was made up as small loaves or rolls about the size of a fist.

From the later 13th century, specialist bakers were making what they called 'raise', 'puff' or French bread, consisting of a kind of milk-enriched bread with butter and eggs made up, like wastel or manchet, into small buns or rolls. Even these best quality breads were creamy in colour rather than white, due to the bran which remained in the flour. Bread described as 'whole wheat', 'chete' or 'cheat' was made of wheat flour more coarsely sieved, while a still coarser wheat bread contained husk as well. Called 'tourte', 'trete', 'treet', or 'brown bread', it may have been the bread used for trenchers. This type of bread was made into round, flattish 2 lb loaves about 10–12 inches across.

Good wheaten bread, leavened and well-baked, was regarded as a digestible and nutritious food. Even in the 12th century, wheaten bread had made its appearance on monastic tables: there was an elaborate gradation of qualities, with the abbot and prior eating the finest quality of pandemain. At the Dissolution of the Monasteries, when inventories were drawn up at Fountains Abbey in Yorkshire, the granaries were found to contain far more wheat than rye: 135 quarters of wheat to only 30 quarters of rye.

But pure wheat was the exception. Commonly, flours were of a variety of grains, mixed by the miller at the mill, or mixed as meal by the baker, in the desired proportion to produce *masdeline*, or *maslin* from the Norman-French *miscelin* meaning mixture. The names were as varied as the mixes. Perhaps the commonest mix was wheat, barley and rye to make maslin bread, generally eaten by servants, labourers and their families. In addition there were also the cheap breads 'of every grain', dark in colour: bran bread made mostly with bran, barley bread from barley flour alone; and rye bread and oatcakes in the north and west where the climate was cold and wet. Very coarse breads were known to be poorly digested: 'Browne bread . . . having much bran . . . filleth the belly with excrements and shortly descendeth from the stomach.'

The lower order of servants and poor country folk could by no means count always on even rye bread. Bolton Priory in Yorkshire issued 'gruel' bread to the poor, made from a mixture of rye, barley and bean (pulse) flour. *Piers Plowman*, written by William Langland *c*.1390, describes a year of dearth when the labourer lived on: '. . . cake of oats, And bread for my bairns of beans and of peas' for some months before the harvest.

Mills to grind corn, powered by wind and water, were increasingly introduced into lowland England in the 13th century. The mill was the property of the landlord, so that he could compel his tenants to bring their corn to the manorial mill, handing over a part of it as a toll for the privilege. The manor mill run by water power from the Morden stream has been grinding corn for the Cotehele estate in Cornwall since medieval times. Hopefully Edgcumbe's miller was more honest than the average, who had a reputation for swindling the peasants by grinding their corn badly and covertly diluting it with sand. Chaucer's Miller was characteristic of the breed: 'Well could he stealen corn and take toll thrice.'

Many medieval towns, particularly in the south, had municipal ovens for those with no oven of their own to bake bread. Professional bakers produced bread from flour they had made up themselves; although they were regarded as superior to millers, they were just as dishonest. Those who were found guilty were condemned to the pillory. Because bread was so important in everybody's diet, its quality and sale were the concern of the governing authorities, and as far back as the reign of King John in the early 13th century, there are records relating to its price. But the most important date is that of the famous Assize of Bread (*Assisa Panis*) in 1266, which fixed the weight of various types of loaves in relation to cost, and authorised the punishment of the pillory for false weight. The Assize ran until the First Bread Act in 1815, obviously changing and modifying as the years went by. Its aim was to try to make sure that everyone paid a fair price for a loaf but it was difficult to enforce, especially in small rural markets where there were variations in the regulations to cover locally made breads.

The baking trade was well-established in London in the 11th century and two guilds, the White Bakers and the Brown Bakers, were incorporated about 1304. A regulation of 1440 laid down that the white bakers 'shall bake all manner of bread that they can make of wheat ... white loaf bread, wastel, buns [French bread], and all manner of white bread that hath been used of old time.' A brown baker 'shall not have a bolter [to sift the flour] nor make white bread.' His brown bread was to include all the husks and bran in the meal, just as it came from the mill, but he was permitted to bake the dough which people brought to him ready made up, and to make horse bread. The brown bakers also baked the 'bread of every grain', which was the cheapest in the Assize of Bread.

Bread-making techniques remained unrecorded for a long time; they were learned by the housewife from her mother and by the baker from the master craftsmen who were his seniors in the 'mystery'. Brewers' yeast, sold by the brewer's wife who carried it to market in earthenware jars covered with a cloth, was used to leaven bread; it was in a semi-liquid state and very different from the compressed yeast of today. In large households, beer was brewed on the premises, so the yeast for bread-making was obtained during the process.

Bread was also a valued ingredient of cookery: crumbs were used to thicken a wide variety of dishes including hot drinks, pottages (stews), sauces and gravies to stop them running off the trencher; for making sausages and stuffings; and for making gingerbread – a favourite medieval sweetmeat. Thin pottages were often poured over 'brewes', or 'sops', which were pieces of bread or toast laid in the bottom of the dish. Toast was very popular, especially the enriched toasts made from white bread soaked in wine and spices, then crisped in front of the fire and served with almond milk or honey. Another well-known bread dish was *pain perdu*, made by dipping slices of pandemain or manchet into beaten yolk of egg, frying them in butter and sprinkling liberally with sugar – the ancestor of our 'poor Knights of Windsor'. Enriched and sweetened doughs were made into 'rastons', where the crumb was removed, mixed with butter and reheated in the oven; the 'buttered loaves' of the 16th century were similar. Wastel bread could also have its crumb removed, and mixed with eggs, spice, fat and currants, then reheated.

The medieval baker also made light, biscuity confections called simnels and cracknels, which were boiled before they were baked; simnels were given an official place in the tables of the Assize of Bread. On occasions, he also baked true biscuits (from the French, *bis-cuit*, twice-baked), which were at first ships' biscuits, put into the ovens to dry out after the bread had been taken out, but by Tudor times were of a finer quality made as sweetmeats for the banquet. Wafers were in great demand because of their use in churches, but were made by the waferer. In towns he was one of the street traders, and an official waferer was attached to the royal court.

Also established in medieval towns were the pie-maker and the London public cookshop, because few houses were adequately equipped with their own ovens. Around 1183, William Fitzstephen in his *Description of London* writes of the advantages of the public cookshop which had been established on the banks of the Thames, where 'according to the season, you may find viands, dishes roast, fried and boiled, fish great and small, the coarser flesh for the poor, the more delicate, for the rich, such as venison, and birds both big and little.' Some pie-makers took advantage of the peppery and spicy recipes of the period to make up their pies from tainted meat, so several regulations were issued during the 14th and 15th centuries to try to prevent such malpractices.

Meat

Much of our information about the foods available at this early period comes from the efforts to stamp out all kinds of tricks. Butchers, who supplied most pork, beef and mutton in towns and cities, often came under suspicion: 'to sell a piece of old cow for a chop of young ox, to wash your old meat that hath hung weltering in the shop with new blood, to truss away an old ewe instead of a young wether.' At one time, there was an ordinance in force prohibiting the sale of meat by candlelight to try to control the quality, but there was no fixed price system except control in times of shortage when there was a temptation to profiteer. London's meat market at St Nicholas near Billingsgate was known as the Shambles because it was a great source of annoyance to the citizens who lived nearby, causing 'abomination and stenches' by throwing 'blood and entrails' into the streets and into the Thames at a place called 'Butchersbridge'. (Shambles became a generic term for meat markets.) The authorities tried to persuade the butchers to slaughter outside the city, but their attempts were constantly frustrated.

Consumption of meat in the Middle Ages very much reflected social class, with great lords enjoying high proportions of meat in their diet, down to the limited proportions of lesser gentry, yeomen and peasants. Indeed, in early medieval times, the peasant seldom seems to have eaten meat at all, except when he did a little successful poaching, or when the lord of the manor gave a feast to celebrate the harvest or some other occasion. Yet, there is now considerable evidence that in the late 14th century, after the Black Death, and during the 15th century, meat was relatively plentiful. Villagers seem usually to have kept pigs and poultry and sometimes an ox, a cow and a few sheep. Chaucer's poor widow in the 'The Nun's Priest's Tale', who was a lowly farm servant, could boast of owning 'three large sows . . . three kine, and eke [even] a sheep,' as well as 'a cock and seven hens'. Protests in the 16th century against enclosures and consequent dearth and high prices, almost invariably declare that the countryman again was no longer able to afford these meats.

As examples of aristocratic meat-eating, nothing could compare with the banquets which marked the climax of the coronation ceremonies of the medieval English kings. Edward I, in preparation for his coronation feast in 1274, is reputed to have directed the sheriffs of several counties 'to produce and send up to London 278 bacon hogs, 450 porkers, 440 fat oxen, 430 sheep, 22,600 hens and capons and 13 fat goats'. Although these quantities were probably exaggerated, great noblemen were loathe to be outdone by their monarch and the lesser nobility tried to excel the hospitality of their betters,

Pig-killing in December, from an early 16th-century Flemish calendar. The poor man's pig was a vital part of his household – the one source of fresh meat, with bacon as a staple part of the diet. The blood was collected to make black puddings and for food colouring. In the background to this picture, large loaves of brown bread for the labourer and his family are being baked in the village or manorial oven.

until Edward II issued a proclamation to restrain 'the outrageous and excessive multitude of meats and dishes which the great men of the kingdom used in their castles.' This had little effect, for the aristocracy continued to eat even more meat, although it was only allowed on four days of the week and not during the six weeks of Lent. Over the whole year, the consumption of meat and fish was probably equally balanced.

The diet observed in Britain's medieval monasteries was based on the Rule of St Benedict, as laid down in AD 529. The meals of the brethren should be scant and frugal, with a prohibition on 'flesh meat', which was understood to include birds and fish. By the 12th century this prohibition had been relaxed as it was considered too difficult to follow in the wet, windy and generally cold climate of Britain. Flesh meat was interpreted as the flesh of 'four-footed beasts' only, so that the vegetarian diet could be enhanced by chickens, pigeons and fish.

Only children, including novices, and the sick and elderly were allowed the 'flesh of quadrupeds'. Thereafter, by gradual degrees, meat-eating crept in, initially for the abbot and his guests and finally for all monks and lay brothers at certain times: after bleeding, for instance, which took place four times a year.

The general standard of livestock at this period would now be regarded as poor. Many animals foraged on waste and common land for all, or part, of the year. Some were fed on meadow, fallow and new grass after the harvest, and occasionally even on specially sown grassland. It was once thought, quite illogically, that almost all domesticated animals were slaughtered at Martinmas – the feast of St Martin which falls on 11 November – but this has been disproved. It is true, however, that animal feed became scarce in the winter as hay and straw were used up. Animals were killed off week by week, so that the meat could be salted and pickled, though the offal had to be eaten fresh. If the weather proved particularly clement, the beasts could be kept longer. The proportion of preserved meat from the 'autumn slaughter' and fresh meat from animals killed at other times of the year can be judged from the household accounts of Alice de Bryene of Acton in Suffolk. In 1418–19 we are given the dates when 17 cattle were slaughtered: 10 were killed in October and November and the rest at other times of year.

For larger households, meat came either from stock which had been bought in well in advance and kept in home pastures, or from smaller quantities of daily or weekly purchases. According to the early 16th-century Household Book of Henry Percy, 5th Earl of Northumberland, 34 'lean beifs' half-starved on their winter diet were purchased in May and fattened in the Earl's pastures to supply his household in Yorkshire from midsummer to Michaelmas, when a further 100 fat cattle were acquired to last until the following midsummer. In addition, joints of fresh meat were 'regularly bought from the butchers'.

As cows' milk began to replace ewes' as the common drink, the number of cattle increased and beef emerged as the Englishman's favourite meat. Sir Thomas Elyot wrote in *The Castel of Helth*, in 1539, 'Beef of England to Englishmen which are in health, bringeth strong nourishing', but it was only for the wealthy Englishman. 'If the peasant reared cattle it was largely for the privileged, the nobility, and the burghers'.

By Tudor times a system had virtually been established whereby beasts bred and raised on the upland pastures of Wales and the North were driven in the summer to the Home Counties, where they were grazed and fattened up before moving to the great London meat market of Smithfield, and to other towns, for final sale to butchers. The country house of the Abbot of Westminster, the Neat House, was located in what is now

Victoria in London. 'Neat' meant ox or cow, so it may have got its name because it was used in the 14th century as a cattle depot for the royal kitchens. Drovers also brought sheep southwards to market from the more distant pastures. In the 13th and 14th centuries, many farmers switched from cereal-growing to sheep-farming because of the lucrative wool trade, so more mutton became available.

Pigs were plentiful, providing the most consistent source of more delicate meat. Often slaughtered in their first or second year, they were seldom specially fed, unless they belonged to a manor where grain, skimmed milk or brewing residues might be available. Animals owned by villagers scavenged the byways and rooted in the woods, in the charge of the village swineherd. If the poor ate fresh meat at all, it was likely to be pork, but bacon formed their staple meat. One of the dishes for which Britain is famous, bacon and eggs, or 'collops' and eggs, was the early medieval peasant's food. But as the woods were cleared for timber and for arable land, so the number of pigs diminished. Pigs were banned in towns because they roamed the streets causing havoc; if the town-dweller wanted fresh pork, he had to buy it from the shambles. As time went on, the consumption of pigs in both towns and the country declined; bacon and ham were rejected in favour of beef and mutton.

Meat was cooked by roasting, broiling on a gridiron, frying, boiling and stewing. Roasting joints and juicy steaks came from young beasts. According to Andrew Boorde, a physician who published in 1542 his *Dyettary of Helth*, one of the earliest English books on diet, 'Young kids' flesh is praised above all other flesh.' Roasted or stewed, it was a favourite springtime dish when Lent was over. Older animals, worn out by a lifetime's work, were tough. Those who could afford better things used mature animals to make strong broth in which to cook other meats or roots. Feet and ears were made into savoury jellies, which were highly prized in medieval times. Offal went into pottages or puddings and were stewed or fried. Suet made the strong paste for standing pies, and lard was an alternative to butter for the pastry of more delicate pies and tarts. Finally, the marrow was extracted from the cracked bones and put into pottages, pies and stuffings.

In Saxon times, hunting had been a pastime shared by rich and poor alike, but the Norman kings and their successors enforced their personal ownership of all forest lands and game. When poachers were caught, they were blinded or otherwise maimed as punishment. Later, occasional days of hunting were conceded, like the annual day in Epping Forest granted by Henry I to the citizens of London. By 1217 the most stringent of the game laws were repealed and hares, coneys (adult rabbits) and rabbits (coneys under a year old) could be pursued by all on foot with dogs. Hunting the wild bull, boar and deer remained an aristocratic privilege, however.

Many landowners enclosed areas of waste land to make parks for their game. The present park of 460 acres at Chirk Castle in Clwyd has developed from a comparatively small medieval hunting park, enclosed by the Mortimers in the early 14th century. An account of 1329 mentions a park keeper, retained at 30s 5d a year, and two carpenters who received 10s a year for repairing the gates and palisade fencing. The account also refers to hunting activity – the keeping of the lord's greyhound bitch and her eight puppies for coursing hares and the lord's nine sparrow-hawks.

Andrew Boorde recommended for the country estate: 'Also a park replete with deer and conies is a necessary and a pleasant thing.' Deer abounded in many monastery parks too and venison would have formed a treat for the abbot's table: the bursar's

King John hunting, from a 14th-century manuscript. The Plantagenets enforced their personal ownership of all forest lands and game. If caught, poachers were blinded or otherwise maimed.

accounts for 1457 at Fountains Abbey mention 'divers bringing venison to the Abbot [Greenwell] – 10d.'

Venison's status led to its use as a gift and its consumption on special occasions, although only at the high table; humble pies made from liver and lights were given to the huntsmen and the lower tables. Because venison was rarely bought or sold on the open market, but taken from parks or exchanged as gifts, it is rarely recorded in contemporary household accounts. When it is, the quantities seem small compared with the meat of domesticated animals. The Earl of Northumberland in 1512 expected to consume 49 deer, which was a small percentage of his meat supply.

Venison was roasted, accompanied by a strong pepper and vinegar sauce called 'peverade', or salt and cinnamon, or powdered ginger. Boiled venison was almost invariably accompanied by frumenty (see p.50) served separately. The less desirable pieces were stewed in well-spiced broth. Some deer were often killed in the autumn with the other farm stock and salted; the meat was then stewed or put into pasties, an extremely popular dish.

While the poor might catch a rabbit on the common, only the lord of the manor, or a monastery in later medieval times, was allowed to have a specially constructed warren or 'coney hayes' attached to the estate. A 'warrener' was usually employed to keep it in good order and protect it from poachers. 'Conies' flesh is good, but rabbits' flesh is best of all wild beasts,' said Andrew Boorde. Both hares and conies went into pottages, like 'civey' and 'gravey' and into stews, and were so popular that Henry VIII had to bring in a close season as they had become 'decayed and almost destroyed' at the hands of hunters.

Wild boar, common until the 15th century, provided the traditional Christmas brawn, made from the heads and shoulders, for all large feudal households. Red squirrel was also a dish for the lord until Tudor times when they went out of favour.

Estate rivers and ponds, as well as the moats of castles and manor houses, were an attraction to duck, geese, swans and other water-fowl; they provided a welcome addition to the diet, especially in winter. Keeping swans was a right for which one had to pay the Crown, but by 1250 many religious houses and commoners had acquired this right. Henry III was very fond of eating swan and the birds for his meals were provided by his sheriffs: for Christmas dinner at York in 1251, the King summoned no fewer than 125 birds. Swans and peacocks were dressed up and gilded as a processional centrepiece for the high table at a banquet or celebration. Bustards, storks, cranes, herons and, from

Right: Men making nets to catch rabbits, hare and wild fowl. An illustration from Gaston de Foix's *Le Livre de Chasse*, a treatise on hunting written in 1387.

Left: Women catching a rabbit with a net and a ferret: an illustration from the early 14th-century *Queen Mary's Psalter*. While the poor might catch a rabbit on the common in this way, the lord of the manor was allowed to have a specially constructed warren or 'coney hayes' attached to his estate.

the middle of the 15th century, the turkey were other popular 'great fowles' for feasts, where there might be as many as twenty dishes of birds.

Apart from the popular pastime of hunting wild fowl with falcons, a noble household would sometimes employ its own bird-catcher or, at least, have connections with one or more to supply wild fowl. In other households, the steward or a trusted servant went out and bargained where he could for the best and freshest birds. In the Earl of Northumberland's household a cater was appointed so that 'all manner of wild fowl be bought at the first hand where they be gotten', on the grounds that the 'poulters' in the neighbouring villages had been taking 'great advantage of my lord yearly'. The poulters themselves also depended on the catchers of wild fowl for their stock, as they dealt in wild as well as domestic birds.

Poultry-dealing was recognised early as a separate trade from butchery, and in London the Company of Poulters was active from the end of the 13th century. Their shops were in the area still known as Poultry just by the Bank of England, though later they also traded at Leadenhall and Smithfield, and regulations were made in 1345 to try to control the price and quality.

Domestic fowls – hens, ducks, geese, peacocks, pheasants and partridges – and their eggs could be bought from farmers' wives at market. At the manor-house they were kept in the courtyard or in an enclosure, where they were usually the responsibility of the dairymaid. Any that were brought by tenants as gifts or as part of their rent were also kept in the enclosure until wanted for preparation for the table, because fowl were always eaten fresh.

Although most country families, even the poorest, kept hens which wandered freely, and many also kept ducks and geese, their eggs were so precious to the peasants' diet that they were killed only when too old to lay.

As in France, manorial rights included the exclusive ownership of a dovecote, or pigeon loft, to supply pigeons and squabs for the table. They were especially appreciated during the winter. Tenants had to tolerate the loss of their grain to the lord's birds which liked to feed on the standing corn in the open fields. There is a pigeon loft in the top storey of a tower at Bodiam Castle in Sussex, next door to the kitchen and with easy access from there. It contained some 300 nesting boxes, two-thirds of which survive, and must have offered essential supplies should the castle come under siege. A reliable source of water was essential, so the dovecote was often built beside a pond. Besides assisting with the annual moult, baths helped to keep the birds free of vermin. The 15th-century round stone dovecote at Cotehele stands by the side of the fish-pond. Inside is a 'potence', or revolving ladder, for easier access to the higher pigeon holes. A small family of white doves now lives there. The late medieval cote at Snowshill Manor in Gloucestershire has niches for 380 birds and is also home to white doves. An attractive 16th-century half-timbered 'magpie' dovecote survives at Hawford Grange in Worcestershire.

Dovecotes were also a welcome addition to monasteries; monks could eat fowl of all types because they were 'two-legged'. The birds belonged to the abbot as lord of the manor. He was only allowed one pigeon house, although its size was not restricted so some could be very large, housing over a thousand birds. Tithe barns belonging to monasteries often had pigeon houses in the upper part. The superb Great Barn at Buckland Abbey in Devon has porches which project on each side, both of which have pigeon lofts.

An illustration from the early 14th-century *Luttrell Psalter*, showing corn being fed to a hen and her chicks. Most medieval cottagers kept hens, ducks and geese for their own use. Domestic fowl were also kept in the manor courtyard or in an enclosure, where they were usually the responsibility of the dairymaid.

Above: The 16th-century dovecote at Willington, Bedfordshire, was built by Sir John Gostwick, Cardinal Wolsey's Master of the Horse. Its kidney-shaped nesting boxes could accommodate some 1,500 birds.

Left: The 15th-century round stone dovecote at Cotehele, Cornwall, stands by the side of the fish-pond; a reliable source of water was essential for the birds' health.

Fish

Fish was almost as vital as bread to the medieval household and eaten in enormous quantity. The Church ordained that on Fridays, and until early Tudor times, Saturdays and Wednesdays, as well as the six weeks of Lent, no one might eat meat; the purpose was to mortify the flesh and to reduce carnal passions, held to be inflamed by such a diet. In fact, eggs and other dairy foods were also forbidden during Lent. This meant that for about half the days of the year, everyone had to eat fish. Dispensation was granted to the general public only for special reasons by royal edict. A Proclamation of 3 February 1541 announced that because 'hearryng, lynges, salt-fysh, samond, stock-fyshe are skant and dear,' the King dispenses with 'the law of abstinence from white meat [dairy produce] during Lent.' Henry VIII's subjects were allowed to eat milk, eggs, butter and cheese, but not to turn this into a 'carnal liberty'.

Churchmen were supposed to observe even more restrictions. At Fountains Abbey, where a meat diet was not sanctioned until the end of the 14th century, a great deal of fish was eaten. Fishing rights on nearby Malham Tarn were owned by the Abbey and those on the River Tees were shared with Rievaulx Abbey, while the rivers Swale, Wiske, Derwent and the whole course of the Ure and the Ouse from Boroughbridge to York provided further freshwater fish. Sea-fishing was practised off Teesmouth, and footholds were secured in the fish markets of Redcar and Scarborough from where cart-loads of fresh fish for the Abbot, and salted or smoked for the monks, regularly trundled their way to the Abbey. The bursar's accounts for 1457 mention: 'For fresh fish for the Abbot from Scarborough – 4d' and 'bringing shell fish – 20d.'

It was not unusual from the 13th century onwards, when fish became part of the monastic diet, for an abbey to have as many as three freshwater ponds: one would be stocked with pike, a second with less predatory fish and a third, called the 'stew', with fish ready to be taken out for the table (see p.26). The last was often divided into sections to keep different types of fish from eating each other and to make catching them easier. In monasteries like Fountains Abbey, the fish-ponds were managed as carefully as modern fish farms. Several of the nearer granges (farms) belonging to the Abbey also had ponds; the best example is that at Parkhouse Grange, but more important were the 20 acres of artificial ponds managed by the Abbey itself, in an enclosure in Fountains Park, beyond the kitchen, called Pondgate. Abbots often had their ponds stocked with their favourite fish, and for relaxation some abbots would themselves fish for their meals.

Again, at Fountains and most monasteries, there was also a mill pond to hold fish, especially eels which were kept in large quantities until needed for the table. Eels were very popular and were imported from the Low Countries in vast quantities throughout the Middle Ages. They were cheaper than most fish and probably the only fresh variety other than shellfish bought by poor people. At many religious houses, fresh fish was obtained in the form of tithes: Ely in Cambridgeshire is thought to have gained its name because dues were paid to the Abbey in eels. Many abbeys had fish-houses and sometimes curing-houses; the abbots of Glastonbury's stone-built fish-house at Meare in Somerset still survives.

'Of all nations and countries, England is best served of Fysshe not only of all manner of sea-fysshe, but also of fresh-water fysshe, and of all manner of sortes of salt-fysshe,' said Andrew Boorde. But transporting fish over long distances was difficult and expensive, so fresh sea-fish was available only to those living on the coast, or the very wealthy. Fresh fish for inland towns was limited to what could be caught in local rivers and ponds.

Contemporary manuscripts record fish of every kind from minnow to whale on the medieval bill of fare. Alexander Neckham, an Augustinian canon who eventually became Abbot of Cirencester in the early 13th century, lists sole, salmon, conger, lamprey, whale, whitebait, gudgeon, bar, cod, skate, plaice, herring, mullet, mackerel, turbot and even seahorse among the fish commonly found in the kitchen. Seals were also eaten and so were the 'royal' fish, which included whale, porpoise and sturgeon: porpoise was the 'venison of the fish day' and sturgeon was something of a luxury for the average manorial family.

Shellfish was gathered in great quantities for sale in towns near the coast. All through the Middle Ages they were the one product of the sea which poorer people could afford: oysters, priced at 2d a gallon in 1298 or 4d a bushel in 1491, were cheap in comparison with other kinds of fish. For a large household several hundred oysters, cockles or whelks were bought at a time, especially as a treat during Lent.

But for ordinary people, fish meant salted or pickled herrings, or stockfish (dried cod). Britain's herring fleets off the east coast caught thousands of fish throughout the summer, and there was a big salting and pickling industry to process them for travel inland. At first, they were preserved in a very primitive fashion, by salting in heaps on the shore without even being gutted. In the 14th century the methods of a Dutchman, William Beukels, were adopted; the herrings were gutted and soaked for about 15 hours in brine before being barrelled up in rows between layers of salt to produce 'white herrings'. Smoking herrings was a development of the same period: the fish was first soaked in brine, then strung up and smoked in special chimneys for many hours and finally barrelled as 'red herrings'. The centre of the herring industry in Britain was the Norfolk port of Yarmouth. In 1108, when the town was made a borough by Henry I, the annual payment to the Crown for this recognition was 10 'milliards' (defined as one thousand million) of herring. Herring pies were also common medieval rents; the city of Norwich was bound by ancient charter to send 24 herring pies annually to the King, who obviously regarded them as delicacies.

Unlike the herring, white fish could be fished at any time of the year, but until the 15th century were caught almost entirely from the south-east coast of England. Thereafter fishermen began to work Icelandic waters, setting out in February or March, taking provisions and salt for salting the cod on board before drying it. At the end of the summer, when all their salt had been used up, they sailed for home and the autumn markets. The term 'stockfish' applied to several members of the cod family, such as pollock, whiting and milwell; it also applied to wind-cured fish which had not been previously salted. The term 'ling' often meant dried cod in general, but as it sold for twice as much as stockfish, it must have been applied to the better quality preserved fish. 'Haberdin' was another kind of large cod, salted or sun-dried. Much preserved fish was also imported. In most years it was all fairly cheap, and cheaper still if bought at the end of the summer and stored until needed for Lent, when it was necessary to have a large quantity available. In the 15th-century Paston Letters, we learn that Margaret Paston had not been able to purchase her Lenten supply until late in the season, but eventually was able to write to her husband, 'As for herring, I have bought a horse-load for 4s 6d. I can get no eels yet.'

Pickled herrings and salt-fish generally were usually boiled and eaten with mustard

East Riddlesden Hall, Yorkshire, viewed across the pond which in the Middle Ages was used for keeping fish for the kitchen, from a watercolour painted in 1920 by E. Riley.

or butter. John Russell in his *Boke of Nurture* of around 1450 describes how, when the roe and bones have been removed, 'then may your lord endure to eat merrily with mustard'. A delicacy enjoyed by Russell was baked herring 'dressed and dished with white sugar'. On the other hand, medieval stockfish required more drastic treatment to make them edible: 'And when ... it is desired to eat it, it behoves to beat it with a wooden hammer for a full hour, and then set it to soak in warm water for a full two hours or more, then cook and scour it very well like beef; then eat it with mustard or soaked in butter' (*The Goodman of Paris, c.*1393). John Russell said stockfish could be coaxed back to some measure of softness using 'many waters oft times renewed'.

Housewives relied for their supplies mostly on the fishmongers, who had their own guilds in London by the middle of the 12th century. The stockfishmongers dealt mainly in dried fish, while the salt-fishmongers handled the imports of salted and pickled herring, cod, eels, whiting and mackerel from the Low Countries and the Baltic. The sale of fresh fish straight from the fishing grounds off Kent and Essex at this time formed only a small part of the trade. Most of the fish landed at Queenhythe, an inlet in the Thames and the chief watergate of the City of London, was quickly salted, smoked or pickled. In 1536 the two fish companies united to form the present Worshipful Company of Fishmongers. They took a prominent part in providing the public with some measure of protection against fraudulence and the sale of bad fish. There are records of baskets and measures found to hold too small a weight of fish. Unsalted fish was forbidden for sale after the second day, and fish were to be immersed in water twice only. Mackerel, being oily and particularly perishable, could be sold on Sundays, before and after divine service.

Freshwater fish must have come as very welcome relief from the monotony of salted and dried fish. In summer river fish and eels were available to all. The late 15th-century *Treatyse of Fysshynge with an Angle*, which has been attributed to Dame Juliana Berners, said to have been Abbess of Sopwell, lists the fish commonly caught for the table: salmon, trout, grayling, barbel, carp, chevin or chub, bream, tench, perch, roach, dace, bleak [small river-fish], ruff, flounder, minnow, eel and pike. Salmon, 'the most stately fish that any man may angle to in fresh water', was in great demand. Scottish and Irish salmon was pickled in brine and transported by sea to London and other southern markets. A single fish could fetch as much as 3 or 5 shillings, making it a delicacy. Lampreys (eel-like fish with sucker mouths) were the favourite fish at court feasts; King John was very fond of them and his great-grandfather, Henry I, is said to have died from a surfeit of them. The finest lamprey were considered to be those caught in the Severn, although they were also very common in the Thames. Until Elizabeth I's reign, it was customary for the city of Gloucester as a token of loyalty to present the monarch with a lamprey pie, a much-loved delicacy, at Christmas.

Like the monasteries, most estates of any size had large artificial freshwater ponds, known as 'stews', which were carefully managed to provide an unfailing supply of fresh fish for fast days. Very large households included a fisherman as a permanent member of staff and it was his job to catch fish from the ponds as they were needed.

The visitor's first view of East Riddlesden Hall in Yorkshire is from across the ancient fish-pond; the 'Stagnum de Ridlesden' mentioned in the Compotus of Bolton Priory in the year 1320 when the canons spent 4s 3d in clearing fish from the fish-ponds of Skipton, Riddlesden and Bolton.

An extensive chain of ponds linked by sluices can still be seen at Baddesley Clinton in

The moated medieval manor house of Baddesley Clinton, Warwickshire, from a late 19th-century watercolour by Rebecca Dulcibella Dering. Castle and manor-house moats provided a source of freshwater fish, as well as water-fowl, for the table.

Warwickshire. John Brome, a wealthy lawyer of Warwick, owned the estate in the middle of the 15th century, and his bailiff's accounts for certain years between 1442 and 1458 survive. They include references to the expenses involved in forming and stocking the three domestic fish-ponds. The digging of the ponds, entirely man-made, began in 1444 and it is clear from the names listed that teams of Welshmen did the 'navvying'.

A similar chain of fish-ponds exists at Canons Ashby in Northamptonshire – perhaps 'ye Canalls' mentioned in a survey of 1711, whose straight edges later blurred to give them the appearance of more conventional lakes.

The two large, rectangular stewponds at Ightham Mote in Kent were probably originally fed by a stream. Like Baddesley Clinton, the half-timbered manor house is also surrounded by a moat, another useful source of fresh fish for the table. In his *Dyettary*, Andrew Boorde warned: 'let not the filth of the kitchen descend in the moat,' for obvious reasons.

Dairy Produce

Generally known as 'white meat', dairy produce, including eggs, seems to have been eaten extensively by all classes, including monks, in early medieval times. But with rising prosperity in the 14th century, it came to be regarded as inferior food, fit only for common people.

From early times well-to-do adults thought fresh milk was a drink fit only for children, the old and invalids because 'it engendered wind in the stomach'. Women's milk and asses' milk were regarded as the most digestible, and women acted as wet nurses to adult invalids as well as to babies. Goats' and ewes' milk were originally more popular than cows', which was rightly thought to be more nutritious in spring and summer than in winter. Townspeople bought milk in the markets or walked out to neighbouring farms to ensure fresh supplies.

Although the wealthy drank very little milk in its raw state, they did use it to make hot beverages called possets or caudles, creamy pottages and custards. But what they really enjoyed was rich cream and curdled cream. Alexander Neckham described how cream and curds from the 12th-century manorial dairy were brought in on large round platters to be eaten by the lord and his fellow diners. Cream was used in cooking to enrich 'made' dishes like rich custards and custard tarts, and curds to make tarts and fritters.

Butter was also produced on the manor. The chief innovation adopted early in the Middle Ages was the wooden plunger, which passed through a hole in the lid of the tall churn and was worked up and down by hand to bring the cream to a solid state more quickly. Sweet butter for immediate consumption was beaten in fresh water until it was free of butter milk and then slightly salted. Salt butter for long keeping was made by working out the butter-milk and then beating a lot of salt or strong brine into it. It was packed into well-glazed earthenware pots or wooden casks with more salt strewn over it. In spite of this procedure, the butter often became rancid.

Butter was regarded as unwholesome for grown men to eat from midday onwards, so it was taken as an aperitif before dinner with fresh fruit: 'It is good to eat in the morning before other meals' advised Andrew Boorde. Butter was recommended for growing pains in children, who were given it with bread for both breakfast and supper, and as a laxative. For cooking, butter was melted, strained and kept in pots until needed. It was then used to enrich bread dough, make pastry and cakes, baste roasting meat, for frying, and to seal the contents of cold pies for long keeping. During Lent, when butter was forbidden except to the children and the sick, olive oil was bought for fish frying; while almond butter (made from ground almonds) could be served at table.

Only the wealthy were able to enjoy a wide range of cheeses in medieval and early Tudor times. Cheese was then classified according to its texture and not its place of origin. There were three main types produced by the manorial dairy: first, hard cheese, made from skimmed milk; second, soft cheese from whole, or at least only semi-skimmed milk, matured for a time, but still with enough moisture to prevent it being really hard; and lastly, new or 'green' cheese, which was made from curd and had to be eaten quickly, for it was too damp to mature properly. A variety of curd cheese flavoured with herbs was known as 'spermyse'. Most of the full-cream milk cheese was destined for the table of the lord of the manor, while the skimmed or semi-skimmed kinds went to the servants and estate workers.

Throughout most of the medieval period, rennet was probably secured from

The preparation of cheese from the 15th-century *Taciturn Sanitalis*. Three types of cheese were produced in the medieval dairy: hard cheese from skimmed milk for servants and labourers; soft cheese from whole milk; and new or 'green' cheese.

whichever young suckling animal, lamb, calf or kid, could best be spared for slaughter. As cows' milk became popular, more calves were bred and took over as the provider of rennet. Even a medieval peasant kept a cow if he could: curds and whey, butter-milk, heavily salted butter and cheese were his staples. In summer he made green cheese and spermyse, while skimmed-milk cheese kept all winter, formed part of his daily diet in the fields. Langland's *Piers Plowman* deplored his shortage of food; all he had was:

> . . . two grene cheses,
> A few cruddes [curds] and creme,
> And an haver cake [oatcake]
> And two loves of benes and bran.

Beverages

Festivals and holy days were all recognised occasions for feasting and merriment, and none was complete without ale, the national beverage. The drink gave its name to a number of social gatherings in the Church, such as church-ales, Easter-ales and Whitsun-ales, and family rejoicings like wedding-ales and christening-ales. Its importance in the national diet was recognised in 1267, when it was subjected, like bread, to a sliding price scale based upon the seasonal cost of grain by the Assize of Ale.

Large establishments had their own brew-houses where prodigious quantities of ale were brewed regularly, once or twice a month, and even in quite a small household the ale was usually brewed at home. Taverns and village ale-houses were often supplied with ale by the local manor brew-house. In spite of all this, there was still a place for commercial brewers, although their products had to be passed by an 'ale-conner', or taster, before they were sold.

Ale was the name given to any fermented drink brewed from malted grain and water. In the south of England the best ale was made from barley malt, but in parts of northern and western Britain oats were used. Elsewhere mixed cereals were common and wheat, oats and sometimes even beans were added to the malt before it was mashed, although Andrew Boorde advised that 'Barley malt maketh better ale than oaten malt or any other corn doth.' Spices and herbs were often added because ale deteriorated quite rapidly and developed a sour taste. Honey was also added with spices to make 'bragot', popular for festive occasions. The 15th-century feast proposed by John Russell in his *Boke of Nurture* for a franklin (in the social hierarchy, just below the lesser gentry and above the yeoman farmer) ended with special cakes and wafers, accompanied by bragot and mead. Possets and caudles made from spiced milk or eggs curdled with ale were also popular.

Earlier the names ale and beer had been applied to the same drink, but the latter fell into disuse, to be reintroduced in the 15th century, when 'that wicked weed called hops' was added to the brew. Hopped beer, introduced from Flanders, was at first regarded with grave suspicion on health grounds; charges of adulteration were made against brewers in 1424 and protests against the introduction of the new drink were made not only by the ale-brewers, but by the authorities of the City of London. As late as 1542, Andrew Boorde praised ale and condemned beer, which he described as the 'naturall drynke' for a Dutchman:

> Beere, is a Dutch boorish liquor, a thing not known in England, till of late days an
> Alien to our Nation, till such times as Hops and Heresies came against us, it is a

The brewery in the courtyard at Lacock Abbey, Wiltshire, set up by Sir William Sharington in the mid-16th century, and probably still in use two hundred years later. The mash tun, where the ingredients for the beer were heated, the cooling trough and the fermenting vat can still be seen.

saucy intruder in this land ... And now in late days it is much used in England to the detriment of many Englishmen ... for the drink, is a cold drink; yet it doth make a man fat and doth inflate the belly ...

Nevertheless, beer did have a vital advantage over ale; the hops had a preservative quality. So, by the early 16th century hops were being widely cultivated in Kent, and also in Worcestershire, Essex, Yorkshire and Cornwall; beer had begun to take over from ale as the Englishman's natural drink. In 1441 beer had, like ale, been made subject to an assize, and the London beer brewers formed their own guild.

Like ale before it, beer was drunk at all times of the day, for breakfast, dinner and supper. Rules of the Earl of Northumberland's household in 1512 stated that no beer was to be bought in; there are frequent entries in the household book for 'faggots for Brewynge' in the estate brew-house. Beer for the high table was commonly a year old or more, brewed in March and October, the two favourite months in large establishments. Small householders had to brew more frequently as they could not store great quantities of liquor.

One of the guidelines laid down by St Benedict in his Rule for monastic life was that each monk should be allocated a measure of wine each day, but this was impossible to observe in Britain's cold climate. It was agreed therefore that when no wine was available locally, the monks should be served ale, beer or cider instead, but should 'sup sparingly'. At Fountains Abbey, the monks were allowed one pint of ale or beer a day and as at other abbeys the making of it was chiefly in the hands of the monks, who devoted a good deal of attention to the task. The infirmarian took a particular interest for he needed the brew as a medicine for those in his care, when it was flavoured with herbs and plants like mugwort, yarrow, betony and ground ivy. The malt-house and the brew-house stood in the south precinct at Fountains Abbey alongside the other agricultural buildings. In early leases of mills granted by the Abbey, the stipulation is made that the malt belonging to the monks should be ground free of charge.

Cider-making had been introduced into Kent and Sussex from Normandy in the 12th century, and had become immediately popular, spreading to the West Country. It could be made from apples mixed with pears, but if the drink was prepared predominantly from pears, it was called perry. Medical opinion was opposed to both: Sir Thomas Elyot claimed in 1541 that people in cider-making districts looked pale, and had 'the skin of their visage rivelled, although that they be young'. Andrew Boorde was dismissive: 'Cider doth engender evil humours ... and doth hurt the stomach', but advised that it could be drunk at harvest time without harm.

In the monasteries, the monk-gardener was usually responsible for supervising the production of cider from crab apples. Sometimes this took place in the orchard soon after the apples had been gathered, but usually there was a special cider-making area, or house, within the monastery compound, as at Buckland Abbey. During the 12th century the gardener at Glastonbury Abbey in Somerset had his own small cider-house, which can still be seen.

There was a cider-house on the Cotehele estate; apples from the orchard were pulped by a crusher powered by a donkey-wheel. Apple pulp descending from the crusher was built up into a cheese between layers of straw on the wooden tray or vat. When this was complete, the press was screwed down, and the juice collected in a trough below.

The other beverages produced almost universally in medieval households were mead

Left: Drunken revelry from the late 14th-century *Tractatum de Septem Vitiis*. Festivals and holy days were all recognised occasions for drinking and merriment. Ale, the national beverage, gave its name to a number of social gatherings in the Church, such as Whitsun-ales, and family celebrations, like christening-ales.

Below: Beekeepers from an illustration to Virgil's *Georgics* by the mid-15th-century Milanese Master of the Vitae Imperatorum. Bees were kept on a large scale in the Middle Ages for honey and wax. The keepers, dressed in protective clothing, are shown smoking out bees from a straw kep or hive so that the honeycomb can be removed.

and metheglin. Mead, a drink of great antiquity, was made of honey and spring water, boiled together and then fermented. Metheglin was a honey liquor flavoured with herbs, particularly favoured by the Welsh.

Wine was the only beverage drunk by the lord of the manor and his family and guests which was not produced on his own estate. There were vineyards in monasteries in the south of England and records of vineyards as far north as York, but grapes are not thought ever to have been grown at Fountains Abbey. Some good white wine was produced by a few large estates in the Vale of Gloucester, but a high proportion of the crops elsewhere ended up as verjuice (see p.34). Even as late as 1509 there were still 139 good-sized vineyards, although the industry was already in decline.

Henry II's marriage to Eleanor of Aquitaine in 1152 had begun large-scale shipments of wines from Gascony, Burgundy, Poitou and Languedoc, to add to the German wines that were already being imported. The luxury trade in sweet wines from southern Europe and the eastern Mediterranean probably began at the time of the Crusades in the 12th century, but expanded constantly.

These sweet southern wines were described by Andrew Boorde as 'hot wines [which] be not good to drink with meat, but after meat, and with oysters, with salads, with fruit, a drought or two may be suffered.' Also for consumption after meals were spiced wines, the most popular of which were hippocras and clary. The former took its name from the bag through which it was strained, said to resemble Hippocrates' sleeve. Red wine was the base, sometimes further coloured with 'turnsel', or turnsole – a dyestuff from the Mediterranean. Various spices, usually ginger, cinnamon and grains of paradise, were added and it was sweetened by those who could afford it with triple-refined sugar or sugar candy. The poor added pepper instead of the more expensive grains of paradise and sweetened it with honey. Clary was even sweeter, based upon sweet southern wines with extra sugar or honey and a wide range of spices.

Wine was drunk in small quantities in comparison with ale, beer and cider. Only the wealthy were able to afford to lay in the pipes and tuns (barrels contained about 105 gallons and 250 gallons respectively) necessary to maintain regular supplies. At Fountains Abbey the bursar's accounts for 1457 mention the purchase of imported wine for the abbot.

Most medieval wine was drunk raw and strong, usually within the year because the exact nature of fermentation was not understood and older wine soon became undrinkable. There were no glass bottles or corks and travel was very rough. Any wine over a year old was sold off cheaply.

The drink to be avoided at all costs was water, which had an evil reputation. Andrew Boorde stated the case plainly: 'Water is not wholesome, sole by itself, for an Englishman.' He recommended that those who drank their table wine diluted with water should 'let it be purely strained; and then sethe [boil] it.'

Fruit and Vegetables

Inside the walls of London and other cities, and within the confines of monasteries, manors and castles, lay the gardens of merchants, nobles and high churchmen. Sometimes they were of considerable size and tended by expert gardeners. For monastic establishments in particular, the garden was important as it provided the foodstuffs and medicines required by the community. For most castles and fortified manor houses, the garden was perforce of limited size, and seldom tended by anyone with a specialist knowledge.

The gardens of large noble households and monasteries often had surplus fruit and vegetables for sale. By 1345 a regular market for such surpluses had been set up near St Paul's Cathedral in London, and similar markets existed in other large towns. Early in the 16th century the first commercial market gardeners began to grow vegetables for sale in the London suburbs.

Much of our information about medieval gardens comes from monastic accounts. Alexander Neckham claimed a surprisingly comprehensive list of plants in his garden in Cirencester at the beginning of the 13th century. From his own experience, he advised that noble gardens:

> should have parsley and cost and fennel and southernweed [a strewing herb] and coriander, sage, savory, hyssop, rue, dittany, smallage, pellitory, lettuce [used as a vegetable, not in salads], garden cress, peonies. There should also be planted beds with onions, leeks, garlic, pumpkins and shallots, the cucumber [rare at this time] growing in its lap .... There should also be pottage herbs, such as beets, herb-mercury, orach [mountain spinach], sorrel and mallows; anise, mustard, white pepper and wormwood do good service to the gardenlet.

A detailed account of another monastic garden of the same period has survived, from Glastonbury Abbey for the year 1333–4. From this we learn that the gardener, Thomas of Keynesham, was a busy man. With four paid servants working under him, he was responsible for the vegetable and herb garden, orchard and vineyard. Onions, leeks and garlic formed the bulk of the vegetables grown. No less than 11,000 cloves of garlic were distributed as follows: 3,000 for seed for the following year's crop; 2,000 for the abbot's kitchen; and 6,000 to be shared between the larderer for the monks' meals and the infirmarian for making medicines.

In the Glastonbury account, herbs are treated as a single item, so it is difficult to identify which were grown. But, given that imported oriental spices were inevitably more costly than home-produced aromatics, medieval herb gardens were planted with as many varieties as could be persuaded to grow in Britain, including aniseed, licorice, caraway, coriander, cumin, hyssop and mustard. An early 15th-century list of 'herbs necessary for a garden' gives over a hundred, including flowers first arranged alphabetically, and then in classified order according to their usage for pottage, for sauces, for drinks, for distilling, and so forth.

At Ightham Mote in the 14th century, there were six long terraced beds for growing vegetables, pot, medicinal and strewing herbs, and for flowers for cooking and scenting the house. The herbs and the flowers would have been mixed together to produce the salads which were so popular at this period, 'mingled well with raw oil' and sprinkled with vinegar and salt. Herbs and flowers were again mixed and scattered among the rushes in the great hall and other family chambers.

In smaller kitchen gardens and villagers' plots, the emphasis would be upon vegetables for cooking; onions, garlic, red and green cabbages and leeks. Indeed, leeks were so popular that the kitchen garden was often called 'the leek garden'. Green vegetables featured little in diets of all but the poor, for they were thought to cause wind and induce melancholy. But they were widely eaten by the poor, boiled as vegetable pottage. Chaucer speaks of the penniless Griselda in 'The Clerk's Tale', who:

A 15th-century French manuscript showing a garden of medicinal plants.

> Whan she homward came, she wolde bring
> Wortes [cabbages] and other herbes times oft,
> The which she shred and sethe [boil] for hire living

Mayster Jon Gardener, a poem on *The Feate of Gardeninge*, written *c*.1440, devotes a substantial section to 'wortys', explaining how, by sowing seed in succession they could be had the year round, concluding:

> And so fro moneth to moneth
> This schalt bryng thy wurtys forthe

It also mentions radishes, spinach, lettuce, parsnips and carrots, but these were rarities. Peas and broad beans, the basis for pottage, were the only vegetables at this time cultivated as field crops. At least three kinds of peas were grown: green and white, both small varieties, and grey, which were larger and often used as fodder for animals or eaten by the poorest people.

Medieval people were somewhat suspicious of fresh fruit, believing that it was 'the cause of putrified fevers', a theory that held sway for centuries. Wynkyn de Worde advised in his *Boke of Kervynge* of 1508: 'Beware of green sallettes [salads] & raw fruytes for they will make your soverayne seke [your body sick].' Fresh plums, damsons, cherries and grapes and, later, peaches were in fact allowed on rich men's tables as long as they were eaten at the beginning of the meal as appetisers. Small wild strawberries collected from the woods and eaten with cream were much appreciated in the country, for Andrew Boorde tells us that 'Raw creame eaten with strawberries or hurtes [whortleberries] is a rurall mans banquet', although his experience as a physician forced him to add 'I have known such banquets hath put men in jeopardy of their lives.' Strawberries, cherries and pears were grown with great success in the moist valleys of Sir Piers Edgcumbe's estate of Cotehele and transported along the River Tamar; it was a trade that was to continue until very recent times.

After the Norman Conquest, new varieties of apples and pears from France were introduced into British orchards. Pondgarth, the enclosure containing the fish-ponds at Fountains Abbey, was enclosed by 8 acres of orchard known as East Applegarth, and west of this were three more orchards, amounting to 12 acres, called the West Applegarths. The cellarer, who was responsible for the storage and purchase of food for the monks, supplied pears, medlars, apples and plums for the abbot's table – pears were considered a luxury and medlars, unlike most fruit, were thought to comfort the stomach. The orchard at Glastonbury Abbey was planted with over 3 acres of apple and pear trees. In 1333, the weather was hot and dry, so fruit was abundant: 248 quarters of apples were harvested for cider-making, further quantities went to the cook and to the cellarer for storage. It was also recorded that a supply of pears was allocated to the abbot's country residence at Mells.

One of the earliest named apples was the 'pearmain', recorded soon after 1200. The 'costard', a very large, good-keeping apple, became popular in the 13th century; it was sold in the streets of London by 'costermongers', whose wares were later extended to many kinds of fruit and other goods. The supply of both fruit and vegetables seems to have been a limited trade in the hands of a few countrymen or local gardeners, who bought their produce into the towns and hawked it in the streets.

Additional cultivated fruit trees were damsons, bullaces, mulberries and quinces.

An orchard scene from the Croissens manual of agriculture, a late 15th-century French manuscript. After the Norman Conquest, new varieties of apples and pears were introduced into British orchards. Most fruit at this period was cooked to make it digestible.

The 13th-century writer Walter de Biblesworth in his list of fruit-bearing trees that were sometimes brought into gardens and cultivated there, also mentions hedgerow fruits – hawthorn, sloe, briar rose and cornel cherry. By early Tudor times the demand for fruit trees meant that not only were many more orchards being planted in the gardens of mansions, but many market gardens were also being established. The most famous was that made at Tenham Manor in Kent by Richard Harris, gardener to Henry VIII, which is said to have been about 140 acres in extent.

Most fruit was cooked in medieval times to make it more digestible. Apples, quinces, wardens (large hard pears) and other pears were baked in pastry coffins with sugar or honey and spice or pulped and put into tarts. Boiled and sieved apples were made into a well-loved pottage called 'appulmos', which was thickened with breadcrumbs and then sweetened and spiced. Strawberries, mulberries, cherries, plums and bullaces also went into pottages.

Fresh fruit was occasionally used to dress meat, fish and poultry. Much more common was verjuice, an acid liquid rather like mild vinegar, produced from unripe fruit such as grapes, crab-apples and wild gooseberries; the name was taken from the French *vert* for green and *jus* for juice. The fruit was fermented and stored in wooden casks, ready for use in cooking. Often it was added to vinegar to neutralise the flavour of meat and fish past their best, to tenderise tough meat and to make vinegar-based sauces. In addition to verjuice, 14th-century recipes include 'vynegar' or wine vinegar, 'alegar' or malt vinegar and 'aysell' or cider vinegar.

Exotic Fruits and Spices

Exotic fruits had begun to arrive in Britain in the 13th century through trade with southern Europe, where bitter oranges of the Seville type, lemons and pomegranates were cultivated. Some dried fruit, 15 lemons, 7 oranges and 230 pomegranates were bought from a Spanish ship at Portsmouth in 1289 for Edward I's Queen, Eleanor of Castille, homesick for the fruits of her native Spain, but this was a rare exception. From the end of the 14th century, however, the shipments became more frequent, carried in from Spain or Portugal, or on Italian spice ships.

As well as the citrus fruits themselves, confectionery made from them was also imported: quince marmalade or 'marmelada' from Portugal, described about 1450 as being 'comfortable for a man's body and namely for the stomach', and succade, a kind of marmalade using lemons or oranges.

During the 15th century oranges were bought as a treat by solicitous husbands and friends for pregnant wives. So usual was this custom in the Paston family that John the Younger felt he had to apologise when he asked for some to be sent to Elizabeth Calthorpe who 'longeth for oranges, though she be not with child'. When oranges were purchased, the juice went into sauces or pottages, while the lady of the house saved the rinds to make her own succade with a honey or sugar syrup.

Also on the spice ships came 'raisins of Corinth' [currants], prunes, figs and dates, much prized by the wealthy. Poorer people ate them during the twelve days of Christmas in festive pottages and pies, which have come down to us as mincepies, Christmas puddings and cakes. Meatless pottages, such as 'figgey' made from figs, raisins, pine nuts, spices and breadcrumbs boiled in wine, were served at Lent.

Walnuts, sweet chestnuts, hazelnuts and cobnuts were grown to eat whole after a meal to close the stomach, but almonds and pine nuts had to be imported from southern Europe. Pine nuts went into the pies and pottages of the wealthy, while the poor had to make do with cobnuts and hazelnuts. But by far the most versatile luxury import was almonds, brought into Britain on an enormous scale. The royal household consumed no less than 28,500 lb in 1286. Almonds could be added whole to certain dishes, or pieces were blanched, fried and scattered over the top as a decoration. Most often, however, they were pounded in a pestle and mortar to serve as a thickener for pottages and sauces. Almonds were especially useful for Lenten dishes when meat was forbidden, as they were a valuable source of protein: ground almonds could be substituted for pounded chicken or pork flesh, diluted with water or wine to make a substitute for cows' milk, or made into almond butter. Marzipan or 'marchpane' made from ground almonds and sugar was probably created in Italy in the 14th century, but it quickly became popular all over Europe. One of its early uses was to make 'subtleties' placed before an admiring audience at the end of each course of a great medieval feast (see p.67). In the 15th century, a 'marchpane' began to emerge as an object in its own right.

Even further afield, from southern China, the Moluccas, Malaya and India came exotic and expensive spices: pepper, cinnamon, saffron, ginger, cardamom, nutmeg, mace, cloves and others no longer in common use, such as grains of paradise, zedoary and cubebs. Spices, particularly pepper, ruled world markets in the Middle Ages. They were more expensive for the British because spices were not imported in direct shipments but had to be bought at the great Continental fairs until the 14th century, when the Venetian ships sailed as far as London and Southampton with their exotic cargoes.

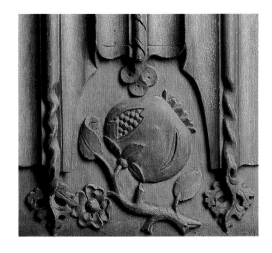

A detail from the early Tudor linenfold panelling in the Oak Gallery at The Vyne, Hampshire, showing a pomegranate, the badge of Catherine of Aragon. From the end of the 14th century, regular shipments of exotic fruits, including pomegranates, were made to Britain from Spain and Portugal.

Spices could be supplied already mixed by the grocer or the merchant; the commonest were 'blanch powder', 'powder fort' and 'powder douce'. Blanch powder was pale-coloured and made from ingredients like sugar, white ginger and cinnamon. In powder fort, hot spices such as ginger and pepper predominated. Powder douce contained some of the milder spices.

London was the centre of England's spice trade and the great importance of this trade is shown by the antiquity of the laws aiming at the control of the quality of spices sold. The London Pipe Roll of 1180 makes mention of a Guild of Pepperers, later to be called 'Grossarii' from which the name grocer is thought to be derived. Outside London, spices could be obtained periodically at the great regional fairs; prices were sometimes keener than those in the capital. But London could supply the rarer, more exotic varieties and they were available there throughout the year; so when a member of a household had to go to London on business, he was often commissioned to send or bring back several different spices. There are constant requests in the Paston letters for such goods: in one letter, Margaret Paston asks her son in London to let her know the price of pepper, cloves, mace, ginger, cinnamon, almonds, rice, saffron, 'raysonys of Corons' and galingale. A few landowners levied rents in agreed weights of pepper, hence 'peppercorn rent'.

The very rich were able to buy enough spices to flavour their food regularly and abundantly. The Duke of Buckingham in 1452–3 used almost 2 lb per day, but quantities were much less in more modest households: the Luttrell household at Dunster Castle used $\frac{1}{2}$ oz a day, but it seems likely that this amount was probably saved up for special meals rather than used every day to provide a light flavouring. For their daily meals a household had to be content with cheaper locally produced flavourings – salt, vinegar, mustard, onions and garlic. Mustard was the cheapest spice of all at less than $\frac{1}{4}$ d a lb in 1418, and was a popular sauce for all sorts of food. In towns it was also obtainable from professional sauce-makers: the Earl of Northumberland's household regulations of 1512 include instructions that mustard was now to be made by the 'Grome of the Skullery', rather than be bought from the 'Sauce-maker'.

Spices appear in every area of cookery: pies and tarts, sweets and even vegetables. The traditional explanation for the generous use of spices in medieval *haute cuisine* is that they were essential to disguise the dullness of salted flesh, or the unpleasant taste of tainted fish and meat. But it is clear from early manuscripts that spices were used just as much to flavour fresh meat and fish. Regular spicing seems to have been appreciated for itself as a status symbol. It is still difficult to judge how heavy this spicing was – in contemporary manuscripts there are vague instructions to 'take cloves, ginger, cinnamon, pepper and sugar,' but few recipes give any quantities and the spices must have varied in quality. So although medieval food was certainly well-seasoned, the result may have been tasty rather than fiery.

Of all the imported foodstuffs, sugar, from Brazil, the Azores, the Canary Islands and later, Cuba and Jamaica, was destined to have the greatest effect on Britain's eating habits. From the 13th century sugar began to replace honey as the standard sweetener, in wealthy households at least. Sugar arrived ready-processed in several grades according to the degree of refining. The coarsest was sold in large cones or loaves, weighing several pounds, which might be brown or almost black in the middle. Finer sugars were produced by a process known as 'claying'. Dark sugar, which included molasses, was also produced. Like spices and other exotic foodstuffs, it was purchased

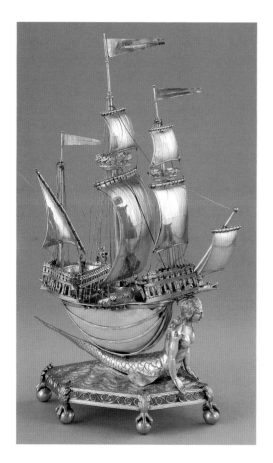

The Burghley Nef, containing a salt cellar.
A nautilus shell is mounted in silver parcel gilt,
French, Paris mark for 1482–3.

in London and requests to relations on business for sugar loaves frequent the Paston correspondence. Margaret Paston would write: 'I pray you that you will vouchsafe to send me another sugar loaf, for my old is done.'

In a great house, sugar was stored alongside the spices and kept locked up to be issued to the cook in relatively small quantities at a time. Sugar was treated as a seasoning, like salt and other spices, and was often sprinkled on a dish at the end of cooking just before it was 'served forth', or added to sauces. But perhaps its most spectacular use was in the making of medieval subtleties. For ordinary people, however, honey remained the universal sweetener. Bees were kept by many, for honey and for wax for candles.

The salt industry was indispensable for the preservation of both fish and meat. Production in Britain could not keep up with the ever-increasing demand, and by the beginning of the 13th century it was necessary to import 'Bay salt', prepared from sea-water drawn off into huge basins on the long level beaches of the French Atlantic coast and the beaches of northern Spain and Portugal. It was coarse, dark salt full of impurities, but much cheaper than carefully prepared table salt, and preferred for preserving purposes because it could penetrate flesh more completely and thus produce a better cure. It is clear from contemporary household accounts that families purchased both salts; Bay salt for preserving and white varieties for the table and cooking.

Visual effects were extremely important. Vivid colours were highly prized and often achieved at the expense of flavour: green from the juice of spinach or parsley was a favourite; brilliant yellow from saffron and egg yolks; red from sanders, a type of sandalwood from India, alkanet root and mulberries; deep purple from indigo, another Indian food colouring, turnsole and heliotrope; white from ground almonds, rice, milk, ground chicken or white fish; and black from pounded figs, dates, raisins and sometimes cooked blood. For special occasions, multi-coloured dishes were produced, such as pottages coloured in stripes, or two different hues. The grandest effects were achieved with gold and silver leaf, laid on the surfaces of gingerbreads and pies, or used to gild the beaks and feet of roast birds, like swan and peacocks for feasts.

It is remarkable that such *haute cuisine* and sophisticated effects could be attained in the relatively primitive facilities of the medieval kitchen.

II

The key factor for a great establishment, whether religious or secular, was that it should have a large kitchen. This was made necessary by the importance attached to food and drink in medieval and early Tudor times, and the manufacture and preserving at home of many more things than are customary today.

Life was largely communal with numerous people to cook for. As J. A. Gotch points out in his *Growth of an English House*: 'as in many other respects so in the kitchens, the great colleges at Oxford and Cambridge afford the best existing illustrations of the internal economy of a medieval house. They still have to cater for some hundreds of people daily, and so it was in the abbeys and great houses of the Middle Ages.' The great kitchen at Christ Church, Oxford, remains as it was in Wolsey's day, except for the introduction of modern equipment.

The great Abbot's Kitchen at Glastonbury, Somerset, dating from the mid-14th century (*left*). It was built to serve a household of about three hundred. Smoke, fumes and steam from the cooking were drawn up primitive flues into the roof, to escape through louvres (*right*).

Until the end of the 15th century, these large kitchens were almost always built some distance away from the house proper, as a precaution against fire. Frequently, they stood directly behind the hall beyond the pantry, buttery and larder, reached by means of a passage or covered way from the back door, or lower end of the hall. The risk of fire was intensified by the flimsy nature of the materials with which they were constructed. The original 14th-century kitchen for Chirk Castle would have been a timber-framed building ranged against the courtyard walls. A wooden kitchen of this type has been found at Weoley Castle, Birmingham; it had a reed-thatch roof and a covered wooden corridor linking it to the stone hall. Temporary wooden kitchens were also erected for great occasions, like those put up in 1273 at Westminster Palace for the coronation feast of Edward I.

In 1245–6, Henry III added a new kitchen to the hall at Clarendon Palace, near Salisbury, leaving the original as a 'privy kitchen' to serve only him, his family and important guests. The new kitchen served the rest of the household and was later to be

known as the 'hall kitchen'. This division was to become the standard pattern for the organisation of the kitchen buildings of royal and very grand courtier and ecclesiastical houses; the privy kitchen was eventually sited far from the hall kitchen and often directly beneath the rooms of the noble personage. Queen Elizabeth I was to object to this arrangement as the smells and noise of the kitchen rose up and disturbed her.

The last great surviving abbot's kitchen in Britain is the famous example at Glastonbury, dating from the mid-14th century. It was built to serve the abbot's household, which at one stage consisted of three hundred people, not counting the numerous guests who were entertained by the abbot at various times. Externally, the stone building is square, the normal shape at this time, measuring about 34 feet across, with an interesting octagonal sloping roof, built of fireproof stone, and a central tower on the top. Inside, the height from the floor to the bottom of the ventilating shaft in the roof is 41 feet, so the building is very lofty. Fireplaces for cooking the abbot's meat, game, fish and other delicacies were built into the far corners of the kitchen, making the

interior octagonal in shape. Smoke and the fumes and steam of the cooking were drawn up through primitive flues to escape through louvres which have now disappeared.

Glastonbury was not a magnificent exception: Gloucester, Durham, Canterbury and Jervaulx abbeys all had kitchens 40 feet long. The abbot's kitchen at Fountains Abbey has not survived, but enough remains of the main kitchen of the monastery for us to have a good idea of how it originally looked. It is not in a separate building, but placed at the west end of the south range where it could serve the refectory of the choir monks on the east and the refectory of the lay-brethren on the west, with a doorway leading into the cloister. Most of the kitchen's internal structures have gone, but their arrangement can be made out. The room, about 50 feet square, was originally whitewashed like the rest of the Ábbey and divided into two parts with two great fireplaces, which stood back to back in the centre of the floor, with a common flue that went up through the middle of the roof. The spaces between the sides of the fireplaces and the east and west walls of the room were vaulted and passaged; the main part of the kitchen was also vaulted. A door in the south wall led out to a covered passageway leading across the kitchen yard to a wooden footbridge over the River Skell; goods and fuel could be brought into the kitchen this way. There was probably a storage loft for flour and other provisions over the south end of the kitchen – beam holes exist at the level of the passage vaults.

Fountains Abbey, Yorkshire, one of the most spectacular medieval monasteries in Britain, founded by the Cistercians in the 12th century (*above*). The huge cellarium was used to store staple foods like flour, fish, dried vegetables and beer (*right*).

Below: The grating in the floor of the infirmary kitchen at Fountains Abbey. Refuse dropped through into a channel of the River Skell, the medieval equivalent of a waste-disposal unit.

Meat was never cooked in the main kitchen at Fountains Abbey, but in the infirmary kitchen which catered for the sick and elderly monks as well as those who had been bled. The present rectangular stone building, separated from the infirmary hall by a small yard as a precaution against fire, replaced an earlier kitchen on this site in the 14th century, when a meat diet was sanctioned in the Abbey. The room is divided into two by a cross-wall. The northern part was the main kitchen with its two kitchen fireplaces built into the cross-wall. Late in the Middle Ages, four ovens were also built. There is a stone grid in the floor, which was once fitted with trap-doors and could be used for the disposal of kitchen waste directly into the river below. The southern part of the building, the scullery, has the remains of the flagged floor with its stone gutters. A narrow recess in one of the corners of the scullery once housed a steep flight of stone steps, perhaps leading up into the flues where bacon could be hung for smoking.

In a great monastery like Fountains Abbey, the cellarer was in charge of all the staple foods like flour, fish, dried vegetables and beer for the monks, the lay brothers, the guests, the poor and for alms. These bulk foodstuffs were stored in the cellarium, which at Fountains Abbey consisted of two storage areas. The kitchener was the caterer for the monks and received a number of perishable foodstuffs, like honey, eggs and milk, directly from its outlying farms, the granges. He also requested bulk goods from the cellarer, and was in charge of all the food from the time it entered the kitchen until it passed into the refectory, although the actual cooking was at first done by lay-brothers, then by servants. The pittancer had charge of all the provisions for the pittances, or individual 'extra' dishes, which supplemented the 'general' dishes laid down by St Benedict's Rule for various feast days, while the almoner dispensed the charity of the abbey, including food, to the regular and casual applicants for help. The infirmarian had complete charge of what gradually became a separate establishment, complete with its own kitchen, refectory and garden.

Many castles also had large lofty kitchens. Defence was the primary consideration in house-planning in the Middle Ages, so doors and windows had to be small and placed where they were least vulnerable; wherever possible, the rooms, including the kitchen, faced inwards on to a courtyard. At Bodiam, a late 14th-century castle in East Sussex,

The three archways of the screens passage at Bodiam Castle, Sussex, connecting the great hall with its service rooms, the kitchen, buttery and pantry.

the central stone corridor between the buttery and the pantry led from the hall to the kitchen, a huge two-storey stone building at the south-west corner of the castle. The kitchen had to cater for about 150 people when the owner, Sir Edward Dalyngrigge, was in residence, and an even greater number when more retainers were called in to man the castle in times of danger. A door in one corner of the stone-flagged kitchen, with a giant four-light window above it, leads into the courtyard; the only other source of light is a tiny opening high up in the west curtain wall. Two great fireplaces, both 12 feet across, face each other on the side walls. The one on the north wall has two ovens adjoining it, both lined with tiles set edgeways to resist the heat during baking.

It was only in the late 15th and early 16th centuries that kitchens began to become an integral part of the house. However, they might still be in tower form and almost detached, such as the magnificent stone kitchen remaining at Stanton Harcourt near Oxford, built in the reign of Edward IV; or completely detached like the later kitchen of the 15th-century fortified manor of Compton Castle in Devon. The original buildings at the screens end of the hall, including the kitchen, had been taken down in about 1520, to be replaced by the new great kitchen. This was built in a separate tower, reached from a back entrance of the hall, and had to provide meals for some 200 people. It is a lofty room with a high vaulted ceiling to improve ventilation and to ensure that any condensation dripped down the walls and not on to the heads of the cook and his scullions. The two windows with ironwork lattice are rather high and small, not only for security but also, having the glassless windows in this position lessened the cross-draughts below, making the master cook's life a little less difficult. The gigantic hearth, extending the full 15 foot width of the room, was constructed by simply setting a beam across and building a double wall. Its open chimney is divided into three flues for the smoke and the smells to escape, presumably to give support to the inside wall and to improve the draught. On each side of the hearth, set into the wall, is a baking oven, one of which dates back to the original building of the house in 1320.

But the standard arrangement for kitchens in most substantial houses of this period was described by Andrew Boorde: 'The buttery and pantry be at the lower end of the hall, the cellar under the pantry, set somewhat lower, the kitchen set somewhat lower from the buttery and pantry coming with an entry by the wall of the buttery.' Doors in the screens passage would lead through from the buttery and pantry into the hall.

When Sir Piers Edgcumbe built himself a new hall at Cotehele around 1520, he produced a variation on this standard arrangement, perhaps because he seems to have left the original kitchen untouched. It is situated at right angles to the service quarters with access to the kitchen court, where there was a supply of water. One service doorway leads from the hall to the buttery, thence to the maze of larders and the scullery; the other to a passage leading to the kitchen at the north-eastern angle of the hall. The room, about 20 feet square, was not especially large as early Tudor manorial kitchens go, but typically it is very high to allow the smoke and cooking smells to drift out through louvred vents. Two enormous hearths on different walls dominate the room: one for boiling and roasting, the other for baking.

In a nobleman's house the clerk of the kitchen was the principal officer in charge of the domestic offices. He was advised and helped by the master cook, also a high-ranking household official in medieval times. One of the master cook's responsibilities was to arrange the menus, which on a feast day especially must have been extremely complicated. There would be guests of different grades and their servants, who all had

An engraving of the magnificent 15th-century stone kitchen at Stanton Harcourt, Oxfordshire. The huge wooden bin on the left is piled high with 5-foot long bundles of timber ready for the fires.

The huge open roasting hearth in the kitchen at Cotehele, Cornwall. The primitive rack above the hearth is typical of the medieval period, and was used for storing smoked and salted sides of meat and fish, bunches of herbs, and strings of onions and garlic. The square hole in the wall at the side of the hearth was traditionally used to keep dry the valuable salt and perhaps to hold the cook's hour-glass, but at Cotehele it may once have penetrated to the hall so that the cook might communicate with the steward.

to be fed different foods, members of clergy who had to have their own menus, as well as young children who had a quite different diet again. To help him prepare this vast range of food, the master cook had a number of assistant cooks and scullions or menials (from the French *meinée* meaning household). All the kitchen staff ate and slept in the kitchen itself, on straw pallets that were often shared.

Furnishings in a medieval kitchen were minimal: one or two heavy trestle tables whose tops were of thick axe-hewn oak planks, known as boards, and a stool placed in the hearth from which the master cook controlled operations. There would also be a large solid chopping-block for preparing meat, poultry and game. At Cotehele, a slice of tree trunk bound with iron hoops, standing next to the pestle and mortar, made a good chopping surface. Rough wooden shelves, pegs and racks on the wall would have held kitchen crockery of earthenware and pewter, wooden bowls, platters, pots and pans and other implements. A 12th-century writer tells us:

> In a kitchen there should be a small table on which cabbage may be minced and also lentils, peas, shelled beans, beans in the pod, millet, onions, and other vegetables of the kind that can be cut up. There should also be pots, tripods, a mortar, a hatchet, a pestle, a stirring stick, a hook, a cauldron, a bronze vessel, small pitchers, a trencher, a bowl, a platter, a pickling vat and knives for cleaning fish . . . . The chief cook should have a cupboard in the kitchen where he may store many aromatic spices, and bread flour sifted through a sieve may be hidden there . . . . Likewise there should be a large spoon for removing foam and skimming.

After the big cauldron, the most important piece of early kitchen equipment was the mortar and pestle. The majority of foods – meat, fish, poultry, game, herbs, spices, almonds, fruit and blacks of salt and sugar – were 'brayed' or pounded in a mortar at some stage in their preparation.

A square hole was traditionally left at the side of the hearth to hold and keep dry the valuable salt in its pot, and perhaps the cook's hour-glass: there were no clocks in private houses at this time, so this large 'egg-timer' filled with sand was the cook's only guidance. At Cotehele, the mysterious hole in the wall to the left of the roasting hearth may have been to store salt, or it may once have penetrated through to the hall so that the cook could communicate with the steward supervising the serving of meals. Smoked and salted sides of meat, dried and smoked fish, bunches of herbs, strings of onions and garlic and many other provisions were hung above the hearth and from the ceiling on wooden racks and pegs; the primitive rack above the hearth at Cotehele, although later in date, is a reminder of these. Bread and flour were kept in boxes or baskets well above floor level as some protection against rats and mice; the covered wooden hutch on a stand in the kitchen at Cotehele stored flour from the estate mill.

The huge open hearths, or 'down-hearths', typical of medieval and Tudor kitchens were the centre of the cook's activities and often the heart of the whole house. The earliest kitchens probably had a central hearth with an iron grate (*caminum ferreum*) and fireback (*reredos*), possibly with a plaster hood above, and a louver, or louvre, in the roof. This would have been the safest position in a wooden building. But where the kitchen was of stone, fires could be placed in the thickness of a wall, and provided with an arch and sometimes a flue. At Stanton Harcourt, there are two large fireplaces, but no chimney.

It was essential that the kitchen fire was kept burning continuously, because this hearth was often the principal source of heat for the house and, before the invention of matches, relighting it with a tinder box was very difficult. At night, the ashes were drawn over the embers to bank the fire down, then a bell-shaped iron, copper or brass cover, or *curfew* from the French *couvre-feu*, was placed over the dying fire to keep it in until the next morning when it would form the basis of the new fire. The curfew was also a sensible fire precaution and was a legal requirement from Norman times. A bell was rung at a fixed hour, telling everyone that it was time to cover their fires. The copper curfew in the fireplace of the dining-room at East Riddlesden Hall in West Yorkshire is a very rare survival from the 16th century, yet they must have been very

At night a bell-shaped iron, copper or brass cover or 'curfew' was placed over the dying kitchen fire to keep it in until the following morning. This copper curfew from East Riddlesden, Yorkshire, is a rare surviving example.

Left: Cardinal Wolsey's kitchen at Hampton Court, Middlesex, dating from *c*.1520. The storage loft above the hearth would be used for dried foodstuffs.

Right: The kitchen at Hampton Court includes the great roasting hearth installed by Henry VIII, after he had taken over the palace from Wolsey. Cauldrons were hung from the horizontal iron bar or 'galley-baulk' on adjustable iron pot-hangers over the fire. The door to the right of the hearth leads into the scullery.

common. In the morning the fire was restarted with a pair of bellows and a bundle of sticks or faggots, then huge logs kept it going throughout the day.

Generally there were at least two fireplaces in a large medieval kitchen ranged side by side, or in adjacent walls: one for roasting, the other for boiling and baking. Roast meat, much-prized in England at this time, was cooked over the open fire on a simple spit with a handle, also called a 'broche', 'broach' or 'flesh-pike', supported either by a pair of cob irons or by a rack fixed with two vertical rows of hooks, which could be leant against the back of the chimney breast. This rack could be taken out of the hearth when not in use, like the unusual racked iron dogs at Cotehele. The fat and juices from the roasting meat were collected in a four-legged dripping pan below, and the job of basting as well as turning the spit was allotted to a scullion called the 'turnspit' or 'child for the Broches', who was protected from the heat of the fire by a shield of wet straw, or a piece of wood with a hole in it, so that he could see to baste the meat with long-handled ladles. Turnspits usually lived in the kitchen and did not penetrate the other rooms in the kitchen complex. At Henry VIII's kitchens at Hampton Court Palace in Middlesex, the spits were turned by one of seven boys employed specifically for the job; the court rules insisted that they all wore clothes and did not relieve themselves in the fireplace when the cooks' backs were turned! The King's Ordinance of 1526 said:

> It is ordeyned by the Kings Highnesse, that the three master cookes of the kitchen shall have everie of them by way of reward yearly twenty marks, to the intent they shall provide and sufficiently furnish the said kitchens of such scolyons as shall not goe *naked or in garments of such vilenesse as they now doe, and have been accustomed to*

doe, nor lie in the nights and dayes in the kitchens or ground by the fireside; but that they of the said money may be found with honest and whole course garments, without such uncleannesse as may be the annoyance of those whom they shall passe . . . .

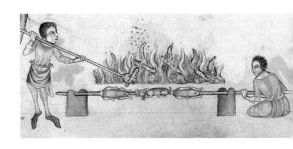

Smaller animals, like coney, rabbit, hare, lamb, kid and sucking pig were spitted whole, often with their heads left on, while larger animals were jointed before being put on the spit. Sometimes meat was parboiled before roasting to ensure tenderness, and lean meats like kid and coney were first larded. Kid and young pig were stuffed with a forcemeat containing dried fruits and spices. Meat balls made from ground pork or beef mixed with currants and spices, called 'pommes dorres', were very popular. They were threaded on to the spit, roasted and then dredged with a mixture of chopped parsley or saffron, flour and beaten egg. A still more exotic set piece was 'urchins' or hedgehogs, made from stuffed pigs' stomachs, pricked all over with holes, and stuck with split blanched almonds, then roasted on a spit. After roasting, the urchins were endored with coloured washes, some golden, some green and some black with blood.

Roast meat was served with a range of sauces, often made entirely separately and served in saucers, which were placed near the diners' trenchers. The sauces were usually vinegar-based, but could be of ale, wine or milk, and all highly seasoned. For wild fowl, roasting was the favourite method of cooking. Large fowls larded with pork fat were roasted on the usual meat spit, or for small birds special little spits were tied on to the full-sized ones. Alexander Neckham in the early 13th century gives us the earliest English examples of these seasonings and sauces: cumin for a boiled hen; a simple sauce without garlic for a roasted hen; a strong garlic sauce made with wine or verjuice or 'gauncil', a thick flour-based sauce flavoured with saffron and garlic, or 'sauce madame' made from herbs, quinces, pears, garlic and grapes mixed with wine for goose. Black sauces, made from the bird's innards boiled with strong spices and vinegar, accompanied roast capon, wild duck, hen and swan. Partridge and pheasant were served with ginger sauce, as were lamb, kid and sucking pig. 'Camelyn', a bread-based spicy sauce, was recommended for heronsewe, egret, crane, bittern, shoveller, plover and bustard. Small birds were served with salt and cinnamon.

The paramount show-piece of the medieval banquet was a 'peacoke in his hakell', that is, in the full glory of his skin and plumage. A manuscript of 1381 tells us how a peacock was prepared at a 'feeste royall': carefully skinned, it was stuffed with spices and roasted; during the roasting, a damp cloth around the bird's head kept it from singeing. When cooked, the bird was allowed to cool and then the skin was carefully sewn on again. Its comb, beak and feet were gilded, the tail feathers spread out and a wad of wool, dipped in spirits or wine, placed in the bird's beak to be set alight as the peacock was ceremonially carried up to the high table, perched upright on a platter 'as he was wont to sit alive'. It must have looked more beautiful than it tasted, because peacock's flesh was said to be tough and flavourless.

Many medieval houses, however, did not have the facilities for spit-roasting. Rural cottagers like the inhabitants of medieval Tŷ Mawr at Wybrnant in Gwynedd cooked over a wood and peat fire placed on a large flat stone in the middle of the hall, or living room; the other part of the house was used for sleeping and for storage. Small birds, eggs, fresh fish, hedgehogs or a poached squirrel might be wrapped in clay and baked in the hottest ashes of the fire. Alternatively, a rough kind of oven was constructed by

Two illustrations from the *Luttrell Psalter*. Small animals were roasted whole on a 'broche' or a 'flesh-pike' over the open fire, turned by a scullion called the 'turnspit' or 'child for the Broaches' who usually lived and slept in the kitchen (*top*). Boiling was the most important daily method of preparing food. Huge metal cauldrons, or 'kytels' with rounded bottoms and three stubby legs, hung over the fire for boiling water and making pottage. Another vital piece of early kitchen equipment was the mortar and pestle (*bottom*).

Dressed peacocks at Hampton Court. The paramount show-piece of the medieval banquet was a 'peacoke in his hakell'. The bird's skin and feathers were replaced after cooking, and it was carried to the high table with gilded comb, beak and feet.

raking a hole in the hot embers, into which the joint was placed, protected by a metal cover. Then the hot ashes were raked over the cover and the whole left to cook slowly.

Despite a popular belief that medieval lords lived entirely on roasts, in fact, many dishes – some extremely elaborate using the most exotic ingredients – were produced by other cooking methods. Boiling was the most important daily method of preparing food, common to rich and poor alike, all over Britain. A stout horizontal iron bar, a 'galley-baulk', or a wooden beam was fixed some distance up the chimney from which huge cauldrons, pots or 'cytels' (hence kettles), could be suspended by their handles over the fire on ropes, chains, iron rods, or adjustable iron 'reckon hooks' or pot-hangers. The chimney crane, a triangular iron bracket fixed to the back of the hearth, which could be swung out horizontally over the fire, provided an alternative method with the advantage that the position of the cauldrons and pots could be altered according to the heat needed. A crane which is adjustable vertically as well as horizontally can be seen in the roasting hearth at Cotehele, as well as adjustable pot-hangers. Cauldrons and pots for use on the fire were made of heavy metal – iron, brass or copper – with rounded bottoms to achieve an even distribution of heat, and usually three stubby legs, so that they could stand securely among the embers. The biggest iron cauldron, which was rarely moved, was used as a water boiler, providing the only source of hot water for washing up, etc. Another, the 'pot au feu' or 'chaudière' (hence chowder), acted as the stock-pot for making stews, broths and pottages.

In poorer households an iron cauldron was a valued possession; kitchen vessels were more usually of wood or leather, with a few earthenware pots to stand in the hot ashes beside the fire, or to balance on a tall stone among the embers. The cottage housewife could seethe or boil her pottage in this way, stirring it with a ladle or spurtle (a wooden stick). If the household did own a cauldron, it could be hung from an iron rod supported by iron firedogs on each side of the down-hearth, or from an iron tripod over the fire, as it probably was at medieval Tŷ Mawr.

In medieval Britain everyone, high and low, ate pottage daily. As late as 1542, Andrew Boorde wrote: 'Potage is not so much used in all Christendom as it is used in England. Potage is made of the liquor in the which flesh is sodden in, with putting-to chopped herbs, and oatmeal and salt.' The ingredients were many and varied. The object was to produce a semi-liquid spoonmeat, which might be a 'running' pottage, where the chunks of meat or fish lay at the bottom of the bowl with the broth or 'sewe' above; it would be almost thick enough to slice – that is, a standing or 'stondynge' pottage. Ordinary people ate simple pottages based on the bread corn of the region, such as 'grewell' made from oatmeal boiled in water with a little meat and a few herbs added, or 'pease potage' from dried peas, or 'porray', which was a thick pottage made from greenstuff. In contrast the nobility and gentry enjoyed some of the rich, spicy meat and fish pottages introduced from Normandy, such as 'civey', 'gravey', 'charlet', 'bukkenade', 'mortrews' and 'blancmange'. Frumenty or 'fyrmente', from the Latin *frumentum* for corn, was almost a national dish amongst the wealthy. It was made by boiling hulled wheat in milk with spices, and was served with venison or porpoise.

Other foods were cooked at hearth level, where irons or trivets, also known as brandises and brandreths, were important aids. Heat-proof pots were set on these three-legged stands (more stable than four-legged) above the hot coals, or the pots had three stubby legs moulded into their bodies so that they could stand in the hot embers. Trivets came in various sizes and heights, ranging from 6 inches to 3 feet. They enabled the cook to control the heat for the particular food or stage of cooking by moving the pot further away or nearer to the fire. Food could also be kept warm in this way. The skillet or posnet was the ancestor of the saucepan (the old name has survived in America) and was used for cooking a smaller quantity of food, or for sauces. It was made of very thick iron or brass, with a long handle and could be used with a trivet, or stood on its three stubby legs right on the edge of the hearth with red-hot ashes raked underneath its rounded base so that the food inside could heat up very gently. Pipkins were vessels of similar shape, but made of earthenware.

Frying-pans were almost identical in shape to those we use today, but with longer handles to protect the cook from the fat. Despite this, the pan was often fitted on to an iron frame and hung over the side of the fire from a pot-hanger as further protection. Many frying-pans, like trivets, were made with legs so that they could stand by the side of the fire. Fried fish was particularly popular; it was first coated in finely grated

The gigantic early 16th-century kitchen hearth at Compton Castle, Devon, with its bread ovens set into each corner. Two small windows with ironwork lattice provided security and lessened cross-draughts below.

breadcrumbs and then fried in olive oil in the rich man's kitchen and rape oil in the poor man's. This would then be garnished with fresh parsley and eaten with 'egerdouce', a spicy, vinegar-based sauce, or 'rapeye', a thick sweet pottage of dried fruit. Other fried dishes included pancakes and fritters, fried eggs, fried lozenges made of flour paste, 'pety pernollys' or 'pety pernauntes' – little pasties made of 'fair flour, saffron, sugar and salt' with a filling of marrow and dried fruits – and 'tansy', a kind of omelette flavoured with the leaves of the herb.

For grilling, the medieval cook had a long-handled, three-legged iron toasting stand or gridiron with horizontal prongs at one end, which could be used to cook pieces of meat and fish or slices of bread over the fire. A similar utensil was a wafering-iron, used to make crisp patterned wafers. It resembled a pair of iron tongs or long-handled scissors, with the insides of the blades cut into decorative patterns, some very beautiful. The salamander was another long-handled implement, named after the mythical lizard reputed to be able to withstand the fiercest flames. At Cotehele a salamander hangs alongside the ovens: its long handle is attached to a heavy disc of iron measuring about 6 inches in diameter and an inch thick, which was made red-hot in the fire and then held just over the top of custards, pastry cheese and cakes to brown or seal their surfaces without overheating the bulk of their contents.

Charcoal produced on the estate of a manor house was very widely used for cooking small quantities of food gently, simmering stews and hashes, making sauces and jellies, boiling preserves, and for grilling meat and fish. Portable charcoal braziers could be used in the open air of the kitchen court or set up in the kitchen itself. Chafing dishes, or chafers, could either stand on a trivet over a grate of charcoal, or glowing charcoal could be placed in the dish itself with a pan placed over the top.

The other cooking facility in the medieval kitchen was the oven. When there was only a central hearth, baking was usually done under an iron cover on the hearth but with wall chimneys and fireplaces, stone or tile ovens could be inserted. At first only the largest houses had their own ovens as part of the kitchen itself, as at Bodiam and Compton castles and at Cotehele. But later, when the kitchen was incorporated into the rest of the house, the bakehouse remained separate, because of the extra fire risk. There is a bakehouse marked on a plan of the 16th-century courtyard of domestic offices at Felbrigg in Norfolk, and there were probably timber bakehouses at Knole and Ightham Mote, both in Kent.

Ovens were large and beehive shaped with a solid oak and, later, metal door or 'stopper' as its only opening. Instead of having a fireplace and flues running beneath it, the oven was heated to the right temperature by kindling a fierce fire of dried faggots,

A detail from a contemporary painting of the Field of Cloth of Gold which took place in 1520. Beehive ovens, for baking bread and pies, and roasting spits have been set up, while finished dishes are set out on a serving-table.

peat or furze with a piece of burning wood from the kitchen fire on the floor of the oven itself. When the oven was hot enough, the ashes were scraped out with long-handled rakes and the floor cleaned with a mop of rags on a pole known in some parts of the country as a 'huzzy'. The weekly or twice weekly bake was then put in with a long-handled flat spade, called a 'peel' or 'peeler', from the French *pelle*, a spade. The handle was often 7 feet long, because the oven threw out a great heat. The door was then closed and sealed with clay. No further fuel was added: the heat stored in the bricks or stones was sufficient to cook all the bread required for the household, as well as pies, tarts, pastries and cakes, although considerable skill was needed to make the ovens work efficiently and to know when they were heated through. One method was to observe changes in the colour of the brick or stone as it got hotter. Some bakers threw a handful of flour against the side of the oven to see if it burned with a blaze of sparks, which meant that the oven was ready for baking. In some regions, a large white or light-coloured stone was built into the wall opposite the oven door, or in the side or top of the oven, which served as a crude thermometer by changing colour as the oven heated up: in Buckinghamshire this was called a 'wise man'. After the baking was finished, the residual heat would be used for various purposes, such as drying herbs, making charcoal, and for drying the wood for next baking day.

The bread was baked first when the oven was at its hottest, then pies, tarts and pastries, followed by the small spiced cakes which were served as an alternative to wafers to accompany the wine, bragot and mead that ended the medieval feast. Large cakes were made only for special occasions. Pies were usually made with savoury fillings, rarely with fruit. The pastry was made strong and plastic enough to be moulded into free-standing containers, called 'coffins', which were filled with a mixture of ingredients. In the *Forme of Cury* compiled *c.*1390 by Richard II's cooks, the cook was advised to prevent the lid sinking, to 'blow in the coffin with thine mouth a good blast of wind. And suddenly stop the hole, that the wind abide within, to raise up the coffin, that he fall not down'. For open pies or tarts, the shell was baked blind, then filled with a mixture of eggs with dried fruits and spices and occasionally small birds, or with cheese.

Because of the fire hazard, and the skills and costs involved in the construction, smaller houses usually did not have their own ovens. Peasants either brought their dough to the manorial bakehouse or open-air communal ovens which served the villages and hamlets, or they baked their bread at home on bakestones and iron griddles over the fire, or on the down-hearth under an up-turned pot.

The medieval scullery, named after the Norman-French 'escuelerie', from *escuele* meaning dish, was where all the washing up was done. If there was no separate scalding house, poultry, game and fish would also be cleaned here. A 12th-century anonymous writer recommends: 'Let there also be a cleaning place where the entrails and feathers of ducks and other domestic fowl can be removed and the birds cleaned'. It was essential to have at least one sink or the medieval equivalents – a wooden bench with wooden tubs on it, or a stone slab set on supports of some kind, hollowed out into a shallow trough with a drain at one end, called a 'gutterstone'. Tubs would stand in the trough for washing dishes and cloths: meat and fish could be cleaned in it and knives could be sharpened on the front edge. All kitchen utensils and equipment were cleaned with black soap – a mixture of sand, sifted ashes and linseed oil. The waste water was carried in a channel outside, where it soaked into the ground.

All the water needed in the kitchen and scullery might be carried in from a well

Steps lead down from the kitchen at Bodiam Castle to the well in the basement of the south-west tower. Eight feet in diameter and eleven feet deep, it provided all the water needed in the kitchen and scullery.

nearby, as at Compton Castle, or from the courtyard, as at Chirk Castle where a 93-foot shaft tapped an underground stream. As pumping techniques became more sophisticated in the 16th century, a pump might be positioned just outside the door.

Large lead rainwater cisterns fed from roof gutters, and drain-pipes were part of the ordinary furnishing of the kitchen court. The lead cistern in the kitchen courtyard at Cotehele is dated 1639 and bears the initials of Sir Thomas Coteel; it would certainly have had a predecessor. Andrew Boorde advised 'The water the which every man ought to dresse his meat with all, or shall use bakynge or brewynge, let it be runnynge; and put it in vesselles that it may stand there two or three hours . . . ; then strayne the upper parte throughe a thycke lynnen cloth, and cast the inferior parte away.'

In the early Middle Ages, the space under the first-floor solar of a large house, the 'undercroft', was used for the storage of winter supplies of grain and preserved meats and luxuries, like spices and fine wines. In many houses, like Compton Castle, the undercroft was later made into a parlour or withdrawing room and a larder had to be built instead. Even the humblest home had its larder where the bacon was kept after it had been salted down – hence 'larder' from the Norman-French 'lard', meaning 'bacon'. In Sir John Fastolf's larder at Caister Castle in Norfolk in the 13th century, he had '3 great standing tubs, 2 salting tubs, 1 barrel and 1 butcher's axe'. After salting, beef, pork, ham, bacon, tongues and sausages, and fish for Lenten use, were hung in the kitchen chimney for several days to smoke, then hung from racks or hooks in the kitchen, away from vermin. Green vegetables were salted down in crocks, cucumbers were pickled in brine, and root vegetables and pulses were stored alongside dried herbs, mushrooms and orchard fruit.

In larger houses like Knole, and Bodiam and Compton castles, ale, cider and wine were stored and dispensed from the 'buttery', or 'butlery', from the French *bouteillerie*, for a bottle store. This was a room leading off from the service end of the hall, often with a cellar underneath the buttery for additional storage, presided over by the butler. Opposite the buttery was the pantry, from the Norman-French *paneterie*, meaning breadstore. Here the bread was kept, as well as the table-ware, linen and candles ready to be taken into the hall at mealtimes by the pantler. He kept the bread in huge wooden chests known as 'arks' and it was his job to see that the bread was properly leavened and baked, and to apportion it among the household. John Russell, usher and marshal to Humphrey, Duke of Gloucester, wrote a *Boke of Nurture*, a complete manual for the upper servants of a mid-15th-century nobleman. The pantler's duties were:

> In the pantry, you must always keep three sharp knives, one to chop the loaves, another to pare them, and a third sharp and keen, to smooth and square the trenchers with . . . . Look that your salt be fine, white, fair, and dry . . . and see to it that the lid of the salt-cellar touch not the salt. Good son, look that your napery be sweet and clean, and that your table-cloth, towel and napkin be folded exactly, your table-knives brightly polished, and your spoon fair washed – ye wot well what I mean.

From the 15th century, especially in smaller houses, one office was often made to serve both as a buttery and pantry. In some of the largest houses, a separate confectionery or 'confectory' was provided, where the delicacies for the final course and the subtleties for a feast (see p.67) were prepared. At other times, pastry might also be produced here.

Food was served out of the kitchen through a wooden hatch or 'dresser window', as at

Great households like Hampton Court had a separate room, a confectionery, to prepare the subtleties and sweetstuff for the table. Sugar was purchased in large cones or loaves, in grades according to degree of refining. A salamander for browning the tops of custards and pies, and an iron for making wafers, stand on the shelf under the window.

The serving place built at Hampton Court by Cardinal Wolsey. Food from the kitchen was assembled on dresser hatches or serving tables before being carried into the hall.

Compton Castle, under the control of the clerk of the kitchen. He tried to ensure that exactly the right amount of food and no more, left the kitchens. In the 15th century dishes became more elaborate; coupled with the ceremony with which it was customary to bring them into the hall, this called for the creation of intermediate serving areas between the hall and the kitchen where both the food and the procession could assemble. Here the food could be checked more thoroughly, and given to the correct waiters to ensure that it reached its correct destination. Part of the kitchen at Knole was blocked off to make a large servery or 'surveying place', by Archbishop Bourchier in the late 15th century. This was equipped with a 'master cook's gallery' for him to make sure that the food was correctly dressed for the table. R. Warner in his *Antiquitates Culinariae* of 1791, remarks how much the tables of our ancestors exceeded his in the splendour of their appearance:

> Every decoration was added to the different dishes that the cook's imagination suggested to gratify the eye. The frequent use of gold and silver, the splendid representations of armorial cognizances, and the grand devices in pastry and sugar, which they termed 'sotelties', must have given a magnificence to the ancient English table of which we at present have no idea.

The following recipes are taken from three medieval cookery manuscripts. The *Forme of Cury* was complied *c.*1390 by master cooks to Richard II, well known for his interest in food. The other two collections are taken from the Harleian collection in the British Museum. The last recipe, dating from the 17th century, features a favourite medieval drink.

Chaucer's Cook from the Prologue to *The Canterbury Tales*, in the Ellesmere Manuscript:

For boiling chicken with a marrow-bone,
Sharp flavouring-powder and a spice for savour.
He could distinguish London ale by flavour,
And he could roast and seethe and broil and fry,
Make good thick soup and bake a tasty pie.
But what a pity – so it seemed to me,
That he should have an ulcer on his knee.

Spiced Mussel and Leek Broth

Cawdel of muskels

'Take and seeth muskels [mussels];
pyke hem clene, and waisshe hem clene
in wyne. Take almaundes & bray hem.
Take somme of the muskels and grynde
hem, & some hewe smale; drawe the
muskels yground with the self broth.
Wryng the almondes with faire water.
Do alle thise togider; do therto verious
[verjuice] and vyneger. Take whyte of
lekes & perboile hem wel; wryng oute
the water and hewe hem smale. Cast
oile therto, with oynouns perboiled &
mynced smale; do therto powdour fort,
safroun & salt a lytel. Seeth it, not to
stondying, & messe it forth.'

From the *Forme of Cury*, c.1390

Shellfish were a special treat during
Lent: cooked either in a single broth of
their own juice with perhaps a little ale,
or in rich spicy pottages like this recipe.

3 lb (1.5 kg) fresh mussels
2 tablespoons (30 ml) dry white wine
1 small onion, very finely chopped
8 oz (225 g) leeks, very finely sliced
2 tablespoons (30 ml) olive oil
1½ oz (40 g) ground almonds
2 teaspoons (10 ml) ground ginger
good pinch of saffron
¾ pt (450 ml) fish stock
salt and freshly milled black pepper
1 tablespoon (15 ml) white wine vinegar
4 tablespoons (60 ml) double cream

Thoroughly wash and scrub the mussels, scraping off any barnacles. Remove the beards and discard any mussels that do not close when given a good tap. Place in a large pan and add a dash of the wine. Cover with a lid and cook over a high heat for 4–5 minutes, shaking the pan until the mussels have opened. Strain the liquor through a colander into a bowl, reserving it. Heat the oil in a saucepan and soften the leeks and onions in it for about 3 minutes. Add the remaining wine and let it reduce by half. Stir in the ground almonds and spices. Mix the reserved cooking liquor with the fish stock and gradually add it to the pan, stirring well. Leave to simmer gently for 25 minutes.

Liquidise the soup and strain through a sieve into a clean saucepan. Taste and season as necessary, and sharpen with wine vinegar.

Discard one half of each mussel shell. Reheat the soup and stir in the cream and mussels. Serve immediately in bowls, with plenty of fresh crusty bread. Serves 4–6.

Sweet-Sour Sauce for Fish

Egerdouce of Fysshe

'Take loches or roches other tenches
other soles; smyte hem on pecys.
Fry hem in oyle. Take half wyne, half
vynegar, and sugur, & make a sirup;
do therto oynouns icorue, raisouns
coraunce, and grete raysouns. Do therto
hole spices, gode powdours and slat;
messe the fyssh & lay the sewe above
and serve forth.'

From the *Forme of Cury*, c.1390

'Egerdouce' was a sweet-sour pottage
in which kid, rabbit or sliced brawn
was cooked, but it also provided a spicy
sauce to accompany fried fish. The
sour element came from the red wine
or vinegar, the sweet from honey and
dried fruits.

6 fillets of sole
1 oz (25 g) butter and oil for frying

FOR THE SAUCE

2 tablespoons (30 ml) olive oil
3 oz (75 ml) onions, chopped
1 oz (25 g) large raisins, stoned
1 oz (25 g) currants
½ teaspoon ground ginger
½ teaspoon ground mace
good pinch of ground cloves
½ teaspoon salt
1 oz (25 g) sugar
4 fl oz (120 ml) dry red wine
3 fl oz (90 ml) red wine vinegar
3 oz (75 g) fresh breadcrumbs
water

Make the sauce first. Gently cook the onions in the oil until soft, then add the dried fruit, spices and salt. Cook for a few minutes. Heat the sugar gently with the wine and wine vinegar in another saucepan until the sugar has dissolved, then add to the onion mixture. Simmer together, covered, for about 15 minutes, then liquidise in a blender or food processor. Return the sauce to a saucepan and stir in the breadcrumbs. Thin with a little water, then taste and adjust the seasoning as necessary.

Fry the fillets of sole in a little butter and oil and arrange on a hot serving plate. Serve the sauce separately. Serves 6.

The dovecote at Ightham Mote, Kent.

Peiouns ystewed

'Take peiouns [pigeons] and stop hem with garlec ypylld [peeled] and with gode erbis ihewe [chopped herbs], and do hem in an erthen pot; cast therto gode broth and whyte grece [lard], powdour fort [a mixture of hot spices such as pepper and ginger], saffron, verious [verjuice] & salt.'

From the *Forme of Cury, c.*1390

Casseroled Pigeon with Herbs and Spices

4 oven-ready pigeons
12 large garlic cloves
4 teaspoons (20 ml) chopped fresh thyme
2 tablespoons (30 ml) chopped fresh parsley
salt and freshly milled black pepper
dripping or lard for frying
½ pt (300 ml) chicken stock
juice of ½ lemon
large pinch of ground ginger
pinch of saffron strands
½ teaspoon ground cinnamon
fresh herbs to garnish

Stuff each pigeon with 3 garlic cloves, 1 teaspoon (15 ml) chopped fresh thyme and ½ tablespoon (7½ ml) chopped fresh parsley. Season with a little salt and freshly milled black pepper, then brown the pigeons all over in a little dripping or lard in a heavy flame-proof casserole which is just big enough to take them. Pour over the stock, then add the lemon juice, ginger, saffron and cinnamon. Cover with a lid and cook in the centre of a moderate oven (180°C, 350°F, gas mark 4) for 1–1½ hours or until very tender. Taste the gravy and adjust the seasoning as necessary. Serve each person with a pigeon arranged on a slice of wholemeal toast with a little gravy poured over. Garnish with fresh herbs. Serves 4.

Chicken in Sauce of Three Colours

Capoun in Salome
'Take a Capon & skalde hym, Roste hym, then take thikke Almeunde mylke [almond-milk] temper it wyth wyne Whyte other Red; take a lytel Saunderys & a lytyl safroun, & make it a marbyl cloure, & so atte the dressoure throw on hym in ye kychoun, & throw the Mylke a-boue, & that is most commelyche, & serve fresh.'

British Library *Harleian Ms 279, c.*1430

Multi-coloured dishes like this were made for special occasions. A final garnishing with spice powder would take place at the dresser, before the dish was served at the second course.

$3\frac{1}{2}$–4 lb (1.75–2 kg) chicken
2 oz (50 g) ground almonds
1 oz (25 g) cornflour
$\frac{1}{4}$ pt (75 ml) water
$\frac{1}{2}$ pt (150 ml) dry white wine
pinch of salt
red food colouring
little powdered saffron
little powdered cinnamon
little white pepper
little powdered mace
2 oz (50 g) whole almonds, blanched and fried gently in butter
few whole cloves

Roast the chicken in the normal way.

Blend the ground almonds with the cornflour and water, then stir in the wine. Pour into a saucepan and cook gently until the sauce comes to the boil, stirring continuously. Simmer for 10 minutes taking care it does not stick, then add salt to taste. Divide the sauce into three. Leave one-third white; colour one-third red with food colouring; colour the final third yellow with saffron. Keep the sauces warm until the chicken is cooked.

Skin and carve the cooked chicken into 8 pieces. Arrange on a hot serving dish and sprinkle with white pepper and powdered mace. Pour the three sauces into a large warm bowl and swirl together gently to make a marbled effect. Pour over the chicken and decorate with the fried almonds and a few whole cloves and serve immediately. Serves 4.

Herb and Flower Salad

Salat
'Take persel [parsley], sawge, grene garlec, chibolles [spring onions], oynouns, leek, borage, myntes, porrettes [a type of leek], fennel, and town cressis, rew, rosemaye, purslayne; lave and wasche hem clene. Pike hem. Pluk hem small with thyme hande, and mingle hem wel with rawe oile; lay on vynegar and salt, and serve it forth.'

From the *Forme of Cury, c.*1390

This is the earliest salad recipe in English. Mixed herb and flower salads proved so popular that they continued in fashion through to the 17th century. The salad would change according to the season and what grew in each cook's herb garden, so adapt and experiment with the basic recipe as you wish, as long as the result is colourful.

2 bunches watercress
1 carton mustard and cress
2 oz (50 g) fresh parsley in sprigs
1 small leek, finely sliced
6 spring onions, chopped
1 oz (25 g) sorrel leaves, coarsely chopped
1 oz (25 g) dandelion leaves, finely chopped
1 small bulb fennel, sliced into matchsticks
1 oz (25 g) daisy leaves, finely chopped
few red sage leaves
few mint leaves
1 sprig of fresh rosemary, chopped
1 garlic clove
2 tablespoons (30 ml) wine vinegar
sea salt and freshly milled black pepper
6 tablespoons (90 ml) olive oil
violets, primroses, daisies, blue borage flowers, dandelions and alexander buds to decorate.

Wash and dry all the salad stuff and prepare it. Mix together in a large bowl, which has been rubbed well with a garlic clove, reserving the flowers. Place the wine vinegar, seasoning and olive oil into a screw-topped jar and shake well to blend. Pour over the salad just before serving and mix again carefully. Decorate with flowers as you wish and serve immediately. Serves 6.

Rich Custard Pie with Date and Prunes

Crustard Lumbard in paste

'Take good creme, and yolkes And white of egges, and breke hem thereto, and streyne hem all thorgh a straynour till hit be so thik that it will bere him self; And take faire Mary [marrow], And Dates, cutte in 2 or 3 and prunes, and put hem in faire coffyns of paast [pastry cases]; And then put the coffyn in an oven, And lete hem bake till they be hard, And then drove hem oute, and putte the licoure into the Coffyns, And put hem into the oven ayen, And lete hem bake till they be ynogh, byt cast sugur and salt in the licour whan ye putte hit into the coffyns; And if hit be in lenton [Lent], take creme of Almondes, And leve the egges And the Mary.'

British Museum *Harleian Ms 4016, c.*1450

Flaunes and crustards were the ancestors of our modern flans and custards; delicious titbits of meat, vegetables, fish and fruit set with egg yolks and cream and baked in pastry cases (coffyns). Crustard Lumbard was considered fine enough to appear in the third course at Henry IV's coronation feast in 1399, with its filling of strained eggs and cream, sliced dates, prunes and marrow. In Lent, when rich dairy products were forbidden, almond milk or cream was used instead.

FOR THE PASTRY

8 oz (225 g) plain flour
5 oz (150 g) unsalted butter
½ oz (12 g) icing sugar
1 egg yolk
about 3 tablespoons (45 ml) cold water

FOR THE FILLING

1 level teaspoon (5 ml) cornflour
about 1 oz (25 g) caster sugar
3 large egg yolks
1 pt (600 ml) double cream
a good pinch of saffron
2 oz (50 g) stoned dates, chopped
2 oz (50 g) no-soak prunes, chopped

First make the pastry. Rub the butter into the flour and sieve in the sugar. Stir together, then beat the egg yolk with most of the cold water. Add to the mixture and work quickly to a firm dough with a fork, adding the remaining water if necessary. Do not overwork the pastry, but knead lightly until smooth.

Roll out on a lightly floured board and line a greased deep 8-in (20-cm) flan ring or cake tin with a loose bottom. Pinch the top edge to decorate, prick the base and leave to rest in a cool place for about 30 minutes.

Line the pastry case with foil or greaseproof paper and baking beans, place on a pre-heated baking sheet and bake in a fairly hot oven (200°C, 400°F, gas mark 6) for 25 minutes, removing the foil or paper and beans for the last 5 minutes.

Meanwhile, make the filling. Mix together the cornflour and the sugar in a bowl; add the egg yolks one at a time, beating until all the sugar has dissolved. Heat the cream with the saffron slowly until just on the point of boiling, stirring to get the best possible colour from the saffron. Allow to cool for about 5 minutes, then strain on to the egg mixture and whisk. Taste the custard and add more sugar if you like. Sprinkle the chopped dried fruit on to the pastry base and pour over the custard. Return to a moderate oven (180°C, 350°F, gas mark 4) for about 30 minutes or until just firm, but a little wobbly in the centre. Remove from the oven and cool. Serve slightly warm, or cold. Serves 6–8.

Sir Geoffrey Luttrell and his family at dinner, from the *Luttrell Psalter*.

Frutours

'Take yolkes of egges drawe hem together through s streynour, caste there-to faire floure, berme [brewer's yeast] and ale; stere it togidre til hit be thik. Take pared appelles, cut hem thyn like obleies [communion wafers], ley hem in the batur; then put hem into a ffrying pan, and fry hem in faire grece or butter til they be browne yelowe; then put hem in disshes, and strawe Sugur on hem ynogh, And serve them forthe.'

British Museum *Harleian Ms 4016*, c.1450

Egg-batter fritters raised with ale-barm regularly appeared in medieval menus, usually as part of the last course. Apple fritters, strewn with sugar when available, were perhaps the best loved, but fritters of root vegetables – skirrets, parsnips or 'pasternakes' – were well liked too.

Wardonys in Syrup

'Take wardonys [wardens or hard pears], and caste on a potte, and boyle hen till they ben tender; then take hem up and pare hem, and kyttle [cut] hem in two pecys; take y-now of powder of canel [cinnamon], a good quantyte, and caste it on red wyne, and draw it throw [through] a strynour; caste sugre ther-to, and put it [in] an erthen pot, and let it boyle: and thanne caste the perys [pears] ther-to, and let boyle togederys [together], and when they have boyle a whyle, take pouder of gyngere and caste ther-to, and a lytil venegre [vinegar], and a lytil safron; and loke that it be poynaunt and dowcet.'

British Museum *Harleian MS 279*, c.1430

Warden pears were hard and much larger than any other varieties.

Pears in Wine Syrup

6 large firm pears
about ¾ pt (450 ml) dry red wine
4 oz (125 g) caster sugar
½ teaspoon ground cinnamon
pinch of ground ginger
red food colouring (optional)
small bay leaves to decorate

Put the wine, sugar and spices in an enamel-lined or stainless steel saucepan just large enough to hold pears standing upright. Heat gently until the sugar has dissolved, then bring to the boil and simmer for 5 minutes.

Meanwhile, peel the pears as thickly as possible, leaving the stalks on. Core them from the base if you wish. Put the pears into the hot syrup, cover and simmer very gently for 15–20 minutes, or until just tender, basting the pears to a serving dish. Taste the syrup and stir in a little more sugar to taste, then boil rapidly without covering until reduced by half and of a coating consistency. Cool a little, then spoon over the pears to give them an attractive reddish gleam. If the colour of the syrup does not seem bright enough, intensify it with 2 or 3 drops of red food colouring. Continue to baste the pears with the syrup until cold, then chill until ready to serve. Decorate with bay leaves stuck into the stalk ends of the pears. Serves 6.

Apple Fritters in Ale Batter

4 medium cooking or crisp, tart, eating apples
1 tablespoon (15 ml) lemon juice
caster sugar

FOR THE BATTER

4 oz (125 g) plain flour
½ teaspoon ground cinnamon
2 tablespoons (30 ml) sunflower oil
¼ pt (150 ml) pale ale, or still dry cider
2 egg whites
oil for deep-frying
caster sugar and ground cinnamon for
   sprinkling

Make the fritter batter first so that it has time to rest for at least 30 minutes before using. Sieve the flour and cinnamon together into a bowl. Make a well in the centre, pour the oil into this, followed by the pale ale or cider. Gradually beat the liquids into the dry ingredients, to make a smooth creamy batter. Set aside for 30 minutes.

When ready to cook, heat the oil for deep-frying to 190°C (375°F). Peel, core and slice the apples into ¼-in (7-mm) thick rings and sprinkle with lemon juice and caster sugar. Whisk the egg whites until stiff and fold them into the batter to make it extra light. Make the fritters in small batches, 3 or 4 at a time. Pat the apple slices with kitchen paper to mop up any excess lemon juice, dip them into the batter using a skewer or kitchen tongs, then shake off any excess batter. Lower carefully into the hot fat and fry for about 4 minutes or until golden brown and crisp. Drain well on kitchen paper and keep hot in a single, uncovered layer in the oven until all are cooked. Serve piping hot, dusted with caster sugar and cinnamon. Serves 6.

Red and White Gingerbread

Gyngerbrede

'Take a quart of hony, & sethe it, & skeme it clene; take Safroun, poudir Pepir & throw ther-on; take gratyd Brede & make it so chargeaunt [thick] that it wol be y-leched; then take pouder Canelle [cinnamon] & straw ther-on y-now; then make yt square, lyke as thou wolt leche yt; take when thou lechyst hyt, an caste Box [garden box] leves a-bouyn, y-stykyd ther-on, on clowys [cloves]. And if thou wolt have it Red, coloure it with Saunderys [sandalwood] y-now.'

British Museum *Harleian Ms 279, c.*1430

Gingerbread, both red and white, was a favourite medieval sweetmeat. Home-made gingerbread could be prepared by mixing breadcrumbs to a stiff paste with honey, pepper, saffron and cinnamon. Ginger is omitted from the earliest recipe we have (see above), but this may be due to an accidental slip on the part of the scribe. Once made, it was shaped into a square, sliced and decorated with box leaves impaled on cloves.

1 lb (450 g) clear honey
tiny pinch of powdered saffron
1 teaspoon (5 ml) ground black pepper
2 teaspoons (10 ml) ground ginger
2 teaspoons (10 ml) ground cinnamon
about 1 lb (450 g) fresh white breadcrumbs
box leaves, or small bay leaves, and whole
  cloves to decorate

Warm the honey over a gentle heat until quite runny, then stir in the saffron and pepper. Pour into a large bowl and add the ginger and cinnamon, then mix in the breadcrumbs. It is impossible to say exactly how many bread-crumbs the honey will absorb because it varies, but the mixture should be very stiff. If not, add a few more breadcrumbs. Line a shallow gingerbread tin with baking parchment and press the mixture into it with your fingers. Level the top and leave to firm up in the fridge for several hours, then turn out on to another sheet of paper and cut into small squares. Arrange the gingerbread on a large plate, then decorate each square with two box or small bay leaves and a whole clove stuck in the centre. You can achieve an even prettier effect by gilding a few of the leaves or painting the ends of some of the cloves red.

If you want to achieve a chequerboard effect, make the mixture up in two lots, adding a few drops of red colouring to one quantity of honey before mixing, then continue as before. Arrange the red and white squares of gingerbread alternately on the serving plate. Makes 12 servings.

Spiced Red Wine

To Make Ipocras

'Take a galon of claret or white wine and put there in 4 ounces of ginger, an ounce and half of nutmegs, of cloves, an quarter of Sugar, 4 pound. Let all this stand togeather in a pot at least twelve houers, then take it and put it in a clere bage made for the purpose so that the wine may come with good coller from the wine.'

From a manuscript at Erddig, *c.*1686

Hippocras, a rich sweetened and spiced wine drunk after meals was still in vogue during the 17th century.

3 pt (1.5 litre) bottle dry red wine
8 oz (225 g) granulated sugar
1 oz (25 g) ground ginger
¼ oz (6 g) ground cinnamon
¼ oz (6 g) ground cloves

Heat the wine gently with the sugar until it has dissolved, stirring frequently. Mix in the spices, then allow to stand for 24 hours, stirring occasionally, then strain through a jelly bag or a double layer of muslin into a jug or bowl.

Pour back into the wine bottle and recork until needed. Makes 10–12 glasses.

A monk in the wine cellar,
from a 14th-century manuscript.

III

Then forth came the first course with fanfare of trumpets,
on which many bright banners bravely were hanging . . .
Then forth was brought the feast, fare of the noblest,
multitude of fresh meats on so many dishes

Sir Gawain and the Green Knight

The medieval and early Tudor emphasis on hospitality as both a social duty and a means of displaying one's power, meant that everyone, whether rich or poor, took pride in giving the best they could afford to all their visitors; but the number of people who had to be accommodated unexpectedly in large households must have put a severe strain on even the best regulated. On one day in the 15th century, the Duke of Buckingham apparently had 319 'strangers' or visitors to dine with him and 279 guests to supper the same evening. By this time, however, there was evidence of a new stringency in attitudes towards guests and hospitality. Households began to charge visitors for their keep. When Lady Harington stayed with the Luttrells at Dunster Castle for eight months in 1423–4, she gave Sir Hugh £32.

The strangers might be influential guests, or messengers, or work people from outside the lord's immediate domain who had to be fed and given accommodation because transport was so difficult. Hospitality was also extended to tenants, notably the Christmas feasts given by lords, who expected their generosity to be reciprocated by feelings of respect, loyalty and deference.

In days before hotels, the abbeys and other religious houses scattered throughout the country were of great service to travellers, of the highest rank downwards. In Cistercian abbeys the guest-house tended to be a separate building, usually in the outer court, as at Fountains Abbey in Yorkshire, where two remain. The abbot also regularly invited the local gentry and fellow clergymen to dinner in the same way as a lord of the manor.

Medieval households varied enormously in size, from the royal establishments which might number as many as 400 in the late 14th century to as few as 20 in the manor houses of the lesser gentry. Sir Hugh Luttrell of Dunster Castle, a modest knight, gave liveries in 1425–6 to four gentlemen, eleven yeomen and four grooms.

The number of retainers demonstrated to visitors a lord's importance; his status was further enhanced by the degree of ceremony and ritual attending the serving of meals. Great feasts were, above all, occasions for display: the brilliance of the surroundings, the costume of the diners, the liveries of the many servers and the tableware, were matched by an abundance of food based on substantial pottages and good roasts, served on a lavish scale. Feasts held in smaller manor houses were more modest, but ritual and ceremony remained extremely important. Even if the food was simple and the home poor, every time the table was laid for meal it was a reflection of the Last Supper.

Three meals a day were eaten by most people in medieval and early Tudor times: *Jantaculum*, or breakfast, taken at sunrise; *Prandium*, or dinner, taken about midday; and *Cena*, or supper, eaten in the early evening about 5pm or 6pm.

Breakfast was a substantial meal for those who could afford to make it so, consisting of bread, cold meats, fish, cheese and ale, beer or wine. The Northumberland

The Duc de Berry dining at high table, from the 15th-century *Très Riches Heures*, showing fine white damask tablecloths, silver and gold serving dishes, the gold or silver-gilt nef and the pile of spare bread trenchers. The carver, equipped with a towel and napkin draped over one shoulder and a handsome set of knives at his waist, works at the open front of the high table. The butler serves the drinks at the 'cupboard' or buffet, also used to display plate.

Household Book lists the provisions for breakfast for the members of the family of the 5th Earl of Northumberland in 1512: 'For Braikfaste for my Lorde and my Ladye on Flesche days dayly throwte the Yere' they were served 'Furste a loif of bred in trenchors [bread sliced into trenchers], 2 manchets [round loaves of the finest wheat bread], a quart of bere, a quart of wyne, half a chyne of mutton or ells a chyne of beif boiled'. On fast or 'meagre' days, the meat was replaced with '2 peces of salt fyshce, 6 baconn'd [red] herryng, 4 white [pickled] herryng or dysche of sproits [sprats].' For 'my Lady's Gentylwomen', her bodyservant, 'A loif of houshold breid, a pottell [½ gallon] of bere and 3 mutton bonys boyled, or ells a pece of beif boyled.' The children in the nursery were given 'a manchet, one quart of bere, a dysche of butter, a pece of saltfish, a dysche of sproittes, or 3 white herryng' on fish days, and 'a manchet, one quart of bere and 3 mutton bonys boyled' on flesh days. Everyone took breakfast informally; the lord and his family in their private chamber, while the children ate in the nursery. For poorer households, breakfast consisted simply of bread with ale or wine.

Dinner was the chief meal of the day. The first course in a nobleman's house according to John Russell in his *Boke of Nurture*, c.1450, was made up of 'such potage as the cooke hath made of yerbis [vegetables], spiece and wyn', and a handsome assortment of the more substantial foods, like roasted and boiled meats, pies and brawn: there was little in the way of fish in any course on flesh days. This substantial first course of the menu was the everyday, basic meal for many members of the household. The more delicate dishes of game birds, poultry and rabbits, and rich sweet items like custards, tarts and fritters were served as second and third courses, reserved for the higher ranks and honoured guests. A late 14th-century menu for a feast on an ordinary flesh day appended to copies of the *Forme of Cury*, c.1390, reads:

1st Course

Boars' head enarmed [larded]

Bruet of Almayne to pottage
  [coneys or kids cut into small pieces and parboiled in broth, then reboiled with
  almond milk, galingale, ginger and rice-flour and coloured red with alkanet]

Teals baked and woodcocks

Pheasants and curlews

2nd Course

Partridge, coneys and mallard

Blank dessorré
  [a pottage of ground almonds and white wine or broth, thickened with
  rice-flour and ground chicken flesh, seasoned with sugar, salt and saffron]

Cawdel ferry
  [wine sweetened with sugar or honey, thickened with fine white flour and
  heated with saffron and egg yolks, with ginger and sugar sprinkled on the top]

with Flampoyntes of cream and Tarts
  [open tarts with a creamy filling including ground pork flesh and cheese and
  sometimes ground figs and spices, with small points of pastry stuck into them]

3rd Course

Plovers, laverocks [larks] and chicken forced [stuffed]

Mawmenny
   [a pottage of shredded chicken or pheasant flesh, sweetened wine, fried pine
   nuts and dates, and spices, coloured red with sanders – a type of sandalwood
   – or yellow with saffron]

A subtlety would have followed each course [see p.67].

A fish day menu for a great medieval feast runs:

1st Course

Vyaund Ryal
   [sweetened wine, spiced and thickened with rice-flour, coloured red with
   mulberries or sanders]

Sew Lumbarde [broth]

Salt fish and Salt Lampreys

Pike, Bream and Roast Salmon

Crustarde Lumbarde [an egg custard tart with dried fruits]

A subtlety

2nd Course

Porpoise with Furmenty
   [a dish of boiled, hulled wheat resembling a modern wheat porridge with
   ground almonds and pieces of porpoise]

Geleye [a fish jelly]

Bream, salmon, conger eel, gurnard and plaice

Lamprey pie

Leche frys [tarts of cheese, butter and egg yolk]

A subtlety in the shape of a crowned panther

3rd Course

Creme of Almaundys
   [thickened confection of almond milk and sugar curdled with vinegar]

Pears in syrup

Tench, trout, fried flanders, perch

Roast lampreys and roast eels

Sturgeon and boiled crab

Graspeys [Royal fish like sturgeon or whale]

A subtlety in the shape of a crowned eagle.

Before it left the kitchen each dish was portioned into helpings, or 'messes', designed to be shared by two or four people, who ate from a shared platter or bowl, or transferred pieces of food to their trenchers. For a great feast there might be up to twenty dishes in a course and three main courses, as well as a 'sotelte', or subtlety – an elaborate sculpture of sugar and almond paste, sometimes combined with jelly and gilded – at the end of each course. The sotelte, a food made to look like something else, was created with loving care by the master cook, or the confectioner, to honour the principal guest.

The subjects, however, were not always subtle: 'At a bridal feast', writes John C. Jeaffreson in *A Book about the Table* of 1875, 'one at least of the subtleties always pointed with greater, or less (usually less) delicacy to what dear old Samuel Richardson calls in one of this models 'the parturient circumstances of matrimony'. Other subjects might be hunting scenes, fully armed ships, castles or religious scenes. The subtlety brought in at the end of the first course of the feast given to celebrate the installation of John Stafford as Archbishop of Canterbury in 1443 was composed of eleven dishes described as: 'Seint Andrew sitting on hie Auter of a-state, with bemes of golde; afore him knelyng ye Bisshopppe in pontificolibus; his Croser kneling behinde him coped'. However, this was probably modelled in plaster and wood rather than in marzipan, as were most of the complicated subtleties by the end of the Middle Ages.

We know a great deal more about medieval feasts, especially grand ones, than ordinary dinners because the method of serving, the seating arrangements and the menus of some of them were recorded in detail at the time. The quantities of food were enormous and although such gargantuan meals marked special occasions, there was a good deal of extravagance and luxury at the tables of both secular lords and of the Church. Edward III passed sumptuary laws regulating food of citizens:

> No man, of what estate or condition so ever he be, shall cause himself to be served in his own house or elsewhere, at dinner, meal or supper, or at any other time, with more than 2 courses, and each mess of 2 sorts of victuals at the utmost, be it of flesh, or of fish, with the common sorts of pottage, without sauce or any other sorts of victuals. And if any man choose to have sauce for his mess he may, provided it be not made at great cost; and if fish or flesh be to be mixed therein, it shall be of 2 sorts only at the utmost, either fish or flesh and shall stand instead of a mess, except only the principal feasts of the year, on which days every man may be served with 3 courses at the utmost after the manner aforesaid.

In contrast to all this extravagance, the peasant's dinner would consist of cereal or vegetable pottage with a little salt bacon, rabbit or fowl added occasionally, and accompanied by coarse bread and cheese. Milk or ale was drunk with the meal, which in summer might end with fresh fruit gathered from the woods and hedgerows.

Supper for the wealthy also consisted of two courses, each made up of a number of meat or fish, poultry and game dishes, though lighter than those for dinner:

> In seemly enough style servants brought him
> Several fine soups, seasoned lavishly
> Twice-fold as is fitting, and fish of all kinds –
> Some baked in bread, some browned on coals,
> Some seethed, some stewed and savoured with spice,
> But always subtly sauced, and so the man liked it.

This meatless supper from *Sir Gawain and the Green Knight*, written in the 14th century by an unknown author, was served to Sir Gawain in a private chamber on Christmas Eve, a semi-fasting day.

On some fasting days, such as Fridays in Lent, supper was missed out altogether, or replaced by a warm drink. Supper was taken in the early evening, but in large households each member was also provided with an allowance of bread, meat and ale to consume in their quarters before retiring. A departing guest would be given a light repast, or 'voyde', consisting of roast apples, pears, 'blaunche powder' – powder of cinnamon, ginger and nutmegs – for the digestion and hippocras. On special occasions, fruit, both fresh and dried, was also served, with sugar plate (similar to modern fondant icing), comfits, spices served on silver plates, hard cheese, wine and a subtlety. By early Tudor times, the voyde had become an informal snack to be enjoyed between meals as well as after supper, and on important occasions was known as a 'banquet'. In Henry VIII's reign banquets followed masques and pageants, and were noted for their lavish display of plate and confectionery.

Throughout the Middle Ages and well into the 16th century, the hall was the centre, literally and metaphorically of every home of any importance. The largest room, it acted as estate office, parish hall, court room, living-room, dining-room, bedroom for servants and thoroughfare for people passing into the inner chambers of the building. Here, twice a day, at noon for dinner and early evening for supper, the lord, or in his absence, his steward, presided at the high table over communal meals; every member of the household – the whole 'family', as the lord would have called those in his employment – was expected to attend. Contemporary households' regulations make it clear that being absent from hall at meal times was a serious offence.

From the late 11th century, the hall could be at first-floor level, allowing for storage, or servants' quarters underneath. Such arrangements were ideal in a monastery, where the abbot's quarter could be incorporated into the monastic cloister; the abbot's house at Fountains Abbey was of this type, as are the two guest-houses. However, most great halls were built on the ground floor and extended to the full height of the house, like Thomas Tropnell's 15th-century hall at Great Chalfield Manor near Melksham in Wiltshire. The proportions of these medieval halls were impressive: Great Chalfield, Cotehele and Rufford in Lancashire all measure about 40 feet in length, 20 feet in width and 30 feet in height. Fourteenth-century halls, like those at Ightham Mote and Compton and Bodiam castles had to be high so that smoke from the central fire would rise well above people's heads and not choke them, before it drifted out of the roof through 'louvres', or smoke turret which could be regulated by 'louerstrynges'. But height was also important as a status symbol and halls continued to be lofty after the central fireplace had been replaced by the wall fireplace from the 15th century onwards.

The high table was placed crossways, often on a raised platform or dais, and this came to be known as the 'high end' of the hall even when the table was placed directly on the ground, as at Ightham Mote. The fireplace was built in a wall near the high table to warm the lord, his family and guests, and in grander establishments large windows threw sunlight on the dais – again, a sign of status. In the hall at Cotehele, panels of heraldic glass are emblazoned with the arms of important Edgcumbe connections and relations proclaiming the owner's standing. Walls were whitewashed or colour-washed, either with a mixture of powdered chalk and water, or with a mixture of lime, sand and hair. From the 12th century, the high table was often emphasised with arcading or

Although this lithograph by Nicholas Condy depicts the hall at Cotehele, Cornwall, arranged for a tenants' dinner *c*.1840, the position of the tables shows how it would have looked in the late 15th century, in the time of Sir Piers Edgcumbe, with the high table placed crossways at the top of the hall. Diners would sit on benches on only one side of the tables, with the lord sitting in his chair of state.

special painted wainscotting 'to the extent of five couples beyond the King's seat', as favoured by Henry III.

The use of woollen cloths to cover the walls, and from the 14th century, tapestry, seems to have begun at the upper end of the hall behind the dais, to make it more comfortable and to lessen the draught. This backing fabric became steadily more elaborate, until it was combined with a canopy over the chair of the lord emblazoned

The medieval great hall at Rufford Old Hall, Lancashire. At the 'high' end of the hall is built the great coved canopy, under which Sir Robert Hesketh's chair of state was placed behind the high table (*left*). At the service end stands the early 16th-century movable oak screen with its rich carved decoration (*above*).

with his 'cloth of estate'. At Rufford Hall a magnificent coved canopy has survived: the chair of state belonging to Sir Robert Hesketh would originally have been positioned under this canopy, in the recess which once existed in the centre of the wall-bench behind the high table. When several very grand personages were present, the canopy might extend over a group of people. The most important person present sat on what was usually the only chair on the dais – and often the only one in the house – placed centrally behind the high table, so he was immediately recognisable. This tradition survives in the single chairman of a board and the single occupant of the 'chair' of a university department. Often he was the host, but the exact observance of the rules of precedence meant that this significant place might be occupied by a guest of higher estate than the host, who then had to sit further down the table. The 'chair of estate' could be decorated with knobs and panels of copper or covered with a piece of rich cloth, and often folded flat so that it could be carried in the luggage when the lord moved on to the next castle or manor house.

With this went his other important pieces of furniture, his valuable hangings, bedding, kitchen equipment and his servants. Even in the early 16th century, when progresses between estates were much less frequent, the 5th Earl of Northumberland required a baggage train of some 27 waggons when he moved between houses, taking with him household goods; those included: 'the stuff in the chamber where my Lord dineth . . . the kitchen stuff as pots, pans, trivets, racks and pastry-stuff . . . with the two beds for the three cooks to lie in . . . a bed for the minstrels.'

Diners at the high table, other than the lord or chief personage, sat on stools, chests or coffers, or sometimes two or three of them shared a high-backed settle placed along the wall, facing outwards towards the minstrels' gallery; this was a prime position to look down the length of the hall and watch the servants approaching with the food. If the party was a large one, lesser members took their places at the two short ends of the table, where they sat on stools, but the long front side of the board was left open, so that the servants could approach with food and drink, and to emphasise the fact that the lord was dining in public. Those present were predominantly male; the only women partaking might be the wives of the host and principal guests. Often the lord's wife preferred to eat with her ladies in her chamber.

Most of the furniture associated with dining or feasting was not kept permanently in position because of all the coming and going and the lack of security. In later medieval times the table on the dais might be permanent and was then known as a 'table dormant' or simply as a 'dormant', but otherwise it was a trestle brought out with the other furniture and hangings to adorn the hall for each great feast.

In the body of the hall, simple wooden boards were laid on A-shaped trestle frames, stored nearby when not in use. These 'tables' were placed along one, or both, of the long sides of the hall; that on the lord's right was the most senior and was called the 'Rewarde', because it was served with the dishes from the lord's own table. The table opposite was called the 'Second Messe' and the rest were graded similarly. The lower the rank, the further one was placed from the 'high end'. At a big feast, the lesser guests might spill over into several rooms and even the minstrels' gallery. They all sat on forms or benches on one side only of the long trestle tables, so that they could enjoy a good view of the meal's entertainment – an arrangement still preserved in the halls of many university colleges.

The only other piece of furniture set up in the hall for a feast was the 'cup-board or buffet', literally a board for cups, set on trestles, placed near the high table. It was draped with a cloth of silk, or some other sumptuous material. By the 15th century, illustrations show that it had developed a high-backed frame with tiers of shelves, or stages, and sometimes a canopy. On the shelves was a display of richly decorated gold, silver-gilt or silver cups, bowls and jugs, sometimes encrusted with jewels – a powerful symbol of the wealth and importance of its owner. Lords would accumulate plate partly as a means of storing wealth: Sir Hugh Luttrell of Dunster Castle bought silver plate worth £54 – about one-sixth of his normal annual income – in 1414–15.

The earliest hall floors would have been of hard-beaten earth, chalk and plaster, except for the dais, which was paved with stone or made of wood. Later halls were stone-flagged or tiled although, even in the early 16th century, some were still floored with earth and were strewn with rushes and clippings of pungent shrubs to keep down the dust and sweeten the air. Thomas Tusser in his *A Hundredth Good Pointes of Husbandrie* of 1557, lists 21 herbs suitable for strewing, from basil and camomile to violets and winter savory. Cardinal Wolsey impregnated the rushes on the floors of his apartments at Hampton Court with saffron. The Dutch humanist Erasmus was outraged by the filth in the Englishman's house, complaining in a letter to Wolsey's physician: 'The floors are commonly of clay, strewed with rushes, under which lies unmolested an ancient collection of beer, grease, fragments, bones, spittle [it was perfectly correct to spit as long as you ground the spittle into the floor with your boot], excrement of dogs and cats, and everything that is nasty.' Although there was certainly cause for complaint, archaeologists have been impressed by how the clay floors of medieval houses had been scoured by constant sweeping. Perhaps more housewives than Erasmus realised had heeded the advice of the 16th-century writer Sir Anthony Fitzherbert: 'First sweep thy house, dress up thy dishboard and set all things in good order.'

The far end of the hall, opposite the dais, was the service or low end where there might be as many as five doorways: the two or three service doorways leading to the buttery, pantry and kitchen, the entrance to the hall on a side wall and usually a back door opposite. To control the constant traffic here and to lessen the draught from these openings, the service came to be screened off, thus forming a screens passage or cross-passage. At first the screening was only partial and could be movable, like the wonderfully carved wooden screen at Rufford Old Hall dating from the early 16th century, the only one of its kind known to have survived intact. Later, the screen, usually of carved and panelled wood with two or three doorways built into it, was made permanent, often with a minstrels' gallery. The original screen at Great Chalfield was made in three separate sections with three service doorways and a minstrels' gallery above. There is also a spacious minstrels' gallery above the oak screen at Compton Castle, with two doorways leading into the screens passage.

In the later Middle Ages, the desire for greater privacy and comfort caused the lord and his family to desert the hall at mealtimes, except on special occasions, in order to dine privately in a parlour, or 'great chamber'. Many great men deplored the new fashion and felt that a lord should always be with his people: Robert Grosseteste, who in 1235 became Bishop of Lincoln, said: 'As muche as ye may, withoute peril of sykenes and weryneys, eat ye in the halle afore youre meyny [household] for that schal be to youre profyte and worschippe.' Again, the poet Langland lamented the trend in *Piers Plowman*:

Elynge [wretched] is the halle eche day in the wyke,
There the lord ne the ladye lyketh noughte to sytte
Now hath each riche [person] a reule to eten by hym-selve
In a pryve-parloure, for pore mennes sake
Or in a chamber with a chymneye and leve the chief halle
That was made for meles, men to eten inne

A miniature from the 15th-century *Roman de Renaud de Mountaban* showing ladies at table with servers, a cupbearer and minstrels.

The great chamber was often still the lord's bedchamber and contained his bed with its canopy and hangings – his 'bed of state', in front of which his servants would set up his board for meals. Only important guests were entertained to meals here, while those of slightly lower estate sat in the hall at the high table, with the steward presiding in place of his master. In very large households, like the 5th Earl of Northumberland's, a second table called the 'Knights' Board', was set up in the great chamber for the guests too exalted to eat with the steward in the hall, yet not sufficiently important to join the lord himself at the principal table.

Precedence was as important as ever when it came to seating: the person of highest estate, whether guest or host, sat in the grandest chair, with a smaller one for his lady, perhaps one or two additional chairs for principal guests, and several stools for lesser guests and other members of the host's family. Much of the meal was passed in silence, partly because the rules of precedence strictly defined who might speak to whom first, and partly because of the presence of the serving staff. Even when the lord and lady were dining without guests, the server, the carver, the cup-bearer and their attendant grooms all had to be present.

It was the custom for sons of noble families to be educated in another similar household, or that of a superior, acting as 'Kervers, Sewars, Cupberers and Gentillmen Waiters'. John Paston the Younger seems to have had an education in the household of John Mowbray, 4th Duke of Norfolk, and Thomas Tropnell of Great Chalfield began his social career by serving as steward in the Hungerford household.

A procession of these household officers carried the food from the kitchen, down the length of the hall where the lower orders were assembled in readiness for their own meal. The procession would be met by the marshall of the hall with his rod of office calling, 'By your leave, my masters'. Everyone rose respectfully to their feet, removed their hats (men wore their hats at the table and only took them off when they were drinking a toast), and stood in silence in homage to their lord's food as it passed by. The procession climbed the stone staircase by the high table to the great chamber. Finally, the tepid food was served with virtually as much ritual and ceremony as attended the service of large formal feasts in the hall.

Then the trestles and tables were trimly set out,
complete with cloths and clearly flaming cressets [open bowls
of stone in which the wick floated on liquid wax].
And waxen torches were placed in the wall-brackets

Sir Gawain and the Green Knight

The first stage in preparing the medieval table for a feast was to lay the tablecloths, of fine white linen damask or diaper in wealthy households. With great ceremony, the senior ewerer, in charge of linen and hand-washing, laid the high table, then the other tables, with no fewer than three cloths, each perhaps four to six yards long. The first,

73

called the couch, was laid lengthwise with the other two arranged to hang over the edge of the board or table, one at the front and the other at the back.

Sweet-smelling herbs and flowers were scattered over the cloth to delight the noble diners, purify the air and repel disease. The senior ewerer then covered the cupboard and the ewery with a cloth and brought all the necessary equipment for washing, including a special basin and ewer for his lord, flanked by basins and ewers for high-table guests. When the master dined in his great chamber, only a single cloth appears to have been laid, but the degree of ceremony was still maintained.

The impressive centrepiece of every fine table was the 'Principle Salt' or 'Salter'; a magnificent covered salt cellar, which in the late medieval period sometimes took the form of dogs, elephants, lions or dragons, garnished with pearls, precious stones or enamels, and represented the most important piece of plate in the household. These salts were chiefly of ceremonial rather than practical use, for their place on the high table effectively separated the lord and his guests from the rest of the diners; hence 'above' and 'below the salt'. The principal salt was laid to the right of the lord's place, by the butler or the pantler, and other smaller salts for the diners' use were scattered about the table. But the glory of the table was the 'nef' – a ship made of silver or silver-gilt, which sometimes included a salt-cellar, or even held the lord's knife, spoon and napkin.

Next the pantler brought the lord's bread rolls, or manchets, wrapped in a napkin of linen damask or diaper, his trenchers and his knife and spoon. He laid each in a defined location in front of his lord's place and covered the whole place setting with another napkin. Erasmus advised: 'If a serviette is given, lay it on your left shoulder or arm . . . Your goblet and knife, duly cleansed, should be on the right, your bread on the left.' The rest of the high table was laid in similar manner.

If the household was wealthy enough to employ a carver, it was his task to pare the outsides of the manchets to make them ready for eating by the lord, his family and chief guests. This was evidently done in the interests of hygiene, as the Earl of Northumberland's Household Book of 1512 instructs: 'Touch never the loaf after he is so trimmed.' Bread for the lord had to be new, that for the guests one day old and for the rest of the household three days old. It was also the carver's job to cut the four-day-old trencher loaves into slices about 6 inches wide and 2–3 inches deep, squaring them for the diners' use. Regulations in the Northumberland Household Book instructed that 'the trencher-bread be made of the meal as it cometh from the mill' – in other words, coarse wholemeal bread. 'They sette hemselfe, atte dyner, & made trenchers of brede for to putte theyr mete upon', as William Caxton describes in his *Noble Boke of Curtasye*. If only the lord and his lady were seated at table, they ate straight from the serving dishes, but if there were others with them, each diner had a bread trencher on which the carver placed slices of meat. Since so many medieval and early Tudor dishes consisted of minced meat, or meat chunks, in thick sauce, the trencher easily became saturated, even when it was made of heavy unleavened bread, so it was changed as needed during the meal. When the high table diners had finished with a trencher, it was thrown to the dogs prowling round the table, carried down to the end of the hall to be given to the poorest retainers, the 'trenchermen', or it was collected in a basket and given as alms to the poor. In humbler households the diner might eat his trencher-bread, if he wished, after the main part of the meal was over.

By early Tudor times, the bread trencher was being replaced by a thin wooden board with a hollowed-out middle for the meat and juices: wooden trenchers were already in everyday use at the Earl of Northumberland's table in 1512. There is also a reference in his household book to hiring 'Rough Pewter Vessel' and buying a small quantity to be brought out only for feasts. When not in use, this 'Counterfoot Vessel' was kept with the rest of the plate in the counting house. The first documentary evidence of the use of pewter platters, probably for dining rather than serving, appears to be an entry in the Pewterers' Company accounts for 1553–4, when '2 dozen trenchers weighing 18 lb at 6d per lb' cost 9s; these details suggest that the platters were 7–8 inches in diameter. There are references to silver trenchers as early as 1521, but it is probable that they were for use at the after-dinner banquet course of sweetmeats, rather than at the dinner or supper table proper.

After the pantler had laid the high table, he saw that the other tables were provided with bread, trenchers of salt, spoons and perhaps knives. Cutlery was fairly basic, and usually the diner was expected to provide his own knife, sharpened on a whetstone at the door of the hall, which most carried in a leather sheath attached to the belt. The same knife, which was shaped like a dagger with a sharp point, would perform other duties through the day, including defence. From early Tudor times, major households provided cased sets of matching knives for the use of their guests. Perhaps the most magnificent of these was that owned by Henry VIII, described in his inventory as: '. . . a case of knives garnished with sundry emeralds, pearls and rubies about the next and divers amethysts; jacynths and balases upon the foot thereof furnished with knives having diamonds at the ends of them.' Other sets of knives in Henry VIII's inventory were accompanied by a matching fork, but this was provided only for serving the meat and not intended for eating. The principle of the fork was not new; it had been known as a cooking implement for centuries, but it was a luxury utensil in medieval times, usually of silver, for eating sticky suckets or sweetmeats. Only the Italians used forks for dining at this time; in England fingers were perfectly respectable eating implements even in the reign of Queen Anne in the early 18th century. When dining on the joints of roasted and boiled meats that formed such a substantial part of medieval and early Tudor meals, each person used his long, sharp-pointed knife to cut off the pieces he required; the knife point was then used to transfer the meat on to his trencher, where it was sliced, and to take salt from the salt-cellar as required. As *The Babees Book of Manners* of 1475 advised: 'Do not touch the salt in the salt cellar with any meat, but lay salt honestly on your trencher for that is courtesy.'

Spoons were sometimes provided by the host, but he was under no obligation to do so, and diners often brought their own. In wealthy houses, spoons were of silver, silver-gilt or even gold, crystal and coral; in poorer households they were of pewter or wood. The contemporary saying that 'he was a man who always fed himself with a wooden spoon' was to imply that someone was a person of no account. Spoons were used to eat all the liquid and semi-liquid foods, especially the pottage. The diner was instructed to clean his spoon properly and not leave it in the dish: 'An whenne your potage you shall be brouhte, take your sponys and soupe by no way, and in youre dysshe leve not your spone, I pray' says *The Babees Book*.

Drinking vessels for the richest were of silver and gold, while the cups and beakers for the less exalted were made of horn or wood. But by 1500, the traditional ashwood drinking cups, measuring perhaps 6 inches in diameter were beginning to be superseded by earthenware cups. Liquor was both drunk and served from leather tankards and jugs, called 'black jacks', because they were made from 'jack' leather; that

Liquor was both served and drunk from leather tankards and jugs called 'black jacks' – so called because they were made from 'jack' leather, a hard leather coated with tar or pitch to make it waterproof. This jack is in the kitchen at East Riddlesden Hall, Yorkshire.

is, hard leather coated with tar or pitch to make it waterproof. These vessels must have imparted a strong tang to the liquor until properly seasoned. Examples of black jacks can be seen at Chirk Castle and East Riddlesden Hall.

Fellow diners shared drinking vessels in the same way that they shared serving dishes, hence the advice from *The Babees Book*: 'Whanne ye shalle drynke, your mouth clence withe a clothe.' The butler was in charge of the drinks, and the initial serving of the wine for the high table and senior ranks, and of ale for everyone else, was timed to coincide with the serving of the first roast. The etiquette for drinking, as for eating, was elaborate. Although the courtesy books generally condemned drunkenness, the rules they laid down must have tended to encourage it. It was considered bad manners to drink more than three times during the course of a meal, so those who followed this rule must have felt compelled to quaff a generous amount on each occasion to last them until the next!

When the cooks announced that the meal was ready, it was the job of the marshal, the chief official at dinner, to assemble the company. The lord and his family and principal guests who were to occupy the high table congregated in the solar, or parlour, where they were served with plums and grapes 'to open the stomach'. The musicians took their place in the gallery and, accompanied by a fanfare and silence from everybody else, the lord and his guests entered the hall at the dais end to take their places. Everyone else went off to wash; the server, the carver and cup-bearer going first. Hand-washing before and after dining was a very important social custom when fingers were used to hold meat while it was being carved from communal platters and dipped into communal bowls. Water was sometimes brought by the senior ewerer's assistants for the lowlier guests and retainers, but otherwise they washed at a 'laving place' set in the walls of the hall itself, or in a vestibule very close by, as at Compton Castle.

At the high table, the covered place settings had been uncovered. The carver, equipped with a towel and napkin elaborately draped over one shoulder, advanced towards his master with three bows, then knelt in front of him and uncovered the salt. He unwrapped his bread and cut a small cone or 'cornet' from both the manchet and the trencher bread for the pantler to taste for poison, together with the salt. At the same time, the marshal and cup-bearer, the latter also with a towel and napkin draped over his shoulder, advanced with the lord's hand-washing basin and with a cup tasted the herb-flavoured water in it. Even the linen damask or diaper towel the lord was to use was not exempt: 'Then the Marshall kysseth the towell for his assay [to check for poison], and so layeth it on the left shoulder of the Lorde of the House.' The 'surnappe', a long towel, was spread ceremoniously across the high table in front of the principal diners to protect the place-settings and their clothes, while they washed their hands in water brought by the ewerer. The other guests and the rest of the household with their washed hands were then conducted to their seats, according to their rank and precedence, by the marshal, and a Latin benediction was said by the chaplain.

By this time the food for the first course had been placed on the serving tables, or dressers in the servery. Gold, silver-gilt or silver were used to make the chargers, or serving dishes, used by royalty and some of the highest nobility; otherwise they were of wood, earthenware or even of pewter. From ordinances of the Pewterers' Company of London we know that by 1438 chargers were over 13 inches in diameter, platters for serving from 8 to 13 inches and dishes and saucers down to 4 inches. All serving dishes sent out from the kitchen were covered in the house of a great lord to give some protection against the fear of poisoning, but no person of high rank would eat or drink anything until it too had been assayed. The server gave the chief cook and the lord's chief steward a taste of each dish. Pieces were carved off joints, pies broken open, and into every sauce and pottage, pieces of bread were dipped and eaten.

The first course 'came in with such cracking of trumpets ..., such din of drumming and a deal of fine piping [*Sir Gawain and the Green Knight*]'. The procession was led by the lord's steward, or the chief guest's own taster, followed by the almoner carrying a large silver alms-dish, which was placed on the high table to receive offerings of food or money for distribution to the poor at the gates later in the day. Behind the almoner came the chief cook, the carver and the server, who on great occasions sometimes preceded the first dish mounted on a horse. They were followed by a string of servants in the livery of the household carrying the laden platters and dishes to the high table, where each bowed low and offered his dish on bended knee to the chief guest and then to the lord and his family. *The Noble Boke of Curtasye* by William Caxton offered a useful tip to the server when he had to carry a silver bowl filled with boiling pottage; he should put pieces of bread between the dish and his hands: 'Take the brede carvyn and lay by-twene and kepe the[e] well hit [hidden] be not sene.'

Lesser guests now sat down and watched the food being offered to the high table. The carver, equipped with a handsome set of knives and the knowledge to display 'the fayre handlynge of a knyfe', now came to the fore. Not only whole fish and birds, sometimes with their feathers, but also whole rabbits, lambs and quarters of veal appeared on the table. The animals were actually carved on the high table, the carver usually working at the open front. This is why it was so important for a well-bred man to be good at carving: 'The correct way to carve should be taught from the first years' said Erasmus in 1530. He had to be acquainted with the 'goodly termes of carvynge employed by carvers for centuries before', printed in Wynkyn de Worde's *Boke of Kervynge* in 1508.

As with many of the culinary terms employed in medieval times, a number of carving instructions were derived from the Norman-French: 'alaye' means to remove the wing (*aile*); 'untach that curlewe' means to loosen (*détacher*); 'culpon that troute' is to cut into pieces (*couper*); 'tayme that crabbe' means to open (*étamer*); and 'traunche that sturgyon' is to slice (*trancher*). The *Boke of Kervynge* makes no mention of actual joints of meat, which the artistic carver would not recognise as proper subjects for his art, but each creature was handled differently and a skilled carver prided himself on the speed and dexterity of his performance. He also had to know the 'fumosyties of fysshe, flesshe and foules', because these – the inferior parts such as legs, heads and sinews – were on no account to be offered to the high table. In John Russell's *Boke of Nurture*, the carver was instructed not to touch any viand except beef and mutton with his fingers, and to use only a spoon at moments of difficulty; but Wynkyn de Worde said that he should place two fingers and a thumb on the knife and the same on the bird or animal to be carved and he must wipe the knife on a napkin – not the tablecloth. Once the carver had cut off a proper slice of meat, it was customary for him to cut it into four strips almost to the end and place this on his lord's trencher. The uncut end-piece served as a handle for his master, who held it in his fingers while he dipped it in sauce or salt and nibbled off the strips; he then discarded the 'handle' as unfit to be eaten. When the carver had completed his task, the first course could be served at last.

Only one thing remained to be assayed, and that was the drink. This was performed by the marshal, butler and cup-bearer at the same time as the serving of the first roast and with the same flourishes as the food tastings. The cup-bearer took his lord's great covered cup of wine from the butler and, kneeling at the table, drank a few drops poured into the domed cover of the cup. Whenever his lord drank, it was the duty of the cup-bearer to hold the cover of the cup below to catch any drips. The placing of the lord's cup upon the high table was the signal for the drink to be passed round among the company, the wine cups of the most important guests being assayed by the cup-bearer. Finally, the feasters in the lower hall received their tepid food, placed at intervals along the tables, and were allowed to eat and drink.

Meanwhile, at the high table, the host or hostess would be offering special titbits to favoured guests. The 13th-century rules for the household of the Countess of Lincoln state:

> and order that your dish be so refilled and heaped, up, especially with the 'entremets' [delicacies] that you may courteously give from your dish to right and left to all at your high table and to whom else it pleases you, that they have the same as you had in front of you.

Favoured guests who were sitting on the reward table might also receive titbits. The final left-overs, known as 'manners', were passed down to the servants: good manners, or bad manners, according to the quality. Diners at the high table who cleared their trenchers would have been guilty of extremely bad manners.

Instructions on how to behave when eating and drinking were laboriously written down in contemporary courtesy books for generations of lords and ladies in the making to learn. Most of the rules concerned personal hygiene and how to share one's 'mess' courteously with one's neighbour. The student is told in 1290 by Fra Bonvicino da Riva: 'Let thy hands be clean. Thou must not put either thy fingers into thine ears, or thy hands on thy head. The man who is eating must not be cleaning, by scraping with his fingers at any foul part.' Scratching, in days when fleas and bugs were everywhere, was one of the habits most advised against, especially the habit of scratching with soupy fingers: 'You must not scratch your throat', said Tannhäuser in his 14th-century poem of courtly good manners, *Höfzucht*, 'whilst you eat, with the bare hand. But if it happen that you cannot help scratching, then courteously take a portion of your dress and scratch with that.' The student is told not to blow his nose with his fingers and not to go scraping and scratching at that part of the male anatomy which the Middle Ages called the 'codware'.

But cleanliness was not the only subject under discussion. Diners were told by Fra Bonvicino da Riva 'not to poke about everywhere when thou hast meat, or eggs, or some such dish. He who turns and pokes about on the platter, searching is unpleasant, and annoys his companion at dinner.' But Tannhäuser knew an even better way to offend fellow guests:

> Some people are inclined,
> When they have gnawed a bone;
> To put it back again into the dish.
> This you should consider as acting greatly amiss.

The floor was the place for bones, even in the best-appointed household, and was paradise for the domestic dogs and cats which roamed freely in medieval halls.

On how to behave when drinking, the student was instructed:

In this engraving the cupbearer on bended knee tastes or 'assays' his abbot's wine to check for poison.

with meat in mouth I shall not taste from cup,
lest neighbour find a filthy drink when he shall come to sup.

When diners were sharing serving dishes and cups it was essential that they learnt their table manners as well as Chaucer's Nun:

At meat her manners were well taught withal;
No morsel from her lips did she let fall,
Nor dipped her fingers in the sauce too deep;
But she could carry a morsel up and keep
The smallest drop from falling on her breast...
And she could wipe her upper lip so clean
That not a trace of grease was to be seen
Upon the cup when she had drunk; to eat
She reached a hand sedately for the meat.

The senior officials of the house, including the steward, had to remain standing throughout the meal, making sure that each dish was served with the right sauce, that everyone was served properly and that no important guest was left with an empty cup, or a saturated trencher. Minstrels were present at all the most important feasts and together with jugglers, tumblers, acrobats and mummers enlivened the tedious ritual in the main body of the hall, bringing with them the tabloid news of the day.

Once the first course had been cleared, the subtlety was brought in and presented to the high table; everyone had a good look at it and, if it were edible, might get a taste. Then, when the high table had been relaid for the second course, there might be a procession to bring in a decorated peacock or swan, followed by the rest of the second course. A second subtlety would then follow at the end of the course, followed by the third course if the feast was important enough, after which the tables were 'voided' or cleared, including the cloths. The alms-dish was carried off by the almoner, who distributed the contents to the poor at the gate. If the lord had guests, the feast was rounded off by a final dessert course of sweet wine or hippocras, with wafers, to aid digestion whole or powdered spices, like ginger, cardamon, coriander and cinnamon bark would be served, with perhaps raisins, nuts and a little fruit. On grand occasions, comfits or dragees were handed round in special boxes or 'drageoirs', with separate compartments for the different sugar-coated seeds and spices. Finally the surnappe was spread out once more over the high table and grace was said again. Then, after further assaying of the washing water and the towel, the lord and his chief guests washed again. The lord got on his feet to drink a toast as a signal that dinner was over, after which everyone went off back to work until supper: 'the Lorde must drynke wyne standyng, and all other in lyke maner, and that done, every man departeth at his good pleasure.'

For much of this period, abbots ate with quite as much aplomb as secular nobles. Until the end of the 11th century the abbot of a monastery dined and indeed lived and slept with his monks. But during the reign of Henry I, regulations were introduced dividing the abbey lands and income between the abbot and his community. The abbot, having complete control of his share of the money, set up a private household and ultimately separate quarters. Until the Dissolution of the Monasteries in the 1530s, an abbot lived like a nobleman, only dining with his monks in the refectory on very special occasions. A great feast held at the Islip manor house of Abbot Litlington of

Westminster for the King and his entire household in 1372 shows the luxury to which an abbot was accustomed. Foodstuffs included 77 capons, 156 pullets, 2 pheasants, 5 heron, 6 egrets and 6 curlew-like birds, all brought alive from London; a large quantity of spices – cloves, cinnamon, mace, ginger and galingale – as well as rice, flour, currants, dates, prunes and sugar; salt; 6 gallons of cream and a large quantity of honey. The gardener supplied grapes, apples, pears, cherries, plums and berries. Quantities of fine wine were drunk from silver goblets belonging to Westminster Abbey. Apart from foodstuffs, plate was brought from the abbey and fine linen for tablecloths, napkins and surnappes was specially purchased. The ritual and ceremony would have been the same for a feast given by a secular lord and entertainment would have been provided. In the Bursar's Accounts for Fountains Abbey, during the 15th century, there are many references to 'players': 'to the Fabulator or story-teller of the Earl of Salisbury' who was paid 12d; to 'the minstrels of Lord Arundel' who were paid 16d; 'to a fool called Solomon (who came again) 4d'; and 'to the King's minstrels': all for the entertainment of the abbot and his guests.

The rest of the monastic community ate in the refectory or frater. At Fountains Abbey, when the monks in general were allowed meat, they had to eat it in the misericord or dining-hall near the infirmary. Meat was never served in the choir monks' refectory, one of the noblest rooms in the abbey, measuring 110 feet by 47 feet, entered from the cloister through an elaborately moulded doorway. It was originally divided into two aisles by an arcade carried on four columns, which have now gone. A low platform on either side of the room originally carried two long tables on stone legs, some of which still protrude from the grassy floor. Between the tables there were narrow passages, giving access to the wooden benches covered with reed mats, on which the monks sat with their backs to the walls. Against the south wall at the far end of the room, the platform is broader and higher and this formed the dais for the high table where the prior presided over meals. The marks where the crucifix once hung above the prior's place, acting as a reredos to the high table, can still be seen. On the west wall, the platform extended further to accommodate the sideboard and lockers where the table-linen and spoons were kept. In preparation for a meal the tables were laid with three cloths (as with secular meals), trenchers or plates, simple salts, brown bread wrapped in napkins, double-handed beakers, and spoon. A place setting of six feet was allowed. Monks had their own knives laid aside at night in the dormitory in case of injury; before the meal they were sharpened with sand kept near the refectory door. After dinner, the remains of the bread was given to the poor, if left uncovered, as were the bread trenchers. If a monk wanted bread for supper, he had to wrap it in his napkin to notify the server.

Before entering the refectory for a meal, the monks had to wash their hands at the 'laver', or wash-basins, on either side of the door. At Fountains surviving stone benches once supported lead-lined, semi-circular basins, each one supplied with running water from a lead pipe. The holes for these pipes and the vertical chases for the pipes draining the basins can still be seen; part of the sophisticated system of water engineering at which the Cistercians excelled. After washing, the monks dried their hands on towels from the towel cupboard or 'aumbrey' in the outer wall of the warming house next to the refectory. They then entered the refectory in silence, each one bowing to the high table and stood in their own places until the prior walked to his seat and rang a small bell. At this signal, the priest on duty for that week would say grace, to which all the monks

The towel cupboard in the cloister at Fountains Abbey, Yorkshire. Before entering the refectory, monks had to wash their hands at the 'laver' and dry them on towels from the 'aumbrey' or towel cupboard.

responded. The brothers would then be seated when a monk in the pulpit on the west wall began to read from the Bible or philosophical books. The servers brought the food in from the kitchen next door by means of the 'dumb waiter' set in the wall. Detailed instructions were laid down that the servers should work quickly and quietly and not disturb the diners.

The Cistercians originally aimed at keeping the Rule strictly, so their diet was extremely simple and very sparing until the 14th century, when meat was allowed. Prandium, or dinner, was usually taken at midday, but never less than ten hours after rising, normally at 2am. In winter prandium was at 1.30pm, twelve hours after rising, and was the only meal served. Each monk would be served 1 lb bread and 2 'pulmenta' or dishes of eggs, cheese, fish, cereals, vegetables with ale, and 1 pulmenta of fruit and uncooked vegetables. Nowhere in the Rule does St Benedict give instructions as to the composition of the cena, the second meal eaten in summer at 6pm, except to say that one-third of the bread from prandium was to be reserved for it. Cistercian statutes decreed that this meal was to consist of bread, together with fruit and uncooked vegetables, and that those who needed it might have an extra quantity of coarse-bread. 'Pittances', a little extra food, and an extra $\frac{1}{2}$ lb white bread, were given after blood-letting, which took place four times a year, immediately before the prandium. In winter, after blood-letting, the monk was given a pittance and 1 lb white bread for breakfast (an extra meal not usually eaten) and the usual prandium on the two following days. In summer, for the following three days, he had an extra 1 lb bread and a pittance at dinner and at supper. Pittances were also given to the sick at the abbot's discretion.

Manners were carefully observed in the refectory: no monk was to leave the room or to walk about; salt had to be taken with the point of a knife, not with the fingers, and when a brother drank, he was required to hold the beaker with both hands. He was not permitted to wipe either his knife or his fingers on the tablecloth nor to put his fingers into his cup. Talking was strictly not allowed in the refectory and in the Rule, St Benedict recommended the use of signs. Consequently, the Cistercian sign language in use until very recently tended to be mostly connected with food. When the meal was over, the prior would ring the bell again and the brethren would file out.

This style of dining continues in monasteries – a direct link with the traditions and etiquette of the Middle Ages.

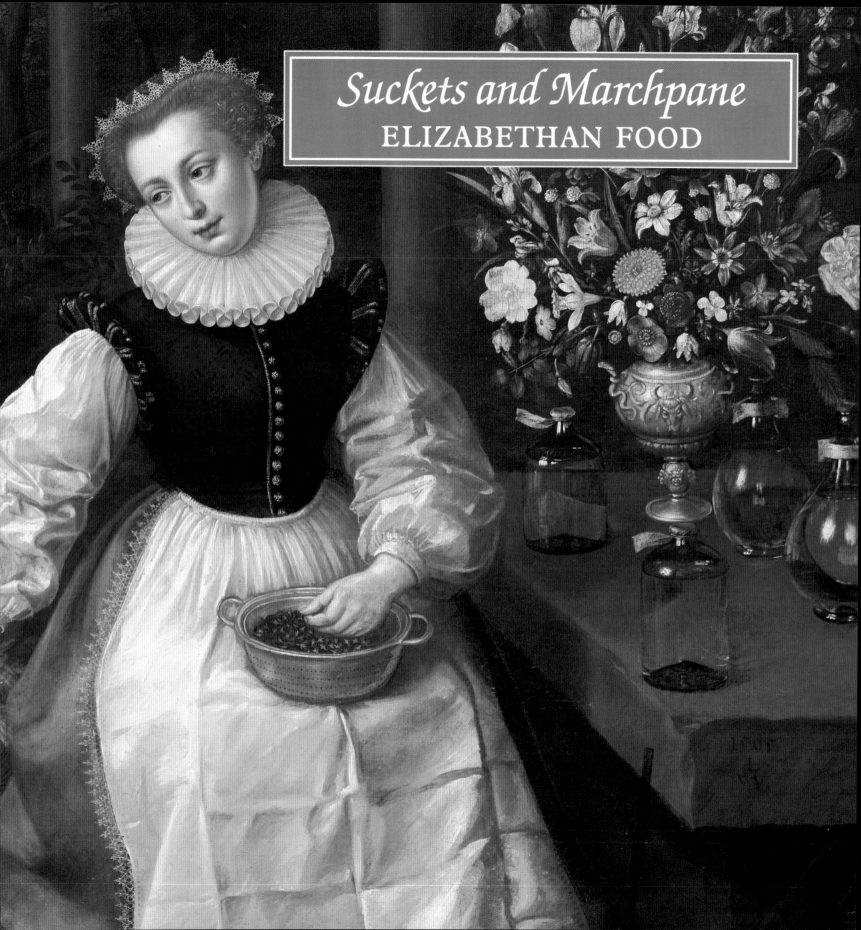

Suckets and Marchpane
ELIZABETHAN FOOD

Suckets and Marchpane

I

Elizabethan England was beset with two problems that are all too familiar today: inflation and unemployment. A doubling of the average market price of all farm crops between 1550 and 1600 hit the poorer farmers and wage labourers particularly hard because their incomes did not rise proportionately. The reasons for the long-term price increases have been much debated by historians, but seem to have stemmed from two causes. Spain's conquests in South and Central America, and their exploitation of the gold and silver deposits there, flooded the European money market, thereby allowing more coinage to be minted. Added to this, a rise in England's population drove up prices, especially of foodstuffs.

An increasing population could not all find work to do, or land to rent. Many disillusioned men and women roamed the countryside as 'rogues and vagabonds', provoking the government at various times to legislate stern measures against them, and to encourage local authorities to set up a system of relief for the poor. Individuals could be unsympathetic to the problem: when Bess of Hardwick was building her New Hall in Derbyshire in the 1590s, she had a wall constructed to enclose the kitchen quarters to stop beggars approaching for food and drink.

Reorganisation of agriculture in the period increased output and productivity, but again increased unemployment. Enclosure of wasteland and a shift to animal husbandry on the heavier clay soils dispossessed many cottagers of their land or rights to keep animals on common ground. Instead they became labourers, dependent on local markets for their food. On the other hand, large farmers and landowners prospered as the main beneficiaries of increased rents and higher prices for produce. Many of the new houses they built, and the additions to old houses they made at this period survive as reminders of this prosperity. They also ate and drank well from the new-found wealth. The household papers of Henry Percy, 9th Earl of Northumberland, describe 'Necessayres' for the provision of his London house for a week in October 1586, which give an idea of the range of foodstuffs enjoyed by the wealthy at this time. A loin of veal was the only 'red' meat eaten, but a wide range of poultry and game was served: a goose, rabbits, pigeons, partridges, pullets, chickens and plovers. The Earl kept Fridays and Saturdays as fish days, when sole, barbel, prawns, roach, oysters and eels were provided. Apart from butter, eggs and bread, other foodstuffs bought were flour, artichokes, mustard, vinegar, cabbage, turnips, rose-water, barberries, capers, yeast and spices. Wine and fruit were purchased by the butler.

Previous pages: Lucas van Valckenborch's late 16th-century painting of Spring shows flowers being prepared for the still-room. Here the lady of the house would distil waters and potions, preserve flowers and make up the rich sweets for the banqueting course.

Some of the luxury items included in the Northumberland household accounts were brought in from Europe, the East and from the Americas. The late 16th century was a period of expansion: new lands were being discovered, new trade routes established and existing links improved. The fall of Constantinople to the Ottoman Turks in 1453 had severed some of the overland spice routes, but these were opened up again in the late 16th century, when Elizabeth I joined with the Ottomans against the common enemy – the Catholic powers – and commercial privileges were given to English merchants. Wars with Spain – and perforce with Portugal following Philip of Spain's accession to the throne in 1580 – meant that England had to rely on Dutch merchants to provide most of their luxury imports from the East, and on parties raiding the Spanish for goods from the West. In 1600 the English East India Company was set up in London with a charter from Queen Elizabeth. Sir Thomas Myddelton of Chirk, who during the 1590s had gained rich rewards from financing the great buccaneering expeditions of Drake, Raleigh and Hawkins, was one of the founders of the Company.

London's population rose from about 120,000 in 1550 to some 200,000 in 1600, when it contained 5 per cent of the population of England. It was by far the largest town and much of the nation's foreign trade passed through its port. London at this time must have had the feel of a large city in the Third World today, a place of bustle and activity where things unobtainable elsewhere in the country were daily bought and sold. For, although internal trade expanded in the 16th century, and coastal shipping in particular moved bulk goods around the coasts, many areas of the country were still almost totally dependent on the local market town and the annual fair for anything which could not be produced at home. Even main highways were described in 1555 as 'very noisome and tedious to travel on and dangerous to all passengers and carriages'.

Bread

As in medieval and early Tudor times, the type of bread was defined by the consumer's status. William Harrison informs us in his *Description of England*, published in 1577: 'of bread made of wheat we have sundry sorts daily brought to the table, whereof the first and most excellent is the manchet, which we commonly call "white bread"'. Manchet at this time was usually prepared with best ale-barm as the 'Godesgoode' or raising agent, and thoroughly kneaded either manually or by foot, when the dough was wrapped in a cloth and trodden 'a good space together'. It was then put to prove for an hour and moulded into 'manchets round and flat, scotch them about the waist to give it leave to rise, and prick it with your knife in the top, and so put it into the oven and bake it with a gentle heat'. Manchets were to weigh '8 oz into the oven, and 6 oz out' and forty were to be made out of the flour bolted from one bushel of corn (1 bushel was 56 lb).

The second quality 'is the cheat, or wheaten bread, so named because the colour thereof resembleth the grey or yellowish wheat, being clean and well dressed, and out of this is the coarsest of the bran (usually called gurgeons or pollard) taken', according to William Harrison. The flour was more coarsely bolted than for manchet and the dough was moulded into 'reasonable big loaves' which were baked at a fairly strong heat. Cheat bread came in more than one grade: 'The ravelled is a kind of cheat bread also, but it retaineth more of the gross and less of the pure substance of the wheat.' This inferior ravelled cheat bread was made in country households and was at least as dark as modern brown bread.

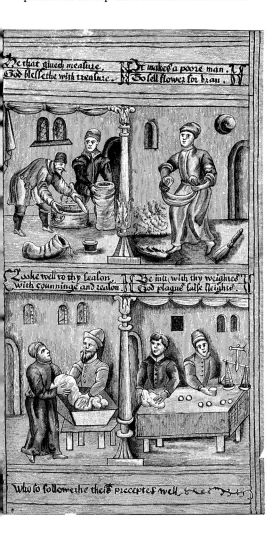

The making of manchet bread from the ordinances of the Bakers' Guild in York, 1595–6. Thoroughly kneaded and proved dough was moulded into individual manchets weighing 8oz each, cut or scotched 'about the waist' to make them rise, pricked on the top and baked in a beehive oven.

William Harrison describes 'the next sort' as 'brown bread':

the colour of which we have two sorts, one baked up as it cometh from the mill, so that neither the bran nor the flour are any whit diminished; the other hath little or no flour left therein at all . . . and it is not only the worst and weakest of all the other sorts, but also appointed in old time for servants, slaves and inferior kind of people to feed upon. Hereunto, likewise, because it is dry and brickle in the working (for it will hardly be made up handsomely into loaves) some add a portion of rye meal, whereby the rough dryness thereof is somewhat qualified, and then it is named miscelin, that is, bread made of mingled corn.

The mid-16th-century kitchen books of Sir William Petre of Ingatestone Hall in Essex, who for a time had been a tenant of Montacute House in his native Somerset, record that three qualities of bread were produced in the bakehouse: 'manchet' for Sir William, his family and guests; 'ravel' or 'yeoman's bread' for his upper servants; and 'tems', an Essex term for maslin, or 'carter's bread' for his lower servants. The quantities baked were reckoned by the 'cast', which was equal to two or three loaves depending on the size and quality of the flour; in 1552 the Hall ovens turned out 1,900 cast of manchet, 5,560 cast of yeoman's bread and 1,480 cast of carter's bread – the equivalent of about 20,000 loaves.

Although many country people still ate bread of branny wheat, maslin or inferior grains, the taste for white bread was growing in London and the large towns. By 1574 there were 62 white bakers in London and 36 brown bakers, a very different proportion from the 32 brown and 21 white of 1307. The wheat for Londoners' bread was coming not only from the Home Counties, but by sea from as far away as East Anglia and Yorkshire. When supplies at home were scarce, which was frequently, the London city companies were responsible for importing grain from Europe. The appeal of white bread was not just its pleasing pale colour and its agreeable taste, but also its greater digestibility. Many of the gentry ate it from necessity as much as preference, for they led less physically demanding lives than those of labourers, and so were unable to digest branny breads.

In the towns, bread was produced by professional bakers. When the Earl of Northumberland of Petworth was staying in his London house at Tottenham, the household's bread was bought from an Islington baker, Thomas Hood: the bill for '306 dozen of bread' between September 1585 and March 1586 totalled £15 6s. Professional bakers were also prepared to bake their customers' own dough.

Dairy Produce

Next in importance to the bakehouse in an Elizabethan house came the dairy, although the enclosure of many commons, and the shortage of cottages with grazing land attached, forced many of the rural poor to give up their cows. Where dairying was practised, whey and buttermilk were drunk in the summer, but for the townspeople, and for most countryfolk, beer became the usual beverage. Milk was rarely drunk by the gentry, but used by their cooks to make rice and sago puddings, the rich posset drinks of milk or cream, mixed with sack or brandy and thickened with eggs, ground almonds or grated Naples biscuits (similar to modern sponge fingers) and syllabubs.

Cream was universally eaten in Elizabethan times. 'Cabbage cream' was made up by

A detail from Pieter Brueghel the Younger's *Harvesters' Lunch*, showing peasants eating a lunch of brown maslin bread, hard skimmed milk cheese, whey and pears.

layers of clotted cream, with sugar and rose-water sprinkled between the layers. Fresh cream was used to make creamy dishes for the final dessert course of dinner, the banquet. Trifles, thick cream seasoned with sugar and ginger, and flavoured with rose-water, were served lukewarm. Other dishes included white pots (cream thickened with eggs and boiled with currants); white leach (cream flavoured with spices, rose-water, and ground almonds and set with isinglass – particularly prized); fools and syllabubs; 'snows' made by whipping cream with egg whites; and junkets, cream curdled with rennet, as in earlier times, but now flavoured with sugar and rose-water.

The poor ate butter, as they had always done, with their bread and their salt-fish, but with a gradual decline in the supply of fresh milk, they became more dependent on it as part of their diet. Army rations in Elizabeth's reign included $\frac{1}{4}$lb butter a day, and butter regularly appears in contemporary institutional diets for hospitals and workhouses. The consumption of butter by the rich was also rising dramatically, used liberally in every possible branch of cookery and setting a trend that was to last until the 19th century. The best summer butter was known to be rich and golden, so marigold petals and carrot juice were used to dye the paler butters, in order that they would sell more readily and expensively. The dairy at Ingatestone Hall, typical of an Elizabethan manorial dairy, produced fresh butter for immediate use, salted butter, pressed into earthenware pots or wooden tubs for keeping, and clarified, potted butter for cooking.

Although the Elizabethans still enjoyed curd fritters, using cheese-curds from the dairy, and fresh curd tarts (like modern cheesecake) also became popular, they did not eat curds as much as their ancestors. On the other hand, cheese was becoming more important in the nation's diet. Cream cheeses, plain or herb-flavoured, were an extra summer-time treat for most people, but mature cheese, from both skimmed and whole milk, was for everyday eating. The usual source of rennet was the stomachbag of a sucking calf, which might be salted, dried and hung in the chimney: a small piece boiled in water produced the rennet. Where farms were small and individuals continued to own single cows, cheese was sometimes produced on a co-operative basis. Local cheeses were becoming more widely known, purchased at cheese fairs, and shipped in some quantity to London from as far afield as Cheshire. The richest were golden in colour, so poorer quality cheeses were, like butter, often dyed with marigold petals or saffron. Some foreign cheeses were imported: Parmesan was greatly admired in Elizabethan times, and early versions of Dutch Edam and Normandy cheese were available.

Fish

Despite Henry VIII's break with the Roman Church in the 1530s, fish days continued to be observed, principally to encourage the nation's seamen. Elizabeth's great minister, Chief Secretary of State William Cecil, ordained: 'Let the old course of fishing be maintained by the straitest observation of fish days for policy's sake; so the sea coasts should be strong with men and habitations and the fleet flourish more than ever.' So, during Elizabeth's reign, Wednesdays and Saturdays were declared fish days, and these were added to, producing the so-called 'political Lent' when more than half the year consisted of fish days. Nevertheless, with no religious sanction behind it, the regulation proved hard to enforce and after 1585 the government let it lapse.

The household accounts of Sir William Petre for 1551–2 show that he strictly observed the Saturday fish day, but a note records: 'Spent this Lent two lambs, three

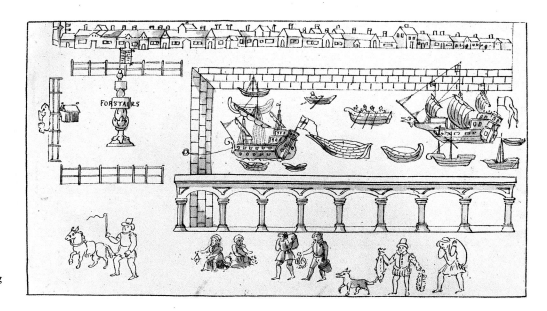

Detail from a drawing of London in 1598 showing the fish market at Billingsgate.

capons, four partridges, six chickens on the children and them that were sick.' The meat would have been served as broths.

Except on the coast, fresh sea-fish sold for more than salt-fish. The carriage of goods by river or road was still very slow, and sea-fish deteriorated too quickly to be brought far inland. In London it was not only sold in open markets and at the fishmonger's stall, but was also hawked through the streets to ensure quick disposal. The variety continued to be wide. The accounts kept by Francis Lucas, clerk of the kitchen to the Earl of Northumberland, paid £52 3s 5d for four months' supply from September 1585 to January 1586: much of the freshwater fish would have come from the fish-ponds at Petworth in Sussex. Between February 1606 and February 1607, work done on the 'fish pondes' amounted to a considerable sum, £59 9s 9d. Very large households, like Petworth and Hardwick, included a fisherman as a permanent member of staff. Hardwick, particularly, was a long way from the sea, and freshwater fish played a large part in the diet of the house: Bess, Countess of Shrewsbury, built five fish-ponds to supply her large household. Sir Edward Phelips also had a number of fish ponds at Montacute: 'two fish ponds all incompassed within a wall. On the West side of the house ... are also severall Fish ponds'. Moats, where they survived, were another source of fresh fish. The site of Speke Hall near Liverpool has almost certainly been moated since medieval times, when it was presumably surrounded on all four sides, although the earliest reference to the moat is in 1693 when it was stocked with carp and perch.

Richard Carew of Antony in his *Survey of Cornwall*, 1602, tells us about the processing of fish in Cornwall in Elizabethan times. The largest part of a catch was processed by the fishermen themselves to preserve it:

Some are polled (that is, beheaded), gutted, split, powdered [salted], and dried in the sun, as the lesser sort of hake. Some headed, gutted, jagged and dried, as rays and thornbacks. Some gutted, split, powdered and dried, as buckthorn made of whitings ... and the smaller sort of conger and hake. Some gutted, split and kept in pickle, as whiting, mackerel, mullet, bass, peal, trout, salmon and conger. Some gutted and kept in pickle, as the lesser whitings, pollocks, eels and squary scads [Spanish mackerel]. Some cut in pieces and powdered as seal and porpoise and lastly some boiled and preserved fresh in vinegar, as tunny and turbot.

It was during Elizabeth's reign that seamen from the West Country began fishing off Newfoundland for cod and other varieties. Red and white herrings were usually salted at sea before they were landed. Mediterranean anchovies, pickled in brine, were occasionally imported, their primary function being to stimulate the thirsts of wine-bibbers at their drinking sessions. Botargo, a relish made from salted mullet or tunny roes from southern Europe, was sold for the same purpose.

The staple Lenten and fasting day foods were salt-fish, red and white herrings and even stockfish, although the last was not much liked. Sir William Petre's cook used a 'stockfish hammer' regularly in the kitchen at Ingatestone Hall (see p.86). Each week in Lent the Petre household bought a barrel of white herring and half a barrel of red: at the beginning of April the week's consumption was 70 white herring and 20 red. In addition, '$29\frac{1}{2}$ couple lings' were recorded in January and a cartload of 'Lenten stuffe' had already arrived in February from London, with '56 couple stockfish, $75\frac{1}{2}$ couple haberdins [large salted cod] and 17 couple lings' – in other words, 300 fish. Week by week, this supply was gradually reduced until October, when there remained 53, made up of '$1\frac{1}{2}$ couple stockfish, 11 couple old ling and 14 couple new ling'.

Ling and stockfish for the Earl of Northumberland's household apparently made the long journey from Tynemouth on the Northumbrian coast: there are several references in the accounts to 'the carriage of 360 salt lings from Tynmouthe' and 'carriage and taking up of linges and saltfish sent from Tynmouthe' to Petworth in Sussex and Syon House just outside London. However, salt-fish, like stockfish, was eaten more for necessity than pleasure. Its exceptional keeping qualities made it invaluable for provisioning army garrisons and ships' crews and Elizabethan mariners took prodigious amounts of salt-fish as well as salted meat with them on their voyages.

Whether fresh or salted, fish was made into well-seasoned broths and stews. A typical Elizabethan broth of carp from *The Good Hous-wives Treasurie* of 1588 might be flavoured with spices, dried fruit, oranges, verjuice or vinegar and butter. Stuffed fish were spit-roasted, or pieces of fish were toasted in front of the fire. Smaller fish could be broiled on a gridiron or fried in butter. Fish was still served on sops of bread, garnished with gooseberries, grapes, barberries or redcurrants, or slices of orange or lemon. Fish pies were a welcome part of Lenten fare, particularly when made with rich herrings, eels, salmon or sturgeon, plus butter, spices and dried fruit. The Lenten ling or salt-fish pie was less sweet and included egg yolks, herbs, spices and butter.

Meat

The increasing population in lowland England, and in particular the dramatic expansion of London, together with the increase in wealth of the better-off, encouraged the long-distance trade in meat animals from the uplands of the north and Wales. Tŷ Mawr, in Gwynedd, the birthplace of Bishop William Morgan who translated the Bible into Welsh in 1588, was in Elizabethan times possibly the most important of a number of farmsteads in a valley on the cattle drovers' route from north-west Wales to the major

Tŷ Mawr in Gwynedd, the birthplace of Bishop William Morgan who translated the Bible into Welsh in 1588. The modest stone cottage formed part of a farmstead on the cattle drovers' route from north-west Wales to the major cattle fairs in England.

Right: Detail from a drawing of London in 1598 showing sheep and cattle being driven down Eastcheap.

cattle fairs of England. Although there were twice as many sheep in the area, cattle were the mainstay of the economy. Because of the lack of winter feed, three-quarters of the farmers had fewer than ten beasts kept penned together within hurdles. Their manure served to improve the land, when the use of lime and fertilizer was unknown. In the summer months many families in the valley continued the medieval practice of taking their animals up into the hills and camping out in the 'hafod' or cabin while tending them. The milk was made into butter and cheese both for consumption over the winter months and for sale in the nearby market.

But the trend towards sheep farming produced a public outcry:

> The more shepe, the dearer is the woll.
> The more shepe, the dearer is the mutton.
> The more shepe, the dearer is the beffe.
> The more shepe, the dearer is the corne.
> The more shepe, the skanter is the white meate [dairy products].
> The more shepe, the fewer egges for a peny.

After 1550, however, cattle were as likely to be the culprits, because beef and veal had become established as the Englishman's favourite meats.

For the poor, little if any meat could be afforded, usually consisting of bacon or a little pork: 'Bacon is good for carters and plowman, the whiche be ever labouringe in the earth or dunge . . . I do say that coloppes [slices of bacon] and egges is as holsome for them as a talowe candell is good for a blereyed mare' said Dr Boorde in his *Dyettary of Helth*; but for the rich there was a wide variety of meat to chose from. According to William Harrison:

> In number of dishes and change of meat, the nobility of England . . . do most exceed, sith there is no day in manner that passeth over their heads wherein they have not only beef, mutton, veal, lamb, kid, pork, cony, capon, pig or so many of these as the season yieldeth, but also some portion of the red or fallow deer, beside great variety of fish and wild fowl and thereto sundry other delicates where in the sweet hand of the seafaring Portugal is not wanting.

Left: Two life-size stags support the coat of arms of Bess of Hardwick in the overmantel of the great hall at Hardwick Hall in Derbyshire. Bess and her fourth husband, the Earl of Shrewsbury, swapped gifts of venison in the honeymoon period of their marriage.

The accounts of the Earl of Northumberland show that from September 1585 to January 1587 an extraordinarily large amount of meat was purchased when it is remembered that half the period consisted of 'non-flesh' days: 2,460 stone of beef costing £152 0s 3d; 427 carcases of mutton costing £166 15s 6d; 78 carcases of veal costing £35 8s 9d; but only £7 14s 7d was spent on pork and £8 16s 10d on lamb. Brawn, costing 20s, was also bought in. Andrew Boorde, like Sir Thomas Elyot (p.18), considered that: 'Beef is a good meate for an Englysshe man, so be it the beest be yonge, and that it be not Kowe-flesh; yf it be moderatly powdered [salted] that the groose blode by salt may be exhaustyd, it doth make an Englysshe man stronge; Veal is good and easily digested; Brawn is an usual meate in winter amonges Englisshe men.'

Game was still plentiful and varied in Elizabethan times, and except for deer, whose meat in theory could neither be bought nor sold, could be taken by all. Great landowners like Bess of Hardwick and the Earl of Northumberland had their parks full of game, especially 'coveted deer'. The sport of stag-hunting was much enjoyed by the rich and powerful, and venison continued to be sent as presents to loved ones and influential friends. In early December 1567, when the marriage of Bess of Hardwick and the Earl of Shrewsbury was still new and affectionate, they swapped gifts of venison. The Earl wrote: 'I thank you, sweet 'none', for your puddings and venison ... The venison is yet at London, but I have sent for it hither.' As in earlier centuries, venison was enjoyed roasted, well-larded if lean and stuck with cloves or sprigs of rosemary and eaten with a sauce of vinegar, sugar, cinnamon and butter, in pasties and stews and for longer preservation, spiced and potted under a protective layer of butter.

According to the unknown author of *A Proper Newe Booke of Cokerye*, the earliest printed English cookery book, probably published *c*.1560: 'A hare is ever good, but best from October to Lent.' Like coneys and rabbits, the hare might be 'given a pudding in his belly', a stuffing of grated bread, suet, herbs and spices, and roasted or stewed whole or hashed in broth and wine with herbs and onions or baked whole in pies, often with the head and ears left on. Rabbits and coneys were kept in warrens on large estates, and looked after by a full-time warrener: both Bess of Hardwick and the Earl of Northumberland employed a warrener, and there are many references in the Percy household accounts to the selling of 'conyskins' as 'kytchen stuffe'.

Right: A late 16th-century embroidered cushion cover from Hardwick Hall, showing fowlers shooting game birds.

A great variety of wild fowl and birds were still eaten. In the Northumberland household papers, the clerk of the kitchen records the 'acates' (fresh provisions) purchased by the 'cater' from September 1585 to January 1586, which included 'pigeons, mallardes, shovellers, herons, curlewes, phesants, woodcocks, snypes, teale, pewetts, partridge, plover, quayles, larkes, small byrdes, and such lyke'. But fewer wild birds were now accepted as a regular part of the diet: blackbirds, thrushes and finches, for instance, were losing their appeal, as were sea-birds and some freshwater varieties, except in the remoter parts of Britain.

Fowlers operating with the aid of nets and decoy birds were first used in Elizabethan times to capture wild fowl in East Anglia. Hawking was still popular: the Petworth estate employed a fowl keeper, a partridge taker, a falconer and a keeper who was paid regularly for 'riding charges into France for partridges'. But already the wind of change was blowing: Sir William Petre's household accounts for Ingatestone Hall mention

The Poultry Vendors by Joachim de Beuckelaer, 1563. Guinea fowl from West Africa and turkeys from Central America were recent introductions to British markets.

payments made as early as 1555 to men for gunpowder with which 'to shoot at crows about the house', and 'to kill fowl'.

Partridges and pheasants were preserved in enclosures for greater convenience. The enclosure at Ingatestone Hall was made of thin wooden lattice, running along the inner side of the orchard wall: 'In this frame both partridges, pheasants, guinea-hens, turkey-hens, and such like do yearly breed and are severally fed and brought up, so as they become tame as other chickens.' Guinea fowl from West Africa and the turkey, a native of Central America and Mexico, had recently been introduced into Britain. The earliest written record of the turkey's existence on English tables was by Archbishop Cranmer in 1541, when, seeking to curb the gluttony of the higher clergy, he mentioned it as one of the 'greater fowls', of which but one was permitted in a dish. Fourteen years later, enough turkeys were sold in the London markets to warrant their price being legally fixed along with other poultry. At that time a turkey-cock cost 6s, while turkey-chicks were 2s 8d, but by 1572 the prices had dropped to 3s 4d for a turkey-cock and 1s 8d for a hen. Turkeys became regular farmyard fowl, regularly appearing roasted at important feasts and entertainments.

Geese were also eaten roasted: the Elizabethan accompaniment to a green goose (killed under four months old) was sorrel sauce; to a stubble goose (over four months old), mustard and vinegar. Most water-birds, after roasting, were served with a sauce made from their own blood mixed with breadcrumbs, or stewed prunes and spices, but new sauces were being added, like the onion sauce served with capon or turkey; or more complex recipes like that containing claret, rosewater, spices and sliced oranges to be served with a capon.

The price of poultry fluctuated greatly in the Elizabethan period. By the end of the century, the price of a hen had risen from 3d or 4d of early 16th-century London to 9d or 10d, making it a luxury food, while 'a capon of grece' was 20d. Pigeons were much cheaper at 8d a dozen and vast numbers were still eaten, although not on quite the same scale as earlier times. Most large houses had their dovecotes, and in 1552 the total number of pigeons taken out of the 'dove-house' at Ingatestone Hall between Easter and Michaelmas was 1,080, many making their appearance on the table as pigeon pie. A working 16th-century stone dovecote at Willington near Bedford is lined internally with nesting boxes for 1,500 pigeons.

Fruit and Vegetables

In Elizabeth's reign no great house was regarded as complete without its garden. The architect of the one was often the designer of the other, as at Hardwick, where the symmetrical arrangement of courts and orchards around the house form an integral part of the design. The gardens at Montacute were probably created around the time of the house in the 1590s, including a kitchen garden to supply the house with fruit and vegetables. John Gerard described the house in his *Herball or Generall Historie of Plantes* of 1597 as having 'large and spacious Courtes, gardens, orchards, a parke', but the first detailed information comes in a survey of 1667:

On the North side of the house is a very faire Spacious Garden walled about and furnished with all sorts of Flowers and fruits and divers mounted walkes without which Garden there is a descent of about 10 stepps into Private walkes walled about

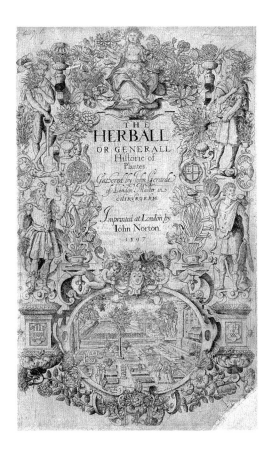

The title-page to John Gerard's *Herball or Generall Historie of Plantes* published in 1597.

Left: Sixteenth-century gardens were formally laid out with herb and kitchen gardens, orchards and flower gardens separated by yew and privet hedges, like this walled garden at Greys Court, Oxfordshire.

and furnished with store of fruite . . . and without the West Walke of the Garden there is a faire Orchard furnished with good fruit and divers pleasant Walks . . . and on the South side . . . are severall Orchards of Cherryes, Pares, Plumbs, others of Apples, and also good kitchen gardens.

It is likely that there was a garden near Speke Hall from at least the Tudor period; in 1624, gardeners were certainly being employed to supply the house with vegetables, herbs and fruit.

Elizabethan gardens were normally formal with the herb and kitchen gardens separated from the house, flower gardens and orchards by yew and privet hedges. A letter written by Peter Kemp to Sir William Cecil in 1561 explains this arrangement: 'for the many different scents that arise from the herbes, as cabbages, onions, etc., are scarce well-pleasing to perfume the lodgings of any house.' A magnificent herb garden, the largest in any National Trust garden, was recreated at Hardwick in the 1960s, using predominantly those plants familiar to an Elizabethan household, both culinary and medicinal. Even the smallest cottages had gardens full of herbs: as in earlier times, in this context herbs included vegetables, flowers and any growing plant whose leaves and stems were used as food.

Not only were vegetables grown in private gardens, but large quantities were raised in the increasing number of market gardens at this period. Around London, and in the suburbs of other major towns like Norwich and Worcester, commercial gardeners grew a variety of vegetables. Some concentrated on cheap, high-yielding crops for the poor – parsnips, carrots, turnips and cabbages – so that in the *Haven of Health*, 1584, Thomas Cogan thought parsnips and carrots 'common meate among the common people, all the time of autumne, and chiefly uppon fish daies'. These roots and cabbages were boiled into pottage by the poor, or, in extremis, eaten raw.

Other market gardeners specialised in producing more delicate vegetables for the richer citizens of the large towns. Such produce, hitherto neglected, found increasing favour at their tables. The chronicler Ralph Holinshed, noted in 1548 that 'melons, pompions [pumpkins], gourdes, cucumbers, radishes, skirets [similar to parsnips], parsnips and turnips' were no longer shunned as food of the poor, but eaten 'as deintie dishes at the tables of delicate merchants, gentlemen and the nobilitie who make their provision yearelie for new seeds out of strange countries.' It is difficult to assess the frequency of these dishes, however, because they were not commonly mentioned on festive menus or in household accounts. But in the opinion of Gervase Markham in *The English Hus-wife* in 1615, the good 'English hus-wife' had to 'have knowledge of all sorts of herbs belonging unto the kitchin whether they be for the Pot, or Sallets, for Sauces, for servings, or for any other seasoning or adorning.'

Protestant refugees fleeing from persecution in The Netherlands and France brought with them to England their sophisticated knowledge of vegetable cultivation. They settled in East Anglia and south-east England, setting up market gardens where they grew produce using new techniques and plants. A number of these new vegetables quickly gained popularity: asparagus; cardoons and globe artichokes, or 'artichoakes' that 'groweth like in the heade unto the Pine apple' (*The Profittable Arte of Gardening* of 1563); cucumbers; cauliflowers; red or Roman beet; white or Italian beet, a kind of chard; spinach; and pumpkins. Poor folk removed the seeds and pith from the last, stuffed them with apples and baked them, while the well-to-do enjoyed them in

A detail from the herb garden outside the Great Barn at Buckland Abbey, Devon, laid out in the formal Elizabethan manner.

elaborate pies: the pumpkin was first sliced and fried with sweet herbs and spices, sugar and beaten eggs, then put in a pastry shell with alternate layers of apples and currants. Pumpkin pie made along similar lines has become a national dish in America, introduced there by the early colonists.

Other new vegetables came from further afield in the New World: the kidney bean, native to Peru, was most often served boiled and buttered as part of a 'sallet'. It was first established in France, hence its alternative name of French bean. The only beans known before the discovery of America had been the broad beans of Europe and the soya beans of the East: now Lima, scarlet runners, string, and haricot as well as kidney beans became common.

But of all the vegetables, or foods, given to the world by America, the most useful was the potato, being easy to cultivate, a prolific cropper, simple to keep and the best assurance against famine. The history of both the sweet and the common potato has never been completely sorted out, but it is thought that the tubers brought back by John Hawkins from his voyage to 'the coast of Guinea and the Indies of Nova Hispania' in 1564 were the sweet potato (*Ipomea batata*), or as Gerard called them 'skyretts of Peru'. The Elizabethan traveller Richard Hakluyt, in his *Principal Navigations, Voiages, and Discoveries of the English Nation* of 1589, described the sweet potato as 'the most delicate rootes that may be eaten, and doe farre exceed our passeneps or carets. Their pines be of the bignes of two fists ... and the inside eateth like an apple, but it is more delicious than any sweet apple sugred.' Most historians agree that the Spaniards brought the common potato or Virginia potato (*Solanum tuberosum*) to Europe from South America about 1580. There is no clear evidence of how it first came to England or Ireland, but it was certainly here by the time Gerard wrote his *Herball* in 1597. Neither variety of potato caught on immediately in England, although the sweet potato was definitely preferred and first appeared in print in *The Good Huswifes Jewell* by Thomas Dawson in 1596 in a recipe for 'a tart that is a courage to a man or a woman'. As well as a potato root, the tart contained borage roots, quinces, dates, egg yolks, wine, sugar, spices and 'the brains of three or four cock sparrows'. But few other recipes made use of either potato during the early years of the 17th century. In spite of many efforts to encourage the cultivation of the common potato, nearly two hundred years were to pass before it became a common field crop in England. The 'potato of Canada', or Jerusalem artichoke, brought back by early French explorers of Canada had much more success. The root vegetable skirret was also extremely popular: 'sweet, white, good to be eaten, and most pleasant in taste'. Like turnips and carrots, skirrets were sliced, boiled and buttered, roasted in the embers of the fire and eaten with melted butter, or baked in elaborate pies.

Vegetable dishes fell under the generic title of 'sallets' and were served raw, boiled or baked. The Elizabethans added new vegetables and fruits to the earlier herb and flower salads, together with hard-boiled eggs and sometimes sliced cold capon, anchovies and other meat or fish delicacies. Such a mixture formed a 'compound sallet', forerunner of the complex 'grand sallet' of the 17th century. Gervase Markham distinguishes between 'compound' and 'simple' salads and for simple recipes suggests:

Chives, Scallions, Radish-rootes, boyled carets, skirrets, and Turnips ... young Lettice, Cabbage-lettice, Purslane and divers other herbs which may be served simply without any thing but a little Vinegar, Sallet Oyle, and Suger: Onions

The potato, a woodcut illustration from Gerard's *Herball*.

boyled and stript from their rind, and served up with Vinegar, Oyle, and Pepper, is a good simple Sallet and so is Samphire, Bean cods, Sparagus, and Cucumbers served in likewise with Oyle, Vinegar, and Pepper, with a world of others, too tedious to nominate.

Many herbs used in salads were believed to have medicinal properties, of special value in the spring, after the salt meat and fish diet of the winter months. Garlic was beginning to go out of favour: Elizabethans called it the poor man's physic, of special value to seafaring men because 'it pacifieth the disposition to vomit'.

Pickled vegetables and fruit were prepared as a garnish for fresh salads and as a winter-time alternative to the 'boyled sallets', which were thought to be better for the digestion. Mushrooms, broom buds, beetroot, red cabbage, samphire, ash-keys and the tops of young greenstuff were preserved in vinegar, stale beer or verjuice, while cucumbers were boiled in vinegar with salt, pepper, fennel, dill and mace. Red beetroot was served as a boiled salad on its own; 'carved and sliced', it supplied a richly coloured garnish for other salads.

Although flowers were grown primarily for decoration – Queen Elizabeth maintained a lady-in-waiting whose sole job was to strew fresh flowers in her path – several were also used in cookery. They took their place along with the fruit bushes in a well-planned kitchen garden, according to Thomas Tusser in 1590:

> The gooseberry, raspberry and roses, all three,
> With strawberries under them trimly agree.

Roses were the source of rose-water, much used as a flavouring in Elizabethan recipes, and rose petals and buds were often candied and eaten as a snack, or served at the banquet course. Marigolds supplied a vegetable dye used in butter and cheese-making and were made into tarts; their petals were dried and used in broths and stews. Violets, primroses, cowslips and borage flowers were candied to preserve them and combined with eggs and cream or curds as fillings for tarts. The flowers for salads had to combine

A detail from Lucas van Valckenborch's *Fruit Market*. A surprising variety of fruit was grown and eaten in Elizabethan England, including the 'apricock' newly arrived from Portugal, the melon from France and the tomato from Mexico – the last was cultivated at this period only as a curiosity.

Lucas van Valckenborch's depiction of Summer, showing the vegetables and fruit grown in an Elizabethan kitchen garden.

visual appeal with an attractive scent: violets, primroses and borage were now joined by cowslips, elder, rosemary, broom and above all, clove gillyflowers:

> Take your herbs and pick them very fine into fine water, and pick your flowers by themselves, and wash them clean, then swing them in a strainer, and when you put them into a dish, mingle them with cucumbers or lemons pared and sliced, also scrape sugar, and put in vinegar and oil, then throw the flowers on the top of the salad, and of every sort of the aforesaid things and garnish the dish about, then take eggs boiled hard, and lay about the dish and upon the salad.

The Good Huswifes Jewell by Thomas Dawson, 1596

For winter salads, flowers were preserved in gallipots topped up with vinegar, 'both for shew and use, for they are more excellent for taste than for to look on.'

Fruit, eaten in ever greater quantities was grown in surprising variety. Thomas Tusser drew up a list of 27 different fruit trees and bushes for the Elizabethan gardener in his *Five Hundreth Pointes of Good Husbandrie* of 1590. Medieval favourites continue to appear: apples, of which Shakespeare mentions 'Codlings, Pippens, Leater Coats [russets], Apple-Johns, Bitter-Sweets, Pomewaters and Costards', as well as 'roasted crabs'; medlars; pears – Gerard mentions an acquaintance who grew in one orchard 'threescore sundry sortes of Peares, and those exceeding good'; quinces, particularly popular in Elizabethan times and eaten at wedding feasts; plums, damsons and bullaces; cherries, now grown in gardens as a commercial crop and used, according to Gerard, to make 'many excellent Tarts and other pleasant meats'; and grapes, strawberries, mulberries, bilberries and gooseberries. Tusser's list also included some relatively new arrivals from southern Europe. Among them was the apricot, or 'apricock' from the Portuguese *albricoque*; in Shakespeare's *Richard II*, the gardener bids his assistant to bind up 'yon dangling apricocks'. New gardening techniques introduced from the Continent encouraged the growing of apricots and quinces against south-facing walls, and even figs were sometimes ripened in sheltered gardens in southern England. Other new exotic fruits were the melon, introduced from France, and the tomato, or 'apple of love' because of its supposed aphrodisiac quality, which was brought back from Mexico, but cultivated in England only as a curiosity until the end of the 18th century. Barberries, which had long been used by apothecaries, now became a popular garnish for meat and fish and began to be grown regularly in gardens.

In the north of England, the variety of fruit grown was perforce more limited. The best fruits to set were 'apples, pears, cherries, red and white plums, damsons, and bullaces .... We do not meddle with apricocks nor peaches nor scarcely with quinces, which will not like our cold parts.' At Hardwick there were originally two orchards, one of which (the south) was probably also the site of the kitchen garden. It is now divided into four by hedged alleys of yew and hornbeam; two parts are occupied by orchards. The more formal, productive one to the south is planted with old varieties of apples, pears, plums, greengages and damsons. The second orchard, next to the house, has pears and ornamental crab apples. A mulberry walk has also been planted by the National Trust beyond the herb garden.

Citrus fruits were imported from Portugal in ever-increasing numbers, although they remained a luxury until well into the 17th century. Oranges, particularly, were extremely fashionable: Sir Hugh Platt in his *Delightes for Ladies* of 1605 (a book on preparing banquetting stuffe), gives instructions for keeping orange juice all the year round to make sauces and cooling drinks, together with a labour-saving tip for snapping up oranges at bargain prices when the first ship-loads arrived in November. Sir Francis Carew is said to have grown the first orange trees in the country on his estate at Beddington near Croydon in Surrey, some time before 1562. The value of oranges and lemons, as well as certain herbs for fighting scurvy, was appreciated at the period. Sir John Hawkins, for example, stipulates that his sailors should eat both fruit on their long voyages, and military commanders recognised their efficacy during sieges.

Elizabethans enjoyed a salad of lemons, thinly sliced, well sugared and garnished with strips of peel. However, uncooked fruit, like raw vegetables was still regarded with suspicion by most. 'Fruites generally are noyfulle to man and do ingender ill humours' wrote Sir Thomas Elyot in his *Castel of Helth* of 1541 – the only fruit he exempted from this ban were peaches, which he declared 'do less harme and do make better juice in the body, for they are not too soone corrupted being eaten'. The dangers were thought to be greatest when epidemics raged: the sale of raw fruit in the streets of London was forbidden during the plague of 1569. To counteract any infection, fruit like apples, pears, wardens and quinces was baked for a long time in pies – for six hours in a 1588 recipe for quince pies. The fruit for pies was usually precooked in a syrup of red wine, sugar or honey and spices, and the Elizabethan fruit tart was often filled with 'tartstuff', a kind of purée, ensuring that the fruit had been well and truly cooked. Apples, cherries, medlars, peaches, damsons, pears, mulberries and rosehips would be boiled, then 'bruised with a ladle' and strained when cold. Red wine was then added and the purée was seasoned with sugar and spices. Boiled and pulped soft fruits were also mingled with cream to make fools and similar dishes, and fruits of all kinds were made into sweetmeats for the banquet.

Nut trees were a feature of the Elizabethan garden. Tusser included on his list chestnuts, filberts, small nuts (perhaps hazelnuts) and walnuts. So, next to the herb garden at Hardwick, the National Trust has planted a nuttery. Almonds were imported in large quantities for the marchpane that was regularly used to make the chief showpiece of the dessert or banquet course in the late 16th century, when the 'subtlety' was becoming archaic (see recipe, p.122).

Exotic Foodstuffs

During Elizabeth's reign the spice trade was still virtually the monopoly of the Portuguese, and thus of Spain since the annexation of Portugal by Philip II in 1580. To get round this English seamen made exploratory voyages to the Far East in the 1590s, and in 1600 the East India Company was set up to try to secure a share in the trade. Despite this, spices remained expensive and were still kept locked away. In the Earl of Northumberland's household account for 1597, there is mention of a payment to 'Griffen of Gilforde' for, amongst other things, 'a little trunck to kepe spyce in the kitchen' at Petworth.

The intriguing spices of medieval cuisine, such as cubebs, galingale and grains of paradise, were no longer imported and, although there was a general decline in spicing food, Elizabethan cooks frequently used the more common spices like cinnamon, mace, nutmeg, cloves, pepper and ginger. The universal use of saffron to colour and season dishes was falling off, although Sir Francis Drake said that 'What made the English people sprightly was the liberal use of saffron in their broths and sweetmeats'. It was,

Right: The 'Cubborde of Boxes', a 16th-century spice cupboard in the great hall at Little Moreton Hall, Cheshire. Spices, which included at this period dried fruit, almonds, walnuts, rice and sugar, were so valuable that they were kept locked up.

Below: A detail from Jan Brueghel's painting, *The Distinguished Visitor*, showing the gift of a sugar loaf. So valuable was sugar at this period that loaves were presented to influential friends and as gifts of love.

however, valued for its restorative properties: Gerard wrote in 1597 that its 'moderate use . . . is good for the head, and maketh the sences more quicke and lively, shaketh off heavy and drosie sleep, and maketh a man merry.'

Dried fruit, almonds, walnuts, rice and sugar continue to appear on the spice list in household accounts: '5 lb sugar 6s 3d; $\frac{3}{4}$ lb pepper 2s 7d; 1 oz Lord's mace 21d; 1 oz cloves 9d; 1 oz nutmeg 6d; 1 oz cinnamon 8d; 4 lb currants 20d; 1 lb raisins 7d; ginger 2d' were purchased for the Percy household at Petworth in 1591. Dried fruits were imported in larger quantities than before and were as often used in recipes as fresh fruit. Sugar was also all the rage, helping to bring about the decline in spices by making bland dishes more appetising. Supplies from the old-established sources were superseded by the quantity of imports from Morocco and Barbary and the new Portuguese and Spanish plantations in the West Indies. In the later years of Elizabeth's reign, much sugar arrived in England not through trade, but in the form of prize cargoes captured by privateers from the Spanish and Portuguese.

In addition to having an enjoyable taste, sugar continued in its reputation as a healthy food. Dr Andrew Boorde had advised in 1542 that: 'All meates and drinkes the which is swete and that suger is in, be nutrytyve', and wealthy Elizabethans followed his advice to excess. Although the national annual consumption averaged no more than a pound per head during this time, the great majority of it was eaten by a few people, whose teeth soon began to tell the tale. As Paul Hentzner, a German visitor, noted, even the Queen's teeth were black from decay, 'a defect the English seem subject to, from their too great use of sugar'.

Beverages

The Elizabethans loved their drink: a 1577 census of drinking establishments shows that over five thousand existed in Kent, Nottinghamshire and Yorkshire alone and, as William Harrison remarked, it was ale and beer 'which nevertheless bear the greatest brunt in drinking'. Hop cultivation had at first been understood so little by English farmers that in 1549 a warrant was issued by the Privy Council, whereby the sum of £140 was authorised 'for charges in bringing over certain hop sellers' from the Low Countries (see p.29). The first book to be published in England entirely on the subject of hop-growing was Reginald Scot's *Perfite Platforme of a Hoppe Garden*, printed in 1574. For some time there was a struggle between ale and beer brewers, but eventually the superiority of beer became so fully recognised that ale was hopped just like beer and the two names became synonymous, so that by 1598 a foreign visitor was writing that: 'The general drink is beer, which is prepared from barley and is excellently well tasted, but strong and what soon fuddles.'

Beer was prepared in three strengths: single or 'small beer'; double or strong; and double-double or very strong. Brewers preferred preparing double-double strength as they could sell it at a high price. The Queen, however, preferred single and in 1560 ordered that the brewing of double-double be stopped and that brewers make 'as much single as double beer and more'. When she went visiting, the Queen was most particular about the quality of her malt liquor and if it did not suit her taste, supplies would be forwarded from London.

Adulteration continued to be a problem: ale-wives were infamous for adding resin and salt to their brews so that they would keep better, thus ruining the flavour. Harrison registers complaints about inns and taverns: 'I find . . . such heady ale and beer in most of them, as for the mightinesse thereof among such as seek it out, is commonly called Huffcap, the Mad Dog, Father Whoresonne and Dragons' Milk . . . .' Such adulteration was punishable by fines, but was difficult to regulate. Measures were also taken against the sellers of indifferent liquor, whether beer or wine: in 1597, an order was made in London that 52 barrels of beer 'being neither fit for man's body nor to be converted into sawce shall have the heads of all the same beaten out, and the beer poured out into the channells part in Cheapside, part in Cornhill, and part in Bishopsgate'.

To avoid adulteration and inferior brews, many Elizabethans brewed their own ale and beer at home. In small households it was normally the housewife's task, but large establishments like Petworth, Hardwick, Montacute and Buckland employed a brewer. Both beer and ale were brewed in the Petworth brew-house using barley grown on the estate, and bought-in hops: 'Paid to Mr Johnson of London on 2nd May 1586 for hoppes, 11s and to Mr Holland of Arundell for hoppes on 2nd July, £4 9s 4d.' Petworth beer was brewed in two qualities: single beer for the household generally and double beer for the Earl and his immediate family. Payment was made to Robert Shawe, the brewer for '52 barrells of single beer, and 1 barrell of double beer' brewed between 9 September 1585 and 1 March 1586. Thirteen years later the quantity had risen significantly. From 6 May 1598 to 18 February 1599, there were 35 brewings, when 12 hogsheads of beer were brewed. A hogshead was $52\frac{1}{2}$ gallons, so we know that roughly 21,000 gallons of beer had been brewed and received into the cellars at Petworth over nine months.

With the disappearance of the monasteries, so too the art of tending vines

A detail from Lucas van Valckenborch's *Fruit Market*, showing wine being tasted in a glass tumbler.

disappeared, and grapes were grown only in the gardens of a few noble households. But a great deal of wine was imported. William Harrison tells us the amount was 'yearlie to the proportion of 20,000 or 30,000 tun [1 tun = 252 gallons] and upwards' and included 56 kinds from France and about 30 from Italy, Greece, Spain, Germany, the Canary Islands and Portugal. Most highly esteemed were the 'mighty great wines' shipped from Bordeaux (the 'Gascoigne' wines) and the sweet, rich malmsies of Crete and Madeira. Wines arriving from Bordeaux were merely labelled red, white or claret; little distinction was made among particular vineyards or regions.

Sack, a dry Spanish wine, was well-established and popular by Elizabethan times, as a look at the drinking habits of Shakespeare's Falstaff reveals. Sir John, with his immoderate love of sack, lived too soon to benefit from the advice of the learned Dr William Vaughan, who in his *Directions for Health* of 1600, warns that 'sacke doth make men fat and foggy', although he admits it 'comforteth the spirits marvellously'.

The Earl of Northumberland's outlay on wine was substantial. In 1598, he purchased for Syon House 3 tuns of claret, 1 butt (30 gallons) of sack, and 1 butt of Canary wine from various vintners, and for Petworth a runlett of Rhenish wine containing 19 gallons; 2 tuns of claret; and 1 tun of 'Gascoigne' wine; the claret sometimes arrived at Southampton and travelled by road to Arundel. All wines were drunk from the wood, but not all were what they were supposed to be: a great many were 'manufactured' by the vintner, the yeoman of the buttery or the butler.

The Elizabethans, like their ancestors, enjoyed hippocras which was served at the banquet. More modest households also made the traditional mead and metheglin and various flower and fruit wines. By the middle of the 16th century, alcohol was being distilled from wine of all qualities. The resultant 'aqua vitae', or 'burning water' was often very crude, but considered an essential ingredient in the healthy diet. Aromatic herbs and spices, such as juniper berries, wormwood, hyssop and mint, were added to disguise the flavour. All such warming drinks were believed to stimulate the heart and they became known as 'cordial waters'. Cordials were sold by distillers and apothecaries, but the distilling apparatus was within reach of any well-equipped household and the 'waters' made at home were usually more wholesome. The 'compleat housewife' had to be able to produce surfeit water, hysterical water, black cherry water, clary water, saffron cordial and a host of others, classified in the anonymous *Newe Jewell of Health* of 1576, as 'laudable, comfortable, commendable and singular'. Spirits were widely drunk in the plague year of 1593, achieving little success as cures, so that the distillers were discredited for a time. But they soon set to work again, encouraged by the soldiers returning from the Dutch wars, who did most to spread the taste for strong liquors among the ordinary people.

II

Hardwick Hall, like other grand Elizabethan households, was a self-sufficient establishment, organised like a trimmed-down version of the Queen's court at Greenwich or Hampton Court. At the centre was Bess herself, and round her radiated three circles: her immediate family, the upper servants and the lower servants. The

Hardwick Hall, Derbyshire (*left*), built by Bess of Hardwick (1527–1628) (*above*) in the 1590s on the site adjoining the manor house where she was born in modest circumstances. Through a series of shrewd marriages, she amassed the fortune that enabled her to create one of the architectural masterpieces of Elizabethan England.

Above right: Henry Percy, 9th Earl of Northumberland (1564–1632), painted by Sir Anthony Van Dyck. His interest in scientific and alchemical experiments earned him the nickname of the 'Wizard Earl'.

division between upper and lower servants was a crucial one in all big Elizabethan households. The upper servants were more like courtiers and were usually the younger sons and daughters of good families wanting to learn household management and ceremonial procedures, just as in medieval times. They were known as 'Mrs' and 'Mr' and counted as gentlewomen or gentlemen, while the lower servants were classed as yeomen. Bess had been in such service herself as a girl in the household of a neighbouring great Derbyshire family, that of Sir John and Lady Zouche of Codnor Castle. Her household at Hardwick was not large, especially when compared with the royal court, which would cater for 1,500 people. Bess's household consisted of about 30 indoor servants of both ranks, including her nephew, the son of her half-sister Jane. The upper servants had their own well-furnished rooms, mostly in the Old Hall, which Bess had begun to refurbish in the 1580s but left unfinished when she started work on the New Hall. The lower servants bedded down on truckle beds or straw pallets on landings on the main staircase, outside Bess's bedchamber door, in the great hall, in the kitchen, pantry or in the scullery. The 1601 inventory lists in the scullery 'a mattriss, a bolster, a blanket, three coverletes'.

The Percies of Petworth were 'one of the greatest families of Christendom', but the 9th Earl also maintained a relatively small household by contemporary standards; the number of servants varied from just under 50 in the late 1580s to over 70 for the year 1603–4. This fell far short of the ideal laid down by Richard Braithwaite in his *Some Rules and Orders for the Government of the House of an Earl* written in the early 17th century, in which he lists more than 100 officers and servants.

In large houses like Hardwick and Petworth, the domestic management was placed in the hands of a senior member of the resident staff, usually the steward. The 9th Earl of Northumberland himself noted what he conceived to be the 'steward's charge' in 1597–8, which included amongst other things, the provision of all household expenses such as wine, corn, hay, spice, wood, coal, beef, mutton and things belonging to the diet, wages and liveries, and plate and furniture for the kitchen. The actual control of the kitchens, provisions and kitchen staff was then delegated to a clerk of the kitchen. William Kenton was clerk of the kitchen at Petworth from 1592–3 and was responsible for some 8 offices concerned with the receipt and storage of supplies of food, fuel and lighting: the granary, cellar, buttery, larder (for dressed meats, fish and dairy produce), pantry, the ewery (for linen and candlesticks), and the scullery and the woodyard. All the purchases were recorded by him daily in a series of 'books of provision' or 'books of daily expenses', so that a check could be kept on the purloining of supplies by unscrupulous servants and an accurate estimate could be made of the requirements of the household. Thomas Blunde, the 'cater', who bought in the 'acates' or fresh provisions, which could not be supplied by the Petworth estate, received his instructions from William Kenton and was accountable to him. So were the master cooks and scullerymen, the yeoman of the cellar and the butler or yeoman of the buttery, the yeoman of the pantry, and the bakers and brewers. Every man in the household from the steward down wore the livery of the Earl (azure blue cloth with the heraldic mark of silver bearing the Percy half-moon), had free board and lodging, and all, except probably 'Harrie' and 'Hugh of the kitchen', were paid quarterly wages. Certain offices also carried 'fees' or perquisites of the office, or their money equivalent: the yeoman of the cellar, the baker and the brewer claimed the profit for selling bran, grain, empty casks and vessels; the cook for selling coneyskins, feathers and tallow.

Women usually played no part in the running of wealthy Elizabethan households, where the cleaning, catering and serving was still done almost exclusively by men, although a 'Joan Dyke' was employed at Petworth to work in the scullery as a 'scourer'. Women were employed in the dairy and to look after poultry, but never as cooks. There were three master cooks at Petworth between 1585 and 1632 – Ralph Christian, Richard Heath and Edward Jones – and the 9th Earl also employed a French cook named Robert Jaggard or Jackett. It was the fashion among many noble households by this time to employ French cooks or chefs, as they were noted for their culinary skills.

The kitchen, which in earlier times would have been housed in a separate building, was now conveniently placed on the ground floor near the great hall, reached via the buttery and pantry. The kitchen at Hardwick is typical of the period, still large and spacious, but smaller than its medieval predecessor. Stone or brick walls were now plaster-covered and whitewashed, and the flat ceiling was of timber beams, or also plastered. The room had a stone-flagged floor and was unusually well-lit, although the windows were placed high up the walls to prevent the scullions and menials from being distracted from their duties. At Hardwick, the architect Robert Smythson sank the floor of the kitchen into a half-basement, thus increasing its height to give the smoke and heat a chance to rise.

The great kitchen at Hardwick with its stone-flagged floor, whitewashed walls and large windows set high to prevent scullions being distracted from their duties. The charcoal stewing stove under the windows was installed in the 18th century.

The kitchen at Canons Ashby, Northamptonshire, built conveniently near to the hall in the 1550s by John Dryden. The narrow mullion windows were replaced by large sashes in 1710 when the kitchen was modernised, but it retains its original shape, and probably its height.

The kitchen at Canons Ashby in Northamptonshire, built in the 1550s by John Dryden, was on the ground floor at one end of the hall. The original screens passage led to the buttery and pantry and a door through to the kitchen; both doors can still be seen. Apart from the passage, widened by Sir Erasmus Dryden in the 1590s, the large stone-flagged kitchen retains its original shape and probably its height. In addition to being placed conveniently for the hall, it was also next to the 'winter parlour', where the family ate their everyday meals when not dining in state in the great chamber.

The domestic offices at Montacute were also divided off from the hall by the screens passage, with a door leading to the buttery, with its cellars underneath, and the pantry, then through finally to the kitchen. The buttery, pantry and passage now form the dining-room. The monastic kitchen at Buckland Abbey would have been sited an inconvenient distance from Sir Richard Grenville's newly converted great hall, so a new kitchen was built allowing easy access to the original screens passage, now the chapel lobby. The 'new' kitchen is large and well-lit with the plastered walls painted an ox-blood colour.

There was no form of running water in the Elizabethan kitchen. It had to be fetched from a well in wooden buckets, earthenware pots and leather bags, and must often have been muddy, polluted and usually twice-used. Nobody would have dreamed of drinking it and many cooks used rose-water in their recipes instead, bought or distilled from flowers from the garden in the still-room each summer and stored in clean, sealed glasses. At Hardwick, water was pumped by means of a horse-operated wheel from a well to a conduit house to the south of the hall. This house, which still survives, originally contained a lead cistern under its canopy. From there, a lead conduit conducted the water to the house, perhaps to the two 'Sesterns of lead in the lower larder' referred to in the 1601 inventory. It must then have been carried to the kitchen and scullery and to the other parts of the house in wooden tubs and containers. There was a 'cestern of lead with a curbe of wood about yt to receive the cundit water' actually in the great kitchen at Petworth in 1574.

The immense open hearths built into the walls of the kitchen dominated the room, providing a fierce, steady, crudely adjustable flame for roasting or boiling, and embers for long slow baking and simmering. The usual fuel for the fire was still wood, although peat was widely used in more remote country areas. Certain woods were preferred for different methods of cooking: ash for roasting because it burns with a hot, clear flame; beech for boiling because it gives an even heat and cherry wood for oven cooking. Conifer and the other resinous woods were avoided, because of the dark smoke and unpleasant smell they produced. Heavy logs and faggots for the fire were still stacked on the floor, or in a small storeroom near the fire, as at Buckland. The kitchen fire was kept burning continuously, covered with a curfew overnight as before, the heavy logs being supported by plain andirons or firedogs.

The basic methods of cooking and preparing food had changed little since medieval times. Enormous joints of meat, poultry and game were roasted on spits, supported by cob irons (see p.47), over a dripping pan in front of the fire. In the kitchen of large houses like Hardwick and Buckland, there were still two open hearths; one for roasting and one for boiling.

To the right of the roasting hearth at Buckland, high up on the wall, is a wooden wheel, possibly the remains of a dog-turnspit cage, although more likely part of a complicated system for hoisting sides of bacon and ham on to hooks ranged along the ceiling bracket. In Elizabethan times, the dog-turnspit frequently replaced the boy, although in smaller houses turning the spit by hand was continued for a long time after, and great houses like Petworth had a 'turnbreach' or turnspit. In his 1570 treatise on dogs, Dr John Caius, physician to Elizabeth I, describes *Canis Veruversator*, the turnspit, as 'a certain dog in kitchen service excellent, for when any meat is to be roasted they go into a wheel, which they, turning about with the weight of their bodies, so diligently look to their business that no drudge or scullion can do the feat more cunningly.' These long-backed and short-legged dogs were bred to work in pairs, taking turns to pad round and round the wooden dog wheel for several hours trying to

The kitchen at Buckland Abbey, Devon, with its ox-blood coloured walls, was built by Sir Richard Grenville in the mid-16th century as part of his conversion of the Cistercian abbey into a private house. This photograph shows the large stout wooden table, roasting hearth with spits, and the remains of the complicated wooden pulley system for the storage of food.

A 16th-century Flemish painting of the *Supper at Emmaus*. On the right, joints of meat and poultry are roasted on spits supported by cob-irons over a dripping pan in front of the fire. The cauldron hangs over the fire on a ratchet hanger from a chimney crane attached to the side of the hearth. At the back is a cupboard for storing food, with shelves to accommodate utensils and serving dishes. Wine jugs are cooling in the cistern in the dining-room.

keep their balance, while the meat roasted. A pulley attached to the end of the spit was connected to another pulley on the hub of the wheel by a leather belt; as the wheel turned, the movement was carried to the spit. Small wonder that the poor dog often tried to hide himself when he caught sight of the spit being prepared, causing the poet Gay to write:

> The dinner must be dish'd at one.
> Where's this vexatious turnspit gone?
> Unless the skulking cur is caught
> The sirloin's spolit and I'm in fault.

The boiling hearth in the Buckland kitchen was put in later than the roasting hearth. It was built into the west wall and included two bread ovens. Joints of meat, poultry, vegetables and puddings were boiled in iron, brass or copper cauldrons or kettles, suspended over the fire from ratchet-hangers, hung from a bar fixed across the chimney, or from a chimney-crane, as in medieval times.

The large fireplace in the hall, or living room, at Tŷ Mawr was used for cooking as well as heating the room. In the wide hearth opening, the fire of wood or peat was burnt on an iron grate above a pit where the ash was collected; it was also sometimes used to rear weak piglets, or chickens. The iron crane fixed to the side of the fireplace was used to hold pots over the fire for making pottage, for boiling ham or bacon, salted fish and vegetables, and to provide hot water for the household. There was no spit, as fresh meat was a very rare addition to the diet of upland North Wales at this time. The pottage was usually thickened with oatmeal, which, along with rye, was the predominant crop in this part of Wales.

Very large houses, like Hardwick, had a separate boiling house for cooking large quantities of meat and making pottage. Both were prepared in a huge copper or brass boiler set into a ventilated masonry structure built in one corner. The copper was heated by means of its own fire on an iron grate beneath, closed off by fire doors. The boiling house of the Tudor kitchens at Hampton Court has been reconstructed recently and shows clearly how it originally operated. Access to the copper, which held 76 gallons, was up a short flight of four stone steps to enable the cook to stir the boiling brew and add new joints of meat with ease. In other houses, like Petworth, a similar copper boiler was placed in the corner of the kitchen itself.

In Elizabethan times, the thick medieval pottages of meat began to yield to fricassées, hashes and 'quelquechoses' (called kickshaws in England) introduced from France. To make a fricassée in 1584, cold mutton or veal was chopped small and fried in 'sweet butter'; then white wine, salt and ginger were added and it was 'served forth in fair dishes'. Hashes were at first prepared from sliced fresh meat, stewed with herbs, spices, broth and often wine. They took their name from the French *hacher*, to chop, and early recipes began: 'Take a couple of legs of lamb, or a leg of young mutton; hash it exceeding thin with your knife', or 'Take your calf's head and . . . hash it in slices as thin as you can'.

The master cooks who worked for the Queen's household were admirably equipped to prepare these elaborate dishes with charcoal stoves, which could cook small quantities of food at a controlled heat in a saucepan or frying pan while being stirred or beaten. Close control of this type was essential when making sauces, egg dishes, pancakes, fritters or many of the sugar-based preserves and confections. In most households, however, 'a chafing-dish of coals' was used for more controlled cooking. This was a portable metal contraption on legs with a lower pan holding coals and an upper lidded pan for cooking. Alternatively, descendants of the medieval brandreths (trivets), or skillets and posnets could hold food just a few inches above the gentle heat of a small fire burning on the hearth.

Pies, pasties, patties, tarts and flans figured among the highlights of Elizabethan cuisine. Huge pies, lavishly decorated, were popular for feasts and country-dwellers would send them as presents to friends or patrons in town. Cooks went to great lengths to make them visually exciting as well as full of flavour: crusts were moulded into the shape of animals and lids were painted and decorated with leaves, flowers, heraldic devices and 'other inventions'. For sweet fillings, the bottom crust was sometimes flavoured with rose-water and sugar. On meat days, these pies were filled with pork, game, mutton, tongue and all kinds of birds, highly spiced, brightly coloured and mixed with dried or fresh fruits. On fish days, they were filled with lampreys, sturgeon, porpoise, ling and cod, again mixed with dried fruits and spices. After baking, they were often filled up with a liquor of white wine, rose-water, sugar, cinnamon and vinegar and the lids were iced with sugar and rose-water. Large pies could also be filled with fruit alone: among the New Year gifts annually presented to the Queen was 'a great pye of quinces oringed', given by her master of the pastry. 'Joke' or 'trick' pies were made for the feasts and revels of the wealthy, especially on Twelfth Night, cut open to reveal a flock of live birds, a troop of live frogs, or even, occasionally, a small human being: the nursery rhyme 'Sing a Song of Sixpence' tells the story of one such pie.

A woodcut from *Opera di M. Bartolomeo Scappi*, 1570, showing a typical contemporary kitchen of a wealthy household, with the turnspit roasting over the open fire protected from the heat by a wooden screen, the charcoal stewing-stove, a curious utensil 'tidy' underneath the wall-safe or bread-car, and the marble or stone cistern with running water.

Hoefnagel's *Fête at Bermondsey* depicts a wedding feast with enormous 'bride pies' being carried in napkins slung around the necks of the servers. Poultry and meat were spit-roasted, while dishes of cooked food were laid out on a white cloth at the serving hatch before being carried to the table.

Recipes for pastry abounded; in some of the earliest, the flour was mixed with a hot liquor of butter and water or ale boiled together in varying proportions. Beef or mutton broth went into some pastries, cream into others, while in Lent, 'thick almond milk seething hot' was combined with 'salad oil fried and saffron'. Various flours were used depending on the contents of the pies: rye for game pies that were to be kept for a long time; wheat for those that were to be eaten more quickly; and fine wheat, dried in the oven first, for those pies to be served hot. Elizabethan dish tarts, such as fruit and flower tarts, florentines (filled with a mixture of veal, kidney, spinach, herbs, spices and dried fruits) were made with short rich pastry, 'driven out so thin that ye may blow it up from

the table' (*A Proper Newe Booke of Cokerye* of about 1560). 'Cut-laid tarts', served for the banquet, had their upper crust removed after baking and replaced by separately baked tart-tops of rich puff paste divided into ornamental patterns with interlaced strips of sugar-glazed pastry and panels of contrasting coloured preserves and marmalades.

Sweet and savoury tarts of custard, curd and vegetables were all popular. Really rich butter paste was often eaten by itself. The flour was mixed with butter, several eggs, rose-water and spices to make a paste which was then divided into two or three pieces. The recipe continues: 'drive out the piece with a rolling pin, and do with butter one piece by another, and then fold up your paste upon the butter and drive it out again, and so do five or six times together . . . There be some that to this paste add sugar, but it is certain to hinder the rising thereof' (Sir Hugh Platt's *Delightes for Ladies*, 1605).

These pies and tarts were baked in a beehive oven if the household was wealthy

A Dutch kitchen scene by Joachim de Beuckelaer, painted in the 1550s, and showing waffles being made. The wafering iron was held in the fire until hot, batter was ladled on to one side of the open iron, and then the other side was brought down to produce crisp patterned wafers.

enough to have one, either built into the wall of the great open hearth as at Buckland, or into the wall of the kitchen. There is such a baking oven to the left of the windows on the north wall of the kitchen at Canons Ashby. In large houses like Montacute and Hardwick, there was often a separate 'pastry', providing pastry cases for pies and tarts as well as baking them. At Hardwick, the 'pastry' was in the north turret leading from the kitchen, where the two great domed, brick-lined ovens have recently been found, side by side. They originally had stone doors, but these had been replaced by later iron doors. The ash was raked out of the ovens and pushed down the slots in front, to be collected in the cellar. There was also 'a borde' in this room in 1601, to provide a working surface.

All kitchens in large houses had separate sculleries for cleaning poultry, game and fish, for scrubbing vegetables, and for washing up. With the disappearance of the bread trencher, more plates and dishes had to be dealt with after a meal but there was little convenience for washing them – just tubs of hot water heated up in large cauldrons over the fire, and an occasional scouring with sand. The Earl of Northumberland employed a sculleryman, an under-sculleryman and a scourer at Petworth. The scullery or 'little kitchen' at Hardwick, which in 1601 had 'three bordes' for working on, lies to the south of the main kitchen.

There were usually two larders, 'wet' and 'dry,' attached to the kitchen of a large Elizabethan house. The wet larder was used to store both salt-fish and fresh fish, sometimes kept wet packed in seaweed, and salted and fresh meat. Animals, other than game, were kept alive until the last moment, so most of the meat in the larders was either very fresh or had been hanging for some weeks: venison was usually hung for at least six weeks before consumption. The salting and pickling of meat, fish and vegetables was also carried out in the wet larder. The 1601 inventory for Hardwick lists the contents of the wet or 'lowe larder' as: 'too Sesterns of lead [for storing water], three bordes [working surfaces], foure tubs [for pickling meat etc], a hogshead [for storing pickled meat etc.], two shelves.' After salting, the meat and fish were smoked and cured in the kitchen chimney. A small house like Tŷ Mawr would not have the luxury of a wet larder, but there are two deep cupboards built into the thickness of the gable wall on the first floor, flanking the chimney, which, because of their soot-blackened walls, may have been used for smoking meat or fish. For centuries salmon have been trapped in 'cists' or cage-traps in the Lledr River below the house and in 1567 William Morgan's father was documented as holding the rights to *piscae in aqua de Conwey et Lledr*. Within living memory, salmon have been smoked in the large chimneys of farmhouses in the area.

The dry larder was used for storing foodstuffs in sacks, nets, tubs, baskets, earthenware pots and barrels on the floor and on shelves and from racks and hooks on the wall. The contents of the 'drie larder' at Hardwick in 1601 were 'three bordes, a cubberd, too shelves [and] a wood Chare'. Sugar loaves were stored in cord cradles suspended from the ceiling and herbs were hung from hooks. Bread was kept in a bread car of slatted oak hanging from the ceiling to keep it safe from rats and mice. Small quantities of salt were taken from the dry larder and stored in a wooden box hung on the wall near the fire in the kitchen to keep it dry for immediate use. The box usually had a leather hinge to avoid rusting.

Many of the ladies serving at court learned the arts of distilling, preserving and candying from the court cooks: 'there is in manner none of them but when they be at home can help to supply the ordinary want of the kitchen with a number of delicate dishes of their own devising, wherein the portingal [Portuguese] is their chief counsellor; as some of them are most commonly with the clerk of the kitchen', as Lucy Aikin noted in her *Memoirs of the Court of Queen Elizabeth* (London, 1819). It was these gentlewomen, rather than the cook, who produced the 'banquetting stuffe', as confectionery was outside the range of the average cook's experience. The lady of the house, assisted by her daughters and maids, gathered the necessary garden produce throughout the summer and autumn, and carried out the sugar work in the still-house. English cookery books began to offer recipes for banqueting fare: 'jellies of all colours ... tarts of divers hues and sundry denominations, conserves of old fruits, foreign and home-bred suckets [candied fruits and vegetables], codiniacs [quince confections], marmalades, marchpane, sugarbread, gingerbread, florentines ... and sundry outlandish confections, altogether seasoned with sugar.' (Gervase Markham's *The English Hus-wife*, 1615.)

Items 'in Ye Still House' recorded in the 1710 inventory of Dyrham Park, near Bath, are typical of those found in an Elizabethan still-house. The 'pewter limbeck' was for distilling cordials and 'waters', including the favourite rose-water, a small fire was used for making sweetmeats and preserves, and the stove or iron cupboard near the fire with shallow tin- or lead-lined shelves was used for stacking confections, etc, ready for the winter banqueting season or to be offered as refreshments to callers at the house throughout the day. Eringo roots (sea-holly), mallow and lettuce stalks, sugar plums and many other fruits were preserved in syrup to be served as 'wet suckets' or 'succade'; 'dry suckets' were candied fruits and vegetables taken out of their syrup and dried off in the bread oven or still-room cupboard, fruit marmalades cut into shapes and crystallised citrus fruit peel. Crystallised orange peel was carried around in courtiers' pockets to eat at the theatre. Candied eringo roots were particularly popular as they were regarded, like much of the 'banquetting stuffe', as an aphrodisiac: 'Let it haile Kissing Comfits, and snow Eringoes' said Shakespeare in *The Merry Wives of Windsor*. 'Comfits' were sugar-coated whole spices, which the ageing Queen Elizabeth is said to have chewed constantly to freshen her breath.

Fortunately for the gentlewoman who was unequal to the task of creating her own banqueting fare, she could purchase it, or commission relations or friends to bring back sweetmeats from professional confectioners, comfit-makers and apothecaries in the larger towns. Even if she did not prepare 'banquetting stuffe', the lady of the house would certainly have dried herbs, fruit, vegetables and flowers for winter salads and have preserved a number of seasonal ingredients for the cook to use throughout the winter months.

After the food had been prepared in a grand kitchen it was assembled on trestle tables in the 'dresser', 'surveying place' or servery, a small room outside the kitchen door under the watchful eye of the clerk of the kitchen. The various dishes were dressed with appropriate sauces and garnished before being passed out for the table. It was the clerk of the kitchen who was responsible for organising the parade of the food to the great chamber or dining parlour.

Some of the following recipes are taken from cookery books compiled for the newly rich merchant classes of Elizabethan England. The other recipes are taken from 17th-century cookery books, and thus strictly are outside the period. Nevertheless they are all typical of dishes enjoyed by the Elizabethans.

Pickled Herring and Fruit Pie

FOR THE PASTRY

12 oz (350 g) plain flour
pinch of salt
freshly milled black pepper
3 oz (75 g) butter
3 oz (75 g) lard
cold water to mix

FOR THE FILLING

1 lb (450 g) pickled herrings or rollmops
1 large cooking pear, peeled, cored and sliced
1 oz (25 g) raisins
1 oz (25 g) currants
2 oz (50 g) dates, pitted and minced
pinch of salt
¼ teaspoon ground cinnamon
2 tablespoons (30 ml) dry white wine
1 oz (25 g) butter, cut into small pieces
beaten egg, or milk, to glaze
1 teaspoon (5 ml) sugar

To make the pastry, sieve the flour and salt together into a bowl. Add a sprinkling of pepper, then rub in the butter and lard until the mixture resembles fine breadcrumbs. Mix with enough cold water to make a firm dough. Knead lightly until smooth, then chill for about 10 minutes.

Line a well-greased 8-in (20-cm) deep flan tin with half the chilled pastry and bake blind in a hot oven (210°C, 425°F, gas mark 7) for 10 minutes. Leave to cool.

Meanwhile, prepare the filling. Unroll the herrings if necessary and remove the onions if there are any, reserving them for later. Rinse the pickled herrings in cold water, then drain. Plunge them into 3 pt (1.5 litres) boiling water in a saucepan. Cook for 1 minute, then remove and drain well. Cut into chunks.

Mix the pear, raisins, currants, dates, salt, cinnamon and wine together in a bowl and add the herring. Using a slotted spoon to drain off any excess liquid, transfer the filling to the pastry-lined flan tin. Dot the mixture with the butter, then roll out the remaining pastry to make a lid. Decorate the top with any pastry trimmings, then brush well with beaten egg or milk. Cut a vent in the lid to allow the steam to escape, then sprinkle it with sugar. Bake in a moderately hot oven (190°C, 375°F, gas mark 5) for 1 hour or until golden brown. Serves 4–6.

Fish being cooked on a gridiron, from a painting by John White.

Spicy Chicken in Orange Sauce

To boyle a Capon with Orenges after Mistress Duffelds Way

'Take a Capon and boyle it with Veale, or with a marie [marrow] bone, or what your fancy is. Then take a good quantitie of that brothe, and put it in an earthen pot by it selfe, and put thereto a good handfull of Currans, and as manie Prunes and a fewe whole maces, and some Marie, and put to this broth a good quantitie of white Wine or of Claret, and so let them seeth softlye together: Then take your Orenges, and with a Knife scrape of all the filthinesse of the outside of them. Then take them in the middest, and wring out the juyce of three or foure of them, put the juyce into your broth with the rest of your stuffe. Then slice your Orenges thinne, and have uppon the fire readie a skillet of faire seething water, and put your sliced Orenges into the water and when that water is bitter, have more readie, and so change them still as long as you can find the great bitternesse in the water, which will be five or seven times, or more. If you find need: then take them from the water, and let that runne cleane from them: then put close orenges into your potte with your broth, and so let them stew together till your Capon be readie. Then make your sops with this broth, and cast on a little Sinamon, Ginger and Sugar, and upon this lay Capon, and some of your Orenges upon it, and some of your Marie, and towarde the end of the boyling of your broth, put in a little Vergious, if you think best.'

From *The Good Huswives Handmaid for Cookerie in her Kitchin*, 1597

4–5 lb (1.8–2.25 kg) chicken, cut into 12 pieces
salt and freshly milled pepper
flour
1 oz (25 g) butter
1 tablespoon (15 ml) vegetable oil
5 fl oz (150 ml) chicken stock
3 fl oz (90 ml) dry white wine
9 fl oz (270 ml) orange juice
2½ teaspoons (12.5 ml) dried orange peel
large pinch of ground mace
pinch of ground rosemary
pinch of ground cinnamon
pinch of ground ginger
1 teaspoon (5 ml) sugar
8 oz (225 g) prunes, stoned
2 oz (50 g) currants
6 slices wholemeal toast
orange slices to garnish

Dust the chicken pieces with seasoned flour. Heat the butter and oil in a heavy casserole and brown the chicken pieces all over, a few at a time, adding more fat if necessary. Remove them from the pan with a slotted spoon and set aside. Add all the other ingredients except the orange slices to the casserole and mix together well. Replace the browned chicken pieces in the casserole, cover with a lid and place in a moderate oven (180°C, 350°F, gas mark 4) for 1–1½ hours, or until the chicken is tender. Adjust the seasoning as necessary and arrange the pieces of chicken on buttered toast. Spoon the orange sauce over and decorate with orange slices. Serves 6.

To Make Stewed Steakes

'Take a peece of Mutton, and cutte it in pieces, and wash it very cleane, and put it in a faire pot with ale, or with halfe Wine, then make it boyle, and skumme it cleyne, and put into your pot a faggot of Rosemary and Time, then some parsely picked fine, and some onyons cut round, and lit them all boyle together, and season it with sinamon and Ginger, Nutmeggs, two or three Cloves and salt, and so serve it on soppes and garnish it with fruite.'

From *The Good Huswife's Jewell*, Thomas Dawson, 1596

Oranges, a woodcut illustration from Gerard's *Herball*.

Lamb Casseroled in Ale with Prunes and Raisins

4 lamb leg steaks, approx. 1½ lb (675 g)
1 oz (25 g) butter
1 tablespoon (15 ml) vegetable oil
1 large onion, finely sliced
1 pint (600 ml) real ale
½ tablespoon fresh rosemary, chopped
    or ½ teaspoon dried rosemary
½ tablespoon fresh thyme, chopped
    or ½ teaspoon dried thyme
2 tablespoons (30 ml) fresh parsley, chopped
¼ teaspoon ground allspice
2 or 3 whole cloves
2 oz (50 g) raisins
freshly milled black pepper and salt
1 oz (25 g) fresh white breadcrumbs
8 oz (225 g) prunes, stoned
4 slices wholemeal toast
orange slices, to garnish

Heat the butter and oil in a heavy casserole dish and brown the lamb steaks quickly on both sides. Remove with a slotted spoon and set on one side. Reduce the heat and cook the onions in the remaining fat until soft. Replace the meat in the casserole and cover with ale. Add the herbs, spices and raisins, then season with salt and pepper. Cover tightly with a lid and place in a moderate oven (180°C, 350°F, gas mark 4) for 30 minutes. Add the breadcrumbs and prunes and return to the oven for a further 30 minutes, or until the lamb is tender. Check the seasoning and adjust as necessary, then serve each lamb steak on a slice of toast. Pour over the gravy and garnish with slices of orange, before serving. Serves 4.

To make Jombils a hundred

'Take twenty Egges and put them into a pot both the yolkes and the white, beat them wel, then take a pound of beaten suger and put to them, and stirre them wel together, then put to it a quarter of a peck of flower, and make a hard paste thereof, and then with Anniseeds moulde it well, ane make it in little rowles beeing long, and tye them in knots, and wet the ends in Rosewater; then put them into a pan of seething water, but even in one waum, then take them out with a Skimmer and lay them in a cloth to drie, this being don lay them in a tart panne, the bottome beeing oyled, then put them into a temperat Oven for one howre, turning them often in the Oven.'

From *The Good Huswifes Jewell*, Thomas Dawson, 1596

To Make Muscadines, commonly called Kissing Comfits

'Then slicke a sheet of white paper, slicked with a slick-stone very smooth, and rowle your sugar paste upon it, then cut it like lozenges with rowel, so dry them upon a stone, and when they bee dry they will serve to garnish a marchpaine, or other dishes, tarts, custards, or whatsoever else, if you will have any red you must mingle Rosa Paris, if blew bottles growing in the corn [cornflowers].'

From *A Delightfull Daily Exercise for Ladies and Gentlewomen*, John Murrell, 1621

Sugar plate, a kind of uncooked fondant, was moulded into all manner of objects – walnuts, eggs, playing cards, Swiss-roll type cakes and ribbons – for banquets. It could be coloured with flower juices and spices.

Jumbles or Knotted Biscuits

1½ oz (40 g) salted butter
1 tablespoon (15 ml) rose-water
4 oz (125 g) caster sugar
1 tablespoon (15 ml) aniseed or caraway seed
2 eggs, beaten
8 oz (225 g) plain flour

Beat the butter with the rose-water, add the sugar and cream together. Mix in the spices, the beaten egg and the flour to form a soft dough. Knead the dough on a lightly floured board and form into rolls, approximately ¼ in (5 mm) in diameter by 4 in (10 cm) in length. Tie each of these into simple knots, rings or plaited strips and arrange on lightly greased baking sheets. Bake in a moderate oven (180°C, 350°F, gas mark 4) for 15–20 minutes, or until golden brown. Cool on a wire rack, then store in an airtight tin until needed. Makes about 15.

Kissing Comfits

1 heaped teaspoon (8 ml) gum tragaconth
2 tablespoons (30 ml) rose-water
1 lb (450 g) icing sugar, sieved
extra rose-water
food colouring

Place the gum in a small basin, cover with rose-water and leave to steep overnight until it has dissolved to form paste.

The next day, add this paste to the sieved icing sugar, working it in with a wooden spoon, and gradually add more rose-water until you have a smooth, pliable modelling dough. Divide the dough into portions and colour with red, blue and yellow food colouring, leaving one portion uncoloured. Roll out the sugar-paste on a board dusted with icing sugar and cut into small diamonds, using a pastry jigger or wheel. Allow to dry, then use as sweets, or to decorate marchpanes (p.122), tarts (p.121) and custards (p.60). Makes 1 lb (450 g) sweets.

To Candy any Roots, Fruits or Flowers

'Dissolve sugar, or sugar-candy in Rose-water. Boile it to an height. Put in your roots, fruits or flowers, the sirrop being cold. Then rest a little, after take them out, and boyl the sirrop again. Then put in more roots, etc. Then boyl the sirrop the third time to an hardnesse, putting in more Sugar, but not Rose-water. Put in the roots, etc. the sirrop being cold, and let them stand till they candy.'

From *The English Hus-wife*, Gervase Markham, 1615

In contrast to the wet suckets, dry suckets or sucket candies were made by draining the fruit, roots, or flowers from their syrup and drying them.

Crystallised Fruit

1 lb (450 g) suitable fruit, prepared
4 oz (125 g) powdered glucose
2½ oz (60 g) granulated sugar for initial boiling
about 14 oz (400 g) granulated sugar for later boilings

Only perfect, firm, ripe fruit should be used and you get the best results by candying each type of fruit separately to keep the individual flavour. Some of the most successful are apricots, cherries, peaches, oranges, grapes and pineapple. Prepare them according to type: small, whole plums and apricots should be pricked all over with a stainless steel fork; cherries and grapes must be stoned; peaches and pears should be peeled and quartered; oranges and pineapple should be peeled and cut into suitable pieces. Chunks of parsnip and baby carrots are also successful.

Place the prepared fruit in a large saucepan and cover with boiling water. Simmer over a gentle heat until the fruit is just tender, but not broken up. This will vary with the type of fruit used. Remove the fruit carefully from the cooking liquor with a slotted spoon and place in a heatproof dish. Reserve the cooking liquor and measure out ½ pt (300 ml) of this

into a saucepan with the glucose and 2½ oz (60 g) sugar. Heat very gently, stirring all the time, until the sugar has dissolved. Then bring to the boil and pour the hot syrup over the fruit making sure that it is completely immersed. Cover and leave for 24 hours.

Place a sieve over a saucepan and carefully drain the syrup from the fruit into the saucepan. Return the fruit to the ovenproof dish. Add another 2 oz (50 g) sugar to the syrup, stir over a gentle heat until this has dissolved, then bring to the boil. Pour over the fruit, cover and leave for a further 24 hours. Repeat the process three more times adding another 2 oz (50 g) sugar each time.

Carefully drain the syrup from the fruit into a saucepan as before. Add 3 oz (75 g) sugar to the syrup, place saucepan over a gentle heat and stir until the sugar has dissolved, then add the fruit and simmer for 3 minutes. Return the fruit and syrup to the heatproof dish. Cover and leave for 48 hours. Repeat the process. The syrup should now be as thick as clear honey. If the syrup is too thin at this stage, add another 3 oz (75 g) sugar to the syrup, dissolve the sugar over a gentle heat, then add the fruit and simmer for 3 minutes. Leave the fruit to soak in the thick syrup for 4 days. Remove the fruit carefully from the syrup with a draining spoon and lay it on a wire rack, placed over a baking tray to catch the drips.

To dry off the fruit, place the tray in a warm place, turning the fruit occasionally during the drying process. The fruit is candied when the surface is no longer sticky. To finish it off, sprinkle some granulated sugar on grease-proof or waxed paper. Lift up each piece of candied fruit on a fine skewer and quickly dip it into boiling water. Allow to drain for a couple of seconds, then roll each piece in sugar until it is evenly, but not thickly coated. Leave to dry on a wire rack.

Serve piled in bowl-shaped champagne glasses, or sundae dishes, as a dessert with fresh cream, yoghurt or ice-cream.

Shred Pyes

'Take 4 pound of a legg of veal parboyled, 4 pound of Beefe suet, 6 pared Aples. Shred altogether, put it through a sieve, season it with 4 pound of Currans, an ounce of beaten Mace, halfe a pound of sugar, six dates, Lemon Pills candyed, a Gill of Rose Watter, as much sack; make them up; a quarter of an hour will bake them.'

From a commonplace book of recipes dated 1699, belonging to Elizabeth Birkett of Townend, Cumbria.

The recipe for these *shred* or *minced* pies harks back to Elizabethan times when they had already become part of traditional Christmas fare. Most mincemeat recipes until the 20th century included a little chopped meat, sometimes raw, sometimes cooked.

Mince Pies

8 oz (225 g) cooked lean veal or beef
8 oz (225 g) cooking apples
8 oz (225 g) large raisins, stoned
2 oz (50 g) dates, stoned
8 oz (225 g) shredded beef suet
8 oz (225 g) currants
1 oz (25 g) candied lemon peel, finely chopped
2 level teaspoons (10 ml) ground mace
2 well rounded teaspoons (15 ml) sugar
3 tablespoons (45 ml) rose-water
3 tablespoons (45 ml) sherry

Mince the meat, cooking apples, raisins and dates into a bowl. Add the suet, currants, peel, spice and sugar and mix together well. Moisten with the rose-water and sherry. Put a spoonful of mincemeat in patty tins lined with shortcrust or puff pastry. Brush the edges of the pastry with beaten egg white and add pastry lids, pinching the two edges together. Make a small slit in the centre of each pie and glaze the top with egg white. Sprinkle with sugar and bake in a hot oven (220°C, 425°F, gas mark 7) for 15–20 minutes. Serve warm. Makes 2½–3 lb (1–1.4 kg).

A Tarte of Borage Flowers

'Take borage floures and perboyle them tender, then strayne them wyth the yolkes of three or foure egges, and swete curdes, or els take three or foure apples and perboyle wythal and strayne them with swete butter and a lyttle mace and so bake it.'

To Make a Tarte of Marigoldes, Prymroses or Couslips

'Take the same stuffe to every of them that you do to the tarte of borage and the same ceasonynge.'

To Make Short Paest For Tarte

'Take fyne floure and a cursey [cup] of fayre water and a dyshe of swete butter and a lyttel saffron, and the yolkes of two egges and make it thynne and as tender as ye maye.'

From *A Proper Newe Booke of Cokerye*. This book, compiled by an unknown hand, probably before 1572, once belonged to the Tudor prelate, Archbishop Parker.

Tarts of flowers were prepared during spring and summer. Cowslips, primroses, borage flowers or marigold petals were beaten small and combined with eggs and cream or curds, then baked in a pastry case. They were served at the second course of the banquet.

Marigolds, a woodcut from Gerard's *Herball*.

Marigold Tart

FOR THE PASTRY

½ teaspoon saffron strands
1 tablespoon (15 ml) warm water
8 oz (225 g) plain flour
2 tablespoons (30 ml) icing sugar
5 oz (150 g) unsalted butter
2 egg yolks

FOR THE FILLING

3 tablespoons (45 ml) dried marigold petals
  (remove from the heads)
water
2 oz (50 g) caster sugar
8 oz (225 g) cream cheese or fromage frais
2 eggs, separated
3 tablespoons (45 ml) single cream
finely grated rind of 1 orange
1 oz (25 g) plain flour
crystallised borage flowers to decorate

Make the pastry first. Crumble the saffron in warm water in a basin and leave until cold.

Sieve the flour and icing sugar together into a bowl, then cut and rub in the butter until it forms fine crumbs. Beat the egg yolks with the saffron water and add to the rubbed-in mixture until it forms a firm dough. Knead lightly until smooth, then wrap in foil or plastic and chill in the fridge for at least 30 minutes. Then roll out the pastry and line a greased 9–10 in (23–25.5 cm) flan tin with a removable base. Prick the base lightly with a fork.

To make the filling, bring a small saucepan of water to simmering point and sprinkle in the marigold petals. Wet thoroughly, then drain and reserve. Beat the sugar with the cream cheese or fromage frais until soft and smooth, then beat in the egg yolks, one at a time, followed by the cream. Stir in the grated orange rind, the marigold petals and the flour. Whisk the egg whites until thick, then fold them into the cream cheese and egg yolk mixture. Pour into the pastry case and cook in the centre of a fairly hot oven (200°C, 400°F, gas mark 6) for 35–40 minutes, or until firm to the touch in the centre. If the top is getting too brown, lay some foil gently over it.

Leave the tart to cool a little in the tin, then loosen the sides with a knife, and transfer to a serving plate. Decorate with crystallised borage flowers and serve lukewarm. Serves 8.

To Make a Dyschefull of Snowe

'Take a pottell [half a gallon] of swete thycke creame and the whytes of eyghte egges, and beate them altogether wyth a spone. Then putte them in youre creame and a saucerful of Rosewater, and a dyshe full of Suger wyth all. Then take a stycke and make it cleane, and then cutte it in the ende foure square, and therwith beate all the aforesayde thynges together, and ever as it ryseth take it of and put it into a Collaunder. This done, take one apple and set it in the myddes of it, and a thicke bushe of Rosemary, and set it in the myddes of the platter. Then cast your Snowe upon the Rosemary and fyll your platter therwith. And yf you have wafers caste some in wyth all and thus serve them forthe.'

From *A Proper Newe Booke of Cokerye*, c.1572

The greatest innovation in Elizabethan cookery was the discovery of eggs as a raising agent. Whites of eggs produced 'Snowe', a centrepiece for the banquet.

Apple Snow

1½ lb (675 g) cooking apples, peeled, cored and
  sliced
1 tablespoon (15 ml) rose-water
caster sugar, to taste
3 egg whites
3 oz (75 g) caster sugar
¼ pint (150 ml) whipping cream
sprigs of fresh rosemary to decorate
gold dragees to decorate

Cook the sliced apples with the rose-water until soft, then rub them through a fine sieve to make a smooth purée. Taste and sweeten with a little sugar if necessary. Leave to get cold, then measure out about ½ pt (300 ml).

In a large clean bowl, beat the egg whites until they stand in soft peaks. Gradually beat in the caster sugar and continue to beat to a stiff, glossy meringue. Gently fold in the measured apple purée, then spoon into individual glasses or sundae dishes. Top with swirls of whipped cream and decorate with rosemary and gold dragees. Serves 4–6.

How to make Marchpane Cake

'Take blancht Almonds and sugar and beat them up into a Past, and when have beaten it into a Past, rowl it out about the thickness that you will have your Marchpane Cakes to be and cut them in 3 square pieces and set an Edge to them of the same past, and Impress the Edges of them, then take Rose Watter and beat searced sugar in it till it be as thick as Pancakes, butter and wet them within it and strew a few of Bisketts in them and set them upon Wafers, and set them againe upon Papers and bake them, and keep them for your use.'

From a commonplace book dated 1699, belonging to Elizabeth Birkett of Townend, Cumbria.

To gild a Marchpane or any other kind of Tart

'Take and cut your leafe of golde, as it lieth upon the booke, into square peeces like Dice and with a Conies tailes end moysted a little, take golde up by the one corner, lay it on the place beeing first made moyste, and with another tayle of a Conie drie presse the golde downe close. And if ye will have the forme of an Harte, or the name of Iesus, or any other thing whatsoever: cut the same through a peece of paper and lay the paper upon your Marchpane or Tart; then make the voide place of the Paper (through which the Marchpane appeareth) moyste with Rose Water, laye on your golde, presse it down, take off your Paper and there remaineth behinde in golde the print cut in the saide paper.'

From *The Treasurie of Commodious Conceits and Hidden Secrets*, John Partridge, 1584.

The marchpane was the centrepiece of any banquet. It was a large flat disc of marzipan, sometimes with a raised rim round the edge, weighing perhaps 3–4 lb (1.5–1.8 kg) or more, which was iced, sumptuously decorated and surmounted for special occasions with three-dimensional figures or models in cast sugar (hot sugar syrup moulded in stone, wooden or pewter shapes); sugar plate (similar to modern fondant icing) or almond paste. Finally, the marchpane was often gilded with gold leaf, readily available but exceedingly expensive in Elizabethan times.

Gilded Marchpane

FOR THE MARCHPANE

8 oz (225 g) caster sugar
1 lb (450 g) ground almonds
2 tablespoons (30 ml) rose-water

FOR THE GLAZE

1 tablespoon (15 ml) rose-water
3 tablespoons (45 ml) icing sugar

Work the sugar, ground almonds and rose-water together to make a stiff paste. Knead until quite smooth. Reserve a little of the marzipan for decorating the marchpane and place the rest on a sheet of greaseproof paper. Roll it into a circle, about $\frac{3}{8}$-in (7.5-mm) thick, then turn up the edge and decorate it with a fork or the back of a knife. Slip the marzipan on to a baking sheet and bake in a cool oven (150°C, 300°F, gas mark 3) for 15 minutes, then open the oven door for a further 15 minutes. Repeat this process until the marchpane is firm and dry but only lightly coloured. Meanwhile, mix the rose-water and icing sugar to a thin paste for the glaze. Brush over the marchpane and continue cooking for 5–10 minutes until dry and glossy. Remove from the oven and leave to cool.

Roll out the reserved marzipan until quite thin and cut out into hearts, diamonds, letters, animals or birds. Paint with edible gold colouring and fix on to the glazed marchpane as it dries to form patterns or pictures. Alternatively, the reserved marzipan can be modelled into figures of animals or birds, or into knots which can be gilded as before. Sugar-coated caraway, fennel or coriander seeds, or confectioners' silver balls can also be used for decoration. Serve as a sweetmeat with coffee at the end of a meal.

A marchpane cake decorated with gold hearts, and wafers.

III

Medieval principles of good lordship and feasting were giving way to a new order which resulted in smaller and more intimate meals. Yet, at all times a nobleman was expected to offer hospitality at his table to any passer-by who could claim the dignity of a gentleman. We learn from an anonymous writer that Henry Percy, 9th Earl of Northumberland, was no exception in this respect and, in fact, kept one of the best tables in the kingdom at Petworth in Sussex: 'Wherein I mean not only the diet of flesh and fish which answer to the stuff of our clothes; but I consider also the bread, wine, salads, oil, vinegar, fruit, sweetmeats, linen, plate and lights, which at the table account as the petty toys of our attire.'

The tradition of the medieval feast lived on for special occasions. Christmas was still the most important of a series of winter feasts when open house was kept as part of the regular hospitality from 1 November to Candlemas on 2 February. A manor house expecting friends, relations, guests, servants, villagers and 'strangers' might easily expect to feed from 50 to 100 people in its hall twice daily for the twelve days of Christmas and for Shrovetide and Easter. William Harrison notes that these feasts were elaborate and abundant, and appetites often prodigious, although the host and his guests ate more moderately. The people who were tempted to over-indulge were poorer neighbours, unused to plenty, who usually had very little left in their own larders by mid-winter.

If breakfast was taken, it was usually served between 6 and 7am. Although eaten regularly in town, it does not seem to have been taken in every house and was probably a matter of personal choice rather than custom. There was a tendency to decrease and regulate the number of meals served throughout the day: 'Whereas of old we had breakfast in the forenoon, beverages or nunchions after dinner, and thereto rear-suppers generally when it was time to go to rest, now these odd repasts, thanked be to God, are very well left and each one in maner (except here and there some young hungry stomach that cannot fast untill dinner-time) contenteth himself with dinner and supper only' wrote William Harrison.

Breakfast was often taken privately, before issuing forth from one's chamber. It could be quite a substantial meal of ale, beer or wine, boiled beef and mutton, with salted or pickled herrings or sprats on fish days, and bread, although Thomas Cogan advises students at Oxford to eat only eggs, milk and butter in the morning in *The Haven of Health* of 1584. Queen Elizabeth, it transpires, was an enthusiastic breakfaster. Her household accounts show that chicken, rabbit, mutton, veal and beef, with ale and wine, were served at Court in the early morning, usually at 8am. When she was entertained at Cowdray Park in Sussex by Viscount Montague in 1591, breakfast for the household consisted of '3 oxen and 140 geese'. The Queen also enjoyed the elaborate outdoor breakfasts which preceded the hunt on her frequent visits to the estates of her loyal subjects. To prepare such a breakfast, the butler would set off into the deer park with a train of waggons, carts and pack-mules carrying all the necessary food and drink, to a carefully chosen place with adequate shade, wild flowers, a nearby spring and sweet-singing birds to make melody. The butler's first task was to place the bottles and barrels of wines and beer in the spring to cool:

That done, he spreads his cloth, upon the grassy bank,
And sets to shewe his dainty drinks, to win his Prince's thanks.
Then comes the Captain Cook, with many a warlike wight,
Which armour bring and weapons both, with hunger for to fight . . .
For whiles cold loins of veal, cold Capon, Beef, and Goose,
With pigeon pies, and mutton cold, are set on hunger loose . . .
First neat's tongues powdered well [pickled ox tongues], then
   gambons of the hog [gammon],
Then sausages and savoury knacks, to set men's minds on gog
Then King or comely Queen, then Lord and Lady look,
To see which side will bear the bell, the Butler or the Cook.
At last the Cook takes flight, but Butlers stils abide,
And sound their drums and make retreat, with bottles by their side.

George Turbevile's The Noble Art of Venerie, 1575

Elizabeth I at a hunting picnic breakfast: a woodcut from George Turbevile's *The Noble Art of Venerie*, published in 1575.

After this huge breakfast, the hunt commenced.

Those of our ancestors who fasted in the early hours certainly made up for it at dinner. This was the main meal of the day for all classes; the gentry usually dined at 11am, while merchants and farmers dined at noon. It was customary to spend two or three hours over this important meal: 'the nobility, gentlemen and merchant men' according to Harrison, 'commonly sitting at the board 'til 2 or 3 of the clock at afternoon, so that with many, it is a hard matter to rise from the table to go to evening prayers.'

Queen Elizabeth dined in her private chamber when she was not dining in state with her courtiers in the 'Presence Chamber' or some suitably impressive apartment. Paul Hentzner, visiting England in 1598, reported that at Greenwich Palace: 'The Queen dines and sups alone, with very few Attendants, and it is very seldom that any Body, Foreigner or Native, is admitted at that Time, and then only at the Intercession of somebody in Power.' The Elizabethan gentleman likewise preferred to dine in privacy with family and special guests in his great chamber, or his new 'dyning parlour'.

The owners of great Elizabethan houses had long ceased to dine in the great hall, except for occasional feasts and celebrations. In some households their place at the high table was taken by the upper servants, as at Knole, presided over by the steward. But at Hardwick and Montacute there was no high table and only the lower ranks of servants and retainers would normally have dined, and probably slept, here. The servants at Montacute ate in the hall until the end of the 17th century when a servants' hall was built. At Hardwick there would probably have been 40 or 50 people regularly eating in the great hall, as the outdoor servants also dined here, as did visiting servants and Bess's little gang of resident craftsmen, busy finishing off the decoration of the house. On feast days and special occasions, the hall would almost certainly have been more crowded, although Bess herself probably never ate here.

The comparatively modest size of the great hall at Hardwick, placed by the architect, Robert Smythson, in the middle of the house, shows its declining role. Yet the hall had to retain its symbolic importance as the grand entrance. At Hardwick, the great hall is dominated by a declaration of ownership in the form of an enormous plasterwork overmantel: two life-size stags wearing collars of eglantine support Bess's coat of arms and coronet. The impressive stone screen supports a gallery connecting Bess's with-

Right: On rare occasions the Norris family of Speke Hall may have dined in state under 'the Great Wainscot' in the great hall.

Below: The round table installed by William Moreton in the bay window of the great hall at Little Moreton Hall, Cheshire, in 1559. This represented a move from dining at the high table to a more private form of eating; the next development was to leave the great hall altogether and take meals in the parlour or the great chamber.

drawing chamber and bedchamber with the 'Low Great Chamber', where she usually dined when she was not entertaining important guests. From the gallery, Bess could survey the diners below in the hall as she crossed over – a deterrent to misbehaviour. A band of musicians would have played here on special feast days to entertain those dining in both the hall and the Low Great Chamber. At the time of the 1601 inventory, the hall was furnished with three long tables and six benches; one Elizabethan oak table and two benches are still there, but the massive oak central table is mid-17th century.

Older halls were embellished to announce the owner's wealth and importance. William Moreton II's alterations to Little Moreton Hall in Cheshire in 1559 included adding a great bay window, the expensive panes of glass proclaiming his ability and readiness to pay for such luxuries. The long refectory table, one of the most elaborate of its kind to survive, helped to keep up the appearance of state to guests passing through to the family apartments. Speke Hall, near Liverpool, was altered by the Norris family during the 16th century when they were at the height of their wealth and influence. It is most unlikely that the family ever lived and ate communally with their servants in the great hall, although on rare occasions they may have dined in state under 'The Great Wainscot'. More likely, this carved oak panelling erected in 1564, and the plaster decoration of the chimney-breast, including a series of heads, traditionally said to represent Sir William Norris and his family, was to impress their guests.

Left: The magnificent High Great Chamber at Hardwick, used by Bess to receive her most distinguished guests and for dining in state.

The grand processional route from the hall at Hardwick Hall, Derbyshire, up to the High Great Chamber.

As well as providing a grand entrance to the house, the hall was the beginning of the great processional route or 'stately ascent' to the apartments above. Distinguished guests would be led up with great solemnity by an entourage of attendants, in strict ascending order of seniority, to be received by the lord or lady of the house. The food for the banquet in the great chamber would also be brought up by the same route from the servery or buttery with appropriate ceremony. Narrow winding stone stairs were giving way to stately flights of broad stone or elaborate wooden stairs. The principal staircase which Sir Edward Phelips, one of the richest and most powerful lawyers of his time in England, and his guests would have taken to the great chamber on the first floor at Montacute, is built of huge slabs of stone, 7 feet wide, winding in short flights round a central pier of solid masonry, decorated at intervals with shell-headed niches.

The upper floor to which these magnificent staircases led began to assume a greater importance, acting as an expression of an owner's wealth and status. These 'rooms of state' gave wider views over the surrounding countryside and gardens, far removed from the smells of the kitchen and everyday bustle of the ground floor, the domain of the lower orders. The most important and the most sumptuously decorated was the great chamber or 'presence chamber', which in all large Elizabethan houses had taken the place of the great hall as the ceremonial pivot of the house. As Viscount Montague's household regulations of 1595 put it: 'In that place there must be no delay, because it is the place of state, which the lord keepeth his presence, and the eyes of all the best sort of strangers be there lookers on ...'. And those eyes were looking about, judging, criticising and taking note of what was new with a view to acquiring furnishings as good, or even better if they could afford them, for their own great chambers.

The scale and splendour of the state apartments on the second floor at Hardwick suggest that they were specifically built in the hope of royal visits. Originally, Bess hoped she would receive the Queen at Hardwick, a wish never to be fulfilled as Elizabeth I travelled no further north than Kenilworth in her entire life. Later, and equally unfulfilled, Bess harboured the ambition that her granddaughter, Arabella Stuart, might succeed to the throne. The 'High Great Chamber' used by Bess to receive her most distinguished guests was the most magnificent. As a tribute to Elizabeth I, Bess adopted the theme of the virgin goddess, Diana the huntress, hunting in a forest with birds and beasts for the great painted plasterwork frieze. Despite the tapestries, richly embroidered curtains, rush matting on the floor and the two huge fireplaces, dining in the High Great Chamber must have been a chilly occasion. The 6th Duke of Devonshire, who inherited Hardwick in 1811, used the room for one winter to dine in with his friends, an experience he described as 'more dignified than entertaining and in spite of all the precautions, exceedingly cold'.

Sir Edward Phelips's great chamber at Montacute, now the library, although on a much smaller scale than Hardwick, was elaborately decorated with its walls hung with '8 peice of arras' topped by an ornate plasterwork frieze, and its spectacular chimney-piece of Portland stone. The windows, set with brightly coloured heraldic stained glass tracing the genealogy of the family and paying tribute to a variety of courtiers and statesmen, as well as friends and neighbours of Sir Edward, must have delighted his guests. Undoubtedly the finest interior at Canons Ashby was also the great chamber, now the drawing-room. The huge chimney-piece and overmantel were built by Sir Erasmus Dryden in the 1580s but the present coved plaster ceiling, perhaps the most elaborate and fantastic of its kind, was added by his son, Sir John, in 1632.

However, not all the gentry houses boasted an upper great chamber. When the Norris family were entertaining formally at Speke Hall, they used the great parlour on the ground floor which had been built in the early 16th century but was added to in late Elizabethan and early Jacobean times to make it more splendid. The ceiling of elaborate stucco depicts, very suitably, pomegranates, roses, lilies, grapes and hazelnuts.

The growing desire for greater privacy and comfort led to the establishment of the 'dyning parlour' on the ground floor of Elizabethan houses. The Norris family used their 'little parlour', as opposed to their 'great parlour', for informal eating, as its contents in 1624 make clear: apart from the three tables, plate cupboard (court cupboard) and stools, either upholstered in blue or covered with blue cloth, there was a toasting fork and 'a tosting iron for cakes', probably used by the family for cosy snacks and suppers. The informal contents of this small intimate room contrast well with the sumptuous furnishings of the great parlour with its extending long table, cupboards covered with green cloths, and stools and chairs upholstered in green silk with fringes. At Canons Ashby the small 'winter parlour' near the kitchen was used by the Dryden family for informal eating. The room has a carved stone chimney surround dating from the 1550s, but the most fascinating features are the painted panels of the 1590s with brightly coloured crests and other devices commemorating the Drydens' ancestry and connections, a similar idea to the windows in the great chamber at Montacute.

Hardwick had the unusual distinction of a second great chamber, as befitted the most wealthy woman in England after the Queen herself. It is referred to in the 1601 inventory as the 'low great chamber', situated on the first floor, and is probably the

Above left: Sir Edward Phelips (1560?–1614), the successful lawyer who built Montacute House, Somerset, c.1600. This portrait shows him in his great chamber with some of the armorial stained glass tracing his family descent and the arms of his friends.

Above right: The great chamber at Canons Ashby, Northamptonshire, from a watercolour by Edward Blore, c.1820, showing the elaborate Tudor chimney-piece and overmantel.

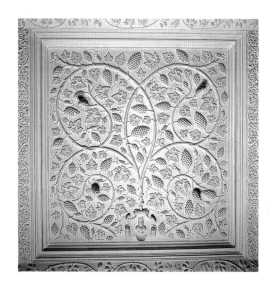

Above: The plaster ceiling of the great chamber at Speke Hall, Merseyside, with its decoration of grapes.

Above right: A narrow back stair leads up from the kitchen to the winter parlour at Canons Ashby, where the family could dine in comfort and privacy. A buffet alcove stands next to the door.

equivalent of the dining parlour in other houses. It was used by Bess for eating on less formal occasions, probably in the summer. The Little Dining Chamber off the Low Great Chamber, now called the 'paved room' because of its stone floor, may have been used as a more intimate 'winter parlour' for the Countess and her family, although its very simple furnishings of 1601, with only one chair and fifteen stools, a long table covered with a Turkey carpet, and 'waynscott rownde about' suggest that it was more likely used as a dining-room for the upper servants. If Bess wanted to eat totally in private, she would use her own withdrawing chamber. In the 1601 inventory, an 'inlayde borde' is listed as being in this room, which may be the table top inlaid with Bess's initials and family arms, now on the landing outside the High Great Chamber. It was probably set up on trestles when she wanted to eat.

In the mid-16th century two new types of dining-tables made their appearance – the drawing table and the square table. The former was supported on a joined frame with elaborate carving, and could be extended by means of extra leaves to nearly double its size. This table was first introduced from the Low Countries, its earliest mention being in an inventory of the goods of the Duke of Somerset in 1552: 'a fayer drawing table of wallnuttree uppon 4 carved pillars with 3 stooles of the same stuffe'. In inventories, drawing tables are usually listed in the hall, the great chamber and particularly in the dining parlour, where space was limited and an extending table would have been a great boon. Square tables, also with joined frames, appear to have been subsidiary to the main dining-table for eating and also for serving food. They appear in 17th-century inventories, such as those for Montacute and Hardwick. All types of table were covered with Turkey or 'table carpets' of velvet, or heavy woollen cloth edged with fringing. Carpets at this time were rarely used as floor-coverings; their normal use was as coverings for tables, cupboards, chests and beds. Thirty-two 'Turkey carpets' were mentioned in the 1601 inventory for Hardwick; most were used to cover furniture, although six were spread on the floors, including one in the High Great Chamber and one in the Low Great Chamber, for Bess's feet as she sat in her chair of state.

The 'court cupboard', or 'side cupboard', developed from the medieval 'cup-board', first appeared with the introduction of the dining parlour. It was still the place where the family plate was displayed and the wine and wine-cups set in readiness on two or three open tiered shelves. Sometimes the middle shelf was enclosed with carved panels of woodwork with one or two doors, to provide storage space for valuable objects. Inventories mention two court cupboards in dining chambers, like that for Montacute, which suggests that one was used for drinking vessels and the basin and ewer for washing, while the other was for the family plate. The drawing table, the square table and the two court cupboards were often made *en suite*.

During Elizabethan times a few more chairs made their appearance in the great chamber, but they were still outnumbered by the 'joint-stools' (wooden stools about 2 foot high, ornamented with carving), on which all but the most distinguished guests sat at table. Precedence was as important as ever when it came to the seating in the great chamber. The person of highest estate, whether host or guest, sat in the grandest chair, often under a canopy or 'cloth of estate'; at Hardwick, one of the canopies listed in the wardrobe in 1601 would have been erected over a dais in the centre of the north wall of the High Great Chamber opposite the door leading from the staircase. Bess would have sat under it on 'a Chare of nedlework with golde and silk frenge' with her feet resting on 'a footestoole of watchet [pale blue] velvet with blewe silk frenge'. For the rest of the company there were 6 forms and 16 stools, elaborately upholstered and cushioned. The only other furniture in the room was a looking glass, a rarity at this period.

In the Low Great Chamber at Hardwick there were five chairs, the grandest being the 'Chare of Cloth of golde and silver with a frett of grene velvet and with grene silk frenge' for Bess. Other seating was provided by richly embroidered and upholstered stools, forms and cushions. When not in use these chairs and stools would be placed around the walls, but the main dining-table remained in the centre of the room. During a meal, diners sat on all four sides of the table with the lord or lady of the house, or the person of highest rank, sitting in the middle of one long side.

Rushes were still strewn on floors in early Elizabethan times, but by the end of the 16th century woven rush matting had become the norm in fine houses like Hardwick and Montacute. Dining chambers and halls were lit by candles set in metal or wooden chandeliers hanging from the ceiling, in wall sconces, in lanterns, or in candlesticks placed on the tables. Four wall sconces and 'too great Copper Candlesticks [chandeliers] with several places to set lightes in' were listed in the great hall at Hardwick in 1601. Scented pastilles, made in the still-room, were burned in perfuming pans.

The first stage in preparing the table for a meal was to cover it with a single cloth over the top of the table-carpet. Bess of Hardwick had many damask and diaper table-cloths, two or three yards wide and six, seven and eight yards long for the long tables, and two-yards square for the square tables. There were also 'six dozen and tenn diaper napkins, six dozen and eleven damask napkins' and damask and diaper 'cubberd cloths' one and a half yards wide and two yards long.

This Turkey carpet at East Riddlesden, Yorkshire, is 17th-century, but shows the custom of the Tudor period when carpets of velvet or heavy woollen cloth edged with fringing were used as table covers.

The degree of ceremony involved in laying the cloth on the table in medieval times was retained. No household manual for Petworth has survived, but one has belonging to the Earl of Northumberland's Sussex neighbour, Anthony Browne, 2nd Viscount Montague of Cowdray. He drew up regulations for the guidance of his household in 1595. He and his family dined in a chamber adjoining the great Buck Hall. In his house, as in any nobleman's, the gentleman usher of the dining chamber assembled the yeomen of the ewery, the pantry, the buttery and the cellar at 10am to prepare the table for dinner. After the yeoman of the ewery had prepared the board with basin, ewer and fine damask towels, the gentleman usher conducted with due reverence: 'that is with two curtesies, one at the middest of the chamber, and an other at the table of my dyett: and that then kissing his hande he laye ytt on the middest of the table in the same place where the yeoman of the ewyre is to laye his cloth, the which he shall helpe to spreade. This service ended, and due curtesie doune, he shall return with him to the ewerye boorde.'

After the cloth had been laid, the first item to be placed on the top was the 'great salt', still the most important piece of plate in the household and the principal decoration on the table. By Elizabethan times this was usually cylindrical or bell-shaped. Three great salts are listed in the 1601 inventory for Hardwick: 'A great guilt salt with a Cover and pictures waying threescore too ounces, . . . a great guilt salt with a Cover and tills waying Fourscore six ounces . . . and a double bell salt with a Cover.' Other similar salts and pepper boxes were arranged at intervals along the table: Hardwick had 'a Salt of golde with a Cover waying fowre ounces, an other Salt of golde and Christall enameled with a Cover' with the Shrewsbury arms, and 'a pepper boxe guilt waying twelve ounces quarter'. After the condiments had been placed on the table, according to Lord Montague's instructions, the yeoman of the pantry approached it and, at each place, arranged a trencher, bread, a napkin, a silver-hafted knife and a spoon (forks were still not considered proper eating utensils for a gentleman), bowing as he placed each article upon the board. Napkins, of damask, diaper or holland, were usually about a yard square and during a meal were either slung over the diner's left shoulder or forearm or, if long enough 'to make both ends meet', were tied around the enormous Elizabethan ruff. The yeoman of the buttery, or butler, would have already prepared the bread by chipping it with a sharp knife to remove any cinders from the crust and squaring each piece neatly.

Wealthy Elizabethans took pride in using their finest tableware at meal-times, continuing to eat from vessels made in gold, silver-gilt or silver. These were available in such quantities in England that a visiting Italian diplomat commented: 'In one single street named the Strand, leading to St Paul's, there are fifty-two goldsmith's shops, so rich and so full of silver vessels great and small, that in all the shops in Milan, Rome, Venice and Florence put together, I do not think there would be found so many of the magnificence that are to be seen in London.'

Bess of Hardwick owned a large amount of plate: the gold items were few – two ceremonial cups, two magnificent salt cellars and a spoon with the Shrewsbury arms – but the silver, gilded, part-gilded and plain, was extensive, including candlesticks, standing cups, bowls, platters, trenchers, dishes, saucers, porringers, cups, sugar boxes, baskets for fruit salts, pepper boxes, posset pots, chafing dishes, toothpicks, jugs and ewers for wine. When not in use for the meal, gilt and silver tableware was set out on the court cupboard or the simple cupboard of earlier times, the shelves of which had been covered with white cloths by the yeoman of the buttery.

Sixteenth-century pewter tableware kept in the great hall at Little Moreton Hall (*left*). Pewter is a soft metal, and therefore susceptible to knife cuts (*above*).

Although this solid gold or silver tableware was obviously restricted to few households, even 'the inferior artificers and many farmers have learnt to furnish their cupboards with a fair garnish of pewter . . . and their tables with carpets and fine napery' according to William Harrison. Composed of tin with a small percentage of lead and copper, pewter cost only 6d or 7d a pound. So those who in earlier times would have used only wooden trenchers could now afford pewter tableware. 'In times past', continues Harrison, 'our pewterers employed the use of pewter only upon dishes, pots and a few other trifles for service here at home, whereas they can now in manner imitate, by infusion, any form or fashion of cup, dish, salt, bowl or goblet, which is made by goldsmith's craft.' When brightly polished, pewter closely resembles silver, but is much softer so that even a moderately hard cut with a knife will score its surface quite deeply. It therefore needed constant maintenance, any cut or scratch being either burnished over, or polished out with fine sand. To save the pewter from the worst cuts, a wooden trencher was often placed at the side of the diner's pewter platter on which he could cut his meat. Wooden trenchers, either square or round, were still used by poorer households in place of bread trenchers which had by now completely disappeared.

Although Henry VIII had six Delftware trenchers in 1542, the use of earthenware plates on the table was virtually unknown in early 16th-century England. The skills and knowledge necessary for the manufacture of pottery were introduced into England by two Dutchmen, Jasper Andries and Jacob Jansen, who sailed from Antwerp in 1567 to escape the attention of the Spanish Inquisition in the Low Countries. They set up a pottery in Norwich 'for the makeing of Galley [Delftware] pavinge tyles and Vessels for potycaries [apothecaries]' which operated up to the end of the 17th century. By 1571, a further pottery had been set up in Duke's Place, Aldgate, London. Dishes and chargers were produced but not used for dining until after the Elizabethan period.

Men still usually carried their knives in a sheath attached to the belt, but large households were now providing cased sets of matching knives for the use of their guests: the Earl of Northumberland purchased 'a case of Knyves and a Kerving Knyffe' for 13s 6d in 1598. These would still have been used for transferring pieces of meat and fish to the trencher and for cutting them up, as well as taking salt, while fingers were used for actually eating the food. The fork was still used only for eating sticky suckets, or sweetmeats, although it was certainly known as a fashionable novelty from 1582 onwards, as is evident from gifts of forks made to the Queen on various New Year's Days. Spoons were used to eat all the liquid and semi-liquid foods of the Elizabethan table, especially the pottages and dishes served on moist sops of bread. In fashionable houses, the fig-shaped spoons were made of silver, or silver-gilt, sometimes with knobs or figures of the apostles at the ends of their handles. Bess of Hardwick had 'thirtie and one guilt spoones waying thirty eight ounces, thirtie and six other spoones whereof eleven with knobs and nyne with thappostles waying fyftie one ounces and a half.'

Although silver and gold drinking vessels remained popular with the wealthy, they had to make way for wine-glasses of sparkling Venetian glass. As William Harrison noted 'It is a world to see in these our days how that the gentility do now generally choose rather the Venice glasses, both for our wine and beer. The poorest will also have glass if they may, but, sith the Venetian is somewhat too dear for them, they content themselves with such as are made at home of fern and burned stone.' The Venetians, jealous of their skills, had made death the penalty for any glassmaker found passing his craft on to any non-Venetian. So when the Venetian Jacomo Verzelini came from The

A Family saying Grace by Gortzius Geldorp. Each diner is provided with a pewter plate, knife and spoon, napkin and bread. The beer glass is a very early example.

Netherlands to establish a glasshouse in London in 1572, he literally took his life in his hands. He produced glasses and bowls of exquisite quality, decorated with intricate engraving. Further glasshouses, outside London, were soon making a wide range of goblets, bottles, distilling equipment and beer glasses. At the other end of the scale, the poor continued to drink from wooden, horn and leather vessels.

Once the table had been laid in a nobleman's dining chamber, the gentleman usher confirmed that the meal was ready in the kitchen before proceeding to inform his master and conduct him and his guests to the table. Washing hands before and after dining was an extremely important part of the proceedings. The yeoman of the ewery brought to the lord and his guests a ewer containing rose-water, a matching basin to catch the falling drops and a clean linen towel from the cupboard or ewery.

On the gentleman usher's command, the sewer next washed his hands at the ewery board, together with the carver. Lord Montague's rules stated: 'I will that my carver, when he cometh to the ewerye boarde, doe there washe together with the Sewer, and that done, be armed with an armeinge towell cast about his necke, and putt under his girdle on both sides, and one napkin on his lefte shoulder, and an other on the same arme.' After washing, the sewer went from the dining chamber, down through the hall, where the usher of the hall cried 'Gentlemen and yeomen wait upon the Sewer for my Lord!'. At least six men then joined the sewer at the dresser board in the servery outside the kitchen, where the cook had set out all the dishes in their correct order for the first course of the meal.

Most great houses, like Hardwick and Petworth, employed a number of serving men trained to carve and serve at table. They wore the livery of their master or mistress and

William Brooke, 10th Lord Cobham, with his family, painted by the Master of the Countess of Warwick in 1567. Lord Cobham is shown with his second wife, her sister and six of his children, eating a dessert of fruit and nuts from pewter plates.

attended him or her on visits to neighbours, or to London, if required. As the sewer's procession returned to the hall with the food, the usher then cried: 'By your leave my masters!', before solemnly leading the procession through the hall and up the stairs to the great chamber, if the lord was dining in state, or into the dining parlour. Those present all stood reverently with their hats off, while the procession passed by. From the dining chamber door, the gentleman usher accompanied the server and his procession to the table, ensuring that the dishes were laid in the correct position. Any meat which had to be carved was taken to a side-table by the carver, the carved meat required at the lord's table being served next, and the gentlemen of the chamber acting as waiters throughout the meal. The lord and his most honoured guest would be served their food by waiters on bended knee.

The food was never placed on the table in a haphazard manner, but skilfully arranged for the convenience of the diners with dishes drawn up symmetrically in ranks of four by four: 'For what availes it our good Housewife to be never so skilfull in the parts of Cookery, if she want skill to marshall the dishes . . .' writes Gervase Markham, in *The English Hus-wife*. 'It is like a Fencer leading a band of men in a rout, who knows the use of the weapon, but not how to put men in order.' Presentation was crucial and each dish was dressed with enormous care both individually and as part of the overall table design. In *The Good Huswife's Jewell* of 1596, Thomas Dawson advised his readers to arrange prunes, yellow barberries, fruit or hard-boiled eggs round the rim of the serving dish to produce colourful and symmetrical patterns.

Wines, ales and drinking vessels were set out on the court cupboard before a meal by the yeoman of the cellar. The goblets, or glasses, were kept cool and fresh in a wooden

A detail of a feast and masque from the painting of the life of Sir Henry Unton, *c.*1596. Those rich enough employed a small permanent orchestra to provide entertainment during the meal and music for dancing afterwards.

tub of water until a diner called for a drink. When the goblet of liquor was brought, the guest never drank all of its contents, for that was considered rude; nor was it polite to request the cup more than twice during an ordinary meal. After the goblet had been handed back, it was rinsed before being refilled.

For dinner, Elizabethans ate two courses: the first consisted of great quantities of 'gross meats', or the equivalent in fish on fish days, while poultry, pies, puddings and salads made up the second. The meal could be extended by a banquet or dessert course if wished. Gervase Markham recommended three courses of 32 dishes each for even a humble feast, but the usual fare of the country gentleman, according to Harrison, was 'four, five or six dishes, when they have but small resort [when not expecting a number of guests]'. When Shakespeare's Justice Shallow invites Falstaff to dinner in *Henry IV, Part 2*, he orders: 'Some pigeons, Davy; a couple of shortlegged hens; a joint of mutton; and any pretty little tiny kickshaws [made dishes] tell William Cook.' Other contemporary accounts indicate the profusion of dishes: the Earl of Northumberland and seven guests dined at his house in Bath on 29 April 1591 on a meal of 'Beef [probably roast], Mutton and Veale [probably boiled], Capons [probably boiled], Rabbits, Pigeons [roast], Chickens [probably boiled], Partridges [roast], fresh Salmon [boiled] Tartes [almond or fruit], Made dishes [carbonadoes, hashes, or fricassées], Butter and Eggs.' Vegetables were not mentioned in the Earl's household papers, but a few would have been served together with some attractive salads. Cheese and fruit would have brought the dinner to a close. The Earl's guests, however, would not have worked their way through this formidable menu; rich men, so Harrison explains, furnished their table in this fashion in order that each man might, in each course, choose the food that pleased him best and that their large retinues of servants might also have sufficient at the second sitting which followed. He assures us that gentlemen did not overeat, but were strictly moderate in their diet, although they 'esteemed highly' both rare foods, like sweet potatoes, and good cooking.

Planned entertainments – *entremets* – kept the diners amused during the interval between courses. (The sense of *entremet* had altered considerably by the 19th century.) Those rich enough, like Bess of Hardwick, employed a small permanent orchestra to entertain through dinner, then to provide music for dancing.

Table manners remained pretty basic, as can be seen from the admonitions of Francis Seager, author of the *Schoole of Vertue and Booke of Goode Nourture for Chyldren* of 1557 who was one of many 'poets' to teach the rules of table etiquette:

> For rudnes it is thy pottage to sup,
> Or speake to any, his head in the cup.
> They knife se be sharpe to cut fayre thy meate;
> Thy mouth not to full when thou dost eate;
> Not smackynge thy lyppes, As commnly do hogges,
> Nor gnawynge the bones As it were dogges;
> Suche rudenes abhorre, Suche beastlynes flie,
> At the table behave thy selfe manerly . . .
> Pyke not thy teethe at the table syttynge,
> Nor use at thy meate Over muche spytynge;
> this rudness of youth Is to be abhorde;
> thy selfe manerly Behave at the borde.

With a final washing of the hands, the meal would end in the dining chamber, but for an entertainment of any quality the best was yet to come. With noble hosts their favoured guests might retire for an ambrosial third course, or 'banquet', of fruit, sweetmeats and sweet spiced wines into the 'withdrawinge chamber'; or go up to intimate banqueting houses, which rose above their house roofs; or, perhaps in the summer, proceed to delightful banqueting houses erected in some secluded corner of their garden or park. Sir William Sharington's banqueting house, built at the top of an octagonal look-out tower at Lacock Abbey in Wiltshire between 1549 and 1553, is the earliest known banqueting house on a roof. It consists of two very small rooms holding only six or seven guests comfortably, although more guests could have attended by walking about on the roof. Both rooms have octagonal, carved, stone tables; one of them is supported by four leering satyrs with baskets of fruit on their heads.

On a fine summer's day, Bess and her guests might progress from the High Great Chamber to the richly decorated banqueting house or 'prospect room' on the roof of the south turret of Hardwick Hall. From there they could survey all Bess's lands and gardens, whilst eating the most delectable sugary sweetmeats. At Hardwick there was also a banqueting house on the ground floor and two others in the gardens, which still survive. Sir Edward Phelips had a permanent banqueting house in his garden at Montacute, but others were 'made with fir poles and decked with birch branches and all manner of flowers both of the field and of the garden, as roses, julyflowers, lavender, marygolds and all manner of strewing herbs and rushes' as Queen Elizabeth had made in Greenwich Park for the reception of the French Embassy in 1560, where she gave a supper followed by a masque and a magnificent banquet.

For a banquet, presentation was crucial and special attention was paid to colour. Gervase Markham gives instructions to the ladies of country houses as to the setting out of their banquet:

> you shall first send forth a dish made for shew only, as Beast, Bird, Fish, Fowl, according to invention: Then your March-pane, then preserved Fruit, then a paste, then a wet sucket, then a dry sucket, Marmalade, comfets, apples, peares, wardens, Oranges and Lemons sliced, and then wafers and another dish of preserved fruits, and so consequently all the rest before, no two dishes of one kind, going or standing together and this will not only appear delicate to the eye, but invite the appetite with the much variety thereof.

A 'fruit banquet' consisting of fresh fruit only, less expensive than sweetmeats, was popular among the middling classes.

Sweetmeats were usually served on glass plates and dishes, which could be hired for the occasion. Dry sweetmeats as well as cheese, fruit, caraways and biscuits were eaten from small, wafer-thin, wooden trenchers of sycamore or beech, with elaborate designs, typically painted and gilded with fruit and flowers of the months and seasons or signs of the zodiac. By the 1580s, these trenchers included a verse or 'poesie' in the middle and were called 'roundels'. In his *Art of English Poesie* of 1589, George Puttenham describes the 'epigrams that were sent usually for New Yeares gifts or to be printed or put upon their banketting dishes of sugar plate or of March paines ... they were called "Apophereta" and never contained above one verse or two at the most, but the shorter the better. We call them poesies, and do paint them now a dayes upon the backe sides of our fruit trenchers of wood.' Guests ate from the plain side, and at the end of the banquet, they turned over their roundel and recited or sang the verse on the other side; hence 'roundelay', meaning a short, simple song with a refrain. Often given as wedding presents or as gifts at New Year, trenchers and roundels were produced in sets in pretty decorated boxes. There is a set of four now hanging in the hall at Castle Drogo in Devon.

While the banqueters were enjoying themselves, often playing games, dancing, singing and listening to music, the carver was supervising the clearing of the table in the great chamber or dining parlour. The meat was taken down to the hall, where it was distributed by the server, with advice from the gentleman usher, to the remainder of the household. Viscount Montague bids his gentleman usher to see that, after every meal, all stools and chairs are put back in their proper places and the rooms 'to be swept and kept clean and sweet with perfumes, flowers, herbs and boughs in their season'. The room was prepared for further music, dancing, games, or plays and masques, until supper was ready to be served.

Gentry took supper between 5 and 6pm; farmers and merchants not before 7 or 8pm, and even later in the summer, when labourers would work until dusk in the fields. Supper was supposed to be a lighter meal than dinner, and might consist of a dish like buttered eggs, with posset, usually served in a special pot at bedtime. Mistress Quickly tells Rugby in the *Merry Wives of Windsor*: 'Go; and we'll have a posset for't soon as night, in faith, at the latter end of a sea coal fire.'

But supper could also be a substantial meal, consisting of two courses that could be further extended by a banquet. The Earl of Northumberland and his guests followed their dinner on 29 April 1591 with a supper of 'Mutton, Capons, Chickens, Rabbits, Pigeons, Calves' feete, baked Lampreys, Butter and Eggs'. There would have been additional vegetables and salads and probably a dessert of cheese and fruit – quite a meal in modern terms!

Above: Montacute House, Somerset, with one of the garden pavilions that was used as a banqueting house.

Left: The octagonal stone table supported by satyrs in Sir William Sharington's banqueting house at the top of the octagonal look-out tower at Lacock Abbey, Wiltshire.

Sweet Herbs and Strong Bitter Brews

STUART FOOD

Sweet Herbs and Strong Bitter Brews

A master-cook! why, he's the man of men,
For a professor! he designs, he draws,
He paints, he carves, he builds, he fortifies,
Makes citadels of curious fowl and fish,
Some he dry-dishes, some motes round with broths;
Mounts marrow bones, cuts fifty-angled custards,
Rears bulwark pies, and for his outer works,
He raiseth ramparts of immortal crust; . . .

Ben Jonson, *The Staple of News*, 1631

I

The Stuarts presided over a century of religious, economic and social turmoil, including the last significant land battles to be fought in England and Wales. For the majority of the population, these upheavals merely intensified the struggle to secure adequate supplies of food and drink.

Epidemics in the late 1590s had temporarily checked population growth, and there was probably a small increase in people's purchasing power in the first 20 years of the 17th century, which saw only two really bad harvests. The overseas cloth trade prospered, giving work to many. But the next two decades brought lean times, with trade depression and bad harvests driving down the purchasing power of the poorer farmers, tradesmen and labourers. The outbreak of the Civil War in the 1640s disrupted the economy, bringing hunger and disease. Robert May, chef to the courtier Sir Kenelm Digby and author of *The Accomplisht Cook*, published in 1660, commenting on the effects of the Civil War, wrote: 'Hospitality which was once a relique of the gentry and a known cognizance to all ancient houses, hath lost her title through the unhappy and cruel disturbances of these times.'

The Restoration of Charles II in 1660 coincided with improved conditions; grain prices fell in the second half of the century, bringing down the prices of bread and beer and enabling the poor to buy a wider range of foodstuffs. On the other hand, the gentry and aristocracy as landlords fared relatively well in the period up to 1660, but thereafter saw a decline in their income from rents. The second half of the century was a time of agricultural innovation. Falling prices for traditional grain crops led enterprising farmers, sometimes actively encouraged by their landlords, to diversify and experiment

Pages 140–1: The first London coffee-house was opened in St Michael's Alley, Cornhill in 1652 by Daniel Edwards, a Turkey merchant. In these houses the exclusively male clientele could enjoy a good fire, a 'Dish of Coffee' with a newspaper and a pipe of tobacco, all for a penny. Little wonder, then, that coffee-houses proliferated and by the time this coloured drawing was done of an interior, *c*.1695, there were said to be three thousand houses in the capital alone.

Right: Stuart sophistication: a family taking tea in their formal garden. In the centre foreground a pageboy has been tripped up by a monkey, upsetting his tray. A parade of orange trees in ceramic pots are ranged along the path. This early 18th-century embroidery, one of the Stoke Edith hangings, now hangs at Montacute House, Somerset. It came originally from Stoke Edith in Herefordshire, a house built *c*.1698 by Paul Foley, and is said to have been worked by the five wives of his grandson, Thomas.

Left: One of a series of *The Cryes of London*, originally drawn by Marcellus Lauron at the end of the 17th century, and copied here by Tempest. This cry depicts the seller of water from the New River Company, set up in the opening years of the 17th century to construct a channel bringing water from fresh springs at Chadwell and Amwell in Hertfordshire to Islington to provide a clean supply for the citizens of London. Hugh Myddelton of Chirk was the leading light in this enterprise.

with new food crops. In the 1690s Gregory King, one of the earliest statisticians, thought that expenditure per capita on food was 1s 3¾d per week, broken down into bread 3½d, meat and fish 4¼d, dairy produce 2d, beer 4d, and vegetables, fruit, salt, pickles and groceries 2d.

The establishment of trading posts and colonies in North America, the Caribbean, Africa and the East led to the appearance of many more exotic foods and condiments in Britain. New delicacies, such as China oranges, soy sauce, Westphalia hams and tea were now sought after by the rich and the discerning.

London remained by far the largest city in England, with a rapidly increasing population, from about 200,000 in 1600 to 375,000 in 1650 and 490,000 by 1700. Large quantities of meat, dairy produce, grain and fish were brought in from all parts of the kingdom to satisfy demand, and London also operated as the principal port of entry for exotic produce. Catherine Verney of Claydon House in Buckinghamshire wrote regularly to her husband in London requesting such delicacies as coffee, saltpetre, candied citron, green and black tea, chocolate, stone pots of anchovies, isinglass, 'good sallyt oyal' and 'shavins of hartshorn'.

The 17th century saw the development of the London 'Season', when entire families of country gentry moved to their own or rented town houses to enjoy a winter of social intercourse. Dining played a prominent part, and new foods, recipes and modes of eating were learned in London to be disseminated later to their more humble country cousins.

French cuisine, that had made some inroads into English kitchens earlier in the century, was given a further boost with the return of Charles II and his courtiers from their exile. 'Meats and Drinks after the French fashion' became very much the mode for those who could afford French chefs. In 1662 the King married the Portuguese princess, Catherine of Braganza, who brought with her a taste for fine Chinese porcelain and for the Chinese drink Tcha, or tea. Both porcelain and tea had made their appearances in England earlier, but the Queen's patronage made them the height of fashion.

Apart from these foreign delicacies, however, a 17th-century country house like Claydon was almost entirely self-supporting, relying on its own fields and stockyards to provide most of its food. The winter stores had to be carefully planned and prepared, for a remote house might easily be cut off for weeks in bad weather. Roads remained deplorably bad: it took four days to travel by coach from London to Dover, although this was considered the best highway in the kingdom; a stage waggon from London carrying passengers and a limited amount of luggage would take seven days to reach York and ten to Liverpool. Margaret Adams, a cousin of Sir John Verney, described a difficult journey home from Claydon: ' the continuall Rain which fell that day had so much swell'd the waters in all places that they were often through the bottom of the Coach amongst us.' They finally had to abandon the coach and continue on foot.

Bread

White wheaten remained the bread that everybody wanted to eat, whether they could afford it or not. In 1616 the Grocers' Company reported that 'the poor would not buy barley or rye, either alone or even if mixed with two-thirds wheat': the blend had to be nearly four-fifths wheat before it could be sold for breadcorn. Moreover, it had to be the whitest, brightest wheat obtainable to please the wheaten bread customers. The separate London guild of the brown bakers, established in the 14th century, disappeared as a result.

The finest white bread was still manchet, sometimes enriched with butter, eggs or milk, like the earlier French bread; in fact, wheaten milk bread was still often called French bread and individual manchets came to be known as French rolls. By the end of the century, spiced bread, caraway-flavoured buns and wigs were fashionable breads to be taken at breakfast.

But in the country such bread was still to be seen only on the tables of the gentry. Country people still made their breads from the local grain. In wheat areas, cheat, ravelled cheat and brown bread were made. The large, flat, circular oatcakes known in Cumberland as 'clapbread' (or 'haverbread' from the Old Norse 'hafri' meaning oats) would have been the predominant bread eaten by the Browne family at Townend near Kendal in Cumbria. In 1615 Gervase Markham wrote in *The English Hus-wife*: 'For your brown bread, or bread for your hind servants, which is the coarsest bread for man's use, you shall take of barley two bushels, of pease two pecks, of wheat or rye a peck, a peck of malt; these you shall grind together and dress it through a meal sieve'. Even coarser breads made entirely of peas and beans were still consumed in times of dearth, and these were frequent. A particularly bad period was from 1693 to the end of the century; in 1694 the Myddelton family was baking bread for the poor in the bakehouse at Chirk Castle: 'Payd for Cutteing wood to bake the poores bread and carreing them 9s.' and 'Payd John Griffith, for a great Loggen [wicker] baskett to carry the poores bread 4d'. To try to counter the price of wheat, rice was imported from China, but the population was not impressed.

Meat and Poultry

With the rise of population in England's towns and cities, the demand for fresh meat grew. Helped by the enclosure of common land, landowners had more space than before in which to nurture animals. The long distance trade in meat animals from upland England, Wales and Scotland continued and grew. But although the animals were fattened up before slaughter, their meat must often have been of poor quality. With increasing use of turnips as fodder and the cultivation of better meadows and lowland grasslands in the second half of the century, it was possible to achieve the tender, well-flavoured meat for which Britain was to become famous. A few of the more progressive farmers then began to pay great attention to the quality of their stock and to improve it by suitable breeding.

Beef and veal were the favoured meats of the period. In 1694 Margaret Bankes recorded purchases of considerable amounts for the Kingston Lacy household in Dorset. The home farm supplied the house with most of its meat and poultry, but beef was usually bought in: on 23 April '£1 4s for beef weighing 117 lb'; a week later, £1 5s 10d for beef weighing 123 lb'; and the following week '£2 1s 0¾d for beef weighing 197 lb'. Large households usually bought an ox or a cow at the end of October to salt down and smoke for the winter: the sides of beef were either boned, ready for rolling into flitches like bacon, or jointed before salting. Large quantities of both salt and saltpetre were bought in the autumn for the Kingston Lacy household to preserve enough meat to last until the spring.

Offal was eaten extensively: such dishes as calves' foot pudding, beef palates (the roof of a cow's or ox's mouth), udder, pigs' ears, tongues, tripe, calves' head hash, or lambs' heads might appear even on the most fashionable tables. One delicacy greatly appreciated was lambs' stones, readily available in the midsummer months when lambs were castrated. Also popular were sausages and the various kidney, liver, black, white and marrow puddings contained within cleaned guts or skins.

The further down the social scale, the less meat was eaten, although the slow-down of population growth and more stable social conditions after 1660 meant that meat could be afforded by more people. Farmers like the Brownes of Townend, who were sheep breeders, were able to eat some kind of joint at least on Sundays. The farm servants at Townend dined at their master's table and shared his fare of oatcake, fresh meat (mainly pork, mutton and beef), cheese, milk and beer. In winter there would have been cured and salt meats.

In large towns meat dishes could be obtained from cookshops. The diarist Samuel Pepys sent out for his dinner in 1663: 'Was vexed that it being washing day, we had not meat dressed; but sent to the cook's and my people had so little wit to send in our meat from abroad in the cook's dishes, which were marked with the name of the cooke upon them ...'.

As in earlier times, game, except for deer, could be taken by all, but in 1671 an act was passed prohibiting the killing of game, except for a very limited group of 'qualified persons', which meant only the aristocracy and gentry, those who were likely to own private hunting parks and chases. However, the act had loopholes and for many years to come poached game was sold openly in the season by London poulterers and at taverns and coffee-houses.

In the 17th century, many of the ancient deer-parks were still in full operation and

The Butcher's Shop, a painting by the Dutch artist Jan Victoors. Offal was eaten extensively at this period.

new ones were being set up by wealthy landowners. William Wyndham I devoted great care to creating his deer-park at Felbrigg Hall in Norfolk: he noted in his ledger that in the winter of 1683, his herd of deer numbered 236. His household was large and consumed great quantities of venison: on average, he would kill about seven brace of bucks and six of does each year. Venison dinners were a regular feature of 17th-century social life. Lady Anne Clifford, then married to the 3rd Earl of Dorset, records one in her diary as part of the Christmas festivities in 1617 at Knole: 'There came to dine Mrs Linsey and a great company of neighbours to eat venison.' Venison pasties were made from a whole boned side enclosed in pastry. It was essential that the crust should be quite strong, for it might have to withstand a long journey by waggon before reaching its destination. As in Elizabethan times, venison, either uncooked, in a pasty, or potted, was a most acceptable gift to an important patron or friend. The Verneys of Claydon had an insatiable requirement for medicines and sent their doctor many gifts of venison: 'Sir, I humbley thank you for the venison which I received yesterday, it is very fatt and sweet' was a typical reply from Dr Peter Gelsthorpe to Sir John.

Rabbits were multiplying 'to the benefit of good housekeeping and the poor's maintenance', and the number of warrens attached to the estates of large houses increased in the later part of the century. Occasionally the right of operating them was farmed out: the warren at Felbrigg was let to Thomas Gosse of Haveringhland, who undertook to supply William Wyndham with 300 rabbits a year and to leave 1300 'breeding conies' upon the premises at the end of his lease. Selling rabbits could be a lucrative business. At Knole, the expenses involved in looking after the conies in 1628 came to exactly £10, including 5 guineas wages for the 'wariner', but this money was well spent, for the revenue from conies sold contributed no less than one-fifth of the estate's total income for that year. Very young rabbits were taken in nets where the ends were drawn together with a string, like a purse: the Chirk Castle accounts records the purchase of 'twelve pursenetts to take suckinge rabbits'.

Game birds for the table were trapped under baited nets or taken by hawks. Five stone cupboards or hatches with arched openings set into the exterior wall at East Riddlesden in Yorkshire are thought to have been used for housing John Murgatroyd's falcons in the early part of the century. The opening below the niches may have been used for his hunting dogs. 'Neither do I marvel,' wrote Thomas Cogan in *The Haven of Health* in 1584, 'considering the goodness of the flesh, that gentlemen be at such cost to keep hawks, and take such toil to kill partridges and pheasants.' After the Civil War, when sporting gentlemen again had leisure to hunt birds, they tended to use fowling pieces instead of birds of prey.

Potting was a popular and fashionable way of preserving foodstuffs, particularly game, for serving among the lighter dishes of the second course. The meat was baked in butter, drained and then sealed under more butter, so that it could keep for up to a year. 'Woodcocks to put into potts' was a very frequent entry in the winter accounts of Chirk Castle, and they were often sent to Sir Richard Myddelton when he was in London.

Pigeons from the woods and dovecotes were eaten in great numbers: by the late 17th century, Britain had an estimated 26,000 dovecotes, large and small, reckoned to be more than in any other kingdom in the world. Some agriculturalists blamed pigeons for the great waste of corn: 'The next great destroyers of Corne . . . are your Pygeons, which the wisdome of our nation hath so well found out that they have provided many wholesome Lawes for the restraint of the great multiplicity thereof', said Gervase

The stone cupboards set into a wall at East Riddlesden, Yorkshire. The arched upper row is thought to have been used for housing falcons, the row below for hunting dogs.

Markham in his *Farewell to Husbandry* of 1620. It was calculated that the grain eaten or destroyed each year by the 250,000 occupants of the cotes could have provided bread for 100,000 people. Like their Tudor predecessors, 17th-century dovecotes were usually built on a square or rectangular plan, sometimes incorporated into another agricultural building. At Belton House in Lincolnshire, for instance, the dovecote forms the second storey of the stable. At Wichenford, near Worcester, it seems likely that the poultry yard was laid out around the half-timbered dovecote, conveniently near the duck pond to provide fresh water for the birds. In the kitchen, pigeons were roasted, stewed with bacon, spices, herbs and wine, made into dumplings or pies, and potted.

The price of poultry in the market continued to rise: a chicken could fetch as much as 1s 4d in 1634, compared with 2d or 4d a century earlier. Poultry was now regarded as a delicacy for the table, so one of the duties of the lady of the house was to supervise the provision of poultry and eggs: hens, ducks, geese and turkeys were all bred and fattened to her order. Chickens and capons were often crammed on pellets of wheatmeal or barleymeal mixed with milk, and geese on oatmeal, barleymeal or ground malt. Sir Kenelm Digby wrote of chickens fed on a soft paste of crushed raisins, white breadcrumbs and milk, and claimed that 'the delight of this meat will make them eat continually and they will be so fat (when they are but the bigness of a blackbird) that they will not be able to stand, but lie down upon their bellies to eat.'

Turkey had almost superseded the old celebratory birds of the Middle Ages – the peacocks and swans of the rich, the bustards and herons of the poor. The peacock was abandoned during the 17th century, but swans still appeared at feasts until the end of the century when they were 'commonly kept for their stateliness and beauty'. Pepys reports in his diary on 14 January 1666: 'At noon eat the second of the two cygnets Mr. Sheply sent us for a New Year's Gift.' Great flocks of up to a thousand turkeys and geese were brought on foot to the London markets from East Anglia, their feet tarred for protection. They began the hundred-mile journey in August at the end of the harvest and took three months to get to Smithfield and Leadenhall in time for Christmas. There they could command up to 3s each.

Fish

James I sought to continue the practices of his cousin, Elizabeth, with proclamations against eating meat in Lent and attempts to enforce fish-eating on Wednesdays, Fridays and Saturdays. Lady Anne Clifford of Knole made a resolution to keep Fridays as fish days in 1617; 'The 25th being Friday I came to keep my Fish Days which I intend to keep all the year long.' Under the Commonwealth, fish days were abolished as a Papish institution, and although at the Restoration in 1660 efforts were made again to revive them to help the fishing industry, they were never successfully re-established as fish was too scarce and expensive. In 1662, Pepys writes 'Our dinner, it being Good Friday, was only sugar sopps and fish; the only time that we have had a Lenten dinner all this Lent.'

Despite the price and scarcity of fish there was enough of a market for the choicer sea and freshwater species to encourage efforts to be made to bring in fish in a fresh condition. Ships were provided with tanks of water in their holds to bring the catch back alive and to transport it to London from distant coasts. Turbot and lobsters taken near Tynemouth were kept alive there in rockpools, until they could be transferred to

The Fish Market by Frans Snyders.

the 'wells' in ships for the London market. London's fish market was Billingsgate, with its wharves on the River Thames. In 1699, an Act of Parliament declared it a free and open market for the sale of fish six days a week, and of mackerel on Sundays because it was so perishable.

Otherwise, newly caught fish was dispatched overland in slow-moving, horse drawn waggons; it would have taken two days to bring the mackerel, the dozen whitings and the quarter of a hundred smelts sent to Lord Fermanagh at Claydon in Buckinghamshire from London 'to assist his weak appetite'. He and his family were 'highly feasted' and 'put half of them in pickle'. People living near the coast, like the Bankes family of Kingston Lacy, ate a large variety of fresh fish, while at Chirk Castle, far inland, the fish eaten was largely freshwater: eels, carp, bream and pike were taken from the various fish-ponds in Black Park. In the 1670s when William Wyndham stocked a group of ponds on his estate at Felbrigg he concentrated on his favourite fish, carp, many score of which were given by his neighbours. Sturgeon was popular enough during the reign of Charles II for Robert May to devote a whole section in his *Accomplisht Cook* of 1660, to 'A-la-Mode ways of Dressing and Ordering of Sturgeon', with no fewer than 30 recipes. John Myddelton bought a firkin (a small barrel) of sturgeon and sent it to Chirk Castle in 1678.

A fish that came to be much used as a garnish and condiment because of Portuguese influence, was the anchovy. It was added to sauces, or made-up dishes not only of fish, but also of meat, as rigid demarcation between fish and meat was breaking down. The oyster too was frequently included in dishes of meat and poultry: 'to boil a capon with oysters and pickled lemons', and 'hashed mutton with oysters'. Oysters were regarded as such a delicacy that they appear in all manner of styles. A suggested menu for a large fish day feast by John Murrell in *A New Booke of Cookerie* of 1638 had stewed oysters in the first course, and oysters fried, pickled and baked in a pie in the second.

During the 17th century, potted fish, like potted meat was fashionable: recipes abounded for the potting of eels, salmon, lampreys, smelts, mackerel, lobsters, crabs, shrimps, mackerel, and any fish that was regarded as particularly desirable. The other usual way to conserve fish was to pickle it. Sides of salmon, sturgeon or pike and large eels and congers split lengthways, were rolled in collars and soused like brawn. Cutlets of salmon were put into liquid pickles based on wine, vinegar or beer. A different method of pickling was applied to flat fish, smaller white fish and pieces of larger ones. The fish was first fried, then put in vinegar 'so you may keep it for the use of your table any reasonable time'. This 'caveached' fish, like pickled and potted fish, was served as a side-dish for the second course.

Fruit and Vegetables

Commercial production of fruit and vegetables greatly expanded in the 17th century, especially after the Civil War. In 1633 an estimated 20,000 cartloads of carrots, parsnips and turnips were brought to London markets from land to the west of the city: thirty years later, an observer remarked it was 'incredible how many poor people in London live thereon, so that in some seasons the gardens feed more people than the field'. Richard Bradley, Professor of Botany at Cambridge, and author of *The Country Housewife*, 1727–32, reckoned that the area of land under market gardens around London increased from 10,000 acres in 1660 to 110,000 acres in 1721.

Above left: *The Fruit Seller* by Jan Victoors. By the end of the 17th century the piazza of Covent Garden had become a thriving market supplying fruit and vegetables to the capital.

Above: 'Fair Lemons & Oranges' from *The Cryes of London* by Tempest after Lauron. In the 17th century hawkers bought from Covent Garden as much fruit and vegetables as they could carry to sell through the city streets.

Townspeople bought their vegetables and fruit from markets and on the streets. Several of London's city markets had sections devoted to such produce, but a specialist fruit and vegetable market, to serve the growing gentry community to the west of the city, started in the piazza of Covent Garden, which had been laid out by Inigo Jones in the 1620s as a centrepiece of a residential development for the Earls of Bedford. The growth of the unofficial market prompted the 5th Earl in 1670 to obtain a licence and, by levying tolls on the traders, he made a fortune for himself. Although it didn't start as a wholesale market, it developed as such, supplying London and much of southern England for centuries until moving to a new site at Nine Elms in the 1970s.

Seventeenth-century hawkers bought from Covent Garden as much fruit and vegetables as they could carry, and went through the streets crying their wares. Nell Gwyn, mistress of Charles Sackville, 6th Earl of Dorset, before transferring her favours to the King, was one of the 'orange girls' who sold their wares in the London theatres.

People were also growing more vegetables for themselves. John Aubrey, writing *Brief Lives*, *c*.1680, thought that 'in the time of Charles II gardening was much improved and become common'. The Earls of Bedford hired an experienced gardener to improve their kitchen gardens at Woburn Abbey, representing a general trend amongst the nobility. John Worlidge, author of *Vinetum Britannicus* in 1676, meanwhile, found 'scarce a cottage in most of the southern parts of England, but hath its proportionate garden, so great a delight do most men take in it.'

Vegetables were becoming an important element of the fare of both the rich and the poor. For the latter, high-yielding root vegetables, simply prepared, provided a valuable supplement to their diet. The potato began also to be cultivated for food in the

The grounds of Old Corney House, Chiswick, 1675, showing the fruit trees and rectangular beds, which suggest a practical rather than decorative purpose. This detail from a painting by Jacob Knyff is the earliest depiction of a London garden.

north of England, although it was not to challenge bread as the staple 'bulk' food of English meals until the 19th century. Sir Ralph Verney of Claydon in a letter refers to the contempt held by English maidservants for the 'potages' and 'legumes' which were the ordinary fare of working people in France, adding that his 'Luce' and 'Besse' demanded meat. But this attitude was declining, and vegetables were finding increasing favour on gentlemen's tables. The 17th-century household accounts of Kingston Lacy record a wide variety of vegetables: samphire, spinach, turnips, parsnips, sprouts, cabbage, artichokes, carrots, peas and asparagus, as well as herbs. Margaret Bankes of Kingston Lacy paid '10d for sallets' every week in 1700, and she may have turned to the first English book devoted to such vegetables, *Acetaria*, written by John Evelyn in 1699. This work sought to encourage the growing popularity of 'grand sallets' with their mixtures of fresh and cold boiled vegetables, cold meats, and fish, towards more simple mixtures of raw green leaves and dressing with which we are familiar today. Evelyn provided detailed practical instruction on salad-making, and thoughtful general advice on the composition of a salad:

> ... every Plant should come in to bear its part, withough being over-power'd by some Herb of a stronger Taste, so as to endanger the native Sapor and Vertue of the rest; but fall into their places, like the Notes on Music, in which there should be nothing harsh or grating.

Although a wide range of herbs was still grown, the 17th-century preference was for those of Mediterranean origin, in particular those described in contemporary French cookery books as 'sweet'. It was at this time that the 'faggot of sweet herbs', the modern bouquet garni, was first used in English cooking.

Seventeenth-century gentlemen delighted in the fruit trees in their gardens, and this is reflected in the increasing number of varieties grown. John Parkinson, a London apothecary, in his herbal, *Paradisi in Sole* of 1629, named 57 kinds of apple, 62 pears, 61 plums, 35 cherries and 22 peaches. 'Damasine [damsons] and red currance and red gusberies plants' were bought at Shrewsbury for the Chirk Castle kitchen garden in 1651, and in the following year Parkinson's *Herball* was purchased, no doubt to help with the development of the garden. In 1674 a number of peach, apricot, warden, plum and cherry trees were planted by John Clifford, the gardener.

The East India companies brought back seeds and plants from the Orient, and although the fruits grown from these were perhaps not very fine, they must have helped to break down the old resistance to fruit as a food and to encourage the import of more luscious varieties from the Mediterranean countries. Citrus fruits were shipped from Portugal in ever-increasing numbers. Oranges had been brought back from Ceylon by the Portuguese during the 16th century, but now sweet China oranges were obtainable: according to John Parkinson in 1629, 'a sort lately had from Portugal, whither it came not many years since from China. This hath the rind so pleasant and free from bitterness that it may be eaten as well as the meat which is sweet, and it is the best kind to preserve whole.' In 1622 'lemons unwasht' were 3s a dozen, while oranges were 1s each, so were still regarded as luxuries. When Edmund Verney went up to Trinity College, Oxford in 1685, his father included oranges and lemons in what appears to have been the equivalent of the schoolboy's tuck-box: 'In your trunk I have put for you, 18 Sevill Oranges, 6 Malaga Lemons, 3 pounds of Brown Sugar, 1 pound of white powdered sugar made up in quarters, 1 lb of brown Sugar Candy, $\frac{1}{4}$ lb of white sugar candy, 1 lb of picked Raisons, good for a Cough, and 4 nutmeggs.' Limes and shaddocks (renamed grapefruit in the 19th century) were imported in the 1680s from the West Indies.

Glasshouses for growing vines, peaches, nectarines and even oranges and lemons were being added to great houses. Following in the footsteps of intrepid pioneers like Sir Francis Carew (see p.102), a few wealthy and enthusiastic garden owners, like the Duchess of Lauderdale at Ham House in Surrey, and the Myddeltons at Chirk, purchased orange and lemon trees on the Continent and tried to persuade them to fruit. In 1684 the Duke of Beaufort was entertained to a banquet by Sir Richard Myddelton in the banqueting-house in the park at Chirk: 'His Grace made an halt at an admirable Walled Garden of Trees, Plants, Flowers and Herbs of the greatest rarity [as well as] Orrenge and Lemon Trees . . . .' But the fruit needed careful tending and the additional

The garden of Westbury Court, Gloucestershire, was laid out by Maynard Colchester between 1696 and 1715, very much on formal Dutch lines. The National Trust has restored the garden, choosing plants known in England before 1700. This espaliered apple tree is a 17th-century variety called 'Reinette'.

warmth of a stove in the cold months, and were not very successful. Pepys first saw oranges growing in Lord Brooke's garden in Hackney: 'some green, some half, some a quarter and some full ripe, on the same tree.'

Although fresh orange juice had been available since the beginning of the century, Pepys first encountered it at the house of his cousin in 1669: 'here, which I never did before, I drank a glass, of a pint, I believe, at one draught, of the juice of oranges, of whose peel they make comfits; and here they drink as wine, with sugar, and it is a very fine drink; but, it being new, I was doubtful whether it might not do me hurt.' Margaret Bankes of Kingston Lacy 'payd 7s. 6d. for quarts of lime juice' in 1697.

Oranges and lemons might have become quite common in England, and within the pockets of the middle classes, but there were two desirable newcomers on the 17th-century fruit dish. The first example of 'a certain delicious fruit called "pina"' was brought to Britain from the West Indies in Cromwell's time, and a queen pine from Barbados was presented to Charles II in 1661. This event, recorded in a painting at Ham House excited great interest, and the pineapple remained a rare and delectable luxury until the 19th century. The banana, first seen in London in 1633, was even rarer, also retaining its curiosity status until the 19th century and the advent of fast steamships, because it was so perishable.

Although a wider variety of fruit was available, the price placed it beyond the reach of the ordinary purse for the greater part of the year. Even in the season when a glut might

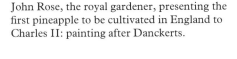

John Rose, the royal gardener, presenting the first pineapple to be cultivated in England to Charles II: painting after Danckerts.

be expected in the markets, it is surprising to find how expensive it was: strawberries and cherries for the Kingston Lacy household in June 1693 cost 1s a pound. Monsieur Misson, a Frenchman who visited England in the 1690s, commented on the rarity of fruit as a dessert: 'The desert they [the English] never dream of, unless it be a piece of Cheese. Fruit is brought only to the Tables of the Great, and of a small Number even among them.' The prudent way to eat fruit was still to cook it first with sugar and spices. Lady Anne Clifford of Knole obviously shared the old suspicion about eating raw fruit: 'While we lay at Barton I kept so ill a Diet with Mrs. Carey and Mrs. Kinson on eating Fruit, so that I shortly fell into the same sickness.' Her mother was worried the fever would turn into the plague, which was rife at the time. Soft fruit was to be blamed too for the outbreak of the Great Plague in 1665.

Dairy Products

Cow's milk virtually superseded all other kinds during the 17th century, although ass's milk still had a great reputation for invalids: Lady Gardiner wrote to Sir Ralph Verney during the trying time of the Buckingham election in 1685: '. . . I am sure if you do not begin to take the asses milk quickly, you will have both a short time to take it.'

In towns milkmaids walked the streets bearing pails slung from yokes across their shoulders, to sell milk from door to door. In Restoration London some may have been based in dairy shops but in smaller towns, the milkmaids brought the milk in from the surrounding countryside. In dairying districts where skimmed milk was sold off locally, whey was a summer drink for country people and in the middle of the century, whey-houses were opened in London.

The 17th century was the beginning of the 'golden age of butter', which continued through the following century. Butter was cheaper than fat, so was used extensively for cooking: not only in pastry and cake-making, fish-frying, meat-basting, in cereal pottages and buttered ales, but also now added to virtually all forms of boiled food, either during the cooking, or 'run over' the dishes afterwards before serving. Boiled salads, herbs and roots, meat and fish in stews, hashes and fricassées were all liberally buttered. No wonder Monsieur Misson viewed the meals of English people with amazement: 'Another time they will have a piece of boiled beef, and then they salt it some days beforehand, and besiege it with five or six heaps of cabbage, carrots, turnips or some other herbs or roots, well peppered and salted, and swimming in butter: a leg of roast or boiled mutton, dished up with the same dainties, fowls, pigs, oxtripes and tongues, rabbits, pigeons, all well moistened with butter, without larding.'

Butter was usually made in quantity in the summer and May butter was considered not only to be the best, but also the most wholesome. For long keeping, it was still salted and pressed into earthenware pots or wooden tubs. It could be purchased in the market places where stone-built butter-markets were erected in the 17th century to protect the perishable butter and cream, and from chandlers' shops. Some was sent for sale far beyond the local market town; much of London's vast amounts of butter came by sea from Suffolk and Yorkshire.

Curds, made into cheesecakes and fritters, became less popular as the consumption of cheese grew. In 1617, Lady Anne Clifford went 'after supper in the Coach to Goodwife Syslies and ate so much cheese there that it made me sick'. Cheddar cheese acquired considerable fame during the 17th century, but at first was 'seldom seen but at

A river landscape by Jan Victoors showing milk being loaded onto a boat. In the 17th century cow's milk virtually superseded all other kinds, brought into towns by milkmaids.

noblemen's tables'. Thomas Cogan commended both Banbury and Cheshire cheeses, but deemed Banbury the best, 'for therein you shall neither taste the rennet nor salt, which be two special properties of good cheese.' Yorkshire cheese, like Wensleydale, Nidderdale, Coverdale and Swaledale, and Scottish cheese were still marketed locally and rarely reached other parts of Britain, but Welsh cheese, described in 1662 as 'very tender and palatable', was shipped from Chester and Liverpool to London and Bristol. Cheeses could be purchased from the noted cheese fairs, such as Weyhill in Wiltshire, Burford in Oxfordshire, St Giles' Hill in Hampshire, Atherstone-on-Stour in Warwickshire, besides the more general fairs, like the famous one at Stourbridge, where dairy produce was always on sale. After the Restoration, Continental influences in cooking led to a greater use of cheese: grated cheese was included in recipes for hashed meat in stuffings and in little pasties.

Beverages

The man in the street of 17th-century Britain was for the most part a beer or ale drinker, except in the West Country and parts of Wales where cider reigned supreme. Initially, brewing was still a small-scale operation carried on by housewives at home, or by the individual ale-house keepers; but a royal edict of 1637 forbade ale-house keepers, taverners, cooks and victuallers to brew their own beer and obliged them to obtain supplies from a common brewer, to make it easier to levy a tax on brewing. The

Parliamentarians subsequently also imposed a duty on beer, later removed on domestic brewing. Beer brewed for sale has paid excise duty ever since.

Every household had its own recipe. It is not surprising that Misson should write: 'There are a hundred and a hundred Sorts of Beer in England.' Its flavour, quality and colour depended on the ingredients, the water, whether the malt was lightly or heavily roasted, the amount of hopping, as well as the particular methods of each brewer. As in earlier centuries, the beer brewed for large households like that of Chirk Castle varied in strength from the 'strong beer' for Sir Thomas Myddelton, to the 'small beer', the ordinary table drink of the servants and children. In her diary for 1617, Lady Anne Clifford records 'upon the 21st, the child [her daughter, Margaret] had an extreme fit of the Ague and the Doctor . . . gave her a Salt Powder to put in her beer'. This small beer probably had a value of 150–200 calories a pint, which meant that a young boy drinking about three pints a day would receive 500–600 calories towards his daily needs of about 2,500. The beer would also supply a little calcium and vitamins, so was a healthy drink, if drunk in reasonable quantities. Molly and Ralph Verney, 'very ill of a feaver and pains with a short Cough very fast', wisely refused to take anything but 'small Beare'.

Chirk Castle grew all the barley and hops for their beer on the estate and employed a full-time brewer at £4 a year and a maltster. There are frequent references in the accounts to buying 'charcoals to drie mault' and 'to dry hopps'. Cider was also made at Chirk: in 1680, '40 dozen of bottles to bottle syder' were brought to the castle from Wrexham. The following year, 'a dozen goulden pippens trees' were collected by horse for the orchard at Chirk: the golden pippin was recommended by John Evelyn for the making of 'the most delicious of that Liquor [cider]'. Extra cider was bought in at Chirk when necessary, as for the funeral of the young Dame Elizabeth Myddelton in 1675.

Herb-flavoured 'physical ales', diet drinks and other specialities, such as 'buttered ale', possets and ale-caudles, 'Lambs Wool', and 'Cock ale' were also very popular. On 9 March 1667, Pepys had a 'great cold, so home late and drank some buttered ale, and so to bed and to sleep'. 'Mum', a strong, heady, herbal ale, first brewed by Christian Mummer of Brunswick, was a popular drink in the later 17th century. For a time, it was retailed at special mum-houses: Pepys recorded a visit in 1664 to 'the Fleece, a mum-house in Leadenhall'. There are references to its purchase in the Chirk Castle accounts, as well as the purchase of two special mum glasses. Flower and fruit ales were usually brewed at home from elderberries and blackberries. For cowslip ale, the flowers were merely left in barrelled ale for a fortnight, then drawn off and put up in bottles.

At the beginning of James I's reign, imported table wines were arriving in bulk from France and in lesser quantities from the Moselle and Rhineland regions, to be drunk by the wealthy. But during the century, the pattern changed. Excise duties were increased on both the English and French sides of the Channel; prohibitions were made at various times against the Dutch merchants who brought most of the German and French wine to British ports; and, finally, trade was affected by William III's campaigns against the French from 1689 to 1697. It was no longer worth importing the *vins ordinaires* of France and those who had previously enjoyed them turned instead to beer and spirits. Better quality French wines still appealed to English connoisseurs and those prepared to pay the new high prices could purchase some fine clarets and burgundy. The wealthy also increasingly enjoyed the sweetish Portuguese wines, allowed preferential duties in 1690 and 1703, and the sweet Levant wines. Bristol was the centre of the trade in sack from Spain and of the dessert wines from Portugal and the Canary Islands: in Pepys'

Painted glass from the King's Room at Oxburgh Hall, Norfolk, showing how drinking glasses were held by the foot.

day, sack was already known as 'Bristol Milk'. Champagne, first popularised at the English court at the time of the Restoration, also won supporters amongst the rich, but, like port and brandy, did not appear significantly in wine accounts until the end of the century. The first reference to 'a flask of shampaigne' in the accounts for Kingston Lacy comes in 1700, while port did not appear in the Chirk accounts until 1716: 'Payd Mr Bennet [merchant] of Chester for 18 gallons port Red £4 10s, And 9 gallons of white £2 5s'. Brandy was extremely expensive at 12s a gallon.

All wines in the 17th century were drunk from the wood as new wine; that is, they were stored in wooden barrels until needed, then transferred to bulbous bottles with conical cork stoppers placed loosely in their necks. The first glass bottles appeared around 1658 and were used alongside the earlier stone variety. Bottles and corks usually arrived by carrier with the wine from the merchant.

Charles Sackville, 6th Earl of Dorset, described by his descendant, Vita Sackville-West, as 'the jolly, loose-living, magnificent Maecenas' – and erstwhile lover of Nell Gwyn – seems to have kept a formidable cellar at Knole. He was a very heavy drinker and entertained lavishly: from July 1690 to November 1691 he spent £598 19s 4d on drink, an alarming sum, when he was paying only 5s 1d for a gallon of red port, 6s 8d for a gallon of sherry and 8s for a gallon of canary. His cellar book for six months lists '425 gallons of red port, 85 gallons of sherry, 72 gallons of canary, 63 gallons of white port and a quart of hock'. Keeping a good cellar was a status symbol in the 17th century and large quantities of liquor were drunk on special occasions to impress guests.

The practice of spicing and sugaring wine remained fashionable. Pepys records that he was offered some hippocras, 'it being, to the best of my judgement, only a mixed compound drink, and not any wine', but he was mistaken – or disingenuous – for it was very potent. Another drink that acquired great popularity in the later 17th century was punch. Introduced by the East Indian merchants it was 'composed of brandy or aquavitae, juice of lemons, oranges or such like'. For some obscure reason, punch-drinking became closely associated with the Whigs, while the Tories remained faithful to their sack and claret.

Fruit cordials and fruit, flower and herb wines were made in the still-room. As sugar became cheaper and more plentiful, wines were made by directly fermenting garden fruits; before this, the juice of the fruit had been simply added to grape wine. At Kingston Lacy, '24 bushels of elderberys' were bought in October 1696 for Margaret Bankes to make wine. In July she also paid '2s for 6 pound of cherrys and 5s for 2 gallons of brandy' and '4s for 12 pound of black cherrys and 12s 6d for 10 quarts of brandy' to make cherry brandy.

Because of the high price of wine, there were many adulterated and artificial products on the market, and much smuggling. To curb the latter, the government encouraged consumption of home-produced corn spirit and spirits of old cider, wine and fermented fruit, or 'aquavitae', already enjoying a brisk trade in London in the early part of the century. This was to lead to a serious social problem in the next century.

However, the greatest revolution in the drinking habits of Britain was brought about by three non-alcoholic beverages – coffee, chocolate and tea. All three were introduced in about the middle of the 17th century, initially as great luxuries, but with widening consumption as prices fell.

For some years, British travellers in the Middle East had spoken of a Turkish drink, 'Coffa, which is a blacke Kind of drinke made of a Kind of Pulse like Pease, called

Coaus'. So perhaps it was curiosity that persuaded gentlemen to visit the new coffee-houses that sprang up in towns everywhere. One of the earliest of these seems to have been in Oxford, for the diarist Anthony à Wood tells us that in 1650: 'Jacob, a Jew, opened a Coffrey house at the Angel, in the parish of St. Peter in the East Oxon, there it was, by some who delighted in novelties, drank.'

The first London coffee-house was opened in St Michael's Alley, Cornhill in 1652 by Daniel Edwards, a Turkey merchant, who launched a 'strong bitter brew' upon a willing public. During the reign of Charles II they multiplied so rapidly in London that by 1675 the city was said to have three thousand coffee-houses. Misson recommended them as pleasant places in which to while away an hour or two: 'You have all Manner of news there: You have a good Fire, which you may sit by as long as you please: You have a Dish of Coffee; you have your friends for the Transaction of Business, and all for a Penny, if you don't care to spend more.' As in the East, coffee-houses had an all-male clientele, who enjoyed the club-like atmosphere where, as Pepys put it, a man could 'toss his mind'. They became the favourite meeting-places of poets, writers, merchants and politicians and proved such hot-beds of political squabbles, that Charles II tried to suppress them in 1675: 'because the multitude of Coffee-Houses lately set up and kept within this Kingdom and the great resort of the idle and dissipated persons in them, having produced very evil and dangerous effects.' But the law suppressing them evoked such strong feelings that it was never enforced: the only people in favour were vintners, who declared that coffee caused the palsy and was a violent enemy to the nerves.

The new drink spread from the coffee-houses to the homes of the gentry, and soon no household of any standing could afford to be without, although coffee remained expensive. The Brownlow family at Belton bought coffee in very small quantities for several years after 1670, but by 1690, Lady Alice was ordering 2 lb of 'coffee berrys' for 8s and a coffee-mill. Individual members of the family had their own personal coffee pots with long spouts and conical covers and china dishes from which to drink the beverage, and coffee and chocolate succeeded ale and beer as their breakfast drinks.

Chocolate was brought to Britain in 1656, this time from the New World. By 1657 an enterprising Frenchman, who owned a house in Queen's Head Alley in Bishopsgate, London, was advertising 'an excellent West India drink called chocolate to be sold, where you may have it ready at any time, and also unmade at reasonable rates'. His blocks of chocolate, which had to be grated to make into a drink, sold for 10 to 15s a pound, so it was only the rich who could afford this exotic brew. Sir Richard Myddelton's new bride must have been exceedingly fond of the drink: a carrier brought 'a box of Chocholett for my Lady weighing 37 pounds' to Chirk Castle on 16 June 1686. It was thought to be very nourishing and good for the health and by the end of the century it was 'much used in England as Diet and Phisick with the Gentry'. Pepys wrote in his diary for 24 April 1661, the day after Charles II's coronation, which he had obviously celebrated merrily: 'Waked in the morning with my head in a sad taking thro' last night's drink, which I am sorry for. So rose and went out [to a chocolate or coffee house] with Mr. Creed to drink our morning draught, which he did give me in chocolate to settle my stomach.'

Like both coffee and tea, all chocolate brewed for sale was made subject to an excise duty in 1660, of 18d a gallon, it being customary, at first, to prepare all three drinks in large quantities and draw them off when ordered, like ale. Early versions of drinking chocolate resembled wine caudle; chocolate was boiled with claret, thickened with

An engraving from the 1690s showing a chocolate party. Chocolate was made in special pots, milled with a 'molinquet' or wooden stick to bring up the froth, and drunk from dainty cups.

egg yolks and sweetened to taste. Perfumed chocolate was popular and even more expensive. To prepare it, chocolate was boiled for several hours with white sugar, cinnamon, pepper, cloves, aniseed, almonds, orange-flower water and vanilla straws, then milk and eggs were beaten into it. Chocolate was made in special pots and drunk from pretty cups in silver holders in the Spanish manner. Chocolate first appears in the accounts of Kingston Lacy in 1693: 'paid for a pound of chocolett 5s; four blue and white chocolate cups and one copper chocolate-pot.' Chocolate-pots were similar to coffee-pots but had removable coves in the lid for stirring and lips rather than spouts.

Tea was introduced about the same time as coffee. It was first advertised in a London journal of about 1660 by Thomas Garway, a coffee-house owner: 'That excellent and by all Physitians approved China drink called by the Chineans *Tcha*, by other nations Tay alias Tee.' Although tea had occasionally been sold in England from as early as 1635, Mr Garway was the first to make regular sales and brew it on the premises. The first supplies were brought from China by the Dutch East Indian merchants and sold in England in the 1660s for the remarkable price of £4 a pound, but the price dropped to around £2 in the next ten years. Further reductions occurred when Britain's own East India Company began to bring home supplies by the end of the century, but it was still very expensive. At first, excise duty was payable on liquid tea as supplied at coffee-houses – 18d a gallon in 1660, raised to 2s in 1670. But, by 1680, enough leaf tea was being bought privately for the duty to be changed to 5s a pound, irrespective of price or quality. For a long time, tea was known as 'Bohea' from 'Thea Bohea' or black shrub. 'Thea Viridis', or green shrub, was simply unripe tea, sold alongside black tea. Both were served in the Chinese fashion – very weak and without milk, although sometimes sugar was added.

Despite the high cost of the leaf, the tea-drinking habit gathered momentum. Its domestic success was ensured with the marriage of the Portuguese princess Catherine of Braganza to Charles II in 1662. Already familiar with tea and the ritual of its preparation she encouraged tea-drinking at court. Wives of courtiers and friends, like the Duchess of Lauderdale at Ham, proceeded to give teas after the newest and most elegant continental manner; the well-to-do ladies of the realm soon followed. Thus, seven years after Pepys drank his first cup of tea, Mrs Pepys enjoyed a similar experience on 28 June 1667: 'By coach home and found my wife making tea; a drink Mr Pelling, the potticary [apothecary], tells her is good for her cold and defluxions.'

Exotic Foods

The apothecary sold a wide range of foodstuffs along with the grocer, the confectioner and the comfit-maker, including spices, banquetting-stuffe, rice and dried fruit. By 1651, Dutch merchants had the virtual monopoly on cloves, nutmegs, mace and cinnamon, but towards the end of the century, the British East India Company at last made some headway. The 17th-century housewife gained new cooking spices, like allspice or Jamaica pepper from the West Indies. Mixed spice powders were still made up, known as 'kitchen pepper', but generally there was a gradual scaling down in the use of spices from the Far East, apart from sugar, with the continued use of sharp fruits to season meat and fish dishes. On 8 April 1694, Margaret Bankes of Kingston Lacy records purchases of spices: 'paid for a quarter of a hundred of brown sugar 15s 2d; for 4 ounces of nutmegs 2s; for 4 ounces of cloaves and mace 3s; for 4 ounces of simmon

Chinamen blending and tasting tea, from an early 18th-century coromandel lacquered screen at Felbrigg Hall, Norfolk.

Sugar-making in the West Indies in the late 17th century. The cane was crushed in a mill between rollers, and the resulting liquor was run off into coppers to be boiled and allowed to crystallise. This engraving is taken from the English edition of Pierre Pomet's *A Compleat History of Druggs*.

[cinnamon] 2s 8d; for a pound of white pepper 2s; and for half a pound of alspice 1s.'

From the 1640s when the English colonists in the West Indies turned their land over to sugar cane, sugar became much more plentiful and cheaper. It was now refined at a number of British ports to varying degrees of whiteness and purity with brown sugar the cheapest. By the end of the 17th century, despite increased import duties, sugar consumption was up to a yearly 4 lb a head, a huge amount when one remembers most people, especially in Wales and Scotland, still met their craving for sweetened food mainly with honey, dried fruits and other fruits and vegetables rich in natural sugars.

An interesting glimpse into the range of foods provided by an apothecary is shown by the ingredients for the banquet served at the funeral of the second Sir Thomas Myddelton in 1666, purchased from Chester: '2 pounds of coloured comfeits for 5s 4d; and for coloured round wafers 4s 8d; for sheete wafers 6d, and red Sanders 6d, a pound of carroway comfeits 18d; perfumed amber comfeits 2s, cloves to burne 10d [to make mulled wine].' Another apothecary in Wrexham supplied '3 ounces of Gum Dragon 16d, 6 graines of musk 2s, 3 lookes [books] of gould for the Cookes 7s 6d, 3 ounces of Amber Comfeitts 18d; halfe a pound of Bisketts comfeits 16d, one pound of Cutchin Eeele 12d [cochineal, derived from the bodies of a coccus insect from Mexico and the West Indies, which replaced sanders and alkanet as a red colouring used in the preparation of banquetting stuffe]; saffron 18d, and 3 booke of large silver 30d [silver leaf for decorating banquetting stuffe].' Further supplies of almond cake, 'naple biskett', and 'six loaves of sugar' were bought from a confectioner for the funeral.

A 17th-century Spanish painted sign for a confectioner. Banqueting stuff could be bought already prepared from the confectioners in large towns.

160

II

Early in the 17th century a nobleman's household, like the 3rd Earl of Dorset's, who lived in great state at Knole, could still consist of at least 100 dependants bound by family ties and fulfilling largely ceremonial functions. As in medieval and Tudor times the clerk of the kitchen was responsible for the cooks and provisions. The cook, in his all-male kitchen, was helped by a collection of scullions and turnspits, some of whom were paid very low wages, while other little boys received no wages but were fed and given presents of clothing. Low wages could be supplemented by 'vails' (from the Latin *vale*, farewells) or tips from visiting gentry. At his departure on 6 July 1627 from Lord St John's Bedfordshire seat of Melchbourne, where he and his family had been staying for a fortnight, Sir John Hobart of Blickling generously handed out over £4 in tips to the servants, including the butler, the pantler, the clerk of the kitchen, four cooks and the usher of the great chamber.

With the Civil War, this social situation changed radically. A comparatively nouveau riche family, like the Brownlows of Belton, or the Bankes of Kingston Lacy had no need of a vast household like the Earl of Dorset. Even the aristocratic Duke and Duchess of Lauderdale employed only about 20 servants at Ham in the 1670s: the number fluctuated according to the time of the year and whether the family was in residence. When the Duke and Duchess were away, a skeleton staff was left in charge on 'board wages' (provided with bed and board only). Extra help in the kitchen was often bought in when entertaining special guests. The Chirk Castle accounts record payment in December 1678 to 'Edward Burges, the cooke, for a fortnight he was assistinge the cooke, my Lord Cholmondeley beinge then at the Castle', and again, to the same Edward Burges 'that came to the Castle against the Duke of Beaufort his coming there'. In the larger cities, the cooks were organised as a company who enjoyed a monopoly in dressing 'any manner of meat'.

In these smaller households, there were fewer gentlemen servants and more women, with a consequent decline in status. Social position was now measured by distinction and seclusion from the lower orders. Roger North, who wrote a treatise on house planning at the end of the 17th century, recommended servants 'should never publicly appear in passing to and from for their occasions', but should keep out of sight, by not, for instance, using the main staircase. Instead, they had their own backstairs. Belton has two staircases at either end of the house rising the whole height of the building from the domestic offices in the basement to the servants' garret bedrooms, as well as a main staircase between the two principal floors only. Servants no longer bedded down in the hall or outside their master's door, or in a truckle bed at his feet.

Often the behaviour of the servants reflected their changing status. The Verneys of Claydon expected and had always received faithful service from those they employed, so it is hardly surprising that Sir John wrote angrily to his steward in 1699 concerning the behaviour of Perry, the footboy: 'Yesterday Perry stayed all the morning out on a small arrant [errand] onely to fetch 3 or 4 Quarts of milk' and being 'half Drunck' ran away, although Sir John had 'no strength too beate him'. Three years later, Lady Verney had to refuse Sir John's invitation to meet him in Bath because of concern over the servants' behaviour at Claydon during her absence: 'The Cook will be drunk, if I

This double portrait of John Maitland, Duke of Lauderdale (1616–82), and his Duchess (*c*.1626–1698?) by Sir Peter Lely hung over the high table in the great dining-room at Ham House, Surrey, in the 1670s.

take out Smith [the butler] and leave the key with Coleman. and then the Charge of Plaite hee has in his keeping, I don't think fitt hee should be out.'

As the century progressed, the social standing of cooks improved, particularly that of the professional elite in the service of members of the upper classes, who could command high wages. A cook in a large house received about £4 a year in 1630, but at Ham in the 1670s John Blangy, the cook, was highly paid at £20 a year (the same wage as the steward), while the housekeeper, who now became a regular member of large households but was ranked low in the hierarchy, earned only £8 and the butler £6. Although large kitchens were still the territory of men, women were usually in charge of the dairy and the still-room and were appearing in the kitchen in menial capacities. John Blangy had two kitchen maids, Mary Trever and Grace Phyllipps, to help him in the kitchen and there was also a dairymaid and a scullerymaid earning £3 10s a year. Pepys engaged a new cookmaid at £4 a year in 1663: 'The first time I ever did give so much', he says. But she proved her worth for a week later he entertained some friends and was:

> very merry at, before, and after dinner, and for the more that my dinner was great, and most neatly dressed by our own only maid. We had a fricasée of rabbit and some chickens, a leg of mutton boiled, three carps in a dish, a great dish of a side of lamb, a dish of roasted pigeons, a dish of four lobsters, three tarts, a lamprey pie (a most rare pie) a dish of anchovies, good wine of several sorts, and all things mighty noble, and to my great content.

As early as 1577, William Harrison in his *Description of England* had complained of the excessively various and abundant diet of 'the nobility of England (whose cooks are for the most part musical-headed Frenchmen and strangers)'. Yet in the early part of the 17th century there was still only slight evidence of the 'courtly' style of cuisine being developed in France and Italy that was soon to spread to England. In 1615, Gervase Markham began *The English Hus-wife* by describing the virtues of a good housewife which included serving home-produced plain food as the English understood it rather than pretentious foreign fare: 'let her diet be wholesome and cleanly prepared ... and cooked with care and diligence; let it be rather to satisfy nature than our affections, and apter to kill hunger than revive new appetites; let it proceed more from the provision of her own yard than the furniture of the markets.' The recipes, for the most part, were of the traditional English country cooking type, including lots of pies, puddings and conserves, and were reproduced for the tables of the gentry, the nobility and probably even of the English court.

With the Restoration of the Stuart monarchy in 1660, however, the style of the French court, where Charles II and his brother James, Duke of York had spent much of their exile, became the fashion amongst the wealthy. No great establishment was complete without a Frenchman presiding over its kitchen, and many English noblemen sent their cooks across the Channel to be trained. Contemporary foreign visitors wrote disparagingly of the food of those who did not: 'The English', observed Sorbetière, a French visitor, in 1663, 'are not very dainty and the greatest lords' tables, who do not keep French cooks, are covered only with large dishes of meat. They are strangers to bisks and pottage ... Their pastry is coarse and ill-baked, their stewed fruits and confectionery ware cannot be eat.' Thirty years later Misson added 'Generally speaking, the English Tables are not delicately served. There are some Noblemen who have both French and English cooks and these eat after the French Manner, but among

THE Accomplisht Cook,

OR THE

ART & MYSTERY

OF

COOKERY.

Wherein the whole A R T is revealed in a more easie and perfect Method, than hath been publisht in any language.

Expert and ready Ways for the Dressing of all Sorts of FLESH, FOWL, and FISH, with variety of SAUCES proper for each of them; and how to raise all manner of *Pastes*; the best Directions for all sorts of *Kickshaws*, also the *Terms* of CARVING and SEWING.

An exact account of all *Dishes* for all *Seasons* of the Year, with other *A-la-mode Curiosities*

The Fifth Edition, with large Additions throughout the whole work: besides two hundred Figures of several Forms for all manner of bak'd Meats, (either Flesh, or Fish) as, Pyes Tarts, Custards; Cheesecakes, and Florentines, placed in Tables, and directed to the Pages they appertain to.

Approved by the fifty five Years Experience and Industry of *ROBERT MAY*, in his Attendance on several Persons of great Honour.

London, Printed for *Obadiah Blagrave* at the *Bear* and *Star* in St. *Pauls Church-Yard*, 1685.

What wouldst thou view but in one face all hospitalitie, the race of those that for the Gusto stand, whose tables a whole Ark comand of Natures plentie wouldst thou see this sight. peruse Mais booke 'tis hee

The title page and frontispiece to *The Accomplisht Cook*, 1685 edition, by Robert May, one of a small number of works by English cooks in the 'courtly genre', addressed primarily to other professionals rather than to housewives.

the Middling Sort of People they have 10 or 12 sorts of common meats which infallibly take their turn at their Tables and two Dishes are their Dinners, a Pudding for instance and a fine Piece of Roast Beef.'

Immediately upon Charles II's return, Pepys's patron, the Earl of Sandwich, was 'very high [elated] how he would have a French cooke'. A few months later, Pepys learned the French manner of drinking healths; he ate 'a fine French dinner'; and on another occasion his wife served him 'a pleasant French fricassé of Veale for dinner'. Several of the most notable French books were translated into English and a small number of works by English cooks in the 'courtly genre' were published, usually written by professional chefs and addressed primarily to other professional chefs rather than to housewives. One example is Robert May's *The Accomplisht Cook* of 1660. Yet, even in these, the recipes are more like variations on traditional English cookery than adaptations to the French models: the old pies and joints of meat remained the centre of the English meal, whereas in France attention was focused on the delicate made dishes.

Great care was now taken in planning the kitchen facilities. In addition to providing ample work space, fireplaces and ovens, there were extensive stores for food, drink, fuel and kitchen equipment, copious supplies of water, good drainage and means of waste disposal, all within fairly easy reach of the dining-room. One of the 'rules of building' most strongly urged by the architect Roger Pratt, who designed Kingston Lacy for Sir Ralph Bankes from 1663 to 1665, was that the ground floor should be raised and approached by a flight of steps, not only to add 'height and majesty' to the house, but also to supply 'a very good storey' below for the domestic offices. As a result, the kitchen was usually a large, airy, well-lit room, as at Ham House. The walls and ceilings were plastered and whitewashed and the ceiling was much lower that those of the earlier kitchens. Although the windows 'below stairs' and in the attic bedrooms were smaller

Sir Roger Pratt's drawing of the front elevation for Kingston Lacy, Dorset, which he designed for Sir Ralph Bankes in the 1660s. One of the 'rules of building' most strongly urged by Pratt was that the ground floor should be raised and approached by a flight of steps to add 'height and majesty' and to supply 'a very good storey' below for the domestic offices.

The kitchen at Ham House, Surrey. Activity in the 17th-century kitchen still centred around the great arched fireplace, which would be fired with coal in a wealthy household like Ham. Here, an advanced hob grate was used, with a moveable side to allow the cook to make up the size of fire required. Equally advanced was the mechanical jack to turn the spits. The charcoal stewing stove under the window allowed noxious fumes to escape.

than those in the family apartments, as can be clearly seen at Ham, they were still larger then before, to give more light for working. Additional light was still provided, when needed, by rushlight or tallow candles. Unhygienic rushes, harbouring dirt and rubbish, were a thing of the past and the stone floor would be thickly strewn with sand, frequently replaced. Strips of rush matting, strategically placed in front of main working areas, provided a little comfort.

Round the walls of the kitchen were built wooden cupboards and shelves for storing tableware, utensils and equipment for preparing food. The dresser make its appearance in the 17th century: at first, it consisted of only a flat wooden board, or table, fixed to the wall with shelves above; food was prepared, or 'dressed' on the dresser board, covered with a clean white dresser cloth. The dresser and shelves to the right of the door of the kitchen at Ham date from the 1670s when the kitchen was modernised by the Duke and Duchess of Lauderdale: there were '4 dresser boards' at this time. In later Stuart times, the dresser board, the shelves above and some cupboards below, were united to become one piece of furniture – the dresser – which often reached the ceiling. The back part was boarded and in the upper part, shelves of different widths were graded to suit dishes and platters of different sizes, while below the flat worktop were capacious cupboards for the storage of food and linen.

Activity in the 17th-century kitchen still centred around the great broad-arched fireplace. Here a great log fire supported on firedogs or andirons provided all the heat necessary for boiling, roasting and grilling. Wood was still the fuel in general use, but coal was frequently used for both cooking and heating in wealthy households like Ham in the second half of the century, particularly in London.

The replacement of wood by coal meant a change in the construction of the fireplace, since it was almost impossible to kindle coal on a flat hearth. Andirons were found unsuitable and were replaced by various types of brazier or fire basket raised above the hearth to allow an up-draught. The ingenious Sir Hugh Platt had already, in 1594, introduced a grate with brick sides and back, but it was a Frenchman, Louis Savot, who in 1624 suggested that coal should be burned on a raised perforated plate. The dog-grate as seen in the kitchen fireplace of East Riddlesden was the most common: it comprised a free-standing wrought-iron basket raised on four legs and placed in the centre of the hearthstone, with a fireback behind.

The kitchen at Ham boasted an iron hob-grate with a moveable 'cheek', or side, allowing the cook to make up the size of coal fire required. Few other kitchens at this time were furnished with such an advanced grate, which came into general use in the next century. Equally advanced was the mechanical jack which turned the spits. The jack was wound up using a handle with a heavy weight on a cord around a drum. The gradual descent of the weight, controlled by the balance wheel, turned cog-wheels which kept the spit, loaded with meat, poultry or fish, revolving for up to 25 minutes. In less sophisticated households spits turned by children or dogs continued in use. All roasting at Townend, for instance, took place in front of the open fire in the fire house, where the household also ate. The andirons and roasting spit remain, although a Victorian cast-iron grate now stands in the original open flagged hearth, once covered by a large stone chimney-hood projecting into the room.

To roast in front of a hob-grate or dog-grate, the spits were supported by hooks on a pair of cobirons, stands or racks with the dripping pan standing between to catch the juices. In 1615 Gervase Markham published comprehensive advice on successful

The 17th-century oak spice cupboard in the cook's closet at Calke Abbey, Derbyshire, probably removed from an earlier kitchen. Blue was often chosen for kitchens as it was believed to be the colour that repelled flies.

A mid-17th-century steel jack and wax jack holder from Cotehele, Cornwall.

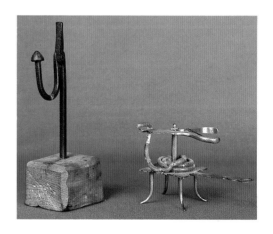

The Fat Kitchen by Jan Steen, showing fresh meat, bacon, poultry and game hanging from hooks and game birds in a rack. The baskets are used to transport birds from market. Birds are being spit-roasted over the open fire, with a dripping-pan beneath to catch the fat and juices. The table is laid with a cloth, pewter plates and spoons, but each diner carries his own knife at his waist.

roasting in *The English Hus-wife*: 'For the good handling of meat', he said, 'the spits and cobirons are to be kept clean and scoured; the meat neatly picked and washed and firmly spitted so that it did not shrink from the spit or fail to turn with it'. Many joints, small animals, birds and fish were stuffed before roasting and served with a wide range of pungent sauces, like the sugared and spiced wine and vinegar sauce thickened with breadcrumbs that was served with venison. But as the quality of meat improved, sauces became simpler.

The kitchen at Ham had '1 fire fork, 2 Gridirons and 1 toasting iron' for toasting, grilling or boiling over the fire, or over the charcoal stove. Slices of bread, pieces of fish and bacon could be toasted on a 'fire fork' or toasting iron: there was a number of designs for the latter, which was basically a stand with pronged attachments fixed at different levels. Gridirons were used to grill or broil steaks of beef, mutton, lamb or veal: these were established dishes in medieval times which had become very popular in the 16th and 17th centuries under the name of 'carbonadoes'. The steak was cut on both sides with the back of a knife to tenderise it, or cooked, before being broiled: 'For there is no meat either boiled or roasted whatever, but may afterwards be broiled,' says Markham. Small fish and birds, sausages, black and white puddings and Bologna or Polony smoked sausage could also be broiled. The vertical broiling iron was an early prototype of the 18th-century hastener or roasting screen. It occurs in some 17th-century inventories, but was far less common for roasting than the spit. Wafering irons were still used to cook sweet, crisp patterned biscuits and were amongst the utensils taken by early settlers to America. In due course they became waffle irons and interestingly have returned to England in this form. The salamander still stood by the fire for browning pastry and custards.

A kitchen interior by Cornelis Lelienbergh, showing utensils typical of the period: brass pestle and mortar, brass pans, iron cauldrons and griddle, earthenware jugs, strainers and pots, baskets for storage, wooden tubs, bellows, skimmers and cutlery.

A more efficient chimney crane was developed in the 17th century, which could raise or lower the level of pots and cauldrons over the fire and also move them along the bar towards, or away, from the centre of the heat source. Some examples were plain workman-like contrivances, others were decorative. Each customer ordered a design from his local blacksmith according to his taste, needs and pocket. The large chimney crane and adjustable pothooks, known locally as 'ratten-crooks', overhanging the 19th-century range in the kitchen at Townend are 17th-century in design. Chains and adjustable pothooks hanging from iron bars in the chimney were used to suspend iron or brass cauldrons or kettles over the fire.

The cauldron was still essential for boiling all the hot water needed, but remained the most economical and simple way of cooking a complete meal in a single container, ideal for a household like the Brownes of Townend. Joints of meat could be plunged into boiling water, together with dumplings, vegetables in net bags, and puddings, either tied up in cloths ('pudding-pokes') or floating in wooden bowls. A 'skummer', a perforated saucer of brass or iron mounted at the end of a long handle, was used to scoop out the food and to skim off any scum. The cauldron had to be covered with a wooden lid to stop soot falling down the chimney into it. Sometimes, poultry, game or small quantities of meat could be placed with herbs and root vegetables in a sealed earthenware or metal pot, and immersed in the cauldron for a few hours to make the richly flavoured 'daubes' and 'casseroles' adopted from France in the latter part of the century. The more delicately flavoured soups were also made in this way. A similar principle was employed in one of the most ingenious culinary inventions of this period, the pressure cooker or 'digester', invented in 1660 by Denys Papin, a French physicist living in London. He discovered that most foodstuffs could be efficiently cooked in a totally sealed vessel, saving time and fuel. Papin's digester was a cast-iron saucepan with a light lid bearing a valve which was forced to open when the steam pressure was too high. It was originally made for obtaining gelatine from bones and was so efficient that when Pepys ate a meal cooked in it, he remarked with wonder that the bones were rendered as soft as butter. Centuries were to pass before pressure-cooking finally became an everyday method of cooking.

Elaborate made dishes like 'olios' from Spain, and 'bisks' from France (from *bisque*, a rich shellfish soup), so popular with the gentry and those of middling rank after the Restoration, were also cooked in pots suspended above the fire. Olios contained a large number of separate ingredients: wild and tame fowl of different types, pieces of pork, veal, lamb and bacon, with sweetbreads, palates and other ingredients which were piled up on the serving dish to form a magnificent pyramid. Part of the broth was poured over the pyramid; the rest was strained and offered separately in a silver cup, or china basin. To make bisks, the larger fleshmeats were stewed to make broth, then pigeons or other small birds were stewed in the resulting broth. Bisks could also be made of fish, especially crustaceans. The fricassées and hashes of the late 16th century continued in favour, prepared from fresh meat or game, either sliced or whole if small, like rabbits and hares. The introduction of the table fork into England in 1611 encouraged the popularity of these Continental dishes; food didn't have to be mashed and 'brayed' for eating with a spoon.

Puddings could be cooked either in the cauldron, or in metal pots over the fire. The future of the boiled suet pudding as one of England's national dishes was assured only with the development of the pudding-cloth, which received one of its earliest mentions in a recipe of 1617 for 'Cambridge pudding', made with suet, breadcrumbs, flour, dried fruit, sugar and eggs; it was also called 'college pudding' because it was served to the students in their college halls. Different regions of the country developed their own specialities, but a uniting factor was that they were almost all rich in fat and carbohydrates to keep out the cold and in sugar and fruit to build up energy: the Englishman's pudding filled his stomach and satisfied his appetite. Foreigners, like Monsieur Misson, also appreciated it: 'They [the English] bake them in an oven, they boil them with meat, they make them fifty several ways: BLESSED BE HE THAT INVENTED PUDDING, for it is a manna that hits the palates of all sorts of people ... Ah, what an excellent thing is an English pudding! To come in pudding-time, is as much as to say, to come in the most lucky moment in the world.'

A large establishment like Ham, where entertainment on a lavish scale was expected, would usually have a charcoal or stewing stove. It was usually built against a wall, often being placed close to a window to ensure adequate ventilation from the noxious fumes produced by the burning charcoal. Once the fire-baskets or 'chaffing dishes' had been filled with glowing charcoal, they gave a clean and easily controlled heat, providing the cook with a very useful facility for preparing delicate soups, made dishes like ragôuts, fricassées, hashes, sauces, and for frying omelettes, pancakes and fritters. Iron trivets, or briggs, were used to support saucepans, frying-pans and stewpans over the fire-baskets, and extra fuel was stored underneath them. The stewing stove was very much a French import and never became very popular outside grand establishments in the 17th century.

In other houses, the chafing dish was still used to heat a small quantity of food gently, or to cook delicate sauces. It was also used for keeping dishes warm on their long

Right: An engraving of a Parisian dining-room of the 1630s, showing a frying-pan over an open fire. A salamander is being used to brown the surface of the food.

Ici, viennent à la haste
Les Enfans de Mardy gras
Mettre la main à la paste.
S'escriment à tour de bras.

La Cuisine les attire,
Soit par coustume, ou par jeu;
Et les bignets les font rire,
Tandis qu'ils sont pres du feu.

L'HYVER

Monsieur, dict vne Maistresse,
Si vous touchez mon tetin,
Ie repandray de la graisse
Sur vostre habit de fatin.

Mais cette picoterie
Se termine incontinent,
Et toute leur raillerie
Est de Caresme-prenant.

Below: This photograph was taken at Rook Howe Meeting House, Rusland in Cumbria, in 1901, but illustrates a method of making bread that goes back through the centuries. Houses without ovens could bake a loaf of barley or rye bread, a pie or a large cake, in an iron pan or griddle covered with a lid, hanging over the open fire, or standing on the hearth with hot ashes or peat piled around it.

journey to the dining-room and for the preparation of snacks outside the kitchen. Smaller quantities of food and sauces could also be cooked in saucepans supported over the fire on an iron brigg bridging the topmost firebars, on a tall trivet standing in front of the fire, or in three-legged posnets standing in the embers of the open fire.

The sauce was an important part of the popular French-style dishes. Towards the end of the 17th century, it took on a new consistency, for French cooks, rather than using breadcrumbs or egg yolks, had begun to thicken their ragôuts with a liaison of flour and lard or butter (*roux*), fried together, and then combined with a little broth. The flour and butter liaison, called at first 'fried flour', came into universal use as a thickener, not only for stews and made dishes, but for sauces to accompany meat, fish and vegetables. At the same period there was a proliferation of thinner sauces based on gravy, squeezed from half-roasted meat, wine, verjuice, orange or lemon juice, or a combination of some of these, with capers, herbs, fruit and spices added.

Methods of baking in the 17th century were regional. Cumbrian Townend did not have an oven until the 19th century; the Brownes would have used an iron bakestone (girdle or griddle) to bake their clapbread, and oat or barley bannocks. The bakestone was heated up over the fire in the kitchen, while oatmeal was mixed with water, buttermilk and salt to make a stiff dough, then shaped on a riddle-board and rolled out to wafer fineness, by a ridged rolling pin. The ridges left by the roller enabled air to pass under the oatcakes, making them lighter. An example of a metal oatcake roller can be seen in the kitchen of East Riddlesden. Each oatcake was baked slowly and gently on the

bakestone until 'they were very pale when done, more a matter of drying than baking'. The traditional method of finishing the oatcakes was to toast them on a cake stool, a wooden easel which supported them in front of the fire. Once cooked, they were stored in a cupboard near the fire as at Townend, and were served at every meal in a special wickerwork basket.

Oatcakes were very important as the staple diet of the working population in northern England. The oats had to be ground into meal at the local mill, then stored in a meal ark, or chest in the kitchen, or in a loft above the kitchen, as at Townend. The most notable piece of furniture in the kitchen at East Riddlesden is the 'Great Arke', a large oak chest, or kist, with a sloping lid, used for storing grain or meal. Possibly this chest once stood with others in the entrance chamber where the air circulating from below would have kept its contents dry.

At Townend and other houses without ovens, cakes, buns, biscuits, puddings and bread continued to be baked in an overturned iron pot if the bakestone was not suitable; alternatively it was covered with a metal lid and hot embers of burning peat or wood were piled around it to maintain the heat. In some remote areas of Wales, Ireland, Cornwall, Scotland and the north of England, baking continued to be done in this way until this century.

The beehive oven was still used for baking in wealthier households, either set into the thickness of one of the walls of the kitchen, or in a separate bakehouse as at Ham, which had two brick ovens with metal doors. The equipment and methods used in baking bread, one of the most important tasks in any household, were clearly described in Randle Holme's *Academy of Armory* of 1688. The baker first transferred a batch of flour from the storage chest or ark into a wooden kneading-trough, where it was blended with warm water, salt or spices and yeast that had been made by dissolving a piece of old sour dough in water. The soft dough was then removed from the trough with a dough-scraper and transferred to the 'brake', a strong table fitted with a long

Above left: The kitchen at East Riddlesden, showing the 'Great Arke', a large oak chest or kist, used for storing grain or meal. It possibly once stood in the entrance chamber of the house.

Above: To make oatcakes, the dough was shaped on a riddle-board and, before baking, rolled out to wafer fineness with a ridged rolling pin, like this 17th-century example in the kitchen at East Riddlesden, Yorkshire.

Right: An engraving by Abraham Bosse of baking pastry. The beehive oven was still used in wealthier households, either set into the wall of the kitchen or in a separate bakehouse. After the bread, rich pies, cheesecakes and pasties were baked as the oven cooled.

Below: The engraved title-page of Hannah Woolley's *The Accomplisht Lady's Delight*, published in 1685, showing candying and distilling above, baking pies in the bread oven and roasting and boiling over the open fire below.

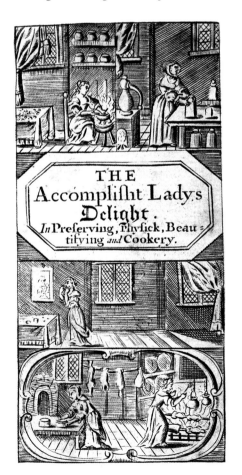

hinged roller with which the dough was kneaded until ready for moulding. On the moulding table, a dough knife, or 'pairing shovel', was used to divide the dough, so that it could be weighed and moulded into loaves, or rolls. Then the bread was baked in a hot oven. After the bread had been removed with a peel, rich pies, patties, pastries, cheesecakes and 'pudding pies' [puddings baked in a pastry case], were baked as the oven cooled. As the oven cooled further, a variety of puddings could be baked slowly in specially turned wooden dishes: rich rice puddings including spices, rose-water, egg yolks, marrow and ambergris; 'whitepots' made with cream, eggs, breadcrumbs or rice, dried fruits and spices; and custards.

Great cakes containing enormous quantities of dried fruit or caraway comfits and raised with ale barm were also baked in the cooling bread oven. At first they were laid on buttered papers, but by the end of the century the tin hoop had come into use to hold a cake in shape and help it to rise evenly. After baking, these large cakes were frosted over with beaten egg white, rose-water and sugar, then put back in the oven (see recipe, p.179). As baking skills developed, areas acquired a reputation for their own local specialities: Banbury cake, Eccles cakes, Shrewsbury cakes and Chorley cakes.

The still-house was the province of the mistress of the house, where, with the help of her maids, she concocted medicines and perfumes, and preserves and sweetmeats for the banquet course, using recipes handed down to her from her mother, collected from friends or taken from contemporary cookery books. As the range of new dishes, new foods and new methods of cookery began to expand, the mistress of the house had to acquire the appropriate recipes, which might be exchanged at dinner and supper parties during the season in London, or while visiting the country houses of friends and neighbours. The everyday processes such as bread-making and roasting were rarely recorded in recipe form because they were already well known, whereas the richer and more elaborate dishes were not in regular use and so were carefully noted down in manuscript books: cooking was becoming a fashionable hobby.

To roast a Pike

'Take your pike and rub him well with salt, then take forth his Gutts and cut out of his belly. Then take a good quantity of sweet herbs. If your Pike is large put in the greater quantity of all these things that are here named, a quantity of Garlicke, take some Anchovyse, and some butter and all sortes of spices beaten togeether, mix these and fill his belly full and for spike him on the spit, and that which spares of filling his belly, put it on a dish and a little wine, and baste him with it, then put all on the dish with him and send him up in that sauce, you may after put in a quantity of pickled Herrings.'

From a commonplace book of recipes, medicinal, domestic and culinary of 1699, belonging to Elizabeth Birkett from Townend in Cumbria.

Freshwater fish, including pike from nearby Lake Windermere, would have been abundant at Townend. Pike was roasted on a spit in front of the fire with a stuffing of butter, highly flavoured with herbs, garlic, spices, pickled oysters and anchovies in its belly, which was later served up as a sauce to accompany the fish at the first course of dinner.

To Rost Venison

'After you have washed your venison clear from the blood, stick it with cloves on the outside and lard it with mutton larde or porke larde, but mutton is the best. Then spit it and rost it by a socking [slow] fire. Take vinegar, bread crums and the gravy which comes from the venison and boyle them in a dishe, then season it with sugare, cinamon, ginger and salt, and serve the venison upon the sauce.'

Erddig MS 1203, c.1685

The venison eaten at Erddig came from the deer park at Chirk Castle. Venison was highly prized by the gentry in the 17th century and brought social cachet to anyone able to offer it to guests. The roast venison of Stuart England was well larded, if lean, and stuck with cloves or sprigs of rosemary. A sugared and spiced wine and vinegar sauce, thickened with breadcrumbs, was commonly served with it.

Roast Venison with Cloves

3½–4½ lb (1.65–2 kg) haunch venison
6 oz (175 g) butter, softened
few whole cloves
1 oz (25 g) plain flour
sprigs of fresh rosemary to decorate

FOR THE MARINADE
½ pt (300 ml) red wine
1 carrot, peeled and sliced
1 medium onion, sliced
1 sprig of fresh thyme
1 bay leaf
pinch of ground cinnamon
pinch of ground ginger
1 teaspoon (5 ml) black peppercorns
2 tablespoons (30 ml) red wine vinegar
2 tablespoons (30 ml) olive oil
1 clove garlic
2 teaspoons (10 ml) soft brown sugar

The day before you intend to serve the venison, place all the marinade ingredients in a saucepan and bring to the boil. Boil for 20 minutes, then allow to cool.

Place the venison in a large china bowl, pour over the marinade and stand in a cool place for 24 hours. Turn the joint and spoon the marinade over it from time to time.

When ready to cook the venison, remove it from the marinade. Spread it with the softened butter, stick it with a few cloves and lay it in a roasting tin. Roast in a moderate oven (180°C, 350°F, gas mark 4) for 2–2¼ hours, basting several times during cooking.

Remove the venison from the roasting tin and keep warm on a serving dish. Pour off any surplus fat from the tin and stir the flour into the pan juices over a gentle heat. Strain the marinade liquor and add it very gradually to the roasting tin stirring continuously until smooth. Taste for seasoning and adjust as necessary, then simmer for 5 minutes. Serve the sauce separately. Decorate the venison with sprigs of rosemary. Serves 6.

Pike in Red Wine with Anchovy

2–3 lb (1–1.5 kg) pike, cleaned but not scaled
  (Note: cod may be used instead)
salt and freshly milled black pepper
1 sprig each parsley, thyme, marjoram and
  rosemary
blade of mace
1 garlic clove
a little flour
2 oz (50 g) anchovies
8 oz (225 g) melted butter
½ pt (300 ml) claret
fresh herbs to garnish

Sprinkle the inside of the fish with salt and pepper and add the fresh herbs, mace and garlic. Rub the fish all over with flour, salt and pepper and lay it in a buttered ovenproof dish. Place the anchovies with the melted butter and claret in a saucepan, heating gently to dissolve them. Pour over the fish and bake in a fairly hot oven (190°C, 375°F, gas mark 5) for about 35 minutes, basting from time to time. Test with a skewer; the flesh should move easily from the backbone.

Lift the fish very carefully on to a warm serving plate, remove the stuffing and discard. Strain the sauce, taste and adjust seasoning as necessary, then pour over the waiting fish. Garnish with fresh herbs. Serves 6.

A detail of fish from the carving attributed to Grinling Gibbons in the King's Room, Oxburgh Hall, Norfolk.

A Dish of Scotch Collops

'Take a Legg of Veale and slice it very thin, then beat them to make them tender, then shred a little Orange Pill very small, then mix a little thyme with them, and so season. Then frye them. When they are fryed very well, beat some yolks of Eggs, and a little wine, and so put them into the frying pan, and toss all together, and so dish them and lay some shred Lemon upon the Top and garnish your dish with what you think fit.'

From Elizabeth Birkett's commonplace book, 1699

Collops was the old word for slices of meat and this dish is again 'after the French fashion'. Wafer-thin slices of lamb, mutton or veal were rapidly stir-fried before being immersed in rich, piquant sauces of wine, spices and highly flavoured items such as garlic, onions and anchovies. The dish was often accompanied by forcemeat balls and was usually served at the first course of dinner.

The Balls for the Collops

'Take some lean veal and so mach pound them very well with a bit of Lemmond rind, a little onion and a few sweet herbs. Season it with pepper and salt, then put to it, two eggs and mix it up; roll it into little balls and fry them.'

From a bundle of 40 recipes written by various hands and thought to have belonged to Sarah Lowry Corry who married Galbraith Lowry of Castle Coole, Co. Fermanagh in 1733. Although the recipe is early 18th-century, it is very similar to 17th-century recipes for forcemeat balls.

Scotch Collops with Forcemeat Balls

2 lb (1 kg) frying steak
3 oz (75 g) butter
1 oz (25 g) flour
¾ pt (450 ml) beef stock
¼ pt (150 ml) dry white wine
1 teaspoon (5 ml) fresh thyme, chopped
thinly cut peel of 1 orange, preferably a Seville
a little shredded lemon peel to garnish

FOR THE FORCEMEAT BALLS

6 oz (175 g) fresh white breadcrumbs
2 oz (50 g) shredded suet
2 oz (50 g) lean veal, minced or bacon, finely
    chopped
1 tablespoon (15 ml) parsley, chopped
1 teaspoon (5 ml) fresh thyme, finely chopped
grated rind of ½ lemon
salt and freshly milled black pepper
1 large egg, beaten
1½ oz (40 g) butter or lard for frying

Although the original recipe uses veal, it is not easy to buy today, so I have used frying steak. Cut the steak into strips of about 5x2-ins (13x5-cms) and ¼-in (5-cm). Melt the butter in a large frying pan and fry the collops of meat for a few minutes on each side until evenly brown. Transfer to a large shallow saucepan or sauté-pan. Stir the flour into the frying-pan juices and cook for a few seconds, then add the stock gradually, stirring continuously, followed by the wine, the thyme and the orange peel. Bring just to the boil so that it thickens to the consistency of thin cream, then pour over the collops.

Prepare the forcemeat balls. Mix together the breadcrumbs, suet, veal or bacon, herbs, lemon rind, and seasoning, then stir the beaten egg into the mixture. Form into 12 small balls about 1-in (2.5-cm) in diameter. Melt the fat in a frying pan, and fry the forcemeat balls for about 6 minutes, or until brown. Add to the collops, season to taste, and cover. Simmer gently for about 10 minutes.

Arrange the collops and forcemeat balls on a warm serving dish and discard the orange peel. Pour over the sauce and serve immediately, garnished with a little shredded lemon peel. Serves 6.

A Compound Sallat

'Take a good quantity of blanched almonds cut coarsely. Then take as many raisins of the sun clean-wasshed and the stones pikt out; as many figs shred like the almonds; as many capers; twice as many olives, and as many currants wasshed clean as all of the rest. Add a good handful of small, tender leaves of red sage and spinach. Mix these all together with a good store of sugar. Lay them in the bottom on a dish, then put unto them vinegar and oyl. Then take oranges and lemons and cut them into thynne slices. Then with those slices cover the sallat over. Cover the oranges and lemons with thinne leaves of red cole-flower, then over these red leaves lay another course of old olives and the slices of well-pickled cucumbers together with the inward hearts of cabbage lettice cut in slices.'

From *The Accomplisht Cook*, Robert May, 1660

Seventeenth-century salads were dressed in patterns as complicated as the contemporary knot gardens. Gervase Markham advised laying out salads for a special occasion to look like bunches of flowers – 'some full blown, some half blown and some in the bud'. Compound salads were first-course dishes and were also popular for suppers.

A Spinage Tart

'Take a good quantity of spinage and boyle it, and when tis boyled, put it into a Cullender, that the water may run out from it, then shred it very small, and season it with good flow of sugar, and a pretty quantity of melted butter, then put in yolks of Eggs, and beat them altogether. Then make a sheet of paste very thin, and put it upon a Dish; so put your Tart Stuff upon it, then another sheet to cover it . . .'

From Elizabeth Birkett's commonplace book, 1699

To Make Pufe Past

'Take a quart of the finest flouer and the whites of three egges and the yolks of fore and a litel colde water and so make it in to past. Then drive it with a roling pine. A broad this put on smale peces of buter, then folde it over. Drive it thine againe. Doue this tenne times always folding the paste and puting buter betwene.'

Erddig MS 1203, *c*.1685

Sweet spinach tarts were popular in 17th-century England. Some included dried fruit, usually currants, almond macaroons, spices and rose-water, and many were iced with rose-water and sugar. They were served at the second course of dinner.

Spiced Spinach Tart

8 oz (225 g) shortcrust or puff pastry
2 lb (1 kg) fresh or frozen spinach
4 oz (125 g) butter
4 eggs
2 tablespoons (30 ml) rose-water
1 teaspoon (5 ml) sugar
good pinch of ground ginger
good pinch of grated nutmeg
salt and freshly milled black pepper

Line a 9-in (22-cm) loose-bottomed flan tin with the pastry and bake blind for 10–15 minutes.

Meanwhile, cook the spinach gently in just the water that clings to the leaves after washing. Drain very thoroughly by pressing out the juice in a colander and dry over a low heat. Melt the butter in another saucepan and add the spinach, stirring until it is mixed well. Beat the eggs with the rose-water, sugar, spices and seasoning. Remove the spinach from the heat and add the egg mixture, stirring well. Taste and adjust the seasoning as necessary. Tip the mixture into the pastry case and bake for 10 minutes in a fairly hot oven (200°C, 400°F, gas mark 6), then turn the heat down to 190°C, 375°F, gas mark 5, and bake for a further 20–30 minutes, or until the filling is well-risen, set and lightly browned on top. Serve warm. Serves 6–8.

Compound Salad

Place a variety of salad leaves including spinach or sorrel, shredded red cabbage and herbs on a large flat dish as a base to the salad. Arrange on top slivers of blanched almonds, chopped figs, large stoned raisins, capers, currants and sliced green olives, then finish with a layer of thinly sliced oranges, lemons and pickled cucumbers. Decorate with thickly sliced lettuce hearts. Serve with a vinaigrette dressing.

An illustration from Robert May's *The Accomplisht Cook*, showing cut-laid tarts. These were served at the banquet with their upper crust removed after cooking and replaced by separately baked, patterned tart-tops of rich puff paste.

Raspbery Creame

'Take a quart of Creame put it to bryle. Beat the whites of 3 Eggs well, and when it hath boyled well, put in your Eggs with a Leafe of Mace and a slice of Lemon pill. Boyle it till it thicken, season it with sugar, then strain it, and beat it well in your dish, then haveing your Rasberryes well stewed, mix them with your Creame, stir it with some of the Juice of them, you must also put in some Amber, and serve it up.'

From Elizabeth Birkett's commonplace book, 1699

Creams and butters formed an important part of the banquet, being either spooned from their dishes, scooped up with wafers, or eaten with brown bread. Creams were also combined with fruit such as gooseberries, pippens, quinces and raspberries to give pleasantly sharp dishes.

To Make a White-Pot

'Take three quarts of Cream, and put into it the yolks of twelve Eggs; the whites of four, being first very well beaten between three quarters of a pound of Sugar, two Nutmegs grated, a little Salt; half a pound of Raisins frist plump'd. These being sliced together, cut some thin slices of a state Manchet; dry them in a dish against the fire, and lay them on the top of the Cream, and some Marrow again upon the bread, and so bake it.'

From *The Closet of the Eminently Learned Sir Kenelm Digbie, Kt. Opened*, 1699

Cookery books revealing recipes from the closets of the aristocracy were extremely popular in the 17th century. Sir Kenelm Digby was a prominent figure at the Stuart Court. He married the celebrated beauty and courtesan Venetia Stanley, previously kept by Richard Sackville, the 3rd Earl of Dorset as his concubine and mother to a number of his children. The Earl of Dorset invited the married couple to dinner once a year, when he 'would behold her with much passion yet only kiss her hand'.

Sir Kenelm Digby's recipes are attributed to specific friends and acquaintances ranging from professional cooks to high-ranking members of the aristocracy, but there is little sign of the 'haute cuisine' of France. The dishes are for the most part quite ordinary, using ingredients that would be abundant on any country estate. White pot was one of the popular creamy dishes of the period and ancestor of our modern bread and butter pudding. It was usually served during the second course at dinner or as a supper dish.

Raspberry Cream

3/4 pt (450 ml) double cream
few blades of mace
long strip of lemon peel
1 oz (25 g) caster sugar
1 egg white
3/4 pt (450 ml) lightly sweetened raspberry purée

Boil the mace, lemon peel and sugar with most of the cream for a few minutes until well-flavoured. Beat the egg white with the remaining cream, then mix into the hot sauce. Boil up twice, stirring frequently before straining through muslin into a bowl. Leave to cool. When cold, stir in the raspberry purée. Taste and add extra sugar if necessary, although the dish should be on the sharp side. Pour into a serving dish and chill. Serve with puffs (see below). Serves 6–8.

Bread and Butter Pudding

3 oz (75 g) raisins
1 tablespoon (15 ml) sherry
6 thin slices bread, buttered and crusts removed
grated rind of 1 lemon
freshly grated nutmeg
2 oz (50 g) soft brown sugar
3/4 pt (450 ml) single cream
3 eggs, beaten

Soak the raisins overnight in the sherry.

Next day, prepare the pudding several hours before you want to cook it, to allow the bread to soak up some of the cream and eggs. Butter the bread well and cut into triangles. Butter a 2-pint (1-litre) ovenproof dish and scatter a few of the soaked raisins over the bottom. Fill the dish with layers of buttered bread sprinkled with grated lemon rind, grated nutmeg and the remaining sugar and raisins, finishing with bread, grated nutmeg and sugar. Heat the cream slowly until just reaching boiling point. Leave to cool a little, then pour over the beaten eggs, stirring continuously with a balloon whisk. Ladle this custard over the waiting bread carefully, so that the pieces are not disarranged. Leave to stand for as long as possible, but at least 2 hours.

Place the dish in a roasting tin with warm water to come half-way up the side of the dish, then bake in the centre of a moderate oven (180°C, 350°F, gas mark 4) for about 45 minutes, or until the custard is just set and the bread crisp and golden. Serve warm with cream. Serves 6.

Everlasting Syllabub

To make a Rare Scillybub

'Take a quart of Creame, a pint & half of white wine or Sack, the Juice of 2 Lemons with some of the piell and a branch of Rosemary, Sweeten it very sweet, then put a Little of this Liquer and a Little of the Creame in to a bason. Beat it till it froths, put the froth into the Scillybub and do until the Creame and wine be done, then Cover it Close and let it in a Coole celler, if it stand there 12 hours it will be the better; if you please you may putt in a Little Ambergrese in to the wine.'

From the Arundell family papers. From the 13th to the middle of the 18th century, the Arundells were one of the great families of Cornwall, with one branch of the family established at Trerice by the reign of Edward III. The family archives have recently been acquired jointly by the County Councils of Cornwall and Wiltshire.

Syllabub was a confection of white wine, cider or fruit juice, well-seasoned with sugar and flavoured with lemon, spices or rosemary, to which milk or cream was added with considerable force. Some recipes recommended that the milkmaid milked the cow directly on to the liquor to produce a frothy head with a clear liquid below. The latter was drunk from the miniature spout of special two-handled syllabub glasses, while the creamy foam was eaten as a spoonmeat. The following recipe is for the more solid type of syllabub.

thinly pared rind and juice of 1 lemon
2 oz (50 g) caster sugar
¼ pt (150 ml) medium dry sherry or white wine
sprig of fresh rosemary
½ pt (300 ml) double cream

The day before the syllabub is to be made, put the thinly-pared rind and juice of the lemon in a bowl with the sugar, sherry or white wine and the sprig of rosemary. Cover and leave overnight to let the flavours develop.

Next day, strain the liquid into a large deep bowl and stir in the cream, gradually beating it with a wire whisk until it holds its shape. Be careful not to over-beat or the cream will curdle. Spoon into small glasses – preferably stemmed or custard cups – and serve immediately or keep in a cool place overnight. Decorate each glass with a tiny sprig of rosemary, or a little twist of lemon peel and serve with jumbles (see p.119). Serves 4–6.

Detail from still-life of peaches and plums by Jacques Linard, 1635, now hanging in Snowshill Manor, Gloucestershire.

Fruit Cake

1½ oz (40 g) dried yeast
½ pt (300 ml) warm water
2 eggs
2 egg yolks
4 oz (125 g) caster sugar
pinch of salt
13 oz (375 g) butter, melted
7½ fl oz (225 ml) double cream
3 tablespoons (45 ml) rose-water
1¼ lb (600 g) plain flour
2 teaspoons (10 ml) ground mace
1 lb (450 g) currants
½ lb (225 g) raisins

FOR THE GLAZE

1 tablespoon (15 ml) caster sugar
1 tablespoon (15 ml) rose-water
1 tablespoon (15 ml) butter

Grease and line a 10-in (25.5-cm) round cake tin and wrap a double layer of brown paper around it, tying securely with string. Mix the yeast with the warm water and leave in a warm place to froth.

Beat the whole eggs and the extra egg yolks with the sugar and salt until thoroughly combined. Mix in the melted butter and gradually beat in the cream, followed by the yeast mixture and the rose-water. Stir in the flour, mace and dried fruit and mix well. Cover with a piece of oiled plastic wrap and leave to prove in a warm place for about 30 minutes.

Pour into the prepared tin and bake in the centre of a fairly hot oven (190°C, 375°F, gas mark 5) for 1¼–1½ hours, covering the top of the cake with a double layer of greaseproof paper after the first 15 minutes to prevent it from burning.

To make the glaze, dissolve the sugar in the rose-water over a low heat, then stir in the butter. Brush over the cake immediately after removing it from the oven. Leave to cool in the tin.

Wrap in greaseproof paper and foil and leave to mature for at least 24 hours before cutting.

To Make Puffs

'Take a pound of double refined sugar, beat and sift it fine, then take 2 graynes of Amber greese finely beaten, and mix it with the sugar, then take the White of an Egg, and beat it till it be all a froth. So put in your sugar by degrees, and beat it as you would do Biskett, then take a pretty quantity of Coriander or Carrowayes, put them in And roll it up in little Balls about the bigness of a Nutmegg and lay it upon Wafers, and set them round like Loaves and bake them.'

From Elizabeth Birkett's commonplace book, 1699

Various forms of light sponge biscuit were served at the 17th-century banquet as a crisp, delicate and bland foil to all the rich fruit- and sugar-based dishes. These puffs, or early meringues, were also known as White Bisket Bread, often flavoured with ground almonds, coriander, aniseed, caraway seed, lemon peel or chocolate.

Spiced Meringues

2 egg whites
4 oz (125 g) caster sugar
1 teaspoon (5 ml) ground coriander

Whisk the egg whites until they form stiff peaks and are smooth, then whisk in 2 teaspoons of the sugar. Fold in the remaining sugar and the coriander with a metal spoon. Brush a baking sheet lightly with sunflower oil and line with a sheet of Bakewell paper. Drop small spoonfuls of the meringue mixture on the baking sheet. Dredge with a little extra caster sugar, then place in a very cool oven (125–135°C, 250–275°F, gas mark ½–1) for about 1 hour, until crisp and delicately beige in colour.

To make a Great Cake

'Take 3 pound and a halfe of flower, 2 pound and a halfe of Currans, halfe a pound of Raisons of your sun stoned, halfe a pound of sugar, halfe a pint of Rose Watter, a pint of Creame, a pound of fresh butter, a Gill of Ale barme, yolks of 10 Eggs and 3 whites. Let the Creame boyle and put in the Butter to melt in it, beat 9 Eggs and mingle with the barme, Rose Watter and sugar. Pour in the Cream and butter, and stirr it well together, then take halfe an ounce of Mace, well beaten and throw upon it, then take some of the flower and strew over it, and let it stand till it hath wrought over, then work it together, put in your fruit, and when it is wrought until it will come from your hands in the Bowle, lay it upon a sheet of White Paper buttered, and a browne one under it and let it stand in the Oven an houre, then take some whites of Eggs, melted butter and Rose Watter, beaten together, and wash your Cake over with a bunch of Sage, and throw over it sugar, and let stand in the Oven a little longer.'

From Elizabeth Birkett's commonplace book, 1699

Cakes were still enormous in the 17th century, round or oval in shape and containing prodigious amounts of dried fruit (see p.173). Rose-water was frequently used by cooks instead of water, which was often of dubious quality.

III

Comenius in *The Gate of Languages Unlocked*, 1633, describes the meals taken during the Stuart period:

> Stout feeders eat up all and do nothing else but devour. Betimes in the morning they break their fast; at noon they dine; when the day is far spent they take their beaver [beverage]; late at night they sup; yea, having newly dined they have a stomach for supper; but let them that lead a sitting kind of life and most within doors refrain from breakfast and beaver and let them not sip the least pittance of wine next their hearts. To be often eating, and full fed thrice a day, is hurtful, unless it be sparingly.

Breakfast was usually taken shortly after getting up, between 6am and 7am, and was a relatively light meal by the standards of the day: a selection of cold meats, fish, especially salted and dried herrings, cheese, bread and butter, wine or ale and beer. Poorer people ate cereal pottages based on the local breadcorn, but then, as now, there were great contrasts in breakfast preferences: the Cromwells took rich broth or caudle, followed by a cup of small ale with toast and sugar at mid-morning, while Pepys held a breakfast party on New Year's Day in 1661 of 'a barrel of oysters, a dish of neat's tongues and a dish of anchovies, wine of all sorts and Northdowne ale.' By the end of the century, the Continental style of breakfast had become fashionable amongst the wealthy, with rolls, spiced bread and cakes served with tea, coffee or chocolate. It was then taken later in the morning, between 9.30am and 10am. A gentleman's breakfast table was arranged as a single course, probably set out in the symmetrical patterns of other meals.

At the beginning of the 17th century, dinner was taken at midday, but as the century wore on there was a tendency to dine later among the devotees of tea, coffee and chocolate and the continental-style breakfast. The Duke and Duchess of Lauderdale of Ham House, for instance, dined at 2pm.

Between 5pm and 8pm, or even later on special occasions, supper was eaten. If it was to be served late, it would consist of a very light meal of a drink, sweetmeats and biscuits. Although subsequent changes were taking place in the planning of the large English country house, the medieval idea of a first- or second-floor great chamber died hard. It continued in use as an eating-place for the family and important guests for a surprisingly long time – well into the 18th century in a few houses like East Riddlesden, Blickling and Knole.

The great chamber at Knole has a beautiful plasterwork ceiling, panelled walls decorated with carvings and a remarkable chimney-piece of black marble, providing a background for the delicate alabaster garlands of flowers and musical instruments in the overmantel; a reminder that the Earl of Dorset's private orchestra must frequently have performed here during meals. Leading from the great chamber is the withdrawing room, where guests would have retired after eating, and where the family would have dined informally with a few favoured guests. The walls were probably hung with tapestry for warmth and it would have been a far more intimate room. Lady Anne Clifford often refers in her diary to dining here, particularly in the winter: on 4 April

1617, she records 'This day we began to leave the Little Room and dine and sup in the Great Chamber.' A little later in the month the Earl 'dined abroad in the Great Chamber and supped privately with me in the Drawing Chamber'. The Earl and Countess seem never to have eaten in the parlour, which appears to have been exclusively for the use of the upper servants, although the Earl may occasionally have sat there with his gentlemen. The only time the family would have dined in the great hall with the entire household was on the most festive occasions. A list of seating arrangements for meals at Knole made between 1613 and 1624 tells us that some 21 senior servants, including the steward, the chaplain, the gentleman of the horse and Matthew Caldicott, 'my Lord's favourite', ate in the parlour, while most of the rest of the household ate at three long tables which stretched the length of the main body of the hall; one, 36 feet long, survives.

The most important servants involved in the buying or providing of food and drink, sat together on the clerks' table, while the menials, like Diggory Dyer and Marfidy Snipt, ate in the kitchen.

AT THE CLERK'S TABLE IN THE HALL

Edward Fulks & John Edwards
  Clerks of the Kitchen
Edward Care, Master Cook
William Smith, Yeoman of the
  Buttery
Henry Keble, Yeoman of the
  Pantry
John Mitchell, Pastryman
Thomas Vinson, Cook
John Elnor, Cook
Ralph Hussie, Cook
John Avery, Usher of the Hall

Robert Elnor, Slaughterman
Ben Staples, Groom of the Great
  Chamber
Thomas Petley, Brewer
William Turner, Baker
Francis Steeling, Gardener
Richard Wickling, Gardener
Thomas Clements, Underbrewer
Samuel Vans, Caterer
Edward Small, Groom of the
  Wardrobe
Samuel Southern, Under Baker
Lowry, a French Boy

The servants at East Riddlesden and Chirk also continued to dine in the main hall: at Chirk a new servants' hall was not provided until 1778. But, as the century progressed, the hall in most large houses was no longer a place for the household to eat. The servants were relegated to a steward's room or parlour and a hall of their own for their meals, usually in the basement, close to the other domestic offices.

The hall had become instead a ceremonial entry to the house where important visitors and guests were received, hence the '12 highback chairs' standing round the walls in the Marble Hall at Belton, so named because of its impressive black and white marble floor, like that at Ham. Most halls were now built on a smaller scale, but they still had to be

The Marble Hall at Petworth, Sussex. Most halls were now built on a smaller scale than in medieval and Tudor times, but they still had to be grand. The Proud Duke of Somerset placed the Seymour bull and family coat of arms prominently over the mantelpiece of his 'Hall of State' to impress his visitors.

impressive to display the wealth and importance of the family. The hall at Petworth, appropriately always called the 'Hall of State' in accounts, was created in 1692. Petworth, home of the Percy Earls of Northumberland since the Middle Ages, had passed to Charles Seymour, 6th Duke of Somerset, known as the 'Proud Duke', through his marriage to Elizabeth, the Percy heiress. From 1688 the Duke and Duchess began to remodel the house and to refurbish it in the Baroque style. In the Hall of State, the Seymour bull and coat of arms over the mantelpiece dominate the room and impress the visitor. Guests arriving for a dinner or a fashionable supper party congregated in the hall and, if the family were entertaining them in full state, they were led up a grand staircase to the dining-room, now replacing the great chamber as the principal eating room and forming a very important part of the state suite. Although the special appropriateness of having a room of state elevated a floor above the hall had ceased to exist, now that the servants had stopped eating there, the Proud Duke conceived the painted staircase at Petworth *en route* to the great dining-room on the first floor as, according to Gervase Jackson-Stops in *The English Country House in Perspective*, 'an ascent to Olympus, suggesting to him and his guests that they were leaving the world of mere mortals below, to sup like gods above'.

At Belton in Lincolnshire a fine staircase with walls densely covered with pictures – 44 of them in 1698 – would have led important guests of Sir John Brownlow and his young wife Alice to their newly appointed 'great dining room'. In 1695, William III dined here and was 'mighty nobly entertained' by Sir John, who 'killed 12 fat oxen and 60 sheep besides other victuals ... the King was exceeding merry and drank freely which was the occasion that when he came to Lincoln he could eat nothing but a mess of milk', according to the diarist de la Pryme. The monarch obviously enjoyed himself, despite his over-indulgence, as de la Pryme also records that 'He [the King] has sent up for him [Sir John] to London to honour him the more, and to requite him for his kindnesses'.

When Sir John and his wife were dining a little more informally, but still 'in some state', with a number of guests, they would dine in the 'great parlour' or 'salon' (saloon) on the ground floor behind the Marble Hall and overlooking the garden. The wood

When Sir John Brownlow and his wife were dining less formally but 'in some state' at Belton House, Lincolnshire, they would use the salon or saloon, with its magnificent woodwork and fine marble fireplace.

panelling, marble fireplaces with superb limewood carvings above, suitably composed of fruit and flowers, dead game and ears of wheat, and the family portraits, originally all surrounded by more similar limewood carvings, were 'things necessary for a dineing Room' in the 17th century according to Randle Holme in *The Academy of Armory*. 'The Room well wainscoted about, either with Moonten and panells or carved as the old fashion was; or else in large square panell. The Room hung with pictures of all sorts, as History, Landscapes, etc.'. Panelling, and for the very fashionable, leather hangings, were preferred to textiles for dining-rooms because they did not retain food smells. This preference lasted until the beginning of this century.

If the Brownlows were dining *en famille* they would eat both dinner and supper in the 'little parlour' placed next door to the back staircase with direct access to the kitchen. A small parlour of this type was a common feature from the early 17th century. The Brownlows' little parlour was originally panelled and inventories show that it was more comfortable and informal than the great parlour, as befitted an everyday family eating room. Both parlours had withdrawing-rooms adjoining them, each furnished with tapestries giving added insulation and warmth.

The great dining-room at Ham, together with the other state rooms, was redecorated in the fashionable and lavish Court taste of the Restoration period by the remarkable Countess of Dysart and her second husband, the Duke of Lauderdale, in the 1670s. Originally there was a fireplace facing the windows and, at the end of the room where the high table would have stood, a bay window at each side. Sir Peter Lely's double portrait of the Duke and Duchess was hung at the upper end of the room; the only painting here in the 1670s, it would have had great symbolic importance. After meals in the great dining-room, guests withdrew to the 'north drawing room'.

When the Duke and Duchess of Lauderdale were dining more informally, they used the 'marble dining-room' (saloon) behind the hall on the ground floor. The original black and white marble floor was replaced about 1756 by the present parquet floor, but the oak panelling and carving still exists. In the 1670s, the walls were hung with gilded leather, richly decorated with cherubs, fruit and flowers. After a meal in the marble dining-room, guests would adjourn to the withdrawing-room.

In smaller houses, like Townend, a prime example of a yeoman farmer's dwelling in the 17th century, all the family, servants and farm-hands took their meals together in the 'fire house' or 'House-place'. Originally, this had been the common living-room with the only fireplace in the house where all the cooking was done, until the kitchen was built. A great deal of importance was now being set upon household goods of all kinds, so in the 1670s the fire house at Townend was panelled and a carved oak press or bread cupboard, a common feature of farmhouses in the north, was built into the wall on the left of the fireplace, for the storage of the household's clapboard. The Browne family and their 'boarders' sat at an immense oak table or 'board', which would have been constructed in the room; the servants sat on heavy oak benches in order of seniority, the most important sitting next to his master, George Browne, who probably sat on the only carved oak chair at the end of the table.

At Chirk, Sir Thomas Myddelton's 'greate dyninge roome' contained a single 'greate shuffle boarde Table' probably about 30 feet long, placed in the centre of the room, but the 1662 inventory for East Riddlesden Hall shows that John Murgatroyd had three tables in his dining parlour: 'one Draweinge [draw-leaf] Table with Carpett, one Round Table and Carpett, one Square Table with Cloath and quishens [cushions].'

The fire house at Townend, Cumbria. The Browne family, their servants and farmworkers took their meals together in this room, sitting at the immense oak table on benches, with George Browne, as befitted the head of the household, on the only chair.

Late 17th-century dining-rooms still contained at least two tables, and if the latest style was being sought, they would be round or oval and gate-legged, turned in oak or walnut. The gate-legged table, so named because its hinged legs opened like a gate to support a flat top, was invented for convenience; it could be folded up and stored either in the room, or elsewhere, and brought in when needed. Chairs would be placed round the walls when not in use. The great parlour at Belton in 1698 contained 24 'dutch' or rush chairs and three or four separate tables which were brought in for meals, giving some idea of the number of diners who might be entertained here. (At this time, the most prestigious entertainments were for relatively few people, but on an elaborate scale.) The little parlour contained two oval tables, two caned armchairs for Sir John and his wife, and 15 single chairs for the rest of the family and close friends. In the marble dining-room at Ham, the gate-leg table of oak and pine is one of three that stood in the recesses between the windows until needed, and in 1679 there were 18 walnut caned chairs round the walls. Cane-seated chairs were introduced from the Continent after the Restoration and became extremely fashionable. In 1688 Randle Holme describes the seating necessary for the dining-room as: 'Chaires and stooles of Turky work, Russia or calves Leather, cloth or stuffe, or of needlework. Or els made all of Joynt work or cane chaires.' The armless dining-chair, also known in the 17th century as a 'back stool' because it had developed from the stool, had a straight, not very high back which might be decorated with carving. Its four legs were linked by stretchers near ground level, like those of the joined stool of Elizabethan times, to lift the diner's feet above the rushes and debris on the floor. It quickly became the commonest form of seating alongside the stool. Later in the century, back stools were often upholstered in cloth, or leather (which did not retain the smell of food), to match the dining-chairs with arms and the stools. Six armchairs covered with crimson velvet and '12 backstools of

Left: The dining-room at Blickling Hall, Norfolk, showing the 17th-century chairs. The dining-table is mid-18th-century.

the same' appear in the 1677 inventory of furnishings for the great dining-room at Ham House; the Duke and Duchess of Lauderdale and their most important guests would have sat on the armchairs. In the same room, eight cedar tables were listed in the 1679 inventory and 11 in 1683, which were probably folding tables kept behind the Indian screens in the room and set up when needed.

By 1688, the court cupboard was about to be superseded by the side-table in fashionable homes, as Randle Holme's list of furniture for the dining-room shows: 'Sides tables, or court cubberts, for cups and Glasses to drink in, Spoons, Sugar Box, Viall and Cruces for Vinegar, Oyle and Mustard Pot.' There was no room in the new dining-room, or parlour, for a court cupboard, so the family plate was displayed in a 'beaufet' or buffet, an open alcove with shelves, either fitted in the wainscot, or enclosed by a pair of doors set in a corner cupboard. The interior of these buffets was painted to match the painted wainscot. The new-fangled 'Cistern of Brass, Pewter or Lead to set Flagons of Beer and Bottles of wine in' was kept underneath the buffet or side-table. In the marble dining-room at Ham, the two cedarwood side-tables of about 1675 were designed to stand in the alcoves; below one of them is a marble cistern. Towards the end of the century, the buffet took on a new form. It was usually made of marble and could contain a supply of running water, shelves for the display of glasses, plate or china and a basin or cistern in which to wash hands, faces or glasses. This type of buffet was installed in the family eating parlour or in a separate small room known as the 'beaufet' next to the great dining-room.

The principal means of lighting rooms was still by candle or rushlight. In the dining-rooms of those who could afford it, sconces of silver were used on the walls, the polished back-plate reflecting the light of the candle. Twenty-six survive at Knole including the armorial set of twelve, dated 1685, that are amongst the finest of their kind. There is also a fine pair at Erddig in North Wales of about the same date. The increasing availability

The buffet and side-table in William III's private dining-room at Hampton Court Palace. The buffet is piled with gilt plate and an oriental ceramic vase (*below*). On the side-table is a monteith, with glasses, a basin for washing the hands and a napkin holder (*below right*).

of mirrors and their strategic placing in the dining-room also helped to maximise the candlelight. These pier-glasses flanked by tall candlestands, known as torchères, transformed evening parties, particularly the card parties now so much in vogue. In 1698, the great parlour at Belton contained 'Two large seeing glasses all japanned' on the piers between the windows with matching tables and candlestands below them.

The tables were arranged for a meal with the finest reserved for the host and his most important guests – the top table; the others were arranged round the room a little like a modern restaurant, with separate tables for gentlemen and ladies. The tables were first covered by the assistant in charge of linen, with a single fine linen cloth, probably woven with a damask design. Until the middle of the century much of the food was still eaten with the fingers, so every diner was provided with a clean white linen napkin for each course. With the introduction of the fork, napkins were no longer used in some houses, as a fairly careful eater might retire from a meal with clean hands. In the fashionable homes of the wealthy, they became wholly decorative and were folded in elaborate ways to be put away at the end of the meal for the next. No-one ever unfolded his own napkin; this would have been frowned on by the host and cursed by his butler who did the folding! Descriptions regarding the folding do not appear to have been printed in England until 1682, when *A Perfect School of Instructions for the Officers of the Mouth* was translated from the French by Giles Rose. Minute instructions for folding dinner napkins in 26 different fashions were provided, ranging from those 'in the form of two Capons in a Pye' and a 'Cross of Lorraine', which were intended to enclose a roll, or piece of bread to the purely decorative 'excellent Heart' and a 'Cockleshell'.

Pepys considered it very remiss of the Lord Mayor not to have set out more napkins for the guests at his banquet in the Guildhall in 1663: 'none in the Hall, but the Mayor's and the Lords of the Privy Council that had napkins or knives . . .', for the 'laying of napkins' was both an art and a profession and Pepys himself would have felt dishonoured if he had failed to provide them at his dinners. He tells us that he employed a professional 'to lay the cloth and fold the napkins' the day before giving a dinner party. On retiring to his house, 'I there found one laying of my napkins against tomorrow, in figures of all sorts, which is mighty pretty, and it seems, is his trade, and he gets much money by it.'

Until the Restoration, the only items of cutlery in common use were the knife and spoon. Knives for the wealthy had steel blades set in handles of crystal, carved bone, ivory, ebony or silver: a present from a groom to his bride was often a fine pair of knives. For the less wealthy, they were functional utensils, their steel blades firmly secured into a handle of wood or bone. In fashionable households, spoons were made of silver or silver-gilt, their handles decorated with figures, but usually a silver spoon was a personal item, often the only piece of plate the diner possessed. In most households, the majority of everyday spoons were of pewter, often cast from worn-out dishes by an itinerant metalworker who carried a set of moulds as part of his equipment.

The most significant change in tableware was the introduction of the fork into English society by the eccentric traveller Thomas Coryat. After a tour of the Continent, he described its use in his *Crudities* of 1611: 'The Italians do always at their meals, use a little fork, when they cut their meat. For while with their knife, which they hold in one hand, they cut the meat out of the dish, they fasten their fork, which they hold in their other hand upon the same dish . . . .' The conservative English were very slow to adopt this Continental fashion and for a long time it was regarded as an affectation fit only for

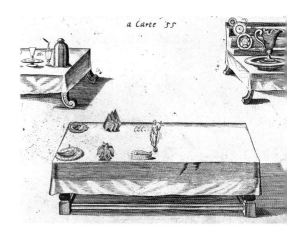

An illustration from Mattia Geigher's *Lo Scalco* published in Padua in 1621 and showing a dining-room arrangement of the period. Tables were now elaborately dressed with fancily folded napkins and figures in wax and sugar-paste. Above the main dining-table are side-tables, one for serving wine, the other a buffet or cupboard for the display of plate, all covered with a cloth.

fops and ultra-refined persons: 'we need no little forks to make hay with our mouths, to throw our meat into them.' (*The Courtier and the Countryman* by Breton.) As late as 1669, foreigners touring England complained that there were no forks on English tables and that only the basin and ewer were supplied for a large supper party; most people were expected to bring their own knife and spoon. Eventually common sense and practicality prevailed, although it was to be many more years before the fork was adopted by working men and women.

The earliest English hallmarked table-fork, dating from about 1632, is in the Victoria & Albert Museum in London. It consists of a simple bar of silver divided at one end into two prongs, based on the design of the earlier carving and cooking-forks. Most of the forks in the latter part of the century were made with long, two-pronged hafts fitted into decorative handles of enamelled silver or carved ivory, to match the knives. As the fork had now taken over the knife's role of spearing meat and transferring it to the mouth, the end of the knife lost its point and became rounded. Toothpicks were now provided on the side-table as the diner could no longer pick his teeth with the point of his knife.

After the cutlery had been arranged at each place, the fork to the left and knife and spoon to the right, the salt was added. In a household like Knole, it was still the most important item until the middle of the century, for it effectively separated the lord and his chief guests from the remainder of the diners. The great salt slowly passed out of use as communal dining came to an end. Smaller salts for individual use were provided instead, in silver and silver-gilt, triangular or round. It was probably a salt of this type that Pepys noted in his diary for 9 October 1663, when he found that 'Under every salt there was a bill of fare'. Cheaper salts could be made in pewter, wood or glazed pottery, including Delftware.

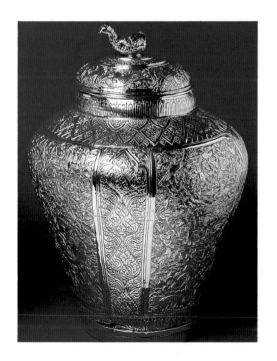

A late 17th-century silver ginger jar from Knole, Kent.

During the Civil War, much of the plate that had adorned dining-rooms in great houses like Knole was melted down in the King's cause. As soon as Charles II was restored to the throne, Dutch and French silversmiths came to England to fulfil commissions to replace dinner plates, bowls, porringers, tankards and chafing-dishes. Much of this domestic tableware was made in London, but regional centres like Newcastle, Chester, York, Norwich and Exeter also produced a significant amount of silverware of the highest standard.

Solid silver tableware was obviously restricted to the wealthiest and most fashionable households, but pewter made an excellent substitute; thus in 1686, a pewterer, George Sherwynn of Salop, supplied Chirk Castle with '98 lb of pewter Dishes at 12d per pound' together with '3 Dozen of Plates costing 44s'. At the same time, Mrs Foulkes the housekeeper ordered 'sand and rotten stone to scowre the pewter'. This troublesome operation could be avoided by using Delftware plates made at Southwark and Lambeth in London, or in Bristol; their glossy white surfaces being hard enough to resist most knife-cuts and scratches. A number of small dishes of this type, about 7 inches in diameter, were certainly in use during the Civil War, but their popularity increased at the Restoration and references to 'white plates' began to appear in inventories. The potters of Staffordshire, the West Country, Kent and Essex were also producing tableware. Accounts for Kingston Lacy list the purchase in 1693 of '2 earthen porringers and plate' but it was used mostly on the tables of the lesser gentry as a substitute for finer Delftwares: '4 delph dishes' were purchased at the same time for Kingston Lacy.

In many households, like Townend, wooden tableware was still in use, the square

An earthenware posset cup, Lambeth *c.*1700, with an English delft charger, now in Lady Betty Germain's Closet at Knole, Kent.

wooden trencher now being replaced by circular wooden plates or platters. Although the Brownes probably abandoned wood for pewter as they rose in social status, many servants' halls, farmhouses and cottages continued to use trenchers right through to the beginning of the 20th century. The Myddeltons of Chirk bought 'six dozen of siccamore Trenchers of a round fashion' and '3 dozen of Square Trenchers with hollowe in the middle' from Thomas Jones of Pennyclawdd in 1674, probably for the use of their servants.

Basketwork also made a limited appearance in the dining-room, to hold bread and to carry plates. An example of the latter was bought for Chirk in 1684. Wicker 'voiders' were used to collect bones, cores or leftovers during the meal.

In the early years of the century, the rich drank from fine Venetian glasses and silver tankards, while poorer citizens contented themselves with coarser home-produced glass, pewter and wood. After the Restoration, British glass began to challenge the best Italy could offer, with the revolutionary use of lead oxide by the glassmaker George Ravenscroft, who was based at the London Glass Sellers' Company's works at Henley-on-Thames in Oxfordshire. Glass was used for glasses to hold wine and water, and for sweetmeats, jellies and syllabubs.

It was still, however, only the wealthy who could afford individual glasses for their guests. These were laid out on a side-table or on the buffet. 'The butler filleth strong wine out of a cruse, or wine pot, or flagon, into cups or glasses, which stand on a cup board, and he reacheth them to the master of the feast, who drinketh to his guests', described Comenius in 1633. After this toast, a guest was obliged to call for a drink

Above: *The Hunt Picnic* by Carlo Cane, with bread on individual plates, covered with napkins, and wine cooling in a cistern.

Below: Wines were preferred as cold as possible, so glasses were suspended by the foot in a 'montieth' of iced water. The Yorkes of Erddig, Clwyd, owned this superb late 17th-century example in silver, engraved with Chinese figures.

when he wanted it, and when a lady drank at table there was always a servant beside her to hold a napkin under her chin. Wine glasses were always held by the base.

Wines at this period were preferred as cold as possible, so glasses were placed in iced water before use. A receptacle was evolved for this purpose, recorded in 1683 by the Oxford diarist Anthony à Wood: 'This year in the summer time, came up a vessel or bason notched at the brims to let drinking vessels hang there by the foot, so that the body or drinking place might hang into the water to cool them. Such a bason was called a 'Monteigh' from a fantastical Scot called Monsieur Monteigh who at that time or a little before wore the bottome of his cloacke or coate so notched.' Bailey in his *Dictionary* of 1721 defines 'monteith' as 'a scallop'd Bason to cool Glasses in'. Early monteiths were of silver, sometimes gold: the Yorkes at Erddig owned a superb late 17th-century example in silver, engraved with Chinese-style figures, which is now displayed in the butler's pantry. There is also a monteith of 1693 in the dining-room at Petworth.

The medieval custom of hand washing before and after the meal survived until the widespread use of dining forks in the middle of the century. 'And when they [the diners] have washed over a bason out of a ewer and have wiped on a towel, they sit down upon benches or stools set in order with cushions,' commented Comenius. Once the guests had washed, grace was said. The gentlemen removed their hats, but replaced them when they sat down and wore them throughout the meal, except during toasts. Only the King ate bare-headed.

Dinner was so substantial as to cause the good Monsieur Misson to shake his head:

Painting of the interior of an inn by Wolfgang Heimbach. After the Restoration, glasses for wine and beer came into common use in Britain with the revolutionary use of lead oxide.

'the English eat a great deal at Dinner; they rest a while and to it again, till they have quite stuff'd their Paunch'. As before, the meal was divided into two or, at the most, three courses, each made up of a number of dishes, both sweet and savoury. The first course included most of the major meat dishes, together with fish and soups, or pottage, which were 'changed' halfway through the course and replaced with a further dish of meat or fish. In the second course would be a range of light meats, game and sweetstuff; but this division of dishes was only a general rule, leaving plenty of scope to include whatever might be available at the time. The third course or banquet was made up of fruit, cheese and sweetmeats. After the Restoration, when words of French origin became fashionable, this course was called 'dessert' from *desservir*, to clear away.

A diary entry for November 1622 records that Henry Ferrers, squire of Baddesley Clinton in Warwickshire 'had to dinner a neck of mutton and potage, a piece of powdered [salted] biefe and cabbage [for the first course], a leg of goose broyled, a rabbet, a piece of an apple tart [for the second course], cheese, apples and peares [for the third course].' For his wedding anniversary on 26 March 1662, Pepys entertained guests to a 'pretty dinner; viz. a brace of stewed carps, 6 roasted chickens and a jowl of salmon, hot, for the first course; a tanzy [eggs and cream flavoured with the herb tansy] and two neat's [ox's] tongues; and cheese for the second.'

Edward Sackville, 4th Earl of Dorset, conducted his affairs at Knole on a suitably lavish scale. A bill of fare for a banquet on 3 July 1636 begins: 'To perfume the room often in the meal with orange flower water upon a hot pan. To have fresh bowls in every corner and flowers tied upon them, and sweet briar, stock, gilly-flowers, pinks, wall-flowers and any other sweet flowers in glasses and pots in every window and chimney.' The menu follows:

First Course

Rice Pottage	Hash of mutton with Anchovies
Barley Broth	[a stew of mutton with anchovies
Buttered pickrell [young pike]	in the sauce]
Buttered and burned eggs [scrambled]	Great Pike
Boiled teats [cow's udders]	Fish chuits [small pasties]
Roast tongues	Roast venison, in blood
Bream	Capons (2)
Perches	Wild Duck (3)
Chine of Veal roast	Salmon whole, hot

Second Course

Tenches, boiled	Grand sallet [an elaborate salad
Crabs [boiled]	including eggs, poultry, fish]
Tench pie	Redeeve pie, hot [a small bird]
Venison pasty of a doe	Almond pudding [egg and cream
Sawns [roast swans]	pudding flavoured with almonds]
Herons (3) [roasted]	Made dishes [fricassées, hashes
Cold lamb	ragôuts, and olios of meat]
Custard [an egg custard]	Boiled salad [a vegetable]
Venison, boiled	Pig whole [roasted]
Potatoes, stewed	Rabbits [probably roasted]

All the dishes of each course were laid out on the table at the same time, in a neat symmetrical pattern as in Elizabethan times. Gervase Markham in *The English Hus-wife* of 1615 describes the process:

She [the good House-wife] shall first marshall her sallets, delivering the grand sallet first, which is ever more compound; then greene sallets, then boyld sallets, then some smaller compound sallets. Next unto sallets she shall deliver foorth all her fricases, the simple first, as collops, rashers, and such like; then compound fricases, after them all her boyld meats in their degree, as simple broths, stewed broth, and the boylings of sundry fowles. Next them all sorts of rost meates, of which the greatest first, as chine of Beefe, or surloyne, the gigget or Legges of Mutton, Goose, Swan, Veale, Pig, Capon and such like. Then bak't meates, the hot first as Fallow-deere in Pastry . . . Then cold bak't meates, Pheasant Partridges . . . Then lastly Carbonados both simple and compound.

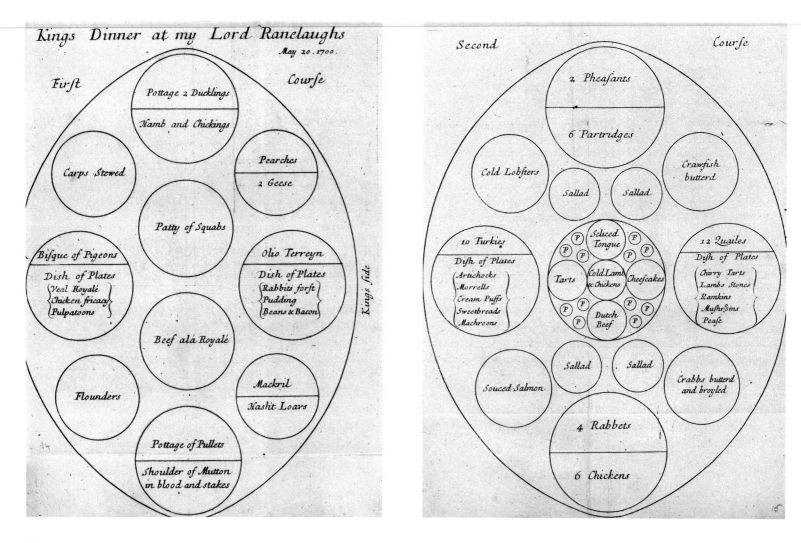

The following labels appear within the first course diagram:

Kings Dinner at my Lord Ranelaughs
May 20. 1700.

First Course

Pottage 2 Ducklings
Lamb and Chickings
Carps Stewed
Pearches
2 Geese
Patty of Squabs
Bisque of Pigeons
Dish of Plates
Veal Royalé
Chicken fricacy
Pulpatoons
Olio Terreyn
Dish of Plates
Rabbits forst
Pudding
Beans & Bacon
Beef alá Royalé
Flounders
Mackril
Hasht Loavs
Pottage of Pullets
Shoulder of Mutton in blood and stakes

Kings side

The following labels appear within the second course diagram:

Second Course

2 Pheasants
6 Partridges
Cold Lobsters
Crawfish butterd
Sallad   Sallad
10 Turkies
Dish of Plates
Artichocks
Morrells
Cream Puffs
Sweetbreads
Machroons
Sliced Tongue
Tarts
Cold Lamb & Chickens
Cheesecakes
Dutch Beef
12 Quailes
Dish of Plates
Chirry Tarts
Lambs Stones
Ramkins
Mushrooms
Pease
Sallad   Sallad
Souced Salmon
Crabbs butterd and broyled
4 Rabbets
6 Chickens

The dishes were assembled in correct order on the dresser in the buttery by the clerk of the kitchen, and handed to the sewer, who, continues Markham, 'shall not set them down as he receive them, but setting the sallets extravagantly about the table, mixe the Fricases aboute them, then the boild meates among the Fricases, rost meates amongst the boild, bak't amongst the rost, and Carbonadoes among the bak't.' In this way 'before every trencher, stand a Sallet, a Fricase, a Boild meate, a Rost meate, a Bak't meate, and a Carbonado' to give 'very great contentment to the Guests'.

The second course was laid out in a similar way. Seventeenth-century cookery books contained designs for the arrangement of dishes. Some of the most magnificent were by Patrick Lamb, for 50 years Master Cook to Charles II, James II, William and Mary, and Queen Anne. His *Royal Cookery*, published posthumously in 1710, included detailed table plans for coronation dinners, wedding suppers, royal feasts, with the positions of anything up to 114 dishes. Similar schemes were followed on tables at every level of polite society, even when only five dishes appeared at each course.

The 'dish ring' was developed late in the century to enable dishes of food to be elevated above the table level, making an impressive display and saving valuable space. Randle Holme describes this as a circular, hexagonal or octagonal stand, the top and

First and second course layouts from Patrick Lamb's *Royal Cookery*, published after his death in 1710. All the dishes for each course were laid out symmetrically on the table. The first included most of the major meat dishes, together with fish and soups, while the second consisted of the lighter meats, game and sweet dishes.

194

Gerrit Houckgeest's painting of Charles I and Henrietta Maria dining in public at Whitehall. The dishes are laid symmetrically on the table, in a careful arrangement. The wine, cooled in a cistern, is served from the cupboard or side-table.

bottom identical so that it could be used either way up, its purpose being to 'make the feast look full and noble': '3 rings for table of French pewter' were bought for the Kingston Lacy dining-table in July 1693.

The reduction in the number of servants after the Restoration led also to a reduction in ceremony during meals: all the panoply of bowing, kissing and kneeling, of sewers, carvers, cupbearers and gentlemen waiters disappeared. The butler absorbed the jobs of the yeomen of the buttery, ewery and pantry, beginning the rise that was to lead to his 19th-century eminence. Footmen, from a lower social class and therefore cheaper, were brought in to wait at less important tables. By the end of the century, they, helped by extra pages, were waiting at the first table under the butler and the under-butler.

Both carving and distributing the meat were particular honours reserved for the master of the house or distinguished guests. Gentlemen were still supposed to know the exact way to carve any dish set before them. Robert May includes a chapter on 'The most Exact, or A la Mode Ways of Carving' in his *Accomplisht Cook* of 1660. The diners helped themselves, or each other (often the gentlemen served the ladies first), on to plates that had been warmed by the fire in an iron frame. 'When serving' said Antoine de Courtin in his book of manners of 1672, 'one must alway give away the best portion and keep the smallest, and touch nothing except with the fork.' Primarily, guests would help themselves to what they could reach (known retrospectively as *service à la française*): if they wished for something else, a servant was summoned to fetch it, though it was not considered good manners to do this too often. Antoine de Courtin further instructed the diner

> to take food only from the part of the dish opposite you; still less should you take the best pieces, even though you might be the last to help yourself . . . . Also, in many places, spoons are brought in with the dishes, and these serve only for taking soup and sauce . . . . You should not eat soup from the dish, but put it neatly of your plate . . . . To wipe your fingers on your bread, again is very improper . . . . Formerly one was permitted to dip one's bread into the sauce, provided only that one had not already bitten it. Nowadays that would be a kind of rusticity. Formerly, one was allowed to take from one's mouth what one could not eat and drop it on the floor . . . . Now that would be very disgusting . . . .

After the main courses had been served, the company might retire from the dining-room to a separate apartment where the ever popular banquet was laid out. However, in most households, particularly after the Restoration, the third course or dessert began to be served at the dining-table.

Music accompanied the meal. The Chirk Castle accounts refer to many payments made to fiddlers, a 'Bagpipe man' and harpists for playing at the castle. Other entertainments were also provided on special occasions: the Myddeltons 'paid the Fire Eater' 2s 6d in May 1721 for performing at Chirk.

Two or three hours after dinner had begun, the last draughts of spiced wine were drunk and the party staggered to the withdrawing-room, or to a small room in the 'Chinese style' to take tea. These closets, or cabinets, attached to the bedchamber and withdrawing-room, where favoured guests would be received for a tête-à-tête conversation, were a new feature of upper-class life, copied from the French. The Duchess of Lauderdale entertained her close friends in a richly decorated closet attached to her bedchamber. The chairs, still there, form part of the set of 'Six Japan'd backstools with Cane bottoms' kept in this room with the Javanese lacquer tea-table, which had its short legs lengthened by an English joiner in 1680 to bring it to a height suitable for ladies seated on backstools. The miniature cabinet with Chinese incised lacquer, also still in the room, may well be the 'Japan box for Sweetmeats and tea' mentioned in the 17th-century inventories. Tea was extremely expensive and had to be locked up: the Duchess would blend the leaves using her own exact proportions and prepare the new drink by boiling water on a special small heater fuelled by spirits of wine, and brewing it in a teapot. It would then be poured into elegant little handleless cups or 'dishes' of porcelain, all imported from the Far East as ballast on tea clippers, and much more expensive than the china sets provided for chocolate or coffee.

The Duchess of Lauderdale's closet at Ham House, Surrey, where she entertained her close friends to tea. In the foreground is a Javanese lacquer tea-table, *c*.1675, and behind stands a miniature cabinet decorated with Chinese incised lacquer, which may well be the 'Japan box for Sweetmeats and tea' kept in the closet in the 17th century.

Lady Brownlow of Belton would probably have invited her favoured guests to drink tea with her in the room described as 'Ante Room' in 1698. Two chinoiserie tapestries were specially made for the room in 1691 with 'Indian figures according to ye pattern of the Queens which are at Kensington' and the theme was continued in the lacquer and japanned furniture. There was also a little room on the first floor described in 1698 as the 'Sweetmeat Closet', where sweetmeats for the banquet, or dessert course, and for serving with tea, were stored. After Lady Alice had been widowed in 1697, she continued to live at Belton, apparently ruling her daughters with a firm hand. Tradition has it that 'once, when the five sisters were enjoying a surreptitious tea-party in one of their rooms, the dreaded footsteps were heard approaching, and to save detection, the whole tea equipage was promptly thrown out of the window'!

After a few hours of good conversation, music, singing, dancing or cards, accompanied by much alcohol and perhaps tobacco, the guests would be served with a supper to prepare them either for their homeward journey, or for the chill of the bedroom. The meal was always served as a single course, usually of five or seven dishes, consisting of assorted light meats, fish and sweetstuffs, usually leftovers: Misson said in 1690 that the English were 'Gluttons at Noon and abstinent at Night'. If the occasion was very grand, supper could be rapidly expanded to 20 dishes and extended by a banquet. Lady Anne Clifford writes of such an occasion after the funeral of James I's consort, Anne of Denmark, in May 1619: 'This night my Lord [the 3rd Earl of Dorset] made a great Supper to two or three of the Frenchmen that came over with the Ambassador. After Supper there was a Play and then a Banquet.'

A typical supper might consist of roast mutton or poultry, cold bacon, game pie, fish, cheesecakes, sweetmeats and fruit, served with spiced wines and cordials. On special occasions, it concluded with much drinking of toasts. Supper, after a dinner given by Pepys in 1663, was a 'good sack-posset and cold meat', then he sent his guests away 'by about 10 o'clock at night'. A much grander supper was served by the Duke of Somerset when the King of Spain visited Petworth on 28 December 1703. After an exhausting social round involving solemn processions with officials bearing emblems of their office, probably watched by scores of spectators, the participants gathered for supper, almost certainly in the great dining-room. Queen Anne's consort, Prince George of Denmark, took over the role of host as he was of higher rank than the Duke. According to a guest, supper was 'served up with so much splendour and profusion, yet with so much decency and order that I must needs say I never saw the like.' She continued 'the table where they supped was an oval and very large; the King sat about the middle of it, and the Prince almost at the end.'

The banquet could be served as a meal in itself at any time, often to quite small parties of people, as well as a continuation of dinner or supper. Sir Richard Myddelton entertained the Duke of Beaufort in July 1684 with a banquet at Chirk Castle. He paid the enormous sum of £9 15s 4d for 'banquetting stuffe' from Shrewsbury:

for cleare paste; for Jasgies [fruit sweetmeats] and currance paste [currant paste]; for orenge pills [orange peel]; for cittorne [candied citron]; for Jumballs [a biscuit shaped into rings]; for Ice cakes [cakes iced with sugar and egg white]; Jourdan Allmonds [large sweet almonds]; 2 sugar loaves; 6 sillibub glasses; for 2 dozen glasses and a baskett; for one dozen of Oranges; one pound of ringoe roots [candied sea holly]; one pound of green genitens [jennetings – an early variety of apple]; one

A silver tea-kettle, with its own heater fuelled by spirits of wine. This example, from Canons Ashby, Northamptonshire, bears the Dryden arms impaling Allen.

A design sketched by Robert Lyminge, architect of Blickling Hall, Norfolk, for a 'Banketting House' in the garden, *c.*1620. The Gothick scheme was never realised.

pound of Lemon Pills; one pound of red currance paste; one pound of rasperie past; one quart of green past; a quarte of Apricocke; 3 ounces of Edge cakes [expensive edging for cakes]; for sweet lemon.

The habit of Bertie Wooster and his friends in the Drones Club of pelting each other with food and other high jinks is clearly based on an old British tradition. Robert May delighted especially in devising dinner-table novelties and describes banquets at which pasteboard castles were bombarded, ladies threw egg shells filled with rose-water at each other, and '... when lifting first the lid off the one pie, out skip some frogs, which makes the ladies to skip and shreek: next after the other pye, when out come the birds, who by natural instinct flying into the lights will put out the candles, so that what with the flying birds and the skipping frogs, one above the other, beneath, will cause much delight and pleasure to the whole company.' No doubt the 17th-century party-goer was relieved to end the day with a quiet posset or caudle, tea or coffee.

An Elegant Repast
GEORGIAN FOOD

An Elegant Repast

I

The Georgian age – the reigns of the first four Georges and William IV, from 1714 to 1837 – was a boom time for Britain, with the development of the first large, purpose-built factories, rapid urbanisation and a dramatic increase in trade at home and abroad, all accompanied by a big increase in population.

In scarcely more than a century, farming was to advance from methods more or less pertaining in the late Middle Ages to something not greatly inferior to those in use today, helped by improvers like Charles 'Turnip' Townsend, Thomas Coke of Norfolk and Robert Bakewell of Dishley. Land was being enclosed at an alarming rate, including even wastes of heather and furze, moors and marshes. Theresa Parker of Saltram in Devon wrote to her brother in 1773 'amongst the many improvements you will find at this place those in farming are none of the least. The whole Down that you may remember between Boringdon and Cann Quarry, besides 200 acres of the same sort of furze Brake, is now covered with all sorts of corn, and affords a prospect of Plenty that is really very striking.' Her husband, John, was one of many progressively minded landowners willing to put money and effort into the improvement of their land, although John Byng, Lord Torrington, an indefatigable traveller and diarist in the 1780s and 1790s, described the proliferating enclosures as 'the greedy tyrannies of the wealthy few to oppress the indignant many'.

In the second half of the 18th century, many estate owners tried to find ways to provide better carriage for their improved farm produce. Canals were a more dependable method of transport for the movement of perishable foods than the still appalling roads. A canal, for example, was built very near the house at Shugborough in Staffordshire and payments to a person for sitting and waiting for goods on the canal bank were recorded in the Anson accounts. All the major trunk roads connecting

Previous pages: The Traveller's Breakfast, by Edward Villiers Rippingille, 1824. The meal provided includes cold meat, boiled eggs, rolls and tea, with the tea-urn or cistern placed in the middle of the table.

London with cities like Manchester, Birmingham, York, Bristol and Dover had been turnpiked and improved, but off the main roads, transit of goods remained difficult and food often arrived unfit for consumption. It was not until late in the century that engineers like Thomas Telford and John MacAdam substantially improved the surface of the roads, reduced gradients and replaced fords and ferries with bridges.

Despite all these improvements, the bulk of the population saw little significant advance in their standard of living. The aristocracy and the gentry continued to live in style, joined by an expanding middle class of merchants and men of the professions, who had the money to expend on houses, clothes and food. But their wealth was being built upon a sub-structure of poverty more extensive than it had been for centuries.

To educate the newly monied families in the ways of genteel cooking and dining came a plethora of cookery and household management books. Reading these today, it is possible to trace the fashions in cuisine, and sense some of the vitality of the period. Charles Carter, in a preface to his *Complete Practical Cook* of 1730, excused himself for producing yet another new cookery book:

> But when 'tis consider'd, that Variety and Novelty are no small Parts of the Cook's Art, and that no Occupation in the World is more oblig'd to Invention; every Year, and every ingenious Artist constantly producing New Experiments to gratify the Taste of that Part of Mankind, whose splendid Circumstances make them emulous to excel in the Delicacies of this Mystery, especially when they exert their Wealth and their Magnificence to entertain their Friends with grand and sumptuous Repasts; it will be allow'd that no Art can be said less to have reach'd Perfection than this, and that none is more capable of Improvement.

Bread

White wheaten bread continued to be popular amongst all levels of society, especially in the south of England and the Midlands. Encouraged by this demand, farmers grew more wheat; coupled with a preponderance of good harvests in the first half of the century, this helped to ensure that wheat was plentiful and cheap. But in the second half of the century, a number of bad seasons made wheat scarce and dear, as in the 17th century. Grain had either to be imported from abroad, or bakers had to supplement their wheat flour with other cereals and with bean, pease and potato-meal. As ever, this inferior bread was not well-received, neither was the government-sponsored 'standard' loaf, a darker wheat loaf containing more bran, sold at a lower price during the worst times of shortage. Those who had once eaten white wheaten bread refused to be satisfied with anything else: 'rye and barley bread are looked on with horror even by poor cottagers', commented Arthur Young in 1767.

To meet the demand for whiter bread, professional bakers began to add lime, chalk and alum, which not only bleached the bread, but increased the size of the loaf. One anonymous writer, in a pamphlet published in the 1750s and entitled *Poison Detected, or Frightful Truths*, accused bakers of raking the charnel houses of the dead and grinding up the bones to add to their bread. He even went so far as to allege that the population of London had dwindled considerably as a consequence of eating adulterated bread.

Enriched, well-fruited spice breads or cakes, lightly spiced wigs and buns flavoured

The manufacture of Yorkshire oatcakes, from *Costumes of Yorkshire* by George Walker, 1814. The dough was rolled out thinly, and the cakes were cooked on the bakestone heated by its own fire. They were then dried on an easel or the back of a chair, as here, and stored draped over a creel.

Thomas Coke, Earl of Leicester, of Holkham Hall in Norfolk was one of the great agricultural pioneers of the 18th century. He is depicted with his South-down sheep in this painting by William Weaver.

with caraway seeds continued to be served hot and buttered at breakfast for the gentry. Muffins, which originated in the north, were also popular. They formed a regular purchase at 1d each from the 1770s for the Yorke household at Erddig in North Wales. At Saltram, they were eaten at breakfast and supper.

Meat and Poultry

The cattle-droving trade which, as we have seen, developed in the 16th and 17th centuries, continued to grow and in the 18th century developed into an industry, sending thousands of beasts from Scotland, Wales and the North to the south of England. Sheep too came slowly by road, being sold from fair to fair until at last they reached the butchers. It was estimated that during the first half of the century, 75,–80,000 head of cattle came annually to Smithfield Market in London, a figure rising to 100,000 by 1800. By the time the beasts reached London, the quality of their meat was bound to be coarse and inferior. The Duke of Bedford had sheep and cattle driven up from his estate at Woburn and parked in the fields outside his London house so that he did not have to depend upon the doubtful wares of Smithfield. It was, of course, necessary to guard them night and day and in 1759 two labourers were paid 3s for 'sitting up to watch fat cattle in Bedford House paddock'.

One of the most notable changes in diet during the 18th century was that people were no longer so dependent on salted or smoked meat, although ham and pork were still preserved in large quantities. This development was made possible by increasing the area of land under fodder crops, especially high-yielding roots such as turnips and swedes and new types of grasses and clovers. Animals could now be adequately fed year round, and so a greater proportion were not slaughtered during the winter. They, in turn, increased the output of grain by providing more manure to enrich the soil. There

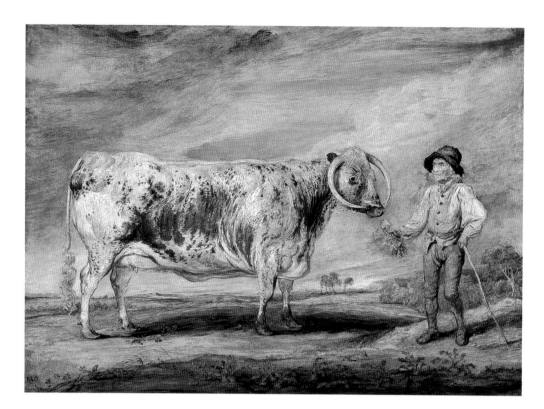

Lord Anson of Shugborough, Staffordshire, was an improving landlord, who set up his own model farm on his estate. This painting by James Ward shows one of Lord Anson's farm labourers, Jerry Hudson, with a longhorn cow.

was, however, an increasing emphasis laid on breeding animals for meat. Many stock farmers bred from selected animals in a small way, whilst some well-off yeomen and gentlemen specialised in such activities. Robert Bakewell of Dishley in Leicestershire, Britain's most prestigious breeder, was able by careful selection and feeding to develop cattle and sheep the like of which had never been seen before, producing high-quality meat that was rich in fat. At Smithfield Market in 1710, the average weight of an ox was 370 lb; by 1795 it had increased to 800 lb. Calves which had weighed 50 lb now averaged 150 lb, and the weight of a sheep increased from 38 to 80 lb. Per Kalm, a visitor from Switzerland, stressed the quality of meat in the *Account of his Visit to England in 1748*: 'All English meat, whether it is of ox, calf, sheep or swine, has a fatness and a delicious taste'.

Consequently, the monied Englishman gained a reputation for devouring enormous quantities of meat, the higher up the social scale, the larger the amount of meat eaten. What Misson declared after travelling England in the 1690s held true for the whole of the 18th century: 'I always heard that they were great flesh-eaters and I found it true. I have known people in England that never eat any bread, and universally they eat very little; they nibble a few crumbs, while they chew meat by whole mouthfuls.' The household of the diarist Parson Woodforde at Weston Longeville in Norfolk consisted of three men, three women and a boy; these seven people, at least five of them engaged in manual work, consumed a mere 13 lb of flour a week, an amount which in previous centuries would have lasted a labourer's family of the same size little more than a day. John Byng tells us of a friend who devoured twelve mutton chops for dinner; 'No man', he adds, 'possesses a healthier appetite.' But it appears there was one, for, according to François de la Rochefoucauld in 1784, the Duke of Grafton ate an ox a day and was taking a course of Bath waters 'to enable himself to eat two'!

The Anson household at Shugborough consumed over 27,000 lb of meat in 1782,

Thomas Rowlandson's depictions of the 18th-century Englishman's ideal diet: roast beef and plum pudding, washed down with claret, madeira and port (*left*); and a busy city chop-house of the 1790s (*right*).

most of which was beef, followed by mutton, pork, veal and lamb. The home farm provided the large part of this; only beef was bought in any quantity and the whole meat bill for that year was valued at around £366. The chef kept a daily record book of the people fed and the amount of meat used; he aimed to supply each person with $1\frac{1}{2}$ lb a day, but it was usually nearer 2 lb. The quality of the meat produced on the estate would have been good, as Lord Anson was one of the 'improving' landlords with a model farm.

Beef was the Englishman's favourite meat in the 18th century and roast beef was his sacramental meal immortalised in Hogarth's prints – Hogarth himself expired soon after finishing a steak – Fielding's song 'The Roast Beef of England', and 'the Sublime Society of Beefsteaks'. Misson noted that in some households Sunday was 'a Day of Beef of which they stuff till they can swallow no more and eat the rest cold without any other Victuals the other six days of the week'. Parson Woodforde scratched this last entry in his diary on Sunday, 17 October 1802: 'Very weak this Morning, scarce able to put on my cloaths and with great difficulty, get down stairs with help . . . Dinner to day, Rost beef, etc.' On New Year's Day 1803, he died.

Fast-food eating shops – cookshops, beefsteak-houses and chop-houses – were London institutions much appreciated by denizens of all classes, and much puzzled over by foreigners. Monsieur Misson deemed the cookshop worthy of a detailed description in 1690:

There are cookshops enow in all parts of the town, where it is very common to go and chuse upon the spit the part you like, and to eat it there . . . . Generally four spits, one over another, carry round each five or six pieces of Butcher's meat (never anything else, if you would have a fowl or a pidgeon, you must bespeak it). Beef, Mutton or Veal, Pork and Lamb; you have what quantity you please cut off, fat, lean, much or little done; with this, a little salt, and mustard upon the side of a plate, a Bottle of beer, and a roll.

Seventy years later, Boswell describes a similar establishment in his *London Journal*: 'You come in thence to a warm, comfortable large room, where a number of people are sitting at table. You take whatever place you find empty, call for what you like, which you get well and cleverly dressed.' He wrote that this type of meal – 'beef, bread and beer and [a penny] for the waiter' – cost a shilling.

Despite the enormous improvements in winter feeding of stock, short-term preservation of meat continued to be an essential domestic craft. For most people it meant salting and smoking: for instance, the contents of the cellar at Springhill near Cookstown in Co. Londonderry in April 1789 included '½ cwt. and 19 lbs of Hung Beef [salted and smoked] and Bacon, Herrings [pickled] and Odd Beef and Pork'. For the wealthy few, ice-houses were built in the grounds of their estates to achieve some degree of refrigeration for the meat. The 18th-century ice-house at Ham House in Surrey is a fine example, consisting of a brick-lined dome covering an ice well, with sides sloping inwards and downwards to a sump or drain at its base. In the winter, ice was taken from the Thames and estate ponds and loaded into the ice well with layers of straw, reeds and bracken, finishing with a final thick layer of straw or reeds. Loading the ice-house was an unpleasant and tedious job: when the large ice-house was filled at Killerton in Devon in 1809, the task took 30 men more than five days to store 40 tons of ice, an amount that it was hoped would last two or three years.

The Yorkes of Erddig, Clwyd, commissioned more portraits of their servants than they did of their own family, and wrote verses praising them, providing an extrordinary record of life below stairs in a Georgian country house. Among the portraits that still hang in the servants' hall, is that of Thomas Jones, the butcher to Erddig, painted in the 1790s.

Meat could be laid directly on the straw or on loose boards laid on top; hung from hooks in the walls or in the dome, or sometimes placed on narrow ledges set into the walls. Originally, however, food preservation was incidental; the 18th-century ice-house was built primarily so that fashionable ices could be served for dessert and wines be cooled.

Game became increasingly the prerogative of the landowner through enclosure and stricter game laws. In the 18th century, further game laws were passed against poachers, including the notorious Black Act of 1723, which allowed an armed or masked poacher to be punished by death if he was taken. Even hares were now legally out of reach of the ordinary family, though rabbits continued to be easy to obtain. Whether acquired legally or not, both rabbits and hares could be trussed and roasted to look like game birds, put into pies, and served as fricassées; jugged hare was an 18th-century speciality.

The number of deer-parks had been greatly reduced by land enclosure, urban spread and industrial development such as the exploitation of coal-mines. It was only in the ornamental parks surrounding major country houses that deer continued to flourish, for here they served as a status symbol for their owners, in addition to providing them with both sport and food for the table. Sir Thomas Myddelton had extended Black Park at Chirk in 1675 to hold five hundred deer and the Yorkes of Erddig always purchased their venison from Chirk. But by 1770 the last forty animals had been given away.

The range of game birds for the table was narrowing; bustards, much prized in the 1690s, were extinct by the end of the 18th century. Pheasants, partridge, grouse or moor-game, plover, quail, lapwing, woodcock, snipe and teal were still enjoyed, but fewer of the small birds were now accepted as a regular part of the diet of the discerning. Thrushes, blackbirds, sparrows and finches were eaten only by the poor. Larks proved the exception to this rule; 15 lark-spits are listed in the 1760 Shugborough inventory.

Shooting had improved so much that the modern techniques of beating flying birds over the guns was developed, and large 'bags' were taken. In 1828, alone, at Lord

Anson's prime shooting estate of Ranton Abbey near Shugborough, 1210 hares, 1975 partridge, 1401 pheasant, 1396 rabbits, 62 woodcock, 74 snipe and 44 duck were shot. Some estates had game larders built a little distance from the house because of the unpleasant smell of large quantities of game, and so that the gamekeeper was able to deposit the bodies without disturbing the kitchen staff. These buildings could be elaborate and decorative, to be visited and enjoyed by the gentry and their guests. Separate game larders of this type can be seen at Kedleston Hall near Derby and Uppark in Sussex. Both face north, with large windows, high ceilings for hanging birds and hares, and rails around the walls for venison. Shelves provide more storage space. Edward Dryden built a small pavilion in the early 18th century as a deer-larder in the park at Canons Ashby.

Once winter feeds for cattle had been developed, large-scale pigeon-keeping declined, except in Scotland where fresh meat was scarcer in winter. A landowner proved less keen on dovecote pigeons when they fed on his own crops rather than peasants' corn in common fields. When dovecotes *were* built, they developed a distinctly ornamental appearance; octagonal brickwork was much favoured, as were classical details. The roof of the dovecote at Erddig is particularly attractive, with its four small dormer windows and decoratively arched cupola topped with a pigeon-shaped weathervane. The dovecote in the kitchen garden at Felbrigg was probably built in the 1750s judging from the 'therm' windows that imitated those found in the baths of classical Rome. Inside there are niches for two thousand stock doves, providing food for the house and rich manure for the kitchen garden. Sometimes, dovecotes were built on two or three storeys, the floors below being used for poultry or even, as at Downhill Castle in Co. Londonderry, as an ice-house.

Despite some specialised poultry breeding, Parson Woodforde could still write of a turkey weighing only 14 lb as 'the finest fatted turkey that ever I saw, it was two inches in fat on the breast after it was roasted', while Lady Fermanagh of Claydon gave 2s 6d apiece for ducks no bigger than pigeons.

Sir John Soane's designs for a poultry yard in the home farm at Wimpole Hall in Cambridgeshire show that both the physical and the aesthetic well-being of its occupants was considered. His drawings provide a symmetrical classical composition of timber boxes with arched openings and neatly sketched nests. From the steward's commonplace book at Chirk Castle, we learn that in 1766 a new poultry yard was begun with 'Houses for the Reception of Pheasants and Fowls', and two years later the Castle employed its first full-time poultry-maid.

Fish

Habits in fish-eating changed during the 18th century. With the end of compulsory fish days and improved transport, freshwater fish, except the choicest varieties, went out of favour. For a time, some kept the stewponds on their estates in operation, but most turned them into ornamental lakes. Several references in the steward's commonplace book to cleaning and enlarging fish-ponds at Chirk in the 1750s make it clear that they were still providing fish for the Myddelton family, while the stewponds at Felbrigg that William Wyndham I had stocked with quantities of carp and tench in the 1670s, were joined together to form an ornamental lake by his grandson in the 1750s.

The two large rectangular brick pools built at Charlecote in Warwickshire by Sir

The elegant Gothic game larder at Uppark, Sussex. These decorative larders were built a little distance from the house, to be visited by the estate owner with his guests.

Sir John Soane's farm buildings at Wimpole Home Farm, Cambridgeshire. His designs for the poultry yard considered both the physical and aesthetic well-being of its occupants.

Thomas Rowlandson's depiction of Billingsgate Fish Market in 1808.

Thomas Lucy in the 16th century were filled in by George Lucy in 1760. Until then his faithful housekeeper, Philippa Hayes, would record in her memorandum book 'fish taken out of the Great Bason in the Court for the master's dinner' and 'Fish taken out of the Old Canal'. We are told he particularly liked 'a whole tench boiled in ale and dressed with lemon and rosemary'.

Salmon and trout were abundant, although the former was still very expensive. The highly regarded sturgeon was occasionally caught in the Severn, Thames and Tyne and several recipes for its preparation are to be found in 18th-century cookery books, as well as recipes for making mock sturgeon, such as Hannah Glasse's 'To souse a Turkey, in Imitation of Sturgeon'. Lampreys were still eaten whole or potted, as were eels and char from Windermere, carried potted or in pies all the way to London.

Fresh sea-fish would still have been difficult to obtain at Chirk and Charlecote, both some distance from the sea. Although transport improved in the 18th century, any journey from the coast with fish was risky, especially in warm weather. Even in London, where there was the advantage of river carriage, stale fish was common and even pickled fish was suspect. Advice was given in 18th-century cookery books on buying fish. Ralph Verney thought the quality of fish was important enough to mention in a letter from Claydon written on 15 September 1743 to his father in London: 'We are now very well serv'd with Fish of all sorts and tolerably reasonable twice a week. Lobsters one shilling per pound, trouts fourteen pence and other fish such as Plaice, Maids [pilchards], Souls, etc; we give according to the size of 'em. There are 2 men who bring 'em from Oxford very fresh, and serve about half a score families.'

Near the coast, a variety of sea-fish was available: regular purchases of mullet, sprats, whiting, pilchards, dories, plaice, turbot, cod, herring and pipers (gurnards) were made for Saltram from a 'man from Plymouth', but on the whole, fish was expensive compared with other foods. John Byng complained of the price of fish at the Weymouth fish market in August 1782: 'large soles at 1s 6d the pair, dories 1s and 2s, mackarel at 1½d or 2d each and 2d the pound for crab'. He thought the fish was 'by no means cheap, at this distance from the Metropolis [London], and on a sea coast'.

Shellfish was as popular as ever, oysters still being the favourite, eaten by rich and poor alike. They were certainly cheap; Dr Johnson fed them to his sick cat! Margaret Davis, the housekeeper at Saltram, records purchases of 'a Hundred of Oysters for 1s on January 1st 1781' followed by a further one hundred the next week. Purchases of this quantity continued on a regular basis throughout the year. Cockles were also purchased in vast quantities for the Great Kitchen at Saltram: '2 Hundred of Cockles for 6d' on 9 July 1781 and again on the 16th, '3 Hundred of Cockels for 9d' on the 30th and a further '4 Hundred for 1s' on the same day. Again, similar purchases continued all year, and would have been eaten boiled, curried or made into sauces. Crayfish was plentiful and would apparently even tempt the appetite of an invalid, for Dr Wells of Oxford sent some to Sir John Verney of Claydon who had 'lost his stomach'.

Although some of the choicer fish were potted to preserve them, dried and salted fish were still eaten, especially in the winter; '16 pound of Salt Fish for 4s 6d' was bought by Elizabeth Edwards, the housekeeper at Chirk on 13 February 1728. Some local dried and salted fish from northern Britain, such as smoked Finnan haddock and Newcastle salted haddock, became more widely known during the century and anchovies remained in great demand. Pickled sprats, herrings, oysters and even salmon were popular among poorer people, who gradually stopped buying the salt-fish on which they had been so dependent.

In the closing years of the century, a new venture was just beginning: packing fish in ice for long-distance transport. This was first practised on Scottish salmon, and proved so successful that ice-houses were built on all the principal salmon rivers in Scotland, and early in the 19th century Londoners were receiving quantities of ice-packed fish claimed to be as fresh as when they were taken out of the water.

It was also discovered in the middle of the century that West Indian green turtles could survive the journey to England if kept in tanks of fresh water. With the turtles came recipes for cooking them 'in West Indian fashion'; a turtle of 60–100 lb was large enough to provide the whole first course of a feast, with a tureen of soup, made from the head and lights, in the place of honour at the centre of the table. The Rev. Thomas Talbot sampled such a dinner at Saltram in 1811:

This popular 18th-century print of *New Mackerel* by Francis Wheatley now hangs in Mr Straw's House in Worksop, Nottinghamshire.

At dinner we had nothing less than two Earls and a Turtle. Lord Paulett [*sic*] (a most profoundly stupid Lord he seems, though very good-natured). Lord Mount Edgecumbe [*sic*] was extremely amusing and gave us some excellent imitations and stories. We dined in the great dining room and had the very best exertions of Mr Howse, the cook, put forth, which he certainly did with considerable effect, being pronounced one of the most accomplished Turtle dressers of the Age, which certainly, and accompanied with Ice Lime Punch, cannot be pronounced a very bad sort of diet.

The 2nd Earl of Egremont of Petworth, whose official duties as an ambassador and government minister involved many banquets, was heard to say genially, 'Well, I have but three turtle dinners to come, and if I survive them, I shall be immortal'. This hope, alas, proved to be in vain, for he died in 1763.

Fruit and Vegetables

Any lingering suspicion of vegetables on the part of medical men disappeared in this period, and they were now part of the daily diet of both rich and poor. The labouring class continued to eat mainly roots and greens. In 1760 Philip Miller, the distinguished gardener, thought that carrots 'provide great comfort to the poor' although in the North potatoes were being more widely eaten. Vegetables were generally not very imaginatively cooked by the lower and middle classes, and such recipes as 'a calves head with cabbage' or 'a large neat's tongue with greens' did not impress foreign visitors. Charles Moritz, an observant Swiss visitor, wrote disparagingly in *Travels through various parts of England in 1782*, of the ordinary Englishman's midday meal which usually consisted of 'a piece of half-boiled or half-roasted meat; and a few cabbage leaves, boiled in plain water; on which they pour a sauce made of flour and butter, the usual method of dressing vegetables in England.'

Turnips and Carrots Ho by Francis Wheatley, part of a series of 18th-century prints of street traders (*see page 211*).

Many of the gentry and aristocracy *were* eating vegetables cooked and served in an imaginative way. There was a growing taste for delicate vegetables such as asparagus, broccoli, mushrooms and globe artichokes, and it was fashionable in London to serve quite ordinary vegetables, like cucumbers, out of season when they were a rarity, raised with difficulty by skilful gardeners. Richard Steele in 1710 summed up the dictates of fashion: 'They are to eat every Thing before it comes in Season, and to leave it off as soon as it is good to be eaten.' In 1719 Richard Bradley wrote that 'the Pride of the Gardeners about London chiefly consists in the production of Melons and Cucumbers at times either before or after the natural Season'.

The gardeners to whom Bradley referred were market gardeners, many of whom now grew good quality and out-of-season vegetables for the tables of the rich, as well as raising large quantities of ordinary vegetables for general consumption. The gardeners at the Neat Houses in Victoria (where the Abbot of Westminster had had his country house in medieval times, p.18) were particularly skilled in raising high-quality produce, and in 1721 it was said, 'there is no where so good a School for a Kitchen Gardener as this Place'. There were, however, complaints from foreign visitors about the quality of some market garden produce. Monsieur Grosley, a Frenchman, complained: 'All that grow in the country about London; cabbage, radishes and spinnage, being impregnated with the smoke of sea-coal, which fills the atmosphere of that town, have a very disagreeable taste.' Some fortunate families were able to ensure quality by having their produce sent up from their country houses when they were resident in London.

At Felbrigg there is a good example of an extensive 18th-century kitchen garden that includes a vegetable plot, orchard, beehives, glasshouse growing Black Hamburg grapes and a herb border, with wall-trained apples, pears, peaches, plums, nectarines, greengages and figs. A walled kitchen garden, laid out in 1805 at Shugborough for Lord Anson, was described by William Pitt the Younger:

> A Kitchen garden of several acres is walled and subdivided: the walls well stocked with the choicest fruit trees, with very extensive ranges of hot-houses, in which the pineapple, the grape, the peach, the fig and other varieties of hot-house fruits, flowers and plants, are cultivated in the highest perfection. One of the hot-houses is heated with steam, in which melons and cucumbers are produced in perfection at all seasons.

The present walled gardens at Calke, built in 1773, include a physic garden, originally intended for the cultivation of medicinal herbs, a large 4-acre kitchen garden and an orchard with fruit stores. Originally there was a vinery in the physic garden and greenhouses, pits and frames were used for growing cucumbers, melons, pineapples and violets. The kitchen garden is again growing a number of 18th-century varieties of fruit and vegetables.

Richard Bradley described his ideal orchard thus: 'Let two Thirds at least bear Apples, and the Remainder be allotted for Pears, Plumbs, Cherries and a Mulberry-Tree or two. The Ground thus planted may be fenced about with Hedges of Filberds and Barberries, to make it still the more compleat and delightful.' The famous Kentish orchards expanded rapidly during the century to meet the demand from the London markets and, with the development of canal systems, apples and plums were carried to the North where fruit was relatively scarce, as a return load on coal barges. As with

Balthasar Nebot's painting of the piazza at Covent Garden with Inigo Jones' St Paul's Church. By the 18th century the vegetables sold here were locally grown, but the fruit was usually supplied from foreign sources.

vegetables, fruit sold in London was expensive and of poor quality; the standard of hygiene in its handling was appallingly low. Tobias Smollett's description in *The Expedition of Humphry Clinker*, written in 1771 of a barrow woman 'cleaning her dusty fruit with her own spittle' was probably not an isolated example.

To supplement home-grown fruit, such popular exotics as lemons, mangoes, limes, melons, pineapples, dates and figs were imported in increasingly large quantities. Glasshouses had been added to houses from the late 16th century, but now orangeries were being specially built to accommodate these exotic fruits. Ashe Windham added an orangery to his estate at Felbrigg in 1705, recorded by his mother, Katherine, in her account book: 'My son laid out on my account for ye Orange House £261 16s 11d'. In November 1771, only two years after her marriage, Theresa Parker wrote from Saltram of the recent addition of 'a delightful Orangery', kitchen garden and grape or peach-houses. The orange trees for the new orangery had been ordered from Genoa and 3 guineas were paid for 'their freight from Falmouth' on 18 October. The trees were placed outside from the end of May for the summer in the grove behind the chapel, which as Theresa's sister Anne wrote in 1782, 'is so warm a situation that we mean to plant all sorts of curious shrubs'. Two years later, in a mild February, the new 'Peach or Grape House' was 'the greatest beauty, the trees in full blossom . . .'.

Oranges from *Illustratio Systematis Sexualis Linnaei* by J. Miller, 1777.

The new orangery for Blickling designed by Samuel Wyatt was probably built in 1782. Ten years later it contained 15 large, 11 young and 6 dwarf orange trees in a variety of boxes and tubs, 3 water pots, a water engine and a brazier. Another member of the prolific architectural family of Wyatts, Sir Jeffry Wyatville, designed an orangery in 1811 for the 1st Earl Brownlow at Belton. Despite all the effort and expense, many of the citrus fruits grown were small and unripe; so both 'China' and 'Sivel' oranges continued to be purchased regularly between 1780 and 1795 at 6 for 1s by the Saltram housekeeper, and lemons at 12 for 2s for use as a flavouring and for garnishing. Lime juice, as we have seen, was imported from the West Indies to make the lime punch that accompanied turtle soup.

Pineries became another fashionable addition to those grand houses that had their own hot-houses. In 1777 new hot-houses and 'Pineries' were built at Knole; £175 was paid for 'two hot-houses full stocked with pine apples and plants'. Pineapples were difficult and expensive to grow and serving them for dessert was a symbol of 18th-century one-upmanship. Fanny Burney, the well-known diarist and Mistress of the Robes to Queen Charlotte, had pineapple every day when she was staying with the Thrales at Streatham, besides grapes, melons, nectarines and peaches – all home-grown. The Rev. Thomas Talbot was obviously disgusted with the dessert he was served at Saltram in October 1811: he wrote '. . . then the Dessert (without Pines as at Port Eliot) still on the cloth . . .'. Port Eliot was a nearby estate in Cornwall, obviously with a pinery.

Dairy Produce

Great houses still prided themselves on their own dairy products. Sometimes ladies turned their dairies into elegant rooms, adorned with pieces of fine china, and took their friends there to drink syllabubs and milk warm from the cow, the real business of the dairy being done in the adjoining scullery. The very attractive dairy at Shugborough once supplied the house with hard cheese, cream cheese, butter, cream and milk.

Originally a banqueting house designed by James 'Athenian' Stuart in the 1760s on the model of the Tower of the Winds in Athens, it was converted into a dairy for Lady Anson by Samuel Wyatt *c*.1805. The basement is lined with Penrhyn slate and has thick shelves and a table also of slate; this was where the real work of the dairy was done by a skilled dairymaid. In contrast the ground floor is elegantly lined with Derbyshire alabaster and lit by stained glass. Round the walls are marble shelves for the milk pans and other dairy pots; a splendid set of pots by Wedgwood in the Egyptian style once stood in the alcoves, but is now stored in the house for safe-keeping. This was the 'fancy dairy' where the mistress of the house could dabble, setting the cream and making flummeries (spiced cream set with calves' foot, hartshorn jelly or isinglass), junkets and syllabubs. A spiral staircase leads up to the banqueting room.

There is an extraordinary 18th-century dairy in the grounds of Ham House, where the tiled walls and marble slabs are improbably supported on delicate cows' legs. The Uppark dairy with its adjoining scullery, designed by Humphry Repton, is one of the best examples of a decorative dairy owned by the National Trust. It was built in the garden, so that Sir Harry Fetherstonhaugh, when entertaining guests outside, could offer them cream and butter freshly made in the little two-roomed dairy, with its windows of Regency glass, blue, orange and white. White tiles with a border of blue convolvulus made a pretty setting for the large bowls and earthenware crocks on the marble tables, full of Guernsey cream and milk, furnished by the Uppark herd. Sir Harry must have delighted in his dairy, for at the age of 70 he married the chief dairymaid, Mary Ann Bullock, aged 18. According to Margaret Meade-Fetherstonhaugh in *Uppark and its People*, legend has it that Sir Harry appeared at the door of the dairy and told Mary Ann he wished to marry her. 'Speechless with surprise, she could not reply. "Don't answer me now", said Sir Harry, "but if you will have me, cut a slice

The interior of the 18th-century dairy at Uppark, Sussex.

out of the leg of Mutton that is coming up for my dinner today . . .'' When the mutton arrived, the slice was cut. Contemporary stories dwell long and lovingly on the rage and surprise of the Cook.'

In large towns cows were kept in sheds and milk was supplied to the citizens either at the dairy or by milkmen and women who took the milk through the streets to customers' houses. There were frequent complaints that town milk was diluted and adulterated – the juice of snails was squeezed and stirred in to give a fresh, frothy appearance, and dark tales were told of mud, stones and all manner of street litter falling into open pails. London milk sellers were said, in 1794, to possess 'neither character, decency, manners or cleanliness. No delicate person could possibly drink milk were they fully acquainted with the filthy habits of these dealers in it.'

If the 17th century was the 'golden age of butter', the 18th century was the age of

Nickolls' painting of St James's Park and the Mall, London, c.1745. In the early 18th century, the park was the place to see and be seen. The promenaders could refresh themselves with milk fresh from the cows that grazed in the park.

A popular print of a milkmaid engraved by Shepherd after H. W. Bunbury. The sentimentality of this scene belies the fact that in cities cows were often kept in unhealthy conditions and that the quality of the milk sold through the streets could well be poor.

cream as far as cookery in wealthy households was concerned. It was added liberally to make dishes like fricassées, ragôuts and braises, to vegetables, to sauces, and to endless puddings and desserts, like snows, flummeries, syllabubs, ice-cream and fruit creams. Cheese was still made on most farms and in many country houses; indeed, on large farms it was made twice a day. Skimmed milk cheeses were very common, although the only one that had a tolerable reputation was the Blue Vinney of Dorset. Whole milk cheeses were being manufactured in large quantities, and in the summer months, soft curd cheeses were produced in all dairy districts.

With improved transport townspeople, particularly Londoners, came to know the many kinds of cheese produced in different parts of the country. Welsh cheese had been shipped from Chester and Liverpool to London and Bristol in the 17th century, but now the trade in Cheshire cheeses was developing: cheese-mongers ran a fleet of no less than 16 ships between London and Liverpool. The organisation also had 'cheese-factors' all over the West Country. It was early in the century that a certain Mrs Paulett, a farmer's wife, supplied her brother-in-law, landlord of the Bell Inn at Stilton near Peterborough in Lincolnshire, with a new variety of cheese that quickly became popular. Daniel Defoe described it as English Parmesan, 'brought to table with the mites or maggots round it so thick that they bring a spoon with them for you to eat the mites with as you do the cheese', but it soon, understandably, was known as Stilton cheese. By the end of the century, Single and Double Gloucester, Wiltshire, Stilton, Wensleydale, Cheshire and Cheddar could be bought in most towns.

For the comfortably off, Per Kalm noted that 'cheese nearly always concludes the meal. Commonly, there is set on the table, whole, a large and strong cheese and each person cuts what he likes from it'. It was also used in cooking to flavour omelettes and hashes; to sprinkle over some vegetables, such as cauliflower and cardoons; as a topping for macaroni; and to make supper dishes. Welsh, Scotch and English Rabbit appeared in Hannah Glasse's *The Art of Cookery*, 1747, for the first time.

Beverages

In 18th-century England, consumption of alcohol reached such an extreme level among all classes that some observers seriously feared for the stability of the social structure. The chief cause of the trouble was unrestricted sale of cheap raw spirit made from the excess grain crops. 'British brandy' paid practically no excise duty – 2d a gallon – and when doctored with juniper it bore a passing resemblance to Dutch gin. It was so cheap that even the poorest, particularly in the towns, felt they could afford to drown their sorrows. Although a licence was needed to sell beer, none was required for spirits. It was estimated that in certain parts of London in the 1750s, one house in every four or five was a gin shop with its shameless signboard proclaiming 'Drunk for a penny; dead drunk for two-pence; clean straw for nothing'.

By the middle of the century, gin-drinking was causing untold misery, disease and thousands of deaths, forcing the government to raise taxation substantially on spirits to try to curb the evil. In fact, it was the sharp rise in the price of grain that achieved this goal. The public in the main returned to beer and other healthier drinks; in 1795 *The Times* advised the poor, under the title 'The Way to Peace and Plenty', 'Go to no gin-shops, or alehouse: but lay out all your earnings in food and clothes for yourself, and your family.'

Cruikshank's portrayal of a London gin shop. It was estimated that in certain parts of the city in the 1750s, one house in four or five was a gin shop, with its shameless sign proclaiming, 'Drunk for a penny; dead drunk for two-pence; clean straw for nothing.'

In Scotland, the problem lay in the illegal distilling of whisky; the increased excise duty had the effect of encouraging the rate of both distilling and drinking because the product of the illicit stills had to be disposed of quickly! Neat whisky became the drink of the poor.

The wealthy, meanwhile, preferred French brandy at 20s a gallon and some of the most important distilleries, such as Hennessy, Gautier and Martell, were founded at this time. John Byng noted in his diary: 'I gave sufficient encouragement to the French by a consumption of their Brandy, of which I commonly call for a Pint per Diem.' Rum at 15s a gallon was imported in large quantities from the West Indian sugar islands, and English punch made from rum or brandy with water or milk, lime or lemon juice, sugar and spices became popular with the middle and upper classes. The Rev. Talbot tells us that Lady Boringdon called for 'a large bowl of Punch' for supper at Saltram in 1811. The drink was always served in a special bowl and transferred by a punch or toddy ladle into large, heavy glasses known as 'rummers' (from the principal ingredient). Punch gradually fell out of favour in the 19th century, becoming a drink chiefly for festive occasions.

Foreign wines were bought by those who could afford them, but they were extremely expensive, especially from France. Champagne, the most expensive, was drunk both red and white, and often still rather than sparkling. It was a regular purchase itemised in John Parker's accounts of 1771–88 for Saltram: on 19 February 1772, £21 was paid 'for champaign' and again on 26 March, a further 15 guineas, with large amounts for burgundy, claret, Madeira and brandy.

The cheapest foreign wine was port. As a result of the Methuen Treaty of 1703, Britain's oldest ally, Portugal, could send port without paying more than a nominal duty. As relations with France worsened, port-drinking became a patriotic gesture. It was drunk by the men all through dinner and all evening too; Dr Johnson spoke with great contempt of claret, as being so weak that 'a man would be drowned by it before it made him drunk ... No sir, claret is the liquor for boys, port for men.' Obviously, William Anson agreed with him for the Shugborough cellar book records that 3 bottles of claret and 59 of port were drunk at his table in August 1787.

Vintage wines were unknown until the invention in 1770 of the cylindrical bottle, with its tightly fitted cork, that could be stored on its side. Before this, all wine was drunk from bulbous bottles that stood upright and were corked comparatively loosely with a conical cork. In large houses the butler was usually put in charge of the wine cellar and was responsible for keeping the cellar book. David Conyngham of Springhill, Co. Londonderry, left a well-stocked cellar in 1789:

> 2 Barrels of Porter [a strong, dark beer], 1 Cag of Rum [16 and a half gallons], 8 gallons of vinegar [purchased from the wine merchant and always kept in the cellar], 1 hogshead of Port wine, and another half full, 1 hogshead of Clarret in bottles, 5 dozen of Sherry, 10 dozen French Clarret in bottles, 2 and a half dozen of Frontiniac, 3 Casks of Cyder, 2 barrels and 2 butts of Cyder, 67 bottles of Ale, 9 Barrels, 4 dozen of and Beer.

Wine was also used for cooking; the butler at Chirk Castle supplied the chef with 4 bottles of white wine, 4 bottles of sherry, 2 bottles of port, 1 bottle of Madeira and 1 bottle of Mountaine (Spanish wine, previously known as malaga) for use in the kitchen during August 1787. At Erddig the Wine Day Book records 'red wine to ye Cooks for Carp' on 19 September 1740; 'white wine for Waffles to ye Cook' the following 4 November; and ' white wine to ye Cooks for Mincepyes' in December.

However, the drink of the ordinary Englishmen remained beer, except in the cider and perry counties. In London alone, the principal brewers produced 1,178,856 barrels of strong beer in 1786, not all of it as good as it should have been. Some of today's large brewing companies like Bass, Charrington, Courage, Tetley, Whitbread, Worthington and Allsopp started up in the 18th century, but even in 1800, at least half the total amount of beer consumed was still home-brewed. The cottager in the south stopped brewing late in the 18th century for the same reason as she stopped baking – lack of fuel and the correct equipment. William Cobbett writing in 1821 estimated that the price of the vats, mash tuns, pails and barrels needed, would have come to about £10, which was a fortune if you were living near subsistence level. The substantial sum of £300 was spent on setting up the Calke Abbey brewhouse in the 1740s. In the North and Scotland where there was cheaper fuel, home-brewing survived longer.

The Shugborough brew-house was set up early in the 18th century as part of strenuous efforts by the estate to become fully self-sufficient, not only in the brewing process itself, but also in the production of malt; the model farm included a malthouse for converting barley grown on the estate into malt. A stocktake of the cellars in 1824 shows that Shugborough's beer was brewed in several qualities. A 'strong very old' sparkling ale from a cask was called 'Old Tom', probably named after Thomas Anson, squire at Shugborough from 1720 until his death in 1773. It would have been drunk exclusively by the family and guests at dinner from small stemmed 'flutes' shaped rather like modern Champagne glasses. It is likely that the '2 dozen of ale glasses for 14s' bought by the household in 1779 were of this type. The second quality brewed was 'Ale', kept in the main ale cellars under the dining-room; the stock included one huge 900 gallon cask called 'Lord Anson', and one 400-gallon cask called 'Lady Anson'. This was probably the main table beer for both the family and the servants: the annual

'A Mansion House Treat or Smoking Attitudes – Sir John Barleycorn, Miss Hop (and their Only Child) Master Porter', from a coloured engraving published by Thomas Tegg. Porter was an almost black beer with a high alcohol content, especially popular with market porters. The Irish version came to be known as Guinness.

production was around 7,000 gallons. The final quality, 'Beer', was the small beer, with an alcohol content as low as 2–3 per cent, that was drunk by the servants at times other than the main meal. As well as being available in the servants' hall, small beer was used as payment for casual labourers. Porter, an almost black beer with a high alcohol content, was also stored in the cellar, but had not been brewed at Shugborough. It was a very popular beer, apparently so named because it was especially liked by market porters. It was brewed in London in the 1720s. The Irish version came to be known as Guinness, after Arthur Guinness, who established a brewery in Dublin in 1759.

The making and care of beer in the cellars was the responsibility of the butler. He controlled the brew, although the practical brewer was usually someone else – at Shugborough he was one of the outdoor staff. At Chirk Castle a brewer, an underbrewer and a hopman were employed, until the hop-yard was ploughed up in 1754. By 1788, the Castle was employing one man, John Jones, as maltster, brewer and baker. It was quite common to have one man acting as brewer and baker, because of the obvious links with yeast. Sir Henry Crewe employed a brewer who also baked. Calke beer was reputed to have been good, although in 1815, Sir Henry expressed great dissatisfaction with both his brewer and his beer: 'you never see a drop sparkle in the glass and it tastes thick and sweet – what I like is a light fine ale; small beer should be brisk and fresh but not tart. As to the Baker, I caution you against any consultation with him. He is the man who has spoiled all my beer for the last 3 years . . . he is neither a good Baker nor a good Brewer . . . and I certainly do not mean to continue him.' The

Above left: The brew-house at Charlecote Park, Warwickshire. Barley was grown on the estate, converted into malt in the village and then carted to the brew-house for the manufacture of ale and beer. When George Lucy died in 1845 it was reckoned that 4,630 gallons of beer and ale were standing in the Charlecote cellars.

Above: The brew-house at Calke Abbey, Derbyshire, was connected to the ale and beer cellars of the house by a brick tunnel, built with a steep slope down which the barrels could be rolled.

brew-house at Calke was connected to the ale and beer cellars of the house by a brick tunnel, built with a steep slope down which the barrels were rolled.

No less noteworthy than the rise in spirit drinking was the phenomenal success of tea as a beverage. In 1717 Thomas Twining opened the first tea shop for ladies in London at Devereux Court near the Aldwych. A few years later the Vauxhall Pleasure Gardens were developed as a tea-garden; it proved so popular that many more such gardens were opened in London and other towns. People of every class from the royal family down, both male and female, could meet here to drink tea together and enjoy the concerts, sports or fireworks provided for their entertainment. 'Throughout the whole of England', wrote La Rochefoucauld in *A Frenchman in England*, 1784, 'the drinking of tea is general. You have it twice a day and, though its expense is considerable, the humblest peasant has twice a day just like the rich man'. Arthur Young thought it was disgraceful that the families of labourers should have started drinking tea, which he insisted was 'an abomination' that would keep them poor.

Indeed, no drink has caused more controversy than tea; doctors, political economists, moralists and the clergy joined with the wine merchants and publicans in condemning it roundly. Jonas Hanway never tired of abusing it, because in his view tea had destroyed the beauty of Englishwomen: 'Your very chambermaids,' he declared in *An Essay on Tea* in 1757, 'have lost their bloom by sipping tea.' Over-indulgence was found to 'hurt the nerves (Bohea especially) and cause various distempers, as tremors, palsies, vapours, fits etc'. From the middle of the century, to counteract the effect of tannin, Per Kalm noted 'most people pour a little cream or sweet milk into the teacup when they are about to drink the tea'. Sugar was also added. The English were already accustomed to sugaring their wine and were quite ready to do the same with other drinks.

Although more and more tea was being drunk – in 1725 a quarter of a million lb was imported into England and by the end of the century more than 24 million lb annually – the price, which included 5s a lb duty, irrespective of quality, remained high. John Parker of Saltram paid 15s a lb for tea in 1774 and bought 10 or 20 lb at a time, probably from London. A visit to the capital was the occasion for settling old bills and giving new orders to the grocer and wine merchant. Philippa Hayes, George Lucy's housekeeper at Charlecote, would make out commissions for George Lucy to execute in London: tea, Bohea and the finest green from Thomas Twining & Son at the Golden Lion, powdered loaf sugar, the best all-nut chocolate, Jordan almonds, French barley, Jamaican pepper, cinnamon, pistachio nuts, coffee beans, hartshorn, white starch and French brandy.

After all the effort and expense of acquiring the tea, it is hardly surprising that even the well-to-do still kept it under lock and key. The price created a black market and an enormous amount was smuggled in from the Continent, especially from Holland. Even Parson Woodforde had no scruples about receiving smuggled tea; 'Andrew the Smuggler [the local blacksmith] brought me this night about 11 o'clock a bag of Hyson tea 6 pound weight. I paid him for the tea at 10s 6d per pound.' The smugglers succeeded mainly because they had the sympathy of the whole country; in 1784 the duty was lowered to a nominal sum and tea-smuggling ended. At the same time the government compelled the East India Company to import enough to satisfy demand without raising prices on the grounds that 'tea has become an economical substitute to the middle and lower classes of society for malt liquor [beer] the price of which renders it impossible for them to procure the quantity sufficient for them as their only drink.' Cooks and servants from wealthy households were allowed to sell used tea-leaves 'to

charwomen' who in turn sold them on to dealers who recoloured them using poisonous dyes, then resold them to the poor.

The American colonists shared Britain's enthusiasm for beverages; in imitation of London, New York came to support numerous coffee-houses and tea-gardens. But in 1766 Parliament declared its right to tax its colonies with a series of annoying duties 'of principle'. These included tea duty of 3d per lb. The colonists reacted in true British fashion and boycotted the taxed goods, and in the case of tea, resorted to smuggling it in from Holland. The East India Company found itself sitting on a huge 8,500 ton surplus of tea in England, and as a result the Tea Act was passed in 1773, authorising the Company to ship it direct to the colonies without paying import duties and selling it through its own American agents – in effect, granting a monopoly. The initial shipment of tea across the Atlantic was destroyed at the famous Boston Tea Party in December 1773. Americans bound themselves not 'to Conform to the Pernicious Custom of Drinking Tea, until such time as all Acts which tend to enslave our Native Country shall be repealed.' Tea became a symbol: to drink it meant to conform to the Mother Country, to turn to coffee represented independence. To this day Americans have tended to take coffee as a result of this extraordinary boycott.

In Britain, on the other hand, tea-drinking spread, and with it sugar consumption. In 1720 sugar consumption was 8 lb a head, but had shot up to 12 lb by the 1770s. As trade with the West Indies developed, so sugar ceased to be a luxury, although many of the poor could still not afford it. Ordinary white sugar candy cost about $6\frac{1}{2}$d a lb with refined varieties about 2d a lb dearer. Treacle, the residue from refining sugar, was much more popular with the poorer classes in the North and was used to sweeten cakes and biscuits

A Tea Garden by George Morland. The first tea-garden at Vauxhall in London proved so popular that many more such gardens were opened. People of every class, both male and female, could meet to drink tea and enjoy the entertainments provided. The tea was taken in tiny, handleless cups, with milk and sugar.

and to add to porridge. The increasing use of sugar and treacle meant a gradual decline in the demand for honey. Nevertheless many country dwellers, especially in Wales and Scotland and the large country estates, still maintained beehives. These were made of wood rather than the traditional skeps of straw and wicker. In June 1771 John Parker paid 3 guineas for new beehives to be placed in the kitchen garden at Saltram.

Chocolate remained fashionable and with coffee succeeded ale as the normal breakfast drink of the gentry. The price had dropped dramatically from the 10-15s a lb in the mid-17th century, so that the Duke of Bedford could buy in bulk 82 lb at 8d a lb in the 1750s. Vanilla imported from Central America, spices and sugar could be added, making it much richer than our modern drinking chocolate. Patrick St Clair, who had accompanied the young Ashe Windham on his Grand Tour in 1693 and had become vicar of Aylmerton in Norfolk, wrote to him at Felbrigg about his daughter's chocolate: 'Thank you for remembering her chocolate; she likes it without sugar and without Veneals [vanilla] and not high burnt.'

Coffee remained expensive at 4s 6d or 5s a lb, yet coffee-houses grew in popularity. Dr Johnson, 'a hardened and shameless tea-drinker', was the century's greatest devotee of 'coffee-house talk'. Ensconced in his favourite chair at the Turk's Head, he would hold forth for hours with Sir Joshua Reynolds, Edmund Burke, David Garrick and fellow writers like Sheridan, Boswell and Goldsmith. John Parker from Saltram and Ashe Windham from Felbrigg must surely have joined him many times, as they numbered all these people among their friends.

Coffee-houses provided a male refuge where a cup of coffee could be had for 2d, chocolate for 2½d, a pipe of tobacco for 1d, and newspapers for free. The Poet Laureate, John Dryden, a relation of the Drydens at Canons Ashby, held court at Will's in Bow Street for years, his armchair in its 'settled and prescriptive place' by the hearth in winter and out on the balcony in summer. Lord Fermanagh of Claydon patronised Thomas Garway's as we read in a letter to him from a relative on 30 June in 1720: 'I lookt narrowly for you in and about Garraway's Coffee House . . . was not so lucky as to find you.'

Properties, commodities and *objets d'art* were commonly auctioned in salerooms attached to coffee-houses and this is how the great auction houses of Sotheby's and Christie's began. One of Thomas Garway's early competitors was Edward Lloyd whose clientele were mainly shipowners, captains, merchants and insurance writers; thus, the foundations were laid for two important institutions – Lloyds Register of Shipping and Lloyds Insurance. The uniformed attendants in the insurance firm's office are still called 'waiters' today, just as in coffee-house times. At the end of the century, however, the coffee-house was declining as an institution and often developed into a private club.

In 1750, William Ellis recommended in *The Country Housewife's Family Companion* that coffee should be made thus:

The right way to make coffee, is to heat the berries in a fire-shovel till they sweat a little, and then grind them, and put the coffee-pot over the fire with water; when hot, throw the water away, and dry the pot by the fire, then put the powder into it, and boiling water immediately over the same; let it stand three or four minutes, and pour off the clear. By this means the hot water meets the spirit of the coffee; whereas if you boil coffee, as the common way is, the spirit goes away, so that it will not be so strong nor quick to the taste.

Rowlandson's print of Lloyds Coffee House.

In spite of this, foreigners like Pastor Moritz condemned British coffee, just as they do today, saying that if you asked for coffee and did not specify how many spoonfuls were to be put in it, you would be given 'a prodigious quantity of brown fluid'. At least coffee remained relatively pure since coffee beans could not easily be faked or adulterated, unlike tea-leaves. It remained a drink of the gentry and middling sort of people, becoming less expensive after the import duties on Jamaican and American coffee had been greatly reduced.

II

Georgian households were usually smaller than those of earlier generations. Fewer servants were employed for financial reasons and because changing ideas of accommodation made it impossible to house as many dependents. The idea of the country estate as a self-sufficient entity was now in decline.

In great houses of the 18th century the domestic offices were kept as far away as possible from the 'superior parts of the house'. Architects were concerned that the state rooms should be protected from the risk of fire and from the noise and smells of the kitchen, rather than in keeping food hot. Verses satirising this concern were penned in 1714 on the building of the ultimate Baroque mansion, Blenheim Palace, by Sir John Vanbrugh for the Duke of Marlborough:

> .... 'tis very fine,
> but where d'ye sleep, or where d'ye dine?
> I find by all you have been telling
> That 'tis a house, but not a dwelling.

Placing the kitchen in a separate pavilion joined to the main house by a corridor was one fashionable solution. This was adopted at Kedleston, where a second pavilion housed the family apartments and Robert Adam's grand design was to have two answering pavilions which were never built. The main block of the house was intended both to entertain important guests and to be a 'temple of arts', open to visitors who have flocked here ever since the builders downed tools. Lord Scarsdale and his family still live in the family wing and had their own kitchen put in as late as 1945. Before this, there was only a butler's pantry to prepare drinks, all their food being cooked in the 18th-century kitchen, and eaten in the state dining-room.

The kitchen at Uppark was also built in a separate pavilion away from the house and not, at first, even connected by a corridor. The food was conveyed to the dining-room in the open air until 1810, when an underground passage lit by cast-iron gratings, still visible on the carriage sweep in front of the house, was built by Repton. The decision to move the kitchen out of the house at Erddig into a separate building may have been influenced by Philip Yorke I's fear of fire; in 1781 he repeated to his agent the need for 'a constant care against the dreadful accident of fire ...'. Indeed, the danger of fire was still very real: John Parker was forced into remodelling the domestic offices at Saltram because fire destroyed the laundry and brew-house in 1788. The new brick kitchen was built on the site, while the laundry and brew-house were moved into a separate block.

The lofty, well-lit kitchen of St James's Palace in London, with its large roasting range, smoke-jack, dripping-pan and roasting screen. The iron oven had its own grate underneath to heat it, a built-in hot plate with its own fire-box. The large copper, again with its own fire-box, was used for boiling vegetables, meat and puddings.

For the 1st Earl Belmore, James Wyatt provided domestic offices in the basement of the east pavilion of Castle Coole in Co. Fermanagh, sinking the kitchen and scullery lower to provide extra height and light for working. The massive stone-vaulted ceilings in the kitchen and throughout the basement were intended as a fire precaution, as well as a means of insulating from the noise and bustle the civilised calm of the state rooms above. Calke also has a basement kitchen, but they were not common. John Byng tried to dissuade a friend from having his kitchen underground, 'for which,' he sensibly remarks, 'there can be no reason in the country'. The reason at Castle Coole was, in fact, disguise; Irish houses tended to have more servants than English, but fewer who were educated or presentable. They were to be seen only when summoned by a bell (bell systems began to appear in the 1760s and 1770s) and their approach to the house was via a long barrel-vaulted tunnel in the stable yard leading to a covered yard outside the kitchen. Despite this, Lord Belmore did not skimp on the decoration of their quarters.

The main features of a Georgian kitchen can be summed up by a description of work carried out between 1748 and 1770 to modernise the kitchen at Chirk Castle: 'A new Flag'd Floor laid in the Kitchen, the same in the Scullery and the same in the upper Larder; a new set of Stewhearths were fixed in the kitchen; a large Press or Cup-board placed on the East Side of the Kitchen to hold Coppers and other Kitchen Furniture . . . and the old Kitchen Dresser demolish'd and a new one fixed in its stead . . . The inside of the Kitchen great Window lower'd dresser height.' The purpose-built 18th-century kitchen was a well-proportioned, high-ceilinged room with large sash windows providing light, good ventilation, and thus better working conditions for the kitchen staff. The Kedleston kitchen, designed of course by Robert Adam, is said to be one of the most perfectly proportioned rooms of its type: '48' by 24' and very lofty' Sir Christopher Sykes noted in 1794, with large sash windows at both ends, and a gallery built for the mistress of the house to watch the cooks and scullions at their work. Horace Walpole spoke of the 'Vast Kitchen with a gallery like a Chapel', always included in the tour of the house made by guests attending the Scarsdales' great parties and by the everyday visitor. The latter was guided by Mrs Garnett, the 'well drest elderly House-keeper, a most distinct Articulator' who took Boswell and Dr Johnson round in 1777.

With its large Venetian windows, more usual in a saloon or on a main staircase, and three great rusticated arches with the words 'Waste not, Want not' written above them, the large kitchen at Erddig is architecturally one of the grandest rooms of the house, demonstrating the high regard Philip Yorke had for his staff. The 'Great Kitchen' at Saltram also provided its staff with the most up-to-date working conditions, with large sash windows and a high coved ceiling with louvres for better ventilation. Extra light

The kitchen at Kedleston, Derbyshire, from a photograph taken in the 1920s at the time the Scarsdales moved from the kitchen pavilion to more modest family quarters. The kitchen was designed by Robert Adam in the 1760s, and was regarded as one of the most perfectly proportioned rooms of its type. On the left can be seen the roasting range, remains of the smoke-jack and the roasting screen or 'baffle'. The large wooden dresser and the stout tables, with fitted butcher's block, are of elm.

Above: When the great kitchen at Saltram, Devon, was built in 1788, it provided all the most modern conveniences – large sash windows, a high ceiling with louvres for better ventilation, and the latest equipment.

Right: The kitchen of the Royal Pavilion, Brighton. The Prince Regent was very interested in his food, engaging the great French chef Antonin Carême at great expense. This kitchen reflects the lavish scale, with its huge roasting range, hot plate and iron ovens, and a vast *batterie de cuisine*. The design of the lamps was copied for the kitchen at Saltram (*see above*).

was provided by candle lamps, or oil lamps developed using colza (rape oil) and whale oil. In the 1780s a Frenchman, Ami Argand, perfected a circular wick which allowed air to pass up the middle of it, giving a brighter flame.

Kitchen walls were white-washed, or painted various shades of blue to repel flies. This is the colour scheme at Erddig and originally was probably used at Calke to match the scullery and pantry. A clock was provided to help the cook, either freestanding or hanging on the wall. It was not unknown for the cook to put back the clock if he or she was running late. Cupboards, shelves and dressers, usually made by estate carpenters, lined all available walls; a prominent place being given to the dresser, on which was displayed the china, copper and pewter. Robert Southey described a kitchen dresser thus: 'a dresser as white as when the wood was new, the copper and tin vessels bright and burnished . . . the plates and dishes hanged in order along the shelves'. Eighteenth-century dressers could be quite elaborate and were invariably fixtures embedded in the wall with the working surface made of unpainted scrubbed wood, usually deal, covered with a white cloth, and the shelves, back legs and drawers generally painted. The dresser in the great kitchen at Saltram is an elegant example, occupying the whole of one wall and displaying china with Lord Boringdon's crest, and copper moulds.

A large wooden scrubbed table or tables, usually of elm or sycamore, in the centre of the kitchen provided the main working surface. Part of the preparation for the day included setting the cook or chef's place at the big table; first, a clean white starched cloth was laid on the table to protect the wood, followed by a chopping board, flanked by all the utensils needed. The first kitchen-maid, or the under-cook if there was a chef, had her place set on the opposite side of the table.

Although in the more remote country areas people continued to burn wood or peat in a great open kitchen hearth until well into the 19th century and beyond, coal had replaced wood as the principal fuel. The design of grates and utensils had altered accordingly, but the methods of cooking and the labour involved in cleaning and preparing remained more or less unchanged. The cradle or basket grate had begun to take over from the dog-grate of the previous century. It was a large oblong iron basket standing on four legs well above the hearth, like the dog-grate, but firmly secured to the back of the fireplace by the iron tie-bars. Such grates meant smaller cooking fires but, because they were shallow from front to back, yet broad and high, they presented the heat in a most efficient and economical way for roasting.

The final stage of the open grate came with the development of the hob-grate in the mid-18th century; panels of cast iron were added to the front on each side of the fire box, with flat iron plates on top to provide hobs for pans and kettles. The cheeks of the fire box could still be wound in or out, under the hobs. Spit-hooks were attached to the sides of the grate and the spit itself could now be turned by the fashionable new smoke-jack. This worked by means of a fan built like a windmill into the chimney and turned by the rising current of hot air from the fire; the power created drove the various gears, chains and pulleys on the chimney-breast that turned the spit.

The roasting range at Saltram, put in about 1810, is equipped with elaborate spits, smoke-jack, large dripping pan and ladles for basting. The width of the fire is adjustable with moveable cheeks worked by a rack and pinion mechanism and the fire is backed by a water tank which delivered piping hot water to the taps in the recess to the left of the great hearth.

The logical progression from the hob-grate was further to enclose the fire, making it more economical in the use of fuel, as well as giving better heat control, and making it possible to have an oven and a boiler for hot water. Inventions were patented in the second half of the century that led to the development of the kitchen range. A precursor of these was an iron oven designed by Hornbuckle, intended to be set at the back of the open grate. It was heated by the fire and also by heat-carrying passages built in behind the grate. In 1793, Langmead patented an oven that could be set at one side of an open fire grate with a boiler for hot water on the other side, but it was Thomas Robinson who took out a patent for the first actual range in 1780. A working reproduction of his range is used still in the kitchen at Shugborough Park Farm House to bake delicious cakes and biscuits. Robinson's range was similar to a hob-grate, having an open coal fire with removable bars, flanked on either side by metal hobs, but at one side he had built an iron oven, which had a hinged door and on the other side, an iron boiler for hot water. The oven was lined with brick and fitted with shelves. A hinged trivet which could be swung forward to take a pan or kettle was fitted to the top bar of the open fire-grate. Although this range was an important step forward, there were considerable drawbacks noted particularly by Count Rumford of Bavaria. The oven was only heated on one side, so that the food tended to be burnt on that side and undercooked on the other. Also, the fire-grate was open, so burned coal extravagantly and created a good deal of smoke. To overcome these defects, the Exeter ironfounder George Bodley introduced a kitchen range owing much to Count Rumford, who had already developed a closed range: this can be taken as the prototype of all 19th-century kitchen ranges.

Roasting was still the most favoured method of cooking meat in England. Hannah Glasse begins her *Art of Cookery made Plain and Easy* of 1747 by giving advice on

The roasting range at Saltram, put in about 1810 and equipped with elaborate spits, smoke-jack, bottle-jacks, a large copper dripping-pan and a brass ladle for basting. The fire is backed by a water tank, delivering piping hot water to the taps to the left of the hearth.

One of the *Cries of London* by J. Harris, 1804, showing a trader selling roasting-jacks.

roasting, 'to instruct the lower Sort' who presumably did not employ cooks: 'If any Thing very little or thin, then a pretty little brisk Fire, that it may be done quick and nice: If a very large Joint, then be sure a good Fire be laid to cake. Let it be clear at the Bottom; and when your Meat is Half done, move the Dripping-pan and Spit a little from the Fire, and stir up a good brisk Fire . . .'. Roast meat, poultry and game was still basted with butter, but a new 'dripping pudding' or 'Yorkshire pudding', described by Mrs Glasse as 'an excellent good pudding; the gravy of the meat eats well with it', was now cooked underneath the meat in the dripping pan, becoming one of Britain's greatest national dishes.

Poultry was usually stuffed before roasting as were some joints of meat, particularly mutton. Stuffings were simpler now and had completely lost their sweet element; oyster and chestnut flavoured only with herbs, a little nutmeg and perhaps a little lemon peel were the most popular. Roast meat was served simply with a well-seasoned buttery sauce made from the basting butter and cooking juices.

The first roasting screens appeared in the 18th century, placed in front of the roasting joint to speed up cooking. The first design, called a 'roaster', 'Dutch oven' or 'hastener' was a polished tin reflector, half-cylindrical in shape, standing on legs, which reflected the radiant heat on to the meat and shielded it from the draughts that blew across the floor and up the chimney; it also shielded the cook from the intense heat of the fire. Alternatively, the joint could be suspended from a hook in the top of the screen and roasted in front of the fire. The fat was collected in a dripping-pan below. The screen often had a small hinged door at the back to allow a basting spoon to be inserted. By the beginning of the 19th century, the joint was turned by means of a bottle-jack, so called because of its shape. This was a spring-driven mechanism wound up by a key, which caused the meat to turn first one way, then back in the opposite direction, for about an hour. Bottle-jacks could also be hooked on a rail running across the mantel of the hearth above the fire; two can be seen in this position at Saltram. A hastener, with a bottle-jack, stands in the Erddig kitchen in front of the Edwardian range which replaced the old roasting range.

Rather confusingly, a Dutch oven was also a portable sheet-metal oven which had a handled spit for roasting fowl or small joints of meat and could be set in front of the fire, or hung on the bars of the grate. Mrs Glasse recommended a Dutch oven or 'tin oven' for making an excellent custard baked in china cups and for baking rice puddings. Even more confusingly, in America the term Dutch oven was applied to a round or oval 'camp oven' made of cast iron which stood in the hot ashes of the open fire.

At the beginning of the 19th century another roasting screen was devised, also called a hastener or a 'haster', described in the 1827 inventory for the kitchen of Attingham Park near Shrewsbury as 'An excellent 6-feet deal panelled Meat Screen, with hot closet at top and iron rack shelves, inside lined tin, enclosed by folding doors, on rollers.' Examples of this screen can be seen at Calke, Kedleston and in other National Trust kitchens.

Built-in charcoal ranges, stew-hearths, stew-holes or stoves, became a more permanent feature in 18th-century kitchens. Edward Dryden modernised the kitchen at Canons Ashby in 1710 by installing two stewing-stoves. In the early 19th century the 6th Duke of Devonshire installed a large charcoal stove under the window in the kitchen at Hardwick, while one of the open hearths in the kitchen at Buckland Abbey was blocked up and replaced by a six-plate stove. Other examples can be seen at Castle

Copper utensils at Felbrigg Hall, Norfolk. The *batterie de cuisine* was an essential for the kitchen of a large country house, especially if there was a French chef.

Coole, Uppark, Dunham Massey and Felbrigg. The last was discovered only recently.

A later improvement on the charcoal range was the built-in hotplate, consisting of a long flat, cast-iron plate, set into a brick base and having a horizontal flue passing under it to connect with a vertical flue in the wall. At one end of the plate was the fire box and the draught was controlled by dampers in the vertical flue. An example can be seen in the kitchen at Calke.

Both the charcoal range and the hotplate were ideal for making dishes that had to be cooked slowly and gently in their own juices, whether of meat, poultry or game. Sauces were also made on them, based now on a roux with added celery, onions, parsley, oysters, chestnuts, anchovies, cockles or eggs, but no spices other than a little pepper; the sweet content had disappeared. The soups particularly fashionable in the 18th century, such as oyster, eel, mussel, crayfish and almond, were better cooked on the charcoal range, especially if they were thickened with flour or egg yolks.

With the development of the hob-grate and more use of the charcoal range, cooking vessels needed to be flat-bottomed and equipped with handles. A huge variety of saucepans and stewpans appeared, culminating in the *batterie de cuisine* so essential to the kitchen of a large country house, especially if there was a French chef. Saltram's superb *batterie* comprises six hundred copper pans, including fish kettles, French stewpans, sauté pans, stock pots, omelette pans, a bain-marie, double saucepans, moulds, skimmers and ladles, many marked 'B' for the owner, Lord Boringdon. It must have been the pride and joy of Mr Howse, the chef, but extremely hard work for the scullery staff to keep clean.

Cooks could command high wages in Georgian times, for really good cooks were scarce. Bachelor George Lucy of Charlecote had many problems with cooks who were dirty, lazy and thriftless, and even the Yorkes of Erddig, who nurtured the tradition of respect and real friendship between family and staff, made similar complaints. Male chefs were paid much more than female cooks. At Chirk Castle, Elizabeth Edwards was paid £8 a year from 1746 to 1761; she was succeeded by a male chef, Thomas Towre, who was paid £47 and was assisted by an undercook, a kitchen-maid and a still-room maid. In the early 19th century, Saltram's Mr Howse, according to Rev. Thomas Talbot, 'combines the Maitre d'Hotel, House Steward and Cook and has a traitment of 130 guineas per Annum'. He was assisted by a kitchen-, scullery- and still-room maids. At this time, the cook earned more than the housekeeper, except in a relatively small country house such as Erddig, where the housekeeper enjoyed a higher position.

As in the 17th century it was considered very fashionable to employ a French male chef. At the beginning of the 18th century the Duke of Bedford paid his French chef £60 pounds a year, while his English cook earned £30. Apart from earning large amounts of money, French chefs gave themselves great airs, tyrannised their underlings and often left at the slightest provocation: Lord Sefton's chef, who had cooked for Louis XIV, threatened to leave after a guest put pepper in the soup! The Ansons of Shugborough retained a male chef, often from Paris, from the 1780s right through to the 1930s, assisted by one or two female cooks and several kitchen-maids. In his raffish youth, when he entertained the Prince of Wales and his circle, Sir Harry Fetherstonhaugh also employed a French chef at Uppark. The Prince himself employed Antonin Carême (the inventor of caramel) to cook for him at the Royal Pavilion in Brighton at a salary of £2,000 a year.

Englishmen under the Hanoverian Georges developed rather an ambivalent attitude towards French cooking, very different from the respect shown in Stuart times. A French chef ranked among the proudest possessions of wealthy aristocrats and yet French cooking, especially the extravagance, was despised. As early as 1710, Patrick Lamb, a veteran among royal cooks, was firing the first shots: Britain's raw materials, he claimed, were unequalled anywhere else and the *quelque choses* of France, 'kickshaws' in England, were no substitute. Eliza Smith, Elizabeth Moxon, Elizabeth Raffald and Hannah Glasse, all early women writers of cookery books, were very bitter on the subjects of 'French messes' and French chefs and yet were quite happy to pinch 'such Receipts of the French cookery as I think may not be disagreeable to English Palates' (Eliza Smith, *The Compleat Housewife*, 1727). Hannah Glasse was forthright in her denunciation of French extravagance: 'Gentlemen will have French Cooks, they must pay for French tricks . . . . I have heard of a Cook that used six Pounds of Butter to fry twelve Eggs, when every Body knows, that understands Cooking, that Half a Pound is full enough.' She continues scornfully, 'So much is the blind Folly of this Age that they would rather be imposed on by a *French* Booby, than give Encouragement to a good *English* cook!' But these ladies were writing for the upper middle classes, not for the aristocracy.

Britain was at war with France for a large part of the century and patriotism was significant in forming public opinion. Plain roast beef was credited with making plain stalwart Englishmen, whereas the French use of elaborate spices and multiple flavourings was viewed with suspicion, even derision. Robert Campbell, author of *The London Tradesman*, opined that, 'Fish when it has passed the hands of a French cook is no more fish; it has neither the taste, smell or appearance of fish. It and everything else is dressed in masquerade, seasoned with slow poisons and every dish pregnant with nothing but the seeds of diseases, both chronic and acute.' Jonathan Swift in his satirical *Directions to Servants*, 1745, advises the cook, if a lump of soot should fall in the soup, to stir it in 'and it will give the soup a high French taste'.

The demand for excellent bakery and puddings in Georgian times brought with it a need for much more efficient ovens. As methods of iron-production improved, cast-iron baking ovens began to replace the old beehive ovens. Some of the earliest were quite separate from the kitchen fire, having their own small grate underneath to heat them, and a separate flue. Inside the oven, a series of narrow ledges was provided along each side to support movable oven shelves, while a hook sliding on a rod fixed across the top of the oven allowed joints of meat to be suspended over a dripping tin. After the development of the range, an oven became an integral part of the fireplace and the separate bakehouse survived only in large establishments.

The usage of an 18th-century scullery depended on the size of the domestic offices. In a large establishment like Dyrham Park, the scullery was called the 'little kitchen' and some of the food preparation and cooking was done here, under the charge of the 'Skullery House-Keeper'. A roomy scullery adjoins the kitchen at Saltram with two pairs of double sinks, one of wood lined with copper, and one of porcelain for washing up, probably put in later in the 19th century. There are two large coppers for boiling vegetables, hams, meat and puddings, and for heating water. The Calke scullery was used only for washing up and vegetable preparation, with two sinks, and plate-racks, a copper boiler for heating water and a few shelves for storing kitchen equipment. There is still a lead-lined chute in the wall, where edible scraps were thrown into an outside tub and collected for the pigs.

Jack Nickolas, the kitchen man. Like Thomas Jones the butcher (*page 207*), his portrait hangs in the servants' hall at Erddig, Clywd. The accompanying verse gives some idea of his tasks:

But him, that waited on the Cook;
And many a walk to Wrexham took;
Whether the season, cold or hot,
A constant Porter to the pot:
Then in the kitchen corner stuck,
He pluck'd the fowl, and drew the duck,
Or with the basket on his knees,
Was sheller-general to the peas.

The bakehouse at Erddig. The scuffle ovens were heated for several hours with faggots; the ashes were then raked or scuffled out onto the floor, and the dough slid in on wooden peels.

The scullery at Attingham Park was also used as the salting room: the 1827 inventory describes the contents as 'A 4-feet square deal Table, and two Vegetable Troughs, with divisions, on tressels; 2 stout 3-feet-10 square Salting Troughs, lined lead, on legs; A stout Table, 10-feet-6 by 5-feet; a 12-feet wood Form; a Chopping Block and a three-stepper [a small step ladder]; Two wicker Meat Baskets, a Meat Hook and four wire Meat Crowns.'

Sinks were made of stone, slate, granite or wood and were supplied with water from a hand pump just outside the door in the kitchen court. Sometimes the sink was fitted with short pipes from which cold water gushed, but this had to be pumped from outside and there was no control of the flow. Until the range arrived with its hot water boilers, all the water needed had to be heated up in cauldrons or fountains over the fire, or in copper boilers in the scullery, heated underneath by their own fire.

In large country houses, there were at least four larders – wet, dry, game and the pastry or pantry. An excellently planned range of larders survives at Dunham Massey, where the bars acting as room dividers are unusual, but would have encouraged air circulation. The first room leading off the kitchen is partly a pastry, where the chef made all his pastry on the cold marble slab set in the corner near the window, with shelves holding crocks for pastry-making ingredients, and partly a dry larder. There is a wire mesh meat safe for storing cooked meat. Susanna Whatman's *Housekeeping Book*, 1776–1800, advised that 'the large joints should not be left open to inferior servants'; there should be two keys, 'one for the Cook and one for the Housekeeper, that there may be no excuse for the leaving roast or boiled beef, legs of pork etc. in the open safe'.

The wet larder at Dunham Massey contains equipment for cleaning and salting down meat and fish: shallow slate sinks, slate-topped tables and a large 6-foot high ice-box (a 19th-century addition). There is also a press for making brawns and potted meats. The 18th-century cookery books and manuscripts belonging to National Trust houses abound in recipes for preserving food of every type: 'to keep Woodcock all year', 'Lobster Sauce that is to keep a year', 'to make Potted Hare', 'to preserve Pigeons', etc.

Behind the wet larder at Dunham Massey is a separate meat larder, with a large rectangular ceiling rack for storing fresh, powdered, smoked and salted meat. Sometimes bacon was stored separately in a cupboard to keep it dry – at Chirk Castle in 1770, 'A large chest made and fixed in the Upper Larder to hold dry Bacon – almost as big as Noah's Ark, which Name it is hereafter to bear' – or hung in the kitchen. There is a complicated pulley system for racks to hang hams, bacon, game, bags of flour, nets of bread and bunches of herbs from the ceiling in the Erddig kitchen, with additional storage in the 'Meat Pantry', also used as a wet larder. On 25 January 1835 there were eight flitches of bacon and eight hams here, as well as a salting coffer, a marble slab, a stool and step-ladder, two colanders and tins, two pewter dishes and earthenware, or the local 'Buckley' pottery, crocks for preserving meat and eggs. The game larder at Dunham Massey is placed away from the kitchen because of the unpleasant smell, but game at Shugborough was hung in a cold room beyond the scullery.

As the century progressed the function of the still-room widened and the housekeeper began to take over here from her mistress. It provided the family's breakfast, light luncheon, and after-dinner tea and coffee, thus freeing the kitchen for the serious business of preparing dinner. The 1827 inventory for the still-room and still-room kitchen at Attingham illustrates the variety of work carried on. The 'very large and expensive copper barrel-shaped Still with large heater under, cover and handles, brass cock, and steam tube' was for distilling essential oils, cordials and medicines, which, with the increasing use of doctors and apothecaries, were becoming less important. The 'large round copper, Preserving Pans and ladles, Saucepans and Sugar Kettle' were for making marmalades, preserves, jellies, ketchups, pickles, and sometimes preserved and candied fruits and sweetmeats for dessert. A pair of scales and weights ensured accuracy when making patent medicines and ointments and a large copper boiler in the still-room kitchen was used for boiling up the raw ingredients for cordials, medicines and pickles. There was a small fireplace and a small baking oven in the still-room itself and a quantity of 'Cake Pans, Patty Pans, Shapes, Moulds, Cutters, Baking Sheets' and a pair of 'Wafer Irons' for the still-room maid to bake rolls, small cakes and biscuits for breakfast, luncheon and dessert. 'A four-foot Deal Table with shelf under and a square Chopping Board' provided a working surface and 'a Sugar Chopping Tray and pair of nippers' were used for breaking up the large quantity of sugar needed. Pounding and grinding the raw ingredients for wines, cordials, medicines and desserts was done in the 'capital 18-inch marble Mortar and Pestle'. Various coffee- and chocolate-pots, china, tea kettles and moulds were kept on the 'high deal painted Press, fitted up with shelves and two drawers, 6-feet wide by 8-feet high' in the still-room. 'A large square Ice Trough lined with lead, on stout legs and cover' in the still-room kitchen and 'a quantity of pewter Ice Moulds, Freezers and Shapes' show that ice-creams, flummeries and other delicious dishes for dessert were prepared here.

The servery, serving room, or service lobby was the link between the kitchen offices and the dining-room. Originally, of course, the buttery had usually fulfilled this function, but once the kitchen was removed to the basement or to a separate pavilion in the grounds, there had to be a staging post where covers could be removed and the final touches given to the food before it was presented at table. In small houses the butler's pantry, if conveniently situated, was adequate, but in larger establishment a separate servery became necessary.

The food from the kitchen at Shugborough was carried by the footmen through an underground cellar passage and up a flight of stone steps into a servery outside the dining-room, where it was assembled on a hot-cupboard heated by charcoal. At Calke, the food had to make the long journey from the basement kitchen, first in a metal hot-cupboard on wheels down the cold passage, then up in a lift to the warmer in the servery on the first floor. At Erddig, the food was also carried some distance along a passage before it was placed on a lift and brought up to the servery. At Belton there is a railway underneath the kitchen courtyard along which food was pushed on a wooden trolley, before being carried upstairs to the serving room. After the tunnel had been built at Uppark, the food was placed in charcoal-heated hot-cupboards and trundled along the tunnel, then carried up the service stairs to the servery which had been built into the house at the same time. The kitchen below the servery was only used to cook for the family, or for still-room work. Despite the use of hot-cupboards, roasting screens, chafing dishes and plate-warmers, much of the food reaching the table must still have been luke-warm at best.

Household management in large houses was now increasingly delegated to the senior servants, although a special understanding of cookery, or at least of menus, was still regarded as falling within the sphere of the mistress of the house who kept a book of the more unusual or particularly fashionable culinary and medical recipes. Here is a small selection of those found in cookery books belonging to the Trust.

Above: The still-room at Uppark, Sussex. As the 18th century progressed, the function of the still-room changed from the distillation of waters and preparation of banqueting stuff to provision of the family's breakfast and after-dinner beverages of tea and coffee.

Below: The Duke of Buccleuch's cook at Drumlanrig, Dumfriesshire, *c*.1817, proudly pointing out his *Gratin à la Drumlanrig* and *Croquette à la Montagu*.

To Make Asparagus Soup

'Take a Hundred of Asparagus, put the Greatest part of them with two Lettuces into three Quarts of Water – Boil them till they are tender enough to pulp thro' a Cullender; they should be Boil'd two or three Hours after they are put thro' the Cullender, add the remainder of the Asparagus, put some Cream and flour to make it a Sufficient thickness, and add pepper and Salt, to your taste – The Asparagus you put in last are to Swim in the Soup.'

From an Erddig recipe book, c.1765

Philip Yorke I was a vegetarian so would have enjoyed this soup.

To Stew Soals

'Cut them across with a knife, fry them in Clarified butter, then put them in a Stewpan then pour over them Clarrett two or three Anchovies let it stew till tis enough. Squeese in the juice of a Lemon, thicken it up with Butter.'

From an 18th-century recipe book at Montacute

As it was still difficult to get fresh sea-fish in the 18th century, frying it and adding strong flavourings was a well known way of masking any unpleasant tainting.

To Stew Cucumbers

'Cut them in Slices and drain them well, shake them in a Frying pan, with some Brown'd Butter, then put in some pepper, salt and some Onions sliced, some Gravy, Stew them 'till they are enough, Squeeze in some Lemon, Thicken them up as you do other Dishes'.

From an Erddig recipe book c.1765, as recommended by Mrs White

Eighteenth-century recipe books abound with recipes for 'stew'd', 'farc'd', baked and 'ragout' of cucumber. Stewed cucumber was served with roast meat.

Asparagus Soup

about 1 lb (450g) fresh asparagus
½ lettuce, washed
1 small onion, finely chopped
1½ pt (900 ml) vegetable or chicken stock
1 oz (25g) butter
¾ oz (18g) plain flour
2 egg yolks
2½ fl oz (about 75 ml) double cream
salt and black pepper

Cut off the tips from the asparagus and reserve for garnishing. Trim the asparagus and cut into 1 in (2.5 cm) pieces. Shred the lettuce finely, then put it with the asparagus and onion in a pan. Pour over the stock, cover the pan and simmer gently until the asparagus is tender. Put through a blender or food processor to make a purée. Steam or simmer the asparagus tips very gently until tender, drain and reserve. Rinse out the pan, then make a roux with the butter and flour, and stir in the purée. Season well, then gently bring to the boil and simmer for a further 2–3 minutes. Mix the egg yolks and cream together and stir into the soup. Reheat carefully without boiling, then taste and adjust seasoning as necessary. Add reserved asparagus tips and serve hot. Serves 4.

Sole in Red Wine with Anchovy

4 fillets of sole, skinned
salt and black pepper
clarified butter for frying
4 dessertspoons (40 ml) melted butter
2½ fl oz (75 ml) claret
4 anchovy fillets
squeeze of lemon juice
lemon slices and deep-fried
    parsley sprigs, to garnish

Season the sole fillets with salt and pepper. Melt a little butter in a large frying pan and fry the fish lightly on both sides, adding more butter as necessary. Remove from the heat and pour off any remaining fat. Add the butter and the claret and arrange the anchovy fillets on top of the fish. Cover the pan and set over a very low heat for about 5 minutes, or until the fish is cooked through. Squeeze over a little lemon juice and serve immediately, garnished with lemon slices and parsley sprigs fried in deep fat (a very common 18th-century garnish for fish). Serves 4.

Ragoût of Cucumber

2 medium cucumbers
2 oz (50g) clarified butter
2 medium onions, sliced
6 tablespoons (90 ml) chicken stock
2 tablespoons (30 ml) dry white wine
salt and pepper
beurre manié to thicken

Slice the cucumbers thickly without peeling them. Melt half the butter in a pan and brown the cucumber lightly. Meanwhile, melt the remaining butter in another pan and brown the onions lightly. When the onions have softened, add them to the cucumber. Add the stock and wine and season well. Cover with a lid and simmer until tender. Remove the lid and thicken with beurre manié until the vegetables are nicely bound together by a little sauce. Check the seasoning again and serve. Serves 4–6.

Chicken or Rabbit Fricassée

Dishes of French origin, like the
fricassée, were still very popular, but
were now made with a thickened sauce to
envelop the meat.

4–6 chicken or rabbit joints
chicken stock or water, to cover
2 medium onions, sliced
1 bouquet garni
salt and black pepper
2 oz (50 g) mushrooms
½ oz (15 g) butter

FOR THE SAUCE
1½ oz (40 g) butter
2 tablespoons (30 ml) flour
1–2 egg yolks
¼ pt (150 ml) single cream
squeeze of lemon juice
slices of lemon, to garnish

Put the chicken or rabbit joints in a shallow pan, cover with stock or water and add the sliced onions and bouquet garni. Season well. Cover and simmer for about 40 minutes, or until very tender. Drain off the cooking liquor into a measuring jug, cover pan again and keep hot. The stock should measure 1 pt (600 ml); if it is more, turn into a saucepan and reduce. To prepare the sauce, melt the butter in a separate pan, stir in the flour, cook for a few seconds, without letting the butter brown, then pour on the stock and stir in well. Cook over a gentle heat stirring all the time until thick. Boil briskly for 3–4 minutes, and then draw aside.

At the same time, sauté the mushrooms in butter in another pan. To finish the sauce, mix the yolks with the cream in a bowl, add a little of the hot sauce, then pour the mixture slowly back into the rest of the sauce. Check the seasoning again and add the lemon juice and mushrooms. Pour the sauce over the joints, shaking the pan gently to mix all together. Cover and keep hot for 15 minutes before serving, so that the flavour of the sauce can penetrate the meat. Garnish with lemon slices. Serves 4–6.

Potato Pudding

Potatoes, like carrots, spinach, and
artichokes were often made into sweet
puddings in the 18th century to serve
alongside the meat and fish in the first
course at dinner.

6 oz (175 g) shortcrust pastry
2 oz (50 g) butter
2 oz (50 g) caster sugar
3 oz (75 g) potatoes, cooked and mashed
good pinch of ground mace
good pinch of ground cinnamon
grated rind of 1 lemon
1 large egg and 1 large egg
  yolk, beaten together
1 tablespoon (15 ml) brandy

Line a 6-in (15-cm) flan ring with the pastry and bake blind in a hot oven (220°C, 425°F, gas mark 7) for 10–15 minutes. Leave to cool.

Cream the butter and sugar until white and fluffy. Beat in the mashed potatoes, spices and lemon rind, followed by the egg mixture and the brandy. Taste and add more spice if you wish. Spoon into the pastry case and bake in a moderate oven (180°C, 350°F, gas mark 4) for about 45 minutes or until risen and golden. Serves 4.

Oyster Loaves

Oyster Loaves

'Take small french rolls, or round loaves, make a hole in the top, take out the crumb, then fry them in butter, and set them before the fire to dry, Stew your Oysters in their own liquor, add the crumbs out of your rolls, and a good piece of butter, stew then 5 or 6 minutes, then put in a spoonful of Cream, fill the loaves and lay on the top.'

From an Erddig recipe book *c.*1765, as recommended by Mrs Hazel

These made 'a pretty Side-dish for a first Course' according to Hannah Glasse. The dish was taken to America and became popular in New Orleans in the 19th century. Oysters were also eaten fresh, fried, 'ragoo'd' or made into sauces and stuffings.

4 miniature cottage loaves or brioches
4 oz (125 g) butter, melted
12 fresh oysters
salt and black pepper
good pinch of grated nutmeg
¼ pt (150 ml) double cream
a little lemon juice

Cut the tops off the rolls or brioches and scoop out most of the crumb. Brush the undersides of the lids and the hollows of the rolls inside and out with butter. Place on a baking sheet in a hot oven (220°C, 425°F, gas mark 7) for about 10 minutes, or until lightly golden and crisp. Meanwhile scrub and open the oysters and drain off the liquor, reserving it. Sauté the oysters in the remaining butter, in a frying pan, for about 1½ minutes, or until they turn opaque. Remove oysters from the pan with a draining spoon, cut them into 2 or 3 pieces, depending on size, and set aside. Add the reserved oyster liquor to the pan with the seasonings and cream. Boil down steadily to a very thick sauce, stirring constantly. Check the seasoning, sharpening with a little lemon juice if you wish, reheat the oysters in the sauce gently and spoon into the warm rolls. Replace the lids and serve immediately for a special first course, or supper dish. Mussels, cockles or mushrooms could be used instead. Serves 4.

The Oyster Lunch by Jean-François de Troy, 1734. England was acknowledged by all – including the French – as the home of the finest oysters in the 18th century. At this feast, prodigious numbers are being consumed, accompanied by champagne. The sealed corks of the bottles are held down by tape and string. Fine export bowls are used to cool and rinse out the glasses. Note the stiletto-bladed knives used in France, and so complained about by English travellers.

Orange Ice Cream

'Squeeze the juice of eight sweet oranges in a bowl, add to it half a pint of water, and as much sugar as will sweeten it; strain it through a sieve, put it into an ice well, and freeze it 'till it is stiff; put it into a lead pine-apple mould, lap it well up in paper, put it into a pail of ice, and salt under and over it, and let it stand for three hours. When you want it, dip your pine-apple in cold water, turn it out on a plate, green the leaves of the pineapple with spinage juice, and garnish it with green leaves. You may put this cream into melon and pear moulds. If a melon, you must green it with spinage juice; – if a pear mould, you must streak it with red.'

From *The Complete House-keeper and Professed Cook, calculated for the greater Use and assistance of Ladies, House-keepers, Cooks, etc.* written by Mary Smith and published in 1772. She had been housekeeper to Sir Walter Blackett at Wallington in Northumberland – it was common for servants to write and publish cookery books.

No fashionable dessert course was served without ices in Georgian times. They could be made at home if you were lucky enough to have an ice-house; if not, confectioners in the largest towns sold a huge variety, for which they had their own stores of ice. Pineapple moulds were particularly popular, because the fruit was a symbol of luxury in the 18th century.

To Make Chocolate Creem

'Take a pint of good Creem, an heaped spoonfull of Chocolate scraped, put it in when the Creem boyls, stir them well together, beat the yolk of 2 eggs and stir it into the Creem, sweeten it to your tast, let the Eggs have a boyl or two to thicken it, put it into a Chocolate pot and Mill it, so hold the Pot high and pour it into a dish.'

From an 18th-century manuscript from Canons Ashby, as recommended by Mrs Martyn

This rich cream made from the fashionable chocolate would have been 'milled', or frothed, with a chocolate mill or molinquet, 'a wooden stick with an head at the end full of notches', and served at the second course.

Plums from *Pomona Franconia* by Mayer, 1776.

Chocolate Cream

6 oz (175 g) plain chocolate
2–3 tablespoons (30–45 ml) water
½ oz (12.5 g) butter
2–3 drops of vanilla essence
3 large eggs, separated
¼ pt (150 ml) double cream

Break the chocolate into small pieces, put in a saucepan with the water and stir continually over very gentle heat until a thick cream. Take off the heat and stir in the butter and vanilla essence, followed by the egg yolks, one at a time, stirring well after each addition. Whisk the egg whites to a firm snow, then stir briskly into the chocolate. When thoroughly mixed, fill 6 small pots or glasses and leave overnight in the cool. Serve with small biscuits. Serves 6.

Orange Ice Cream

1¼ pt (750 ml) water
15 oz (425 g) granulated sugar
finely grated rind and juice of 1 large lemon
finely grated rind and juice of 8 large oranges
drop of red food colouring

Bring the water and sugar to the boil in a heavy saucepan, adding the grated lemon and orange rind as the syrup is heating up. Leave the syrup to boil for exactly 1 minute, then remove from the heat immediately and add the strained lemon and orange juice and food colouring. When the syrup is cold, strain, then set to freeze. After 1 hour, remove and beat thoroughly. Repeat until the mixture begins to harden into ice-cream, which will take 4–5 hours, unless using an ice-cream machine when it will only take 30–45 minutes.

The Duchess of Montagues Receipt to Make Hartshorn Jelly

'Put in one Gallon of watter half a pound of Hartshorn. Let them boyl slowly till the Liquor is a pretty strong Jelly, then strain it off and put in two Quarts of that, the peel of eight oranges and four lemons cut very thin, boyl it a quarter of an hour, then put in the whites of 12 eggs, well beat up in a froth all the Juice of the Oranges and Lemons, and a pound and a quarter of double refined Suger, boyle it a little and then strain it through a Flannell Bagg. You may put wine in it if you wish.'

From an 18th-century manuscript found at Canons Ashby

Jellies set with shavings of hartshorn and calves' feet, and served in glasses, were a popular part of the dessert course. They began to be flavoured with lemon and orange juice in the 18th century.

Lemon Jelly

$1\frac{3}{4}$ oz (45 g) gelatine
$1\frac{1}{2}$ pt (900 ml) water
pared rind and juice of 3 large lemons
7 oz (200 g) lump sugar
2 egg whites, and the shells of the eggs, wiped and lightly crushed
$2\frac{1}{2}$ fl oz (75 ml) white wine

Soak the gelatine in $\frac{1}{4}$ pt (150 ml) of the water. Pour the remaining water into a scalded pan, add the lemon rind, juice and sugar. Warm over gentle heat until the sugar is dissolved. Whip the egg white to a froth, add to the pan with the shells, the gelatine and the white wine. Whisk until the liquid reaches boiling point. Allow to boil up three times, drawing the pan aside between each boiling to allow it to settle. Pour the liquid into a scalded jelly bag with a bowl underneath. Return the liquid several times to the jelly bag until it runs crystal clear. Pour into a mould or into glasses and leave to set. Makes 2 pt (1.2 litres) of jelly.

To Make Ramokins

'Take a Quarter of a pound of Cheshire Cheese, two Ounces of Butter beat together in a Mortar, then lay'd onto a Butter'd Toast. Crisp it with a Salamander.'

From a recipe book at Erddig c.1765

This was a very popular supper dish in the 18th century, particularly in Wales. For the English version, the toast was soaked in red wine.

Savoury Cheese Toast

2 oz (50 g) butter
8 oz (225 g) Cheshire or Cheddar cheese, grated
salt and pepper
2 egg yolks if required
4 slices bread, lightly toasted

Melt the butter in a heavy saucepan, stir in the cheese and season well. Stir over a gentle heat until the cheese melts. If the mixture shows signs of separating, bind together again with the egg yolks. Spread the toast with the mixture and brown under preheated grill for 3–4 minutes. Serve immediately. Serves 2 or 4.

The conservatory at Tatton Park, Cheshire, designed for the Egerton family by Lewis Wyatt and built 1820. This watercolour by Buckler was commissioned to celebrate its completion.

III

The Georgian period was the age of the social round, of theatre and opera, balls and assemblies, and tea, coffee, chocolate and breakfast parties. The large country houses were the centres of local social life whenever the family was in residence. A constant stream of visitors rode up the drive to pay their respects, discuss business or to present requests and complaints.

Christmas was still the traditional time for entertaining on an enormous scale. In the 1730s, Lord Fermanagh entertained 400 people – tenants, labourers, local townspeople and schoolchildren – over several days at Claydon, complaining of the noise caused by the hired musicians with their drums, trumpets, haut-boys, pipes and fiddles; 'that', he said, 'besides the vast expense, has been very tiresome'. A few years later Lord Fermanagh escaped to London for Christmas to enjoy the pleasure of polite entertainment instead of taking part in the traditional festivities alongside his dependents, but his son, Sir Ralph Verney, wrote of the New Year celebrations at Claydon: 'Last Monday I entertain'd the Tenants of Middle Claydon and invited yours at Steeple Claydon who all came and seem'd well pleased. I gave 'em a Sirloin of Beef and five Ribs roasted, four geese and 4 Plumb-Puddings. They behav'd very well and were very moderate both in eating and drinking and came at one o'clock and went away at six. They drank in all but four dozen of Strong Beer and the rest of Ale.'

Weddings, christenings, comings of age and funerals also involved lavish entertainment, and of course visits from royalty were always occasions to push the boat out. The 1st Duke of Dorset reckoned up his expenses at more than £257, including half an ox, 4 sheep and a calf, when visited briefly at Knole by the future George II, then Prince of

Weddings, christening, comings of age and funerals were all traditional times for lavish entertainment. Celebrations for the twenty-first birthday of John Pole of Shute Barton, Devon in 1829 included the open-air spit-roasting of two enormous oxen with gilded horns, captured here in a drawing by George Cruikshank.

240

Wales. In his early life, Sir Harry Fetherstonhaugh introduced an era of lavish hospitality and entertainment at Uppark where he kept a renowned stable. His home was a social and sporting centre receiving large parties of visitors. Sir Harry's mother filled over a hundred lines in her account books for expenditure on food, wine and entertainment in 1784.

The poor, of course, could seldom entertain, but were sometimes entertained by their wealthier neighbours. Boswell tells us 'I once dined at Durham with the prebendary in residence, a number of the poor, who were good, decent old people ate at table and were helped bountifully. After dinner every man of them had a glass of ale and every woman a glass of sweet wine, and then each of them had a paper of tobacco and withdrew to a hall to smoke it.' Many landowners and farmers gave their tenants and labourers annual feasts after sheep-shearing or harvest; those given for his tenants each year by the 3rd Earl of Egremont in the park at Petworth involved hundreds of people in all-day festivities.

At times the constant influx of guests must often have been a burden. Theresa and John Parker of Saltram certainly enjoyed entertaining, but they liked to limit it. Theresa scarcely ever mentioned visiting or receiving company without some expression of reserve: 'We must spend the next week in returning all our Dining visits which we do not enjoy the thought of much . . . Lord and Lady Chatham who are down upon a wedding visit to Mr. J. Pitt have threatened us with their company, I don't love him . . . but the pleasure of being in company with so remarkable a man would make up for the trouble of receiving them.' Sir Joshua Reynolds was a close friend and a constant visitor, as was the Duchess of Devonshire and county families like the Edgcumbes, the Chichesters and Bastards. Naval and militia officers came from nearby Plymouth and Torquay. The house continued as a centre of smart society when their son, the 1st Earl of Morley, succeeded and enjoyed what his brother-in-law, the Rev. Thomas Talbot, described in 1811 as, 'a pretty constant round of visitors'.

In contrast, the Yorkes of Erddig lived a modest life suited to the household of a moderately prosperous Welsh squire. Their disregard for the trappings of formality and the inelegance of their own dress amused some friends and disturbed others; Philip Yorke I's wife Elizabeth, daughter of the Speaker of the House of Commons, Sir John Cust, did her best to make Erddig and her husband presentable, but ultimately had to give up the struggle. Philip Yorke had in 1749 at the age of five, 'chused chiefly to dine on vegetables' and started the preference for vegetarianism and sometimes teetotalism adopted by succeeding generations of Yorkes, making life very difficult both for their cooks and butlers.

Breakfast in most leisured Georgian homes was rather an informal affair taken any time between 9am and 11am although the time was very flexible, especially when entertaining. On a visit to Petworth in 1828, Thomas Creevey went down to breakfast to find 'two gentlemen out of livery, and the foot boy with coffee pots, tea pots, kettles, chafing dishes to keep rolls, etc. hot, and everything in the eatable way, and I was directly asked whether I would breakfast *then*, and *where* I would have it. This, I was told afterwards, always lasts from 9 till 12.' Ladies often breakfasted in their bedrooms, usually on chocolate or tea and bread and butter. A variety of small mahogany breakfast tables were specially designed for the purpose. Theresa Parker often preferred to eat breakfast privately, but we learn from the Rev. Thomas Talbot's letters to his wife some years later that when company was present, breakfast at Saltram was served in the morning or breakfast room, a new feature of 18th-century houses, at about 10.30am or

Breakfast at Saltram, Devon, was served in the morning room, a new feature of 18th-century houses. Informal dinners were also eaten here, with the Parker family serving themselves from the dumb waiter in the corner. The dining-table and chairs are of mahogany, with a Chinese punch-bowl in the centre of the table.

A silver egg boiler with its own spirit lamp, made by John Edwards in 1802, Attingham Park, Shropshire.

'whenever eight or so of the party have appeared'. The great object 'seems to be to avoid constraint or form'. There was 'an Urn and cistern of black tea at one end – ditto of green tea at the other and coffee at the side – the breakfasts and bread by no means good'. Perhaps this was because the breakfast was produced by the still-room maid and not Mr Howse the chef. When there were no guests, 'breakfast of the plainest description' was eaten upstairs in the Blue Bow, now the Chinese Bedroom, appropriately decorated with silk wallpaper depicting the growing, curing and packing of tea. Informal dinners were also eaten here, or in the morning room.

The food consumed during breakfast and the behaviour of the participants clearly surprised foreign observers. La Rochefoucauld noted in 1784 that 'In the houses of the rich you have coffee, chocolate and tea and bread and butter in various forms and the morning newspapers are on the table . . . so that conversation is not of a lively nature.' Pastor Moritz felt he was a long way from his native Switzerland: 'a kind of bread and butter [is] usually eaten with tea, which is toasted by the fire and is incomparably good. You take one slice after the other and hold it to the fire on a fork till the butter is melted, so that it penetrates a number of slices all at once; this is called toast.' Also present on the breakfast table could be, as Boswell wrote in 1763, 'that admirable viand, marmalde', but generally, in polite society it was a light meal of bread and butter, toast, honey, warm rolls, muffins, spiced bread and small cakes of various kinds, with tea, chocolate or coffee, all provided by the still-room rather than the kitchen. Mrs Lybbe Powys, visiting Holkham in Norfolk in 1756, 'had a breakfast in the genteelest taste, with all kinds of cakes and fruit'. This breakfast fare has continued in America in the enormous variety of breakfast breads and hot cakes, such as rice, corn, griddle, buttermilk, buckwheat and hominy cakes, flap-jacks and various waffles and fritters.

The breakfast served to King George III and Queen Charlotte on their visit to Cotehele in August 1789 must have been somewhat more substantial. They were entertained by the Edgcumbes in the drawing-room and the Queen has left us a particularly vivid account of the visit: 'At breakfast we Eat off the Old Family Pewter and used Silver Knives, Forks and Spoons which have been time immemorial in the Family and have always been kept at this place. The Decanters are of the year 1646 the name of the Wines burnt in the Earthenware . . . . The Dessert Plates are Old Delph of a very large Size . . . . We embarked again 10 minutes after 12 . . .'.

Hunting breakfasts were more substantial with cold meats, wine and ale harking back to the meals of earlier centuries. Sir Harry Fetherstonhaugh had to provide 'three hot meat dishes for each morning's breakfast' if the Duc de Chartres accompanied the Prince of Wales on a visit to Uppark. Some people had extraordinary ideas about breakfast fare. According to Theresa Parker, Lord Poulett, a frequent guest at Saltram in the 1770s, 'has continued to find out a nastier breakfast if possible than yellow cucumbers as he now eats every morning a lemon steeped overnight in small beer'.

In the 1770s breakfast parties – the ancestors of today's garden parties – became fashionable. Guests were served cold food and strolled in the house and garden, listening to music. The earliest breakfast parties were given at breakfast time, but they gradually crept into the afternoon. By 1828 a 'Breakfast' given by the Duchess of St Albans at Holly Lodge, on the slopes of Highgate in London, started at 3pm. According to Prince Pückler-Muskau, who toured England in 1826–28, the food was served at 5pm by servants dressed up as gardeners. There was a maypole, archery and dancing in tents. The party ended at midnight.

A party in the grounds at Ham House, Surrey, by Thomas Rowlandson. Many landowners gave their tenants and labourers annual feasts after sheep-shearing or harvest. The popular festive fare was roast beef and plum pudding, served with plenty of beer.

Luncheon in the first half of the 18th century was an informal snack, or accidental happening, taken between meals. It was also called 'nunchin' or 'nunchion', although Dr Johnson's *Dictionary* of 1755 defines 'Nunchin' as 'a piece of victual eaten between meals', but 'Lunch or Luncheon' as 'As much food as one's hand can hold.' The snack usually consisted of a glass of cider, wine, or home-made fruit wine from the still-room with a cake or biscuit, a glass of buttermilk or sweetened whey from the dairy, or a cup of coffee or chocolate at one of the fashionable coffee-houses. As the century progressed, lunch developed into a more substantial midday snack, hence the term 'nooning' referred to by Susanna Whatman in 1776, reflecting the tendency for dinner, the main meal of the day, to be taken later and later, leaving a long gap after breakfast. Lunch towards the end of the century might consist of cold meats, pies, salads, cakes, biscuits and various beverages. Both terms for this midday snack continued in use: Jane Austen uses 'nunchin', spelling it 'noonshine' in a letter written in 1808, and 'nuncheon' in *Sense and Sensibility*, 1811. Gradually nuncheon died out, although it was still in use in rural parts of Wiltshire around Salisbury in the last decade of the 19th century. The verb 'to lunch' seems to have achieved its first, rather hesitant, admission in 1832: reversing the usual process, it began life below stairs, in the servants' hall.

Dinner was the principal vehicle for hospitality as well as the main meal of the day and its hour varied enormously. 'In my memory', wrote Richard Steele, 'the dinner hour has crept from 12 o'clock to 3'. Boswell recorded in 1763 that 'our time of dining is three o'clock', but La Rochefaucauld noted in 1784, that 'five o'clock . . . is the dinner time'. In the country, it was usually earlier, sometimes still at the traditional hour of 12 noon; at Saltram, dinner in the 1770s and '80s was between 2 pm and 4 pm, but by 1811 was always at 7 pm (the normal hour by this time). The hour for dinner was even more susceptible to class differences; labourers eating at 1 pm, while the fashionable aristocracy dined later and later.

An invitation to dinner was usually a lengthy affair covering most of the afternoon and evening. La Rochefaucauld observed 'It is customary to start at three o'clock [and] stay until ten, for in no circumstances will an Englishman hurry over his food and drink.' He was undisguised in his horror of the ordeal: 'Dinner is one of the most wearisome of English experiences lasting, as it does four or five hours.' In the country, guests would travel some miles over bad roads to dinner parties 'though they own to being bruised to death and quite deshabillered by jolts'. Many thoughtful hosts would give their dinner parties at 'the full of the moon' to make the journey home easier. Parson Woodforde's rotation dinners were always at this time and Patrick St Clair writing to Ashe Windham at Felbrigg told him: 'Your cousin invited us to eat a piece of mutton with him, which we design to do next moon.' In Georgian England an invitation 'to eat a piece of mutton' was often the invitation to informal dinners, although there was usually a great deal more than mutton on the table.

In most large 18th-century country houses, a suite of state or public rooms arranged round three sides of the hall on the entrance floor included both a dining-room or 'eating room', meant first and foremost as a showpiece to be used only when entertaining, and a drawing-room. Both were large, important rooms, often set symmetrically opposite one another across the hall. This arrangement had the advantage of muffling the loud conversation of the men who sat smoking and talking long over their after-dinner port, so that it did not impinge too much upon the ladies chatting in the drawing-room. When the plan for Hagley Hall, George Lyttelton's home in Worcestershire, was still being worked out, he wrote to the architect: 'Lady Lyttelton wishes for a room of separation between the eating room and the drawing room, to hinder the ladies from the noise and talk of the men when left to their bottle, which must sometimes happen, even at Hagley.'

The walls of early 18th-century dining-rooms were often panelled or hung with gilt leather set into wooden panelling, but this began to go out of fashion. By 1773, Robert Adam wrote of dining-rooms: 'Instead of being hung with damask, tapestry &c; they are always finished with stucco and adorned with statues and paintings, that they may not retain the smell of the victuals.' Curtains were not hung in dining-rooms for the same reason. The ornate stucco often depicted motifs symbolic of food and drink. Of the new dining-room at Felbrigg created by James Paine, William Windham II wrote at the end of April 1752: 'I have chosen 4 casts of the four seasons for the corners of the ceiling in the new eating parlour.' Spring was garlanded with flowers, summer with ears of corn, balancing fruitful autumn and bearded winter. The theme of the ceiling was echoed in the elaborate plaster swags of fruit and flowers designed to frame the family portraits.

Bacchus, the Roman god of wine, was the tutelary deity of the 18th-century dining-room, and often appeared in paintings, plasterwork and other decoration. James Paine's dining-room at Nostell Priory in Yorkshire includes sideboards with Bacchic

decoration. The elaborate stucco ceiling, the marble chimney-piece, on which the figure of Bacchus is carved, and the pictures in the dining-room at Kedleston were all carefully chosen by Robert Adam. He set the pictures into plaster frames; at the upper level, still-lives of fruit and dead game representing the pleasures of the table, while below landscapes of the park depicting scenes of horticulture, hunting and fishing.

By the 1760s the simple sideboard had been transformed into a suite with a long flat table for displaying the family plate, flanked by two urn-shaped wine-coolers standing on pedestal cupboards used for storing dining-room articles. A separate wine-cooler or cistern beneath the table completed the suite; when filled with crushed ice, it could keep the wine cold for several hours, or, if filled with water, used glasses could be rinsed in it. Examples of this type of sideboard suite can be seen at Castle Coole, Saltram and

The dining-room at Saltram, Devon. Originally Robert Adam designed this room as a library, but he converted it into a dining-room in 1780 when the new kitchen was built. At the end is the magnificent sideboard, built into the bow, flanked by urn-shaped wine coolers. The dining-table is not original, but the sixteen chairs were purchased specially for the room.

Top: Robert Adam placed the dining-room sideboard suite at Kedleston, Derbyshire, in a great domed apse, recalling the ornate Baroque displays of the previous century (*see also frontispiece illustration*).

Bottom: The ornate wine fountain made by the great silversmith Paul de Lamerie in 1719 for Sir John Harpur, 4th Baronet, of Calke Abbey, Derbyshire. These fountains usually stood on pedestals near the sideboard, and dispensed wine through the tap.

Osterley Park. Adam placed the suite at Kedleston in a great domed apse, recalling the Baroque buffet displays of the previous century. In 1766, the Duchess of Northumberland described it as: 'adorn'd with a vast quantity of handsome plate judiciously dispos'd on Tables of beautiful Marble & of very pretty shapes in the midst is Mr Stewarts Tripod the cut Decanters are all bound with Silver which has a mighty pretty effect.' 'Mr Stewarts Tripod' is the magnificent ormolu perfume-burner still on the centre table in the alcove, designed by 'Athenian' Stuart. The earliest pieces of 'handsome plate' acquired by Lord Scarsdale were a rare French silver wine-fountain of the 1660s, and its pair, made to match by the English smith, Ralph Leeke, in the 1690s. Unfortunately, both the fountains (for dispensing wine when a tap was turned), and a pair of cisterns which stood on the pedestals between the tables, were sold in 1947.

At Kedleston, a chestnut roaster stands on the sideboard with charcoal in the bottom and tongs to lift out the contents for dessert. The huge wine cooler of Sicilian jasper has a wooden base to protect the cooling bottles. Sideboards were often made from mahogany or rosewood, two of the new timbers brought back from the great tropical forests through the West Indies trade. The strength of mahogany, particularly, made it possible to use large expanses for massive sideboards and leaves for table tops. Some sideboards had pedestal ends to take wine bottles and decanters, and a spirit lamp to warm dinner plates. There was often a shelf underneath for plates and maybe the dessert, like the sideboard in Chirk Castle dining-room, a copy of an Adam design produced in the 1780s. A lead-lined wine-cooler or cistern of the same wood as the sideboard completed this suite. Other designs had brass rails running along the back for a short curtain to protect the walls from food stains; examples can be seen at Shugborough, where the very large semi-circular sideboard is fitted into the bay window, and at Erddig, Calke and Attingham.

Until the early 19th century no dining-table with accompanying chairs was left standing permanently in the centre of the country-house dining-room to distract from the decoration. Instead, the central space was left open. Chairs would be arranged round the walls, while a number of small gate-leg tables were kept folded in the dining-room or in the passage outside to be brought in when needed for meals. When entertaining on a grand scale, these tables could be put together to make larger tables. Towards the end of the century it became fashionable for the first time to have one large dining-table of the pedestal type. The pedestal dining-table in the dining-room at Kedleston dates from around 1800. In many houses, this table was still dismantled after meals and the two ends could be placed against the walls as pier-tables, or used in other rooms as occasional tables. Extra leaves could be stored. Jane Austen mentions this system of furnishing in a letter of 1800. She wrote 'The two ends put together form one constant table for everything, and the centre-piece stands exceedingly well under glass.'

La Rochefoucauld was very much struck by English dining-rooms. 'The chairs and tables,' he wrote, 'are also made of mahogany of fine quality and have a brilliant polish like that of finely tempered steel.' Elsewhere, he mentions the dining-table as being brilliant 'like the finest of glass' and says that the Englishman seems to be at his happiest when seated around it. Dining-chairs usually had leather or horsehair seats that did not retain the smell of food, or stain easily.

Demand for fine furniture was country-wide and the new styles were disseminated from London to the provinces, so that a number of smaller towns became furniture-making centres of some importance. The mahogany dining-room table and chairs at

Erddig were supplied by Gillow of Lancaster in 1827 at a cost of £110 5s 4d. They were a present to Margaret, the wife of Simon Yorke II, from her brother and the original bill exists for 20 chairs at £4 19s each and 2 carvers at £6 each.

The dining-room was heated by a coal fire and lit by candles in torchères, candlestands and candelabra. Expensive wax candles – the candle tax of 1709 had brought up the price to 5s per 1 lb (about 4 candles) – were used by the wealthy when entertaining and by those less wealthy, only for very special occasions. In the Saltram accounts there are many references to their purchase in large numbers from licensed chandlers. When Thomas Creevey visited Petworth in 1828 'dinner was of the first order, turtle, venison, moor game &c. The servants, too, very numerous tho' most of them very advanced in years and tattered, and comical in their looks. The wax candles too were sufficiently numerous to light us all up well tho' we were at one end of a room 60 feet long . . .'.

The complete change of manners from the informality of breakfast to the scrupulous formality of dinner astounded the foreign visitor. La Rochefoucauld said: 'In the morning you come down to breakfast just as you wished . . . in the evening, unless you have just arrived, you must be well-washed and well-groomed. The standard of politeness is uncomfortably high – strangers go first into the dining-room and sit near the hostess and are served in seniority in accordance with a rigid etiquette. For the first few days I was tempted to think that it was done for a joke.' Even the informal Parkers at Saltram liked people to dress for dinner. Theresa wrote to her brother with much impatience: 'You may judge of the kind of animal Mr Genneys must be who is just come to his estate and just married and puts on a clean pair of boots to come down to dinner! – having never any use for shoes, and not having a pair in the house.'

Guests, in full evening dress, assembled in the drawing-room or saloon and after the footman had announced that 'dinner was upon the table', the important formal progress to the dining-room began. The order in which the guests were dispatched determined their placing at the table, with the ladies sitting together at one end and gentlemen at the other. John Trusler, in his *Honours of the Table* of 1788, explained:

> When dinner is announced, the mistress of the house requests the lady first in rank, in company, to show the way to the rest, and walk first into the room where the table is served; she then asks the second in precedence to follow . . . bringing up the rear herself . . . the master of the house does the same with the gentlemen . . . when they enter the dining room, each takes his place in the same order; the mistress of the table sits at the upper end, those of superior rank next her, right and left; those next in rank following, then the gentlemen and the master at the lower end; and nothing is considered as a greater mark of ill-breeding, than for a person to interrupt this order, or seat himself higher than he ought.

Trusler pointed out that precedence was worked out on the basis that 'women have here always taken place of men, and both men and women have sat above each other, according to the rank they bear in life. Where a company is equal in point of rank, married ladies take place over single ones, and older ones of younger ones'.

This practice must have caused a great deal of friction. In Jane Austen's *Persuasion*, written during 1815–16, two of the female characters fret over the loss of precedence that followed their changing stations in life: one feared losing the right to walk 'immediately after Lady Russell out of all the drawing-rooms and dining-rooms in the country,' while the other felt that her status as daughter-in-law prevented her getting the 'precedence that was her due'. The formal progress was not observed in town houses; guests gathered in the drawing-room, or went straight into the dining-room and sat where they wished.

For most of the century, men and women did not sit alternately around the table unless they were particularly intimate, or if they had left the table for a short time to allow the servants to set up the dessert course, when a more relaxed and convivial attitude might prevail. But by 1788, Trusler was mentioning 'a new promiscuous mode of seating' which had lately been introduced: 'A gentleman and lady sitting alternately round the table, and this for the better convenience of a lady being attended to, and served by the gentleman next to her. But notwithstanding this promiscuous seating, the ladies, whether above or below, are to be served in order, according to their rank or age, and after, the gentlemen in the same manner.'

When the guests entered the dining-room, they were met with a dazzling display. The table would be covered with large, brilliantly white cloths which extended down to the floor. The cloth was important both as a protection for the wood and for hiding any joins in the tables, but also its removal at the end of the main courses signalled a change in the nature of the dinner: before, the business was eating; after, it was drinking. The cloth, to the horror of visiting foreigners, often stood in for napkins, which had gone out of fashion with the introduction of the table fork in the previous century. It seems that the habit was regarded as a national custom and a sign of independence from foreign influence. It is decribed as such by Sophie von la Roche, a visitor from Switzerland: 'The table was covered with a fine big damask cloth on which we all wiped our mouths in old English style.' Another visitor observed: 'Napkins, which have been discussed for 20 years, are beginning to be introduced. Those who are attached to the old customs ridicule the use of them ... they cover themselves with the table-cloth, which is of extraordinary length.'

Napkins were certainly being used again in the fashionable households that employed a French chef and adopted many of the more refined French table manners. This table linen was usually of fine texture, often imported from Flanders where the weavers were celebrated for the delicacy of their work. Some linen had the crest or coat of arms of the owner woven into it, or the designs of the dining-room ceiling. Three or four qualities of fine damask, linen or cotton diaper were used for both table-cloths and large napkins at Shugborough. The linen inventory of 1760 included '37 damask table-cloths; 37 dozen and 2 damask napkins; 14 diaper table-cloths, bird eyes; 4 dozen diaper table-napkins; 6 diaper table cloth, large pattern; 3 dozen and 6 diaper napkins, large pattern; 11 small breakfast table-cloths, damask; and 18 tea napkins'. A mahogany linen-press was kept in the butler's pantry or in the servery to make sure this expensive table-linen was absolutely immaculate. People of more moderate means could not afford these fine elaborate cloths – they had something homespun, or they bought inexpensive cloths in shops or from travelling pedlars. Nancy Woodforde, the Parson's niece, paid 9s 6d each for cloth for the breakfast table. Later in the century, the use of table napkins was more common, as the cheaper cottons from Lancashire began to appear on the market.

At the beginning of the century, the popular table decoration for long narrow tables was a band of alternating features, like silver candelabra and baskets of either fruit or flowers, or sometimes both. The food was then arranged down the length of the tables on either side. If the tables were shorter and wider, the food could be arranged around a central object, of flowers, fruit, confectionery or fancy metalwork. By mid-century, it was fashionable to have miniature landscapes down the middle of the tables, sometimes set out on mirrors to amplify the light. Classical temples were constructed of sugar paste, biscuit dough, or wax cardboard, traced with silk. Later, in 1783 at a very elegant dinner with the Bishop of Norwich, Parson Woodforde described the table as having:

> A most beautiful Artificial Garden in the Center of the Table remained at Dinner and afterwards, it was one of the prettiest things I ever saw, about a Yard long, and about 18 inches wide, in the middle of which was a high round Temple supported on round Pillars, the Pillars were wreathed round with artificial Flowers on one side was a Shepherdess on the other a Shepherd, several handsome Urns decorated with artificial Flowers also &c. &c.

Doccia centrepiece, c.1775, from Ickworth, Suffolk. The sugar figures of the 17th-century dining-table had been displaced by the more delicate productions of the porcelain manufacturers. This Italian centrepiece, with its mermen and shells, would have been filled with various pickles.

The sugar figures had been displaced by the more delicate productions of the porcelain manufacturers and to a lesser extent the silversmiths. Horace Walpole wrote amusingly of this war between sugar and porcelain:

> Jellies, biscuits, sugar plums and creams had long since given way to Turks, Chinese and Shepherdesses of Saxon china. But these, unconnected and only seeming to wander amongst groves of curls of paper and wild flowers, were soon discovered to be too insipid and unmeaning. By degrees, whole meadows of cattle, of the same brittle materials spread themselves over the whole table, cottages rose in sugar and temples in barley sugar, pigmy Neptunes in cars of cockle-shells triumphed over oceans of looking-glass or seas of silver tissue ... confectioners found their trade moulder away, while toy-men and china shops were the only fashionable purveyors of the last stage of polite entertainments.

At a formal dinner at Saltram in 1811, the Rev. Talbot described 'the table of an immense width with a plateau full of biscuit figures and vases with flowers etc. the whole length, leaving merely a room for a dish at each end of a single row of dishes around with 4 Ice vases with Champagne etc. at the corners of it'. Perhaps the biscuit figures were some of those collected by Theresa Parker, who had a penchant for unglazed porcelain and stoneware.

Diners were no longer expected to supply their own cutlery when asked out to dinner, although special travelling sets were still in common use for eating at inns and hostelries. Matching cutlery sets were now being made with family crests for wealthy households and it was fashionable to lay 'the fork always on the left and the knife and spoon on the right hand' face downwards in the English style to avoid catching frills and lace cuffs. As Britain prospered, much more silverware appeared on the table, including cutlery, cruets and casters. A large canteen of early Georgian silver cutlery including 49 tablespoons also used for soup, 39 dessertspoons and 55 table forks, still exists at Saltram. Table knives were an expensive item and were kept in special elaborately decorated or polished wood boxes on the sideboard. There are two knife boxes in Erddig's dining-room with serpentine fronts and silver mounts, complete with table knives, and other examples can be seen in Georgian dining-rooms of National Trust houses. The blades of the knives were wide and rounded at the ends and somehow guests managed to eat peas with them and take up gravy and fruit juice.

The fork started the century as two-pronged, but soon acquired its third prong. In

1784 a Frenchman thought English usage of these instruments worthy of lengthy description:

> I do not like to prick my mouth or my tongue with these little sharp steel tridents which are generally used in England ... I know that this kind of fork is only intended for serving and fixing the pieces of meat while they are cut, and that the English knives being very large and rounded at the point, serve the same purpose to which forks in France are applied, that is, to carry food to the mouth ... The fork seizes, the knife cuts, and the pieces may be carried to the mouth with either. The motion is quick and precise ... In France ... when meat is cut to pieces, the knife is laid down idle on the right side of the plate, while the fork passes from left to right.

In early Georgian times everyday cutlery was made from iron, but just as mahogany was catching the public's imagination, Benjamin Hintsmans developed a harder, sharper low-priced steel and sets of his cutlery soon found their way on to the new mahogany tables. New designs were produced for specialist knives to deal with oysters, cheese and onions. Pewter, still used to make spoons, was superseded by Britannia metal which was much in demand at the end of the century as a cheap substitute for silver. It was tough, versatile and much cheaper than pewter or the new silver-plate. About the year 1742 Thomas Bolsover, a Sheffield cutler, invented a new kind of plate named after his home town. This released a flood of mass-produced silver-plate items for the table, including cutlery, which were within the price range of the middle classes.

Cruets for oil and vinegar were still used, but the cruet frame did not come into fashion until the end of the century. One firm of silversmiths is said to have designed more than 500 cruet frame patterns between 1788 and 1815. In the Victoria & Albert Museum can be seen a late 18th-century stand containing four green glass cruets, which held soy sauce and ketchup as well as oil and vinegar. Casters were still made for sugar and Jamaican and Cayenne peppers, and towards the end of the century, when there was a vogue for sprinkling cinnamon on hot buttered muffins, a small caster was made, known as a 'muffineer'.

By mid-century the wine-glass or tumbler was placed on the table to the right of the diner. Before this, glasses were placed on a cloth-covered sideboard or pier-table until called for. Glass was still expensive and seems to have been quite scarce even in wealthy homes at the beginning of the century, but increasing demand plus the invention of lead crystal led to the production of much beautiful English and Waterford glass. A tax, assessed according to weight, placed on glass in 1745 was responsible for the development of decoration. Until this time, the value of glass tended to be dictated by weight; now, beauty of design and cutting, engraving, gilding and enamelling dictated value. On the dining-table at Shugborough stands a set of rare funnel-shaped glasses with gilt rims dating from about 1740.

In the 18th century, wines were still preferred as cold as possible and the monteith continued to be used for cooling glasses. In fashionable society, their use appears to have become outmoded, following the appearance of individual wine-glass-coolers made of glass at the coronation banquet of George III and Queen Charlotte in 1760. Writers on table etiquette later in the century instructed butlers to place one to the right of each diner. Early in the 19th century, directions were more explicit: 'Hock and champagne glasses are to be placed in the cooler, two wine-glasses upon the table'. Examples of wine-glass-coolers can be seen on a side-table in the dining-room at Chirk

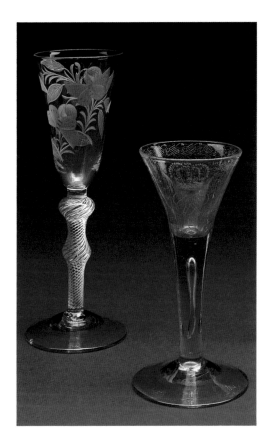
Eighteenth-century glasses from Mompesson House, Salisbury in Wiltshire. A tax, assessed according to weight, placed on glass in 1745 encouraged the development of decoration. Henceforward beauty of design and cutting, engraving and gilding dictated value.

Castle. They were also known as water-glasses, and until about 1790 it was customary for them to be accompanied by glass plates.

When the guests had taken their seats, the servants brought each a dinner plate which had previously been warmed in front of the fire or in a specially designed plate-warmer. A magnificent gunmetal and ormulu plate-warmer in the shape of a Greek vase stands in front of the fireplace at Kedleston. Dinner plates would have been stacked in a space at the back, and either heated with a spirit-lamp in the bottom, or put to warm close to the fire, a highly desirable feature when the kitchen was such a long way from the dining-room.

At the beginning of the century, the newly founded Meissen factory near Dresden in Germany was copying expensive Chinese porcelain, but it was not until the 1770s that this secret formula for true porcelain was acquired by other factories in Europe. Meanwhile, many, such as that at Sèvres and, from the 1740s, those at Chelsea, Bow and Derby in England, were making tea- and dinner-services of exquisite beauty of soft-paste or artificial porcelain. Waddesdon Manor in Buckinghamshire has a magnificent collection of Sèvres, formed during the 19th century by successive generations of the Rothschild family, and many other National Trust houses are rich in English porcelain.

A form of true porcelain, using china clay and soap-rock, was manufactured at Bristol from 1748 and transferred to Worcester in 1752. This porcelain was more resistant to sudden changes of temperature and became the ideal material for tea-services. A Worcester tea- and coffee-service painted in green and black with figures posing among ruins, dating from about 1770, can be seen in the 'mirror room' at Saltram.

A third type of porcelain using bone-ash, was developed at Bow in 1749 and subsequently used at Chelsea and Derby. Josiah Spode adopted this technique to make bone china, the principal medium for English porcelain to this day.

The desire to reproduce Chinese tea-wares was directly responsible for the rise of one of Britain's most prestigious industries – the Staffordshire potteries – in the mid-18th

One of a pair of Chelsea plaice tureens at Erddig, Clwyd. From the 1740s, porcelain factories at Chelsea, Bow and Derby were making tea- and dinner-services of exquisite beauty.

A selection from the Worcester tea- and coffee-service in the Mirror Room at Saltram, Devon. The service was made in about 1770, and painted in black and green with buildings, ruins and figures.

(376)

For J U N E.

FIRST COURSE.

Green peafe foup removed
with mackarel

Fricaffee of chickens

Neck of mutton boiled
with caper fauce

Fish fauce

Hare collops   Calf's head pie   Pigeons in furprize

Tongue boiled   Currant jelly   Papiets de veau

Haunch of venifon roafted

SECOND COURSE.

Two turkey pouts roafted

Cheefe cakes

Ragoo of mufhrooms

Preferved codlins

Potted beef   Crowcant   Collared pig

Compote of apricots

Artichokes   Blamonge

Weat-ears roafted

(377)

For J U L Y.

FIRST COURSE.

Soup with artichoke bottoms
removed with crimp cod

A breaft of veal
ragoo'd   Young potatoes   Beef fteaks
a-la-mode

Anchovy fauce   Parfley fauce

Swine's cheek boil'd   Venifon pafty   Windfor beans

Plain butter   Shrimp fauce

Sallad

Lambs' feet with
muftard   De quez de polard
a-la-fanch herb

Leg of mutton roafted
with ftewed cucumbers

SECOND COURSE.

Two ducklings roafted

Trifle   Dutch flummery

Cray-fith

Green gages   Apricots

Artichoke bottoms
forced   Apricot tart   Ragout mille

Peaches   Potted char   Melon

Cuftards   Italian cream

A leveret roafted

B b b

Suggested menus for June and July from Mary Smith's *Complete Housekeeper*, 1772. Mary Smith had been housekeeper to Sir Walter Calverley Blackett at Wallington, Northumberland.

century. Factories belonging to Spode and Josiah Wedgwood were able to produce 'services' of matching plates, cups and saucers for breakfast, dinner and tea, from earthenware, within the financial reach of all but the poor. Spode's table services, bearing initials or coats of arms, and Wedgwood's fine cream-coloured earthenware, called Queensware following approval by Queen Charlotte, proved highly popular.

However, Chinese porcelain remained sought after and was shipped in quantity. The Parkers acquired at least three Chinese services; the last, an imposing dessert-service, is still in the dining-room at Saltram. An armorial service of oriental porcelain was the height of fashion and some 4,000 were made for British families. With images copied from drawings, engravings, even seals (with mottoes often mis-spelled by the Chinese), these services sailed back at the rate of one every six days for a century. There are fine examples at Shugborough, Uppark, Arlington, Ickworth and Nostell Priory.

As in the previous century formal dinners were divided into two or occasionally three courses, each consisting of a variety of savoury and sweet dishes followed by dessert. The first would comprise of soups, boiled meats and fish, small roast and pies, supplemented with dishes of vegetables, and the occasional sweet pudding. As the first course neared its conclusion, the first 'remove' dish was introduced – the most imposing meat or poultry joint served as a 'conversation piece', like the subtlety of earlier times, to revive interest in the meal. It also helped to span the lengthy time it took to remove the remains of the first course and bring in the second course dishes.

The second course normally concentrated on roasted meats with various 'made' dishes like fricassées and ragôuts, fish, fruit pies and custards. Sometimes the dessert was placed in the centre of the table at the same time as the second course, raised up on dessert frames; 5 glass dessert frames were listed in the Shugborough inventory of 1773. There would be a second remove dish if a third course was to be served. This would be even more spectacular than the first to refresh the flagging palate. If there was no third course the dessert would be served. The 18th-century passion for outward display meant that all the dishes for each course were laid on the table at the same time, as in previous centuries. Folding-plate illustrations and diagrams were included in cookery books of the period to instruct on how to present an artistically balanced picture of colour contrasts and shapes.

A few cookery writers, most notably Hannah Glasse, chose to omit these table diagrams, saying 'Nor shall I take it upon me to direct a Lady how to set out her Table; for that would be impertinent ... Nor indeed do I think it would be pretty, to see a Lady's Table set out after the directions of a Book.' She did, however, describe a particular dish as being suitable for a 'remove', 'side' or 'corner' dish. In some books 'ideal meals' were arranged on a month by month basis. Some hostesses may have followed the suggested menus slavishly, especially those who were trying to rise in the world, but most would probably consult them just to pick up fresh ideas.

Visiting foreigners were deeply impressed and sometimes a little appalled by the suicidally large diet of the English. Parson Woodforde, far from wealthy, thought nothing of entertaining his neighbours in February 1788 to a dinner of: 'some Fish and Oyster Sauce, a nice Piece of Boiled Beef and a fine Neck of Pork rosted and Apple Sauce, some hashed Turkey Mutton Stakes, Sallad &c., a wild Duck rosted, fryed Rabbits, a plumb pudding, and some Tartlets, Desert, some Olives, Nutts, Almonds, and Raisins and Apples', and this was 'not above 3 hours notice of their coming'.

In October 1772 Sir James Caldwell dined with Lord Bangor at Castle Ward in Co. Down:

> There was an excellent dinner, stewed trout at the head, chine of beef at the foot, soup in the middle, a little pie at each side and four trifling things at the corners . . . . The second course of nine dishes [was] made out much in the same way. The cloth was taken away and then the fruit – a pine apple, not good; a small plate of peaches, grapes, and figs (but a few) and the rest, pears and apples. No plate or knives given about; we were served in queen ware . . . . During dinner two French horns of Lady Clanwilliam's played very fairly in the hall next to the parlour which had a good effect . . .

Before the guests began eating Trusler advised: 'The mistress ... should acquaint the company with what is to come ... or if the whole is put on the table at once, should tell her friends they "see the dinner", but they should be told, what wine or other liquor is on the side-board. Sometimes a cold joint of meat, or a sallad is placed on the side-board. In this case it should be announced to the company.'

Although there was a vast quantity of food on offer in each course, the diner was not expected to sample all the dishes. After the soup, each man helped himself from the dish before him and offered some of it to his neighbours; if he wanted something beyond his

Course layouts from Mary Smith's *Complete Housekeeper*, 1772. Folding-plate illustrations and diagrams were included in cookery books to instruct on how to present an artistically balanced arrangement of dishes on a dining-table. The first course would consist of soups, boiled meats and fish, small roasts and pies supplemented with dishes of vegetables and the occasional sweet pudding (*left*). The second course normally concentrated on roast meats with various 'made' dishes like fricassées and ragôuts, fish, fruit pies and custards (*right*).

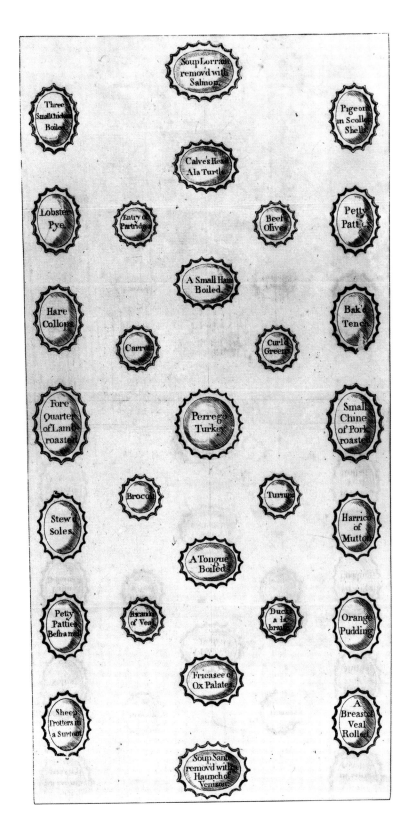

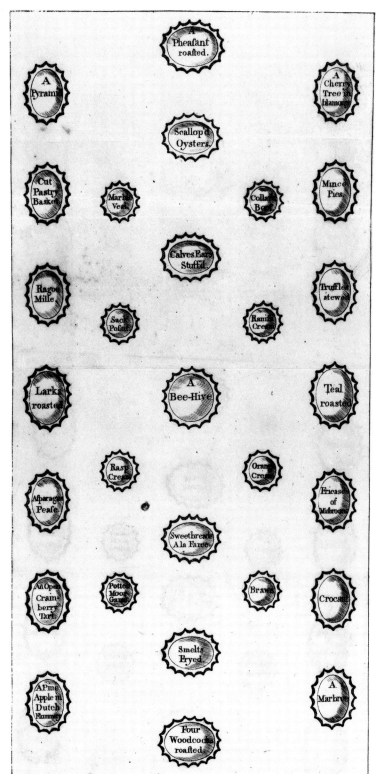

255

reach, it was very much a question of catching the footman's eye. A seasoned diner would make sure the footman was suitably bribed beforehand. When the diner had indicated his next choice of dish, a clean warm plate and the correct cutlery was placed in front of him. Trusler's 'Rules for waiting at table' of 1788 were as follows:

A good servant will be industrious, and attend to the following rules in waiting; but where he is remiss, it is the duty of the master or mistress to remind him.

1. If there is a soup for dinner, according to the number of the company, to lay each person a flat plate, and a soup-plate over it, a napkin, knife, fork and spoon, and to place the chairs. If there is no soup, the soup-plate may be omitted.

2. To stand with his back to the side-board, looking on the table. This is the office of the principal servant. If there are more, then to stand round the table, or, if each person's servant is present, that servant should stand behind his mistress's or master's chair.

3. To keep the dishes in order upon the table, as they were at first put on.

4. If any of the garnish of the dishes falls on the cloth, to remove it from the table in a plate, thus keeping the table free from litter.

5. To change each person's plate, knife, fork and spoon, as soon as they are done with. This will be known, by the person's putting the handles of this knife and fork into his plate.

6. To look round and see if any want bread and help them to it, before it is called for.

7. To hand the decoraments of the table, viz. oyl, vinegar, or mustard, to those who want, anticipating even their wishes. Every one knows with what mustard is eaten, with what vinegar, and so on, and a diligent, attentive servant, will always hand it, before it is asked for.

8. To give the plates, &c. perfectly clean and free from dust, and never give a second glass of wine, in a glass that has been once used. If there is not a sufficient change of glasses, he should have a vessel of water under the sideboard, to dip them in, and wipe them bright.

9. It is genteel to have thin gill-glasses, and the servant should fill them only half full, this prevents spilling, and the foot of the glass should be perfectly dry, before it is given.

10. To give nothing but on a waiter, and always to hand it with the left hand, and on the left side of the person he serves. When serving wine, to put his thumb on the foot of the glass, this will prevent its over-throw.

11. Never to reach across a table, or in serving one person to put his hand or arm before another.

12. To tread lightly across the room, and never to speak, but in reply to a question asked, and then in a modest under-voice.

13. When the dishes are to be removed, to remove them with care, so as not to spill the sauce or gravy over any of the company; to clean the table-cloth from crumbs, if a second course is to be served up, if not, to take away the knives, forks and spoons, in a knife-tray, clear away the plates, take up the pieces of bread with a fork, roll up the cloth to prevent the crumbs falling on the floor, rub the table clean and bright, and put on the wine, &c. from the side-board, with a decanter of water and plenty of clean glasses.

These things are the province of the servants, but as few servants are thorough good waiters, and as the master of the house is responsible for his attendants, it is incumbent on him to see that his company is properly served and attended. For a table ill-served and attended is always a reflection on the good conduct of the mistress or master.

This type of service inevitably ensured that the food would be cold because diners were so dependent on the footmen. The ladies were at particular disadvantage, until the promiscuous seating when they were looked after by their gentlemen neighbours. John Trusler advised the gentleman, 'As eating a great deal is deemed indelicate in a lady (for her character should be rather divine than sensual) it will be ill manners to help her to a large slice of meat at once, or fill her plate too full. When you have served her with meat, she should be asked what kind of vegetables she likes, and the gentleman sitting next to the dish that serves those vegetables should be requested to help her.'

Another factor that held up the meal was the interminable time it took for the host and hostess or principal 'strangers' to practise the 'genteel act of carving'. Eliza Smith in *The Compleat Housewife* of 1727 provided detailed instructions on the art, recording a whole series of terms reminiscent of earlier times: 'to spat a Pike, to roar a Goose, to thigh a Pigeon or to tame a Crab.' By 1788, Trusler was also providing illustrations to assist the aspiring carver.

The butler, if there was one, would look after the wines at the sideboard and ensure

A York dining-room drawn by Mary Ellen Best. Although this drawing was made in 1838, it reflects a late Georgian table arrangement with soup ready on the right for the mistress of the house to serve, and the roast for the host to carve on the left.

Left: *Elegant Merrymaking* by Peter Angellis. All the dishes for each course were laid on the table at once by footmen who also brought clean plates, cutlery and glasses when needed. Wine bottles were not placed on the table at this time.

that everything went smoothly. Placing wine bottles on the table so that guests could help themselves was not normal practice until the beginning of the 19th century, so guests once again had to catch the eye of a footman. Because of the varied nature of dishes in each course, the wine and beer could be taken in whatever order the guests chose throughout the meal, although it was usual to start with champagne, if on offer. Guests could not drink during dinner without being challenged, a peculiarly English custom. 'Each lady must be solicited to drink wine by a gentleman, who first drinks to her, then to the hostess and the master of the house, and so on, until he has gone through the whole company. It would be undecorous,' wrote Goede, 'to touch a glass with your lips previous to such challenges.' Prince Pückler-Muskau described exactly how the procedure worked after his visit to England in 1828: 'When you raise your glass, you look fixedly at the one with whom you are drinking, bow your head and drink with great gravity . . . . It is esteemed a civility to challenge anybody in this way to drink . . . . If the company is small, and a man has drunk to everybody but happens to wish for more wine, he must wait for the dessert (after which he could drink freely), if he does not find in himself courage enough to brave customs.'

The serious business of eating lasted for at least two hours and this, too, bewildered and distressed the foreign visitor: 'You are compelled to extend your stomach to the full in order to please your host. He asks you all the time whether you like the food, and presses you to eat more.' said La Rochefoucauld. Trusler instructed guests to behave properly; it was vulgar to eat too quickly or too slowly, which showed you were either too hungry, or you didn't like the food; it was also vulgar to eat your soup with your nose in the plate. 'It is exceeding rude to scratch any part of your body, to spit, or blow your nose . . . to lean your elbows on the table, to sit too far from it, to pick your teeth before the dishes are removed.' Fanny Burney and Mrs Thrale wondered if the guest who helped herself to loaf sugar with her fingers could be a lady.

Right: Dessert course at Fairfax House, York. The finale of any formal dinner was the dessert. At each place setting the dessert plate is flanked by cutlery displayed face down to avoid lace cuffs, and a clean napkin. The various wine-glasses are accompanied by water-glasses used to rinse the fingers between each delicacy. At the centre of the table is a silver épergne filled with dry sweetmeats.

L'Après-Dinée des Anglais, 1814: the French view of the English, whom they regarded as greedy, drunken, melancholic and unstylish in their dress. After dinner, when the ladies and the servants had left, the men were free to discuss politics and love affairs and drink themselves under the table (*left*). Foreigners were shocked by the fact that chamberpots were provided in the sideboard. Meanwhile the ladies retired to tea and scandal in the drawing-room (*right*).

The finale of any formal dinner was the dessert course. After the dishes from the last main course had been cleared, Trusler instructed the butler, if water and glasses were used after dinner, 'to put on those glasses half full of clean water, when the table is cleared, but before the cloth is removed for dessert'. Water-glasses might serve the double purpose of cleaning the fingers and rinsing the mouth at the end of a meal. Tobias Smollett in his *Travels* of 1766, complained that he knew of 'no custom more beastly than that of using water glasses in which polite company spirt, and squirt and spue the filthy scouring of their gums'. Refined people later in the century would dip merely the tips of their fingers in the glass. 'This ceremony over,' wrote La Rochefoucauld, 'the cloth is removed and you behold the most beautiful table that it is possible to see.' (Once again he extols the shining quality of the wood.) The exposed table was then covered with 'elegant china baskets' of fresh candied and preserved fruit, 'sweetmeat glasses' of dry and wet sweetmeats, 'comfits and licorice in fine porcelain or crystal vases' to aid the digestion, small glass and china plates of olives and nuts, and glasses of sparkling jellies, creams, ices and syllabubs.

Such dessert courses would be by far the most expensive part of the meal and, like the banquet of the previous century, could only be afforded by the wealthy. Boswell tells us of a host who 'is anxious to cover the retreat of some uncut principal dish which may be served up again or is making some fantastic pretence to have the rarest and most valuable fruit in his dessert carried away as he has already had the glory of their being seen by the company, who he flatters himself will talk of it all over the town.' Horace Walpole never at a loss for words, found such creations to be 'puerile puppet-shows'.

Although the making of sweetmeats was sometimes carried out in the still-room, more often the dessert was ordered from outside caterers or confectioners, many of them from the Continent, who had set up in the more fashionable towns. If required, the confectioner would also supply the glass and structures needed to display the

dessert; pyramids of sets of two to six glass salvers or tazze, piled one upon another in gradually diminishing sizes with a master glass in the centre of the topmost, were very fashionable. Lady Grisell Baillie records in her diary of 1719 that at a London dinner party there stood 'in the middle of the table a Pirimide, sillibubs and orange cream in the lower part, above it, sweetmeats dry and wet'. During the 1790s, glass or silver épergnes for holding fruit, flowers and sweetmeats superseded the pyramid and its individual sweetmeat glasses.

At Waddesdon, there is the most exquisite Sèvres dessert service consisting of more than a hundred pieces including fruit stands, compotiers for stewed fruit, ice-pails and ice-cups for serving ice-cream, wine-coolers and monteiths.

Each guest at the table was provided with a dessert plate, a spoon, a small knife and fork, a glass finger-bowl for rinsing the fingers between each delicacy and 'a square and very small serviette' to use as an elegant table towel. The dessert doily had made its appearance by the end of the previous century: Jonathan Swift in his *Journal of Stella*,1711, notes 'after dinner we had coarse D'Oyly napkins fringed at each end upon the table to drink with'. The 'doily' was named after Thomas D'Oyly, a 17th-century linen draper trading at the Nun in Henrietta Street, Covent Garden, who introduced small linen mats to place under finger-bowls and bottles to prevent the soiling of tables. Pückler-Muskau noted that 'three decanters are usually placed before the master of the house [which] generally contain claret, port, sherry or madeira'. These were passed from right to left by being 'pushed . . . on a stand, or in a little silver wagon on wheels'.

When the dessert course was over, La Rochefoucauld tells us that: 'All the servants disappear. The ladies drink a glass or two of wine and at the end of half an hour all go out together'. They retired to the drawing-room for coffee or 'tea and scandal', leaving the 'heroes to their pleasure': to settle the nation's destiny, toast their mistresses and drink themselves under the table. La Rochefoucauld comments:

It is then that real enjoyment begins – there is not an Englishman who is not supremely happy at this particular moment . . . This is the time that I like the best: Conversation is as free as it can be, everyone expresses his political opinions with much frankness. Sometimes conversation becomes extremely free upon highly indecent topics – complete licence is allowed . . . very often I have heard things mentioned in good society which would be in the grossest taste in France.

La Rochefoucauld was also shocked that 'The sideboard is furnished with a number of chamber pots and it is a common practice to relieve oneself while the rest are drinking; one has no kind of concealment and the practice strikes me as most indecent.' There is an example of a sideboard with a pot cupboard at Stourhead. Lord Scarsdale was more delicate; a chamberpot was provided for his guests in a cupboard just outside the door of the dining-room at Kedleston. The company served themselves from wine-coolers and dumb waiters, the bottles making a continuous circuit of the table. A dumb waiter was an English invention consisting of three circular trays in decreasing sizes round a central pillar. It usually stood at the corner of the table to hold plates and cutlery as well as food and drink. The Rev. Talbot described the serving of a typical dinner at Saltram 'in the absence of Company' where 'his Lordship performed by a Dumb Waiter the whole Ceremony himself'.

Towards the end of the century, horseshoe-shaped tables were made for after-dinner drinking round the fire. Some had folding screens as a protection against the heat, and a network bag in the centre to contain biscuits, while coasters attached to a metal rod, or sliding in a well, were provided to hold the bottles.

At the end of two or three hours, at about 9pm, a servant announced that tea and coffee were ready and conducted the gentlemen from their drinking to join the ladies and the card-tables in the drawing-room. The ladies, meanwhile, had been having a

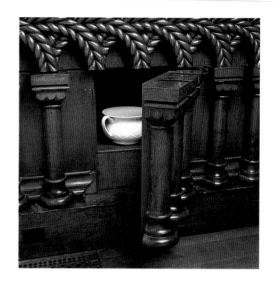

The carved wooden dado in the dining-room at Penrhyn Castle, Gwynedd conceals a cupboard for the chamberpot.

The family of Sir John and Lady Cust of Belton House, Lincolnshire, by Enoch Seeman, 1741. On the tea-table are small, handleless cups, teapot and sugar-bowl with tongs.

John Montagu, 4th Earl of Sandwich (1718–92), who is credited with inventing the sandwich so that he could eat without losing time away from the gambling tables. This portrait, painted in 1740 by Joseph Highmore, hangs at Beningbrough Hall, Yorkshire.

delightful time in the drawing-room, a light feminine room compared with the rather masculine dining-room. 'Nanny' Robinson, who took over as mistress of Saltram after her sister Theresa's death, enjoyed this period of the day more than any other. 'Taking tea' was considered the height of 'English style' much admired across the Channel, and had its own increasingly elaborate ritual, its own equipage and of course its own table, described by Thomas Chippendale as the 'china table', with a low gallery around its edge to stop the expensive tea-china from falling off. English tea-wares had reached their height of beauty and elegance; even tea-caddies in which the precious leaves were locked away were frequently masterpieces of the cabinetmaker's art. At the beginning of the 19th century, the 'tea-poy' was introduced – a small table usually fitted with tea caddies and glass blending bowls where the mistress of the house could blend her own tea. Two can be seen at Calke.

Once the gentlemen had arrived, more tea was made, this time served with cakes, sandwiches (said to have been invented by the 4th Earl of Sandwich so that he could eat meals without having to lose time away from the gambling tables) and bread and butter. 'The slices of bread which they give you with your tea', wrote Pastor Moritz in 1782, 'are as thin as poppy leaves.' At Saltram, muffins, cakes, fruit and wine were placed on a dumb waiter for the evening's entertainment of games of cards or dancing. John Parker, like many of his age, was a great gambler, frequently losing as much as £1,000 a day playing whist at Boodle's, his club in London.

The final event of the evening, some two or three hours later, seems to have been optional; guests stayed on to enjoy a light supper of cold meats, sweets, fruit and wine, or a choice of light hot dishes such as 'ramokins' (see p.239), or went home. Robert Southey explained that 'supper is rather a ceremony than a meal' and was followed by 'wine and water, or spirits'. This was to him the 'pleasantest' hour of the day, ending a short while before midnight.

The Georgians certainly seemed to have had plenty of stamina for entertainment. The Duchess of Northumberland wrote in her diary for 6 May 1760: 'Went home, voided a large stone. Tired to death. Went to a ball; tired to death. A Bad Supper'!

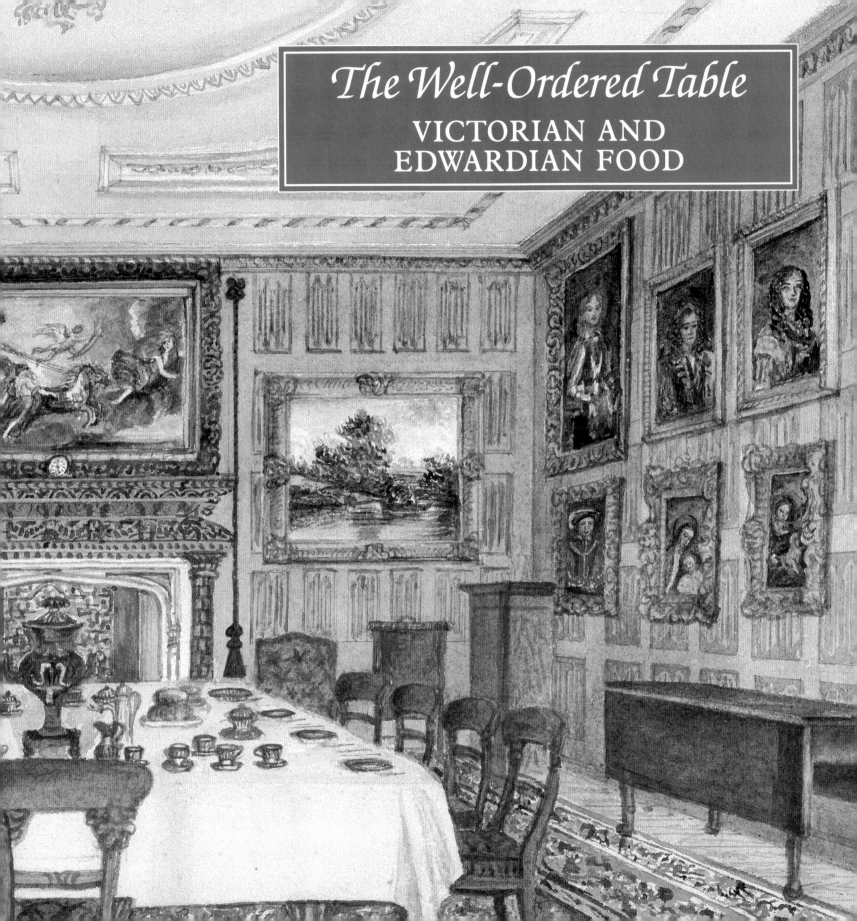

The Well-Ordered Table

VICTORIAN AND EDWARDIAN FOOD

The Well-Ordered Table

*I have always thought that there is no more fruitful
source of family discontent than a housewife's badly
cooked dinners and untidy ways. Men are now so well
served out of doors – at their clubs, well-ordered
taverns, and dining houses – that, in order to
compete with the attractions of these places,
a mistress must be thoroughly acquainted with the
theory and practice of cookery, as well as be
perfectly conversant with all the other arts of
making and keeping a comfortable home.*

The Book of Household Management, by Mrs Isabella Beeton, 1861

I

The seventy-seven years from the accession of Queen Victoria in 1837 to the outbreak of the First World War in 1914 represented an age of unprecedented material progress, in which Britain led the world in industrial production. Overseas trade grew ever wider, drawing in raw materials and food supplies, and providing much of the world with manufactured goods.

The solid prosperity of this period, shades of which are with us today in public buildings and monuments of civil engineering, as well as in more prosaic reminders such as lamp-posts and pillarboxes, could nevertheless not obscure the continuing uneven distribution of wealth. The old landed aristocracy, now joined by an increasing number of industrialists, merchants, bankers and professional men, as ever lived and ate in luxury. Below was a widening stratum of middle-class men and women who also had servants to cook and serve their food, were keen to observe the fashions in eating and drinking, and to follow trends set by their social superiors. It was for these aspirants that the encylopaedic cookery books of the time were written, such as Mrs Beeton's *Book of Household Management*, 1861, and Eliza Acton's *Modern Cookery Book*, 1845.

The expansion of the Empire influenced cooking in Britain. For, although Mrs Beeton maintained that 'Cookery in Australia is to all intents and purposes English.... An Englishman in a good hotel in Sydney or Melbourne would find no difference between that and one of comparable standing at home', where the British colonised a country with a sophisticated cuisine, most notably India, recipes were introduced on to home dining-tables. Most of the cookery books of the period contain a selection of Anglo-Indian dishes: kedgeree for breakfast, pilaus and curries for lunch or dinner,

Previous pages: Mid-19th-century watercolour of the Chapel Parlour at The Vyne, Hampshire, by Martha Chute. Martha was married to William Lyde Wiggett who assumed the name Chute after inheriting The Vyne from his uncle. She has apparently depicted the table laid for breakfast, although the butler appears to be fetching wine.

George Cruikshank's satire on the condition of Thames water. Pollution caused regular outbreaks of cholera and typhus in London in the 19th century. In 1855, therefore, a Metropolitan Board of Works was established to build sewers to carry London's effluent under a new embankment and downstream. The capital's water supply, however, remained in private hands until 1904.

tamarind sauce as a condiment. Mrs Beeton even went so far as to combine colonial ingredients and offer the unlikely dish of 'Curried Kangaroo Tails'.

But for the rest of the population, life was still hard. Widespread unemployment, especially in the crowded industrial cities of the North and the Midlands brought destitution and hunger. Employers were able to impose any conditions they pleased: small children as well as men and women were obliged to accept low wages and long hours of work. Conditions for the agricultural labourer were equally desperate, exacerbated by a succession of bad harvests between 1809 and 1814. 'In little over a generation' wrote the historian A. L. Morton, 'the mass of the rural population passed from a beef, bread and ale standard of living to a potato and tea standard.' Two renowned London chefs, Alexis Soyer and Charles Francatelli, realising the desperation of the situation, designed new soup recipes for cheap mass feeding. These may not have been very nourishing, but marked the start of a new attitude. One enlightened landowner who shared their concern was 'The Great Sir Thomas' Acland, 10th Baronet, of Killerton in Devon. Money that had previously been lavished by his family on stag-hunting and good living was now spent on estate improvements, political elections – Sir Thomas was MP for Devonshire – and the furtherance of good causes. Sir Thomas was extremely concerned about the poor in the nearby village of Broadclyst; an unusually generous amount was paid to the parishioners out of the Poor Rate. Despite this, 400 people were still poor enough to beg for a penny piece from John Veitch, the estate's agent, on Christmas Day and 100 were forced away from the 'birthday beef', which celebrated Sir Thomas's coming-of-age in 1808. Distressed by this, he suggested that a soup-kitchen should be set up to cater for the needs of the whole parish during the winter, but his agent persuaded him that selective grants of food and clothing would do more good.

Great Sir Thomas's son, 'Tom Thumb', continued his father's good works at Killerton. Unlike many county families, the Aclands were 'not a bit grand', their simple style of living being described in a book of instructive stories for mothers' meetings, *Ways and Means in a Devonshire Village*, which was dedicated to Tom Thumb in 1885. Like the lady in the book, his wife Mary personally sold her household dripping at half price to the cottagers of Broadclyst and bought 'comforts' for them out of the profits. The cookery lessons wrapped up in the stories include the same economical dishes of curried cold meat and giblet stew that Sir Thomas had learned to make at 6d a time when he attended classes in London.

In the 19th century, shops began to assume a form that the modern customer would recognise. This Styal Estate shop at Quarry Bank Mill, Cheshire, displays typical Victorian products.

But even the poorer classes felt the influence on their food of Britain as an industrial giant and a world power. By the early 20th century, the man and woman in the street could take advantage of a wide variety of food available through Britain's colonial possessions, from cocoa to bottled sauces based on Indian ingredients. But the staple products were also coming from overseas: 77 per cent of wheat and 80 per cent of beef consumed in Britain in 1911 came from America. Farmers struggled to compete by replacing their workers with machinery such as mechanical reapers, steam ploughs and tractions engines, so that in 1911 only 12 per cent of the population was employed in agriculture. But even with more efficient and larger farms, British agriculture was not prospering, and was forced instead to concentrate on areas where competition from world markets could not penetrate, such as fresh milk and market gardening.

In the 19th century shops began to assume a form that the modern customer would recognise. One development was the introduction of the 'Co-op' or co-operative store, which proved particularly popular in the North. The first Co-op Society opened in Rochdale in Lancashire in 1844. The theory behind these stores was that customers paid a decent cash price for their goods, thereby acquiring a stake in the business. Provided trade was good, they could expect a return in the form of a 'divi' or dividend every six months or year. A central agent purchased goods for a number of stores, thus benefiting from buying in bulk.

A second development in retail shopping resulted from the increase in cheap transport from the 1840s, both in Britain and overseas. Basic foodstuffs could now be imported cheaply, prepared and packed at a central warehouse and delivered, ready to sell, to as many outlets as were available. Thomas Lipton opened the first of these shops in Glasgow in 1872; a quarter of a century later he had 245 branches spread across the country. Perhaps even more spectacular was the career of Julius Drew. He had been sent out to the Far East as a tea buyer by his uncle, a successful importer. On his return to England he opened The Willow Pattern Tea Store in Liverpool in 1878. A mere twelve years later, with his partner John Musker, he had 106 more shops all over the country, known as Home & Colonial Stores. Like Lipton, Drew was able to buy goods cheaply from all over the British Empire and sell directly to the public rather than through a middle man. Drawing on his early experience, Drew did all the tea buying, causing a minor social revolution, since his shops tended to sell Indian rather than China tea, thus encouraging a swing in public taste. At the age of 33 he was able to retire and realise his dream of establishing himself as a landed country gentleman, when Sir Edwin Lutyens designed Castle Drogo for him at Drewsteignton in Devon, where his family considered they had ancient links.

Although by 1900 the poorest groups of the population had greater choice of foodstuffs, this did not necessarily improve their health. Nearly 60 per cent of the population of England and Wales lived in towns of more than 20,000 people. Most of their food had to be bought from shops or street vendors, because few had gardens or patches of land. Convenient and quickly-prepared food was preferred because men and women were still working extremely long hours in factories and offices, and the cooking facilities at home were generally very limited. They went to work early in the morning on nothing more than a cup of strong black tea, followed by a midday meal of bread (usually white not brown or wholemeal) and jam, and more tea. It was only for the evening meal, at the end of a long, tiring day, that any cooked food was eaten, usually quickly fried foodstuffs, such as bacon, a kipper or a few cheap sausages with, perhaps, some highly seasoned pickles. From the late 19th century, frequent trips to the 'fish and chip' shop were a feature of working-class life. These trends even undermined the hitherto healthier diet found in Scotland, where the consumption of wheat bread – little eaten previously in comparison with oats – rose, while the consumption of meat and of vegetable broth fell. The cuts of meat favoured by the Scots took too long to cook on work-days, even if the cooking facilities existed.

Ironically, it was war that raised the nation's consciousness about the bad diet of a large proportion of the population, ushering in a whole series of efforts to counter the problem. Recruitment for the South African War in 1899 revealed the poor physique of many working-class men, and as a result the Inter-Departmental Committee on Physical Deterioration was set up in 1904. Their report revealed that thousands of young children were living on near-starvation diets of mainly bread and jam, and were suffering from rickets, bad teeth and stunted growth. The Committee's findings led to the first National Conference on Infant Mortality held in London and the beginning of the Infant Welfare Movement, which has since saved hundreds of thousands of lives.

Bread

As ever, wheaten white bread was regarded as the standard to which all households should aspire. But the widespread use of wheat flour for baking throughout the country was only made possible after the repeal of the Corn Laws. These had been introduced in 1815, during the Napoleonic Wars, to restrict wheat imports, thus protecting the British farmer. With wholesale disaster facing Ireland following a series of potato famines, the British Prime Minister, Sir Robert Peel, was forced to execute a political U-turn and repeal the Corn Laws in the summer of 1846. 'Tom Thumb' Acland of Killerton voted for the repeal, thus committing political suicide, for he represented a rural constituency where most of his supporters were landowners and farmers who depended on keeping up the price of corn. 'It is a choice of evils,' said a West Country journal, 'in which cheap bread is ruin to the agriculturalist, and dear bread is a calamity to the rest of the population.'

Larger quantities of 'hard' wheat began to be imported from the North American prairies and the vast arable plains of Australia and the Argentine. It rapidly displaced the oats, rye, barley and maslin eaten by previous generations. Nevertheless, brown bread was beginning to come into its own. Without exception, the agricultural writers of the early 19th century praised its wholesome and nutritional qualities, its moisture and its resistance to going stale.

Many large country houses continued to bake their own bread, but there was a general decline in home-baking. One of the problems was the lack of ovens. In old houses, capacious brick ovens had been built in, but this stopped when free-standing iron stoves and ranges became available. The decline in home-brewing had caused a lack of brewers' yeast for baking, but by the 1850s this particular problem had been solved with the introduction of a quick-acting compressed yeast produced by the Dutch distillers, popularly known as 'German' or 'dried' yeast. Cookery writers recommended it for domestic baking, although it was not favoured by professional bakers because of its cost and erratic supplies. It was imported in bulk into Britain, but not manufactured here until 1900. Self-raising flour and baking powder were also introduced about the same time.

Some households still took their own dough to the baker to be baked, but most bought ready-made bread. This, however, was condemned as being worse in Britain than in any other country; unhygienic, unwholesome, bitter, liable to go stale quickly and indigestible. The 18th-century practice of adding lime and chalk, and particularly alum as a bleach had become almost universal. Urban bakeries were generally situated in filthy basements: the state of many London bakeries was first reported by Dr William Guy of King's College Hospital in London, who subsequently became a founding director of the Aerated Bread Company, with its chain of ABC tea-rooms. This was the first firm of bakers to produce bread on a commercial scale using mechanised dough-mixers and efficient and economical gas-fired ovens.

However, bread was one of the foods dramatically changed by technological developments of the Industrial Revolution. The long-standing, if unwholesome, desire for whiter and still whiter bread, and the need of the millers and bakers for a flour which would keep, led to the invention of the roller mill in the 1860s. Instead of the wheat being milled between two stones as it had been for centuries, the roller mill acted as a monster mangle, crushing the wheat-germ between its rollers and allowing the miller access to the pure white starch in the middle of the germ to produce the genuine refined white flour without wheat-germ that we eat today. As a bonus, the flour enjoyed a longer shelf-life, because the wheat-germ contained the natural oils that caused the flour to go rancid. Unfortunately for the poor, with the removal of the wheat-germ went most of the nutritional value, not to be replaced until the next century.

Brown's DM standard bread, as advertised in the 1890s. It was recruitment for the South African War in 1899 that revealed the poor physique of many working-class men who were living on a diet of bread (usually white, with the wheat-germ removed), factory jam, tea, fried fish and bacon.

Meat and Poultry

The amount of meat eaten in 19th-century Britain depended entirely upon circumstance. While the poor in urban slums might taste meat only a few times each year, servants in a large house or on a farm could enjoy meat at three meals a day.

Because of the perishability of meat, until the advent of the railways, it was still brought to the towns on the hoof to be sold directly to butchers, or at spring and autumn fairs held in all the major towns. Families who could afford to buy an entire beast did so, driving it home and fattening it up before killing it. However, most of the animals, thin and exhausted from the long walk to town, were slaughtered by butchers in squalid conditions in the shambles or butchers' shops situated in the centre of most of the market towns.

A considerable quantity of diseased meat was sold. Sausages frequently contained horse-flesh, and horrible were the tales told of shop-made pies. The sale of diseased and tainted meat was made public in the 1840s by a number of investigations and reports. As a result, municipal authorities both tightened up and vigorously enforced the restrictions governing the inspection of meat markets and merchants. The RSPCA, founded in 1824 as a protest against the hardships to which driven animals were subjected, helped to bring about the removal of the live animal market, after eight centuries, from Smithfield, hard by the City of London, to a more rural site at Caledonian Market, just north of King's Cross Station. Here the health threat posed to a densely populated area was diminished. Smithfield remained, and continues to be, a dead meat market.

The railways made a similarly positive contribution to the supply of fresh meat to the cities: consignments of healthy butchered carcasses travelled overnight from the beef farms of Aberdeenshire to be in Smithfield Market by morning. Animals could be sent live by rail to the weekly cattle markets being established on the outskirts of many of the larger towns.

A century of selective breeding and better animal nutrition by feeding roots, improved grasses, clovers and the like, as well as the introduction of cattle cake (crushed oil-seeds) established the quality of British beef and mutton. Whereas excessive fat had been admired in the 18th and early 19th century, now a more moderate ideal was preferred, although it was still much fatter than our modern meat, for the Victorians regarded fat as a sign of health. After fattening, the animals were slaughtered at two to four years of age, then the carcasses were hung for three or four days, and the resulting beef was generally acknowledged as being the best in the world. Sheep were fattened in the same way.

In July 1887 Sir George Otto Trevelyan, who had inherited Wallington the previous year, held a large party to celebrate Queen Victoria's Golden Jubilee. As his wife Caroline recorded in her notebook: 'There were 189 invitations sent out. Nearly all came. They had dinner in two parties and tea afterwards. Calculated 198 head.' The catering arrangements included 138 lb of beef, two legs of mutton, numerous rabbit pies and 'sweets' to follow – probably jellies and blancmanges. Caroline also undertook the major duty entitled 'Xmas beef' in her notebook, which involved the presentation of gifts to employees and widows at an end-of-year party. In 1895 she wrote 'we were abroad so gave no entertainments, but the men employed all had beef', the portions being 4 lb for a single man, 6 lb for a man and wife and 1 lb for every child.

Mutton was the middle-class staple; lamb a seasonal treat. Veal was eaten, especially in wealthy houses where there was a French chef, because it smacked of the Continent. Pork was not only considered 'common', but often unwholesome. As the century progressed, however, demand for pork increased rapidly to add variety at dinner parties. Sucking pig was sufficiently popular for Mrs Beeton to include it among her menus. The more progressive breeders had been improving their stock to produce meat with a higher proportion of lean to fat and a white skin, to make it more saleable.

Whether fashionable or not, the pig was by far the most useful animal for working-class households because it could be fed on scraps. In towns pigs were kept on garden plots or allotments or even lived with the family in cellars and slum dwellings. Frequently they were turned loose to scavenge on the rubbish thrown into the streets. This nuisance continued until the 1870s when medical officers banned pigs from town centres. But those agricultural labourers who could keep a pig, could still enjoy some pork and bacon.

Until 1842, live cattle imports were banned, which effectively cut Britain off from foreign meat supplies. The ban was lifted in that year and live animals began to arrive in

David Copperfield carves a leg of mutton for his guests, from Charles Dickens' novel, published in 1850. When the joint turns out to be undercooked, Mr Micawber grills it on an open fire. Mutton was an immensely popular dish in Victorian Britain.

numbers, about 309,000 coming annually from northern Europe by 1854. In the 1860s, importers brought in cheap fatty American bacon, dried 'Hamburg' beef from Germany and canned boiled beef and mutton from Australia and America in large quantities for the poorer classes.

Salted beef and pickled pork were imported to try to meet the demands of the British market by tapping into the ample supplies of meat available from Australia and America. Although it could be inferior in quality, it was cheap and often the only meat that factory workers could afford. Several attempts were also made to impregnate fresh meat with sulphites, with rather unpalatable results, although it was used a good deal for charity meals and soup kitchens.

One of the great achievements of the 19th century was canning. During the Napoleonic Wars, the British fleet had blockaded the French ports and the consequent food shortages in France encouraged Nicholas Appert to pioneer a method for preserving foods such as meat, fruit, vegetables and even milk in glass bottles by subjecting them to heat. Bryan Donkin, a partner in the firm of John Hall, founder of the Dartford Iron Works, realised that Appert's discovery would be very valuable to his firm if tinned iron containers could be used instead of glass jars. In a few years this process became very widely adopted for the storage of military rations, the provision of ships, and the prevention of food shortages.

The imports of salted and tinned meat from Australia and America fell off rapidly towards the end of Victoria's reign with the development of refrigeration. The difference in price between fresh meat in Australia or America and in England encouraged efforts to find a way of transporting supplies to the expanding cities of Britain. Canning, although cheap, was generally rather unpopular. In 1861 Thomas Sutcliffe Mort, who had emigrated to Australia from Lancashire in 1838, opened the first freezing works at Darling Harbour in Sydney. In 1876 he chartered a sailing ship fitted with a refrigerating machine in an attempt to send supplies of frozen meat to London, but failed. It was only a question of time, however; the first successful journey came in 1880 when the SS *Strathleven* arrived in London with a cargo of 40 tons of Australian beef and mutton in her refrigerating chambers, practically all of it in excellent condition. Although it was certainly inferior to fresh home-produced meat, it sold readily at Smithfield for only 5d–6d per lb, and was certainly good enough for stews, pies and puddings.

The poultry industry too became more highly organised during the 19th century. In 1846 a number of different varieties of birds were introduced, partly to meet the demand from cooks. Chicken was all the rage through the influence of French cookery where it was used much more frequently and imaginatively than in traditional English recipes. Poultry, whether kept on farms, in rural cottages or urban tenements, was always the responsibility of the woman of the house, providing her with a useful source of pin-money and a supply of eggs for her family.

The usual size of hen's eggs in Victorian times seems to have been much smaller than today. Large quantities were imported from France – about 100 million in 1852. Bought eggs were often bad, prompting Soyer to give the classic advice about breaking them into a bowl before using them. Since hens stopped laying through the winter, various methods of preservation were employed. The eggs could be immersed in deep earthenware pots full of water-glass or lime, painted with oil or resin, boiled briefly – according to Mrs Beeton for 20 seconds to 1 minute – or stored in ice-houses.

Rabbits were classified as poultry in Victorian and Edwardian times because they were sold by poulterers as well as being hawked on the streets in towns and cities. Wild rabbits were still kept in warrens, but although Mrs Beeton describes some of these, in the sandy districts of Norfolk and Cambridgeshire, as being as large as 2,000 acres, warrens generally went into a decline during the first half of the century because improving landlords found it difficult to establish hedgerows and protect their crops with such large numbers of rabbits nearby. For the first time, Mrs Beeton mentions the keeping of tame rabbits for the table. These were whiter and more delicate than their wild cousins, although not considered by some to have 'as high a flavour'. She tells us that in the 1820s there were one or two large rabbit-keepers in London with about 2,000 breeding does, but by the 1860s, tame and wild rabbits were both coming in from the country. Tame rabbits were, however, kept 'by a few individuals in almost every town and by a few in almost every part of the country' in gardens, allotments, or in backyards.

Game was not legally saleable until 1831, so theoretically its consumption was limited to the landed gentry, or those with shooting rights, as in previous centuries. It was still a status symbol – a mark of landownership and of gentility, reflected by the savagery of the Acts against poaching. In 1831 the right to kill and sell game was controlled by licence and the penalty for poaching in daylight was reduced, although night-poaching continued to be classified as a crime punishable by prison with hard labour, or even transportation. Game was nurtured as carefully as regular farmstock by a keeper, whose job included not only guarding against poachers, but keeping vermin under control.

One day's bag of a shoot in November 1894 outside the Stag Lodge keeper's house on the Saltram estate, Devon. Scores of pheasants are on display, accompanied by a solitary hare.

Grouse shooting in August and pheasant shooting from October to Christmas became an important part of the social calendar for the leisured classes. At Penrhyn Castle in North Wales, Lord and Lady Penrhyn were usually in residence only for the shooting season. Among the duties of Angus Duncan Webster, the head forester, was the planting of box, privet, yew and holly on the estate for game cover, while Lord Penrhyn's sporting interests were entrusted to Andrew Foster, head keeper for 28 years, and his staff of eight. Five hundred brace of grouse and 3,000 pheasants were reared annually on the southern part of the estates.

Because of its social prestige, game was the *sine qua non* for any dinner party given between August and February. In addition to recipes for venison, hare and leveret, Mrs Beeton describes how to cook and serve a much larger range of game birds than we eat today, including snipe, blackcock, corncrake, teal, widgeon, ptarmigan, grey and green plover and ortolan, which was imported from Europe as a delicacy for upper-class tables. It was so tiny that Soyer's ultimate extravagance, copied by Mrs Beeton, was to stuff them inside truffles, rather than the other way round. Partridges, grouse, woodcock, wild duck and pheasant were very common and quail were imported in large numbers from Egypt when pheasant was not in season.

A distressingly large number of other wild birds continued to find their way on to the table via the poulterers or markets up to the end of the century and beyond, including fieldfares, curlews, ruffs and reeves, dotterels, larks, wheatears, redwings, blackbirds, redshanks, redwings, knots, jackdaws, rooks and goldfinches. Perhaps the most popular was the sparrow put into pies with herbs and spices.

Fish

During the first part of the 19th century, the tainted condition of much meat sold was only equalled by that of the fish; even the pickled herrings offered for sale were partly decomposed owing to faulty preparation. Fresh sea-fish had always presented a problem for inland areas outside London and was still a luxury enjoyed only by those who lived near the coast, until the coming of the railways. Disraeli regularly exchanged trout and partridges from his Hughenden estate in Buckinghamshire with turbot, sole, mullet, lobsters and prawns from his close friend and benefactor, Mrs Brydges Willyams, who lived at Torbay on the south coast of Devon. 'Turbots visiting trout are patricians noticing country cousins', he wrote on one occasion and in a moment of exuberance, thanking her for a basket of prawns described them as 'the rosy coloured tribute of Torbay'.

In the early years of the 19th century, ice was used for transporting fresh fish overland to market but was not carried on the fishing vessels themselves, which normally returned daily to land their catch. As the century wore on, steam trawlers that were capable of ranging further and staying longer at sea began to replace the old sailing boats, but some means of preserving their catches had to be employed. It was Samuel Hewitt, an enterprising fishing-smack owner from Barking in Essex – then a busy fishing port on the Thames – who began bringing fish back to port packed in ice. He also started the system of remaining on the fishing ground for a month or more at a time, the catch being taken to Billingsgate by fast cutters sent out daily to collect it from the fleets of trawlers.

At first the necessary ice was supplied by local farmers who were persuaded to flood their fields in the winter and collect the ice as it formed, which was then cut into blocks, carted to the ports and stored in underground ice-houses. But by 1830 a great deal of ice was being exported into England from America, the fishing industry being the largest consumer. A little later, Norway entered the field and since her freight charges were lower she captured most of the market – by 1899 the amount of ice imported from Scandinavia had reached a huge 500,000 tons.

The availability of cheap Norwegian ice coincided with the expansion in railway communications, which meant that fresh sea-fish began to appear in bulk in the markets of inland towns only a few hours after being landed. This led to the decline in the popularity of salted and pickled herrings, for so many centuries one of the chief foods of the inland population. In addition, new sources of supply were opening up. With ample supplies of Norwegian ice on board, the newly invented deep-sea trawlers began to sweep the rich and scarcely explored banks of the North Sea. By 1891 British trawlers were venturing as far afield as Iceland. This brought a huge glut of fish to the market, lowering prices and turning it into the staple food of the working classes. Fish was quick and easy to cook, with the minimum amount of equipment and fuel, or in the case of shellfish was sold ready-cooked. So fish – grilled, baked, boiled or fried – was eaten at every meal by the urban poor. In 1850 one-third of the entire Billingsgate supply was bought by London fishmongers, one-third was sent to the country and the remaining third was bought by the street-sellers.

Street-sellers bought up the majority of the cheaper kinds of fish – plaice (about 3d each, according to Mrs Beeton), herrings (4 for 1d) sprats and mackerel, shrimps, whelks, cockles, winkles and red herrings – hawking them around the streets of London on barrows or in donkey carts. Whelk stalls were set up in almost every street in certain parts of London, the whelks being sold in saucers at two, three, four, six and eight a penny, according to size. The trade was lucrative and as one costermonger remarked to the writer and journalist, Henry Mayhew: 'Whelks is all the same, good, bad, or middling, when a man's drinking, if they're well seasoned with pepper and vinegar.' Oysters had been so plentiful and cheap at the beginning of the century that they had been a staple food of the very poor, for as Sam Weller put it in *Pickwick Papers*, published in 1836: '. . . poverty and oysters always seem to go together . . . the poorer a place is, the greater call there seems to be for oysters . . .'. As late as 1840 they cost only 8d a bushel, but by 1860, due to over-fishing and pollution, they had become scarce and a luxury only the rich could afford at 1s a dozen.

Freshwater fish – trout, eels and crayfish – now rarely appeared legally on the tables of most working-class families, and the more expensive fish, which included sole, turbot, John Dory, salmon and lobster were seldom even sold on the street. But these choicer fish were much in demand by the middle and upper classes for entertaining and because of faster transport they no longer had to travel to Weymouth to sample red mullet, or Worcester to enjoy lampreys. These could now be brought to their own table in perfect condition: the Carlton Club in London's St James's, for example, made a point of serving for dinner at 7pm salmon caught in the morning in the River Severn. Turbot, known as 'the Pheasant of the Sea', was a particular favourite of Victorian dinner parties, boiled whole in a large diamond-shaped fish kettle and served 'white side' up with lobster sauce. Turtle soup was still fashionable but not recommended by Mrs Beeton for those with 'weak stomachs'. When live turtle was too dear, cooks could use tinned turtle, also sent over from the West Indies.

Fish, together with meat and other perishable goods, could now also be stored in the home thanks to ice. Ice companies were soon boasting that they could provide supplies from their massive depots in cities and ports by rail to town houses and rural ice-houses

Gardeners and estate workmen resting from their labours outside the 18th-century ice-house in the park at Knole, Kent, in a photograph taken *c*.1900. The ice, from shallow ponds, was shovelled into the brick-lined pit below ground level and, firmly packed, would last well into the summer months.

in any part of the country within 24 hours. Smaller ice-houses or temporary ice stores could now be built above or in the ground, covered with a roof of timber or thatch, and stocked with ice brought to the door, at a cost that the middle-classes could afford.

Large estates often had more than one ice-house. At Tatton Park in Cheshire, there are thought to have been at least three ice-houses in the 19th century, as well as an ice store in the basement of the house, although cold storage would seem to have been an Egerton family enthusiasm, for the 3rd Lord Egerton was the first president of the Ice and Cold Storage Association. The use of full ice-houses as stores for all types of food was recommended by John Loudon in his *Cottage, Farm and Village Architecture* of 1833: 'In England, many persons are deterred from forming an ice-house, by the idea that . . . ice is only useful for making ice-creams and cooling wines: but an ice-house may be made anywhere; and as a place for preserving meat, fish, fruit and vegetables, there is not a more useful appendage to a country house . . .'. However, many ice-houses were not used for the storage of food; instead, the ice was taken to the house as required, stored in boxes, bins or refrigerators and then used to prepare iced dishes and cooling beverages, to make table decorations, and to cool rooms in the summer.

Although the first patent for a refrigerating or ice-making machine, invented by an American named Jacob Perkins, was granted in Britain in 1834, it was not until 1876 that it was effectively developed, after Dr Carl Linde introduced ammonia compression. From then until the end of the century, there was a steady increase in the use of mechanical refrigeration for manufacturing substantial quantities of artificial ice, which replaced imported ice from Norway, Iceland and Greenland.

Country houses built after 1850 in locations with good road or rail communications to a town or city, such as Wightwick Manor near Wolverhampton, kept large iceboxes or refrigerators in their larders or cellars supplied frequently from local ice depots. The ice would arrive at the local station and be delivered to the house by cart. As a result, ice-houses fell rapidly into disuse.

Dairy Produce

In Victorian times, the quality of milk drunk by a household and the manner in which it was obtained varied according to region. Even in rural areas, milk might be scarce in one parish while only a mile away there might be a plentiful supply, depending on whether the farmer would sell milk from the farm direct, or found it more economical to feed his milk to the pigs, or sell it in the nearby town. For cities and towns too large for milk to be brought in for sale from the neighbouring countryside before completion of the railway network, cows were still kept all the year round in filthy sheds by town cow-keepers, with no opportunity for summer grazing or exercise. Like cattle kept for meat, their conditions were appalling: 'Two in each seven feet of space . . . no ventilation, save by a tile roof through which the ammoniacal vapours escape . . . . Besides the animals there is . . . a large tank for grains and hay, and between them a receptacle into which the liquid manure drains and the solid is heaped . . . the stench thence arising is insufferable.' The quality of the resulting milk was extremely poor and often carried disease. It could be further adulterated with chalk or flour and, like cream, thinned with water. Even then it was expensive, so seldom drunk by the poor.

From the 1850s, the situation began to improve. Higher rents tended to drive the cow-keepers from the town centres into the more rural suburbs, while the numbers of

Above left: An advertisement for Express Dairies, *c*.1900. These dairies were established in the mid-19th century to bring fresh milk from the country by rail quickly and hygienically into London.

Above: Easy access to ice and the invention of ice-boxes and refrigerators meant that ice-cream, previously a luxury food, was generally available and became very popular, either made at home or bought from commercial confectioners. It was also sold on street corners as 'penny licks' or 'hokey pokey' by Italian immigrants who had a tradition of ice-cream making.

city cattle were diminished by plague. Local authorities were now beginning to impose higher standards of hygiene as a result of Dr Hassall's report on the quality of the 'solids and fluids consumed by all classes of the public' commissioned in 1850 for the *Lancet*. Railways enabled milk to be transported quickly and hygienically from countryside that had hitherto been too distant. Express Dairies, for example, was set up to bring milk from the country into London, and by 1866 over 2 million gallons were arriving annually in the metropolis by rail. Fresh milk also benefitted from the experiments of Louis Pasteur in France, although it was not until the 1890s that pasteurisation (partial sterilisation by heating) became common in British dairies.

Ice-cream, previously the luxury food of the wealthy, was now generally available and became very popular, either made at home or bought from commercial confectioners. It was also sold on the street corners of major cities and ports, like London, Liverpool, Birmingham, Manchester and Leeds, as 'penny licks' or 'hokey pokey', by Italian immigrants who had a tradition of ice-cream making.

'Substitutes have been much spoken of' announced one commentator in the 1870s. Indeed, many food substitutes were developed at this time, often to the detriment of the British diet, especially that of the urban poor. A method of producing powdered milk was invented by an Englishman called Grimwade in 1855 and this became the basis of many infant and invalid foods. Four years earlier, Gail Borden's process for condensing milk had arrived from the United States. Three-quarters of the water content of the milk was removed by evaporation, sugar was added and the milk was hermetically sealed in tinned cans. The Northern armies in the American Civil War of 1861–5 were supplied with condensed milk by Borden. The business was transferred to Switzerland

'The Finishing Touch'. The first edible and cheap substitute for butter dates from the late 1860s. Although neither its flavour nor texture was liked, sales rose steadily and the Margarine Act of 1887 was passed to prevent traders using it to adulterate butter.

in 1865 and factories for the production of the famous 'Swiss milk' were soon established in many other European countries, including Britain, where it sold cheaply enough to became a regular substitute for the genuine article among the poor.

The first edible and cheaper substitute for butter dates from the late 1860s, when a French chemist, Mège-Mouriés, made 'margarinmouries' – from the Greek word *margaron*, a pearl, because at one stage in its manufacture, the fat appeared in pearly drops – using emulsified beef suet and milk. When made in England, it was called 'butterine'. Later certain vegetable oils were added, leading to a further reduction in its nutritional value. Although neither its flavour nor texture was liked, sales rose, and the Margarine Act of 1887 was passed to prevent traders from using it to adulterate butter.

The dairy industry had been rather neglected by agricultural reformers, who preferred to concentrate on improving the production of beef. Perhaps this occurred because the dairy had traditionally been the domain of women. But 'Tom Thumb' Acland of Killerton proved the exception, promoting dairy work and introducing a working dairy into the West Country agricultural shows in which he was involved. 'Everybody laughs at me and the dairymaids,' he once wrote to his wife. Visitors to Killerton who admired at breakfast the cream, and butter stamped with a cow, might be urged to walk down the drive and see for themselves how it was made on the home farm. By the 1880s, educational courses in dairy work were being introduced, and the first of the commercial creameries came into existence, helped by technological advances.

All British cheese was farmhouse-made until 1870 when the first cheese factory was established. The leading varieties had been established by the end of the previous century: Cheddar, Cheshire, Stilton, and double and single Gloucester. But these did not find favour with polite society, who regarded fresh cream cheese as the only acceptable and digestible type. Mrs Beeton pronounced, '. . . cheese, in its commonest shape, is only fit for sedentary people, as an after-dinner stimulant, and in very small quantity. Bread and cheese, as a meal, is only fit for soldiers on march or labourers in the open air . . .'.

Vegetables and Fruit

As the 19th century progressed, and more and more of the population was employed in industry rather than agriculture, there came a decline in the number of working-class people with gardens in which to grow their produce. Even cottages for the poorest rural labourers were often built without a garden. Towards the end of the century, allotments were created in some areas – a field might be set aside by a philanthropic landowner or a local authority, and plots within it rented out as vegetable gardens to labourers. Potatoes became a common crop; they were easy to grow, high yielding and provided sustaining and comforting food. In Ireland the dependence of much of the rural population on this vegetable, almost to the exclusion of any other food, proved disastrous when harvests failed time and time again in the early years of the 19th century, reaching a climax with the devastation of the crop by disease in 1845–6. It was the plight of the Irish, as we have seen, that persuaded Peel to repeal the Corn Laws.

The Poor Law Amendment Act of 1834 also had a profound effect on the diet of the poorest section of the community. The destitute, the sick and the elderly had been able to apply for poor relief from their parish since Tudor times. The 1834 Act proposed to abolish the provision of outdoor relief, sending applicants to workhouses administered by unions of parishes. Diets under the old regime were often not ungenerous – bread, meat, suet dumplings and vegetables – but after 1834 they were made deliberately monotonous, based on bread and gruel with thin vegetable soup, to act as a deterrent to all but the truly destitute.

This was not the style adopted by the industrialist Samuel Greg, when in 1790 he established an Apprentice House at Styal Mill, Quarry Bank in Cheshire. He was not necessarily being philanthropic when he provided 90 pauper child apprentices from the slums of Manchester and Liverpool with a garden for growing their own vegetables and fruit. He wanted them to have a healthy diet so that they could generate energy. The children worked a 13-hour day in the mill, cleaning and carrying out menial jobs, returning to the Apprentice House for a dinner mainly of potatoes, cooked in one of the boilers in the kitchen. 'Sundays' wrote a runaway apprentice, 'we had for dinner boiled pork and potatoes, we had also peas, beans, turnips and cabbage in their season'. All the vegetables and fruit – mainly apples – as well as a wide range of herbs for culinary and medicinal use were grown by the boys in the evenings. Much of the produce was sold in the village rather than providing food for the children, but they were treated with the herbs for various ailments, mostly coughs and eye-trouble. Troublesome children were even sedated with herbs. A store of dried herbs, apples and vegetables were kept in the attic for winter use. The National Trust has recreated the Apprentice House kitchen garden, using 19th-century materials and gardening methods to grow local varieties.

The Victorian grower of fruit and vegetables could glory in the number of varieties available – 30 or 40 types of apple and pears were regularly marketed in different parts of the country, mostly grown with only the help of traditional animal fertilizers. Commercial market gardens flourished on the outskirts of the larger towns and cities and smallholdings grew anything from cauliflower to soft fruits. The development of the railway system made it possible to carry fruit and vegetables long distances. Areas that specialised in delicate produce could therefore supply the burgeoning cities: asparagus from Evesham, strawberries from Southampton, and early potatoes and

Eventide by Sir Hubert von Herkomer, 1878. This is practically the only Victorian oil painting of the dreaded workhouse, and was based on the artist's own observations at the Westminster Union in London.

The Apprentice House at Quarry Bank Mill, Styal, Cheshire. The industrialist Samuel Greg provided 90 pauper apprentices from the slums of Manchester and Liverpool with a garden to grow their own vegetables, fruit and herbs, although much of the produce was sold in the village rather than feeding the children.

broccoli from Cornwall. Nevertheless, there was still a huge market for locally grown produce, taken daily to the towns to be sold either direct from street carts, or wholesale to established shops and market stalls.

Tinned vegetables, mainly tomatoes, began to be exported from America in the 1880s. Asparagus and peas were popular, but all green vegetables lost their colour during the canning process and were recoloured with salts of copper, which rendered them a health hazard. Tinned fruit from America soon followed, the most popular being pears, gooseberries and pineapples. Pineapples had always, hitherto, been available only to the rich, either grown in hot-houses or brought from the West Indies by clipper. This seems to have remained a strong memory, for tinned pineapple has until very recently been regarded as a 'treat' for high tea. The one fruit that could not be tinned was the banana. As it had to be brought to Britain from the Canary Islands and the West Indies on specially equipped steamships to control temperature and stop over-ripening, it could command a very high price.

Tinned pineapple, however, was not likely to appear on the tables of country houses. In their gardens were not only all the standard fruits and vegetables grown for daily use, but magnificent hot-house fruit and forced early vegetables were raised to grace the table when entertaining. Few status symbols were equal to a dish of tiny early peas, or a display of freshly picked, home-nurtured grapes, figs, melons, peaches and pineapples.

Lord Armstrong used his engineering genius to introduce the latest in hydraulic technology to his estate at Cragside in Northumberland. Water was pumped up from the lake on the estate not only to provide lighting for the house but also to rotate the great earthenware pots in his extensive glasshouse or 'orchard house' at Knocklaw. These pots were of two sizes, the larger being about 2 feet in diameter. They were ranged on three splendid stone shelves to grow peaches, figs and other choice fruit. Each pot is supported on a turntable with roller bearings, which made them easy to turn, allowing the quite substantial fruit trees to benefit from the maximum amount of light.

Walter Speed reigned as head gardener at Penrhyn Castle from about 1860 to 1921, under three Lords Penrhyn. He was renowned as a leading expert on the production of flowers, vegetables and particularly fruit, and in 1897 was one of the original recipients of horticulture's highest award, the Victoria Medal of Honour, given by the Royal Horticultural Society. Speed turned the Penrhyn estate into a centre of horticultural excellence famed throughout Britain for the unsurpassed quality of its kitchen garden produce. An obituary in the October 1921 issue of *The Garden* says of him:

> As a gardener nothing that Mr Speed did but he did well. As a Grape grower he was certainly second to none. Who that had seen his old faggot of Vines, pruned in his own inimitable way, will ever forget the monster bunches he grew each year, and their perfect finish? Most of his Peaches under glass he lifted and replanted each year and fed with new loam. I have seen them grown as well, but never better. His Fig trees on walls out of doors, to see them in fruit was a sight never to be forgotten.

When Lord and Lady Penrhyn were absent from the castle, produce from the kitchen garden was sent to them, each fruit individually wrapped so that they arrived in perfect condition, their bloom intact. This custom, which had been adopted in the 18th century amongst the wealthy who spent the 'Season' in London, continued to be observed in Victorian times. When Mary Elizabeth Williams married George Hammond Lucy of Charlecote in 1823, her father advised her: 'For the wages Mr Lucy gives, you ought to have a first class gardener who will produce for you plenty of fruit and have it sent up to you in London where it will be extravagantly dear.'

Like Penrhyn, Wallington was far from any supplier of luxury foods, and therefore had to be largely self sufficient. Heated greenhouses were built so that even in this bleak Northumbrian climate Sir Walter and Lady Trevelyan, who were both very interested in gardening, might grow exotic fruits such as avocados, guavas, passion-fruit and melons. Already avocados were being acclaimed as 'the most delicious [fruit] in the world' by Edwin Lankester in *Vegetable Substances Used for the Food of Man*, 1846. They were not served at the beginning of the meal, when the rule was soup and fish, but dressed with salt, pepper, sugar and lime juice and eaten for dessert.

When Mr Hedley was engaged by Sir Walter as head gardener at Wallington soon after his father's death in 1846, he was encouraged to exhibit at the recently established Newcastle Flower Show. Sir Walter was particularly keen on winning the class for a collection of ripe fruit usually won by the nearby Blagdon estate. After months of work, the day of the show approached and to satisfy his mother, Sir Walter asked Hedley to lay out his collection in the apple house before packing up for the show. In the exhibit was a fine melon and before Hedley realised what was happening, Lady Trevelyan had cut out a slice with a huge knife from her girdle, tasted it and replaced the segment with the

The walled garden and conservatory at Wallington, Northumberland, the domain in the 19th century of Mr Hedley. Magnificent hothouse fruit and forced early vegetables were raised in country-house conservatories to grace the table.

muttered remark, 'The flavour is all right, the fruit will be insipid when it returns.' Then in an authoritative voice she bawled out to the head gardener, standing meekly outside the doorway, 'Tell the judges that the fruit is unbeatable, and that one has said it who knows what she is talking about.' With this, she swept down the stone stairs and disappeared. As the poor gardener had nothing with which to replace the damaged melon, he stayed at home, refusing to enter any other show while the Dowager Lady Trevelyan ruled the roost at Wallington! She, apparently, had no use for shows and believed good fruit was best eaten fresh at home. This story was told in *Memories of Wallington* by Edward Keith, who was, with a short break, gardener there from 1882 to 1933 and head gardener for 43 of those years.

Although Sir Walter and his wife, Pauline, were very hospitable, their way of life was somewhat unusual. On a visit to Wallington in the 1860s, the young Augustus Hare arrived in time for lunch 'which was as peculiar as everything else (Lady Trevelyan and her artists [probably the painters William Bell Scott, Holman Hunt, Ford Madox Brown, Arthur Hughes or the sculptors Thomas Woolner and Alex Munro] feeding solely on artichokes and cauliflowers).' Both vegetables were popular in all grand houses, but Sir Walter had other rather peculiar tastes in vegetables for Victorian times; in spring common sorrel was a favourite as were nettles boiled like spinach. He also regularly gathered edible fungi in the woods and had them cooked for his breakfast without ill effect, although he would not trust the gathering to anyone else.

However, most of the gentry still held to the belief that many vegetables were indigestible and food for the poor. Onions, leeks and above all garlic, were treated with great caution by everyone with any social pretensions because of the danger of smelly breath. The last two were used sparingly in soups and stews, particularly when entertaining. Although garlic was sometimes discreetly introduced into elaborate dishes created by chefs, it was never found in middle-class kitchens. The only vegetables guaranteed as perfectly digestible were old potatoes, mushrooms, cauliflowers, broccoli, French beans and asparagus, which consequently were relatively fashionable; cauliflowers were expensive at 6d compared with 2d for a cabbage, and asparagus cost 2s 6d for 100 heads.

Potatoes were served in the dining-room of a fashionable household three times a day and it was *de rigueur* to serve them in a different way each time; contemporary recipe books give instructions for preparing many potato dishes. But on the whole, vegetables were not very important to those who could afford more desirable foodstuffs.

Salads were regarded with even more suspicion because, according to Mrs Beeton, 'vegetables eaten in a raw state are apt to ferment on the stomach.' To counteract this 'they are usually dressed with some condiments, such as pepper, vinegar, salt, mustard, and oil.' A Victorian salad might consist of lettuce, mustard and cress, radishes, cucumber, endive, red cabbage, beetroot, potato and celery, but not tomatoes until after 1880 when they were being offered for sale in most of the fruit markets.

In 1847, a group of enthusiasts launched the Vegetarian Society of England. Within 20 years, it had a fair number of supporters particularly in intellectual circles, although the medical profession as a whole ridiculed the new ideas. A contemporary cartoon records a meeting of vegetarians held in Fleet Street in London. A speaker had 'gravely made the statement that "all forms of flesh were effete and imperfect materials for human nourishment, whilst fruits, nuts and grains were complete and could alone make the best of the vitality remaining in man". The response was, "Humph! Nuts!

No, thank you no nuts. Nuts are associated with chatter and the zoo.'" The first *Vegetarian Cookery Book*, written by Martha Brotherton, was published in 1866. The savoury dishes were rather restricted as there were few cheese recipes, and certainly none using rice.

Beverages

In an attempt to decrease the consumption of spirits, the Prime Minister, the Duke of Wellington, passed the Beer-house Act of 1830, which encouraged beer-houses to spring up all over the country, especially in rundown areas. Any householder assessed for the poor rate was now entitled to obtain an excise licence for 2 guineas, which enabled him to retail beer on or off his premises between 4 am and 10 pm. The working population flocked to these beer-houses both for the beer and the good company, especially those who had not been able to afford the higher prices of licensed public houses. Much of the beer and ale drunk was purchased from commercial brewers, who were able to double their capacity when they discovered that by using ice to cool the wort and to regulate the temperature of the fermenting rooms, they could make beer the whole year round instead of only in the coolest weather.

To compete with the newly opened beer-houses, the first of the famous Victorian gin-palaces opened in the 1830s. In 1835 Cruikshank published a cartoon showing a gin palace mounted on barrels crushing the people in its path: 'Its progress,' says the caption, 'is marked with desolation, misery and crime.' But instead of the dirt and dampness of cellars and slums, the rooms of the gin-palaces were brightly painted and

The Gin Juggarnath by George Cruikshank, 1835, showing a gin-palace mounted on barrels and crushing the people in its path.

pretty girls provided a glamorous atmosphere; the poor could forget for a time the misery of their condition. 'Gin drinking is a great vice in England' Charles Dickens wrote in 1835, 'but wretchedness and dirt are a greater.' He continued: 'If Temperance Societies would suggest an antidote against hunger, filth and foul air, or could establish dispensaries for the gratuitous distribution of bottles of lethe-water [to make the poor forget their problems] gin palaces would be numbered among the things that were.'

It was estimated that in early Victorian times about one-fifth of all the wine drunk was fake in one way or another. The average customer was unlikely to know the difference through lack of experience, as the duty on foreign wines and therefore the price, remained high. Sherry and port formed 80 per cent of wine drunk by the British, due to continued discrimination against French wines as well as their economy – they went further and kept well after being opened. These, and Champagne, the next most popular wine with the wealthy, were also the most commonly adulterated. The most frequently mentioned imitation for Champagne was gooseberry wine: a number of apparently sophisticated people testified that it could be remarkably like the real thing, although the quality of the 'real thing' at this time may have been poor. The taxes which Gladstone imposed in 1861 on alcoholic beverages helped to bring French wines back into favour as the duty payable was based on strength, which meant that fortified wines, such as port, paid a heavier duty than the lighter table wines. The sales' outlets for wine were extended by allowing eating-house owners, grocers and other retailers of food to take out licences. At once the imports of French wine doubled and ten years later had almost doubled again, far ahead of port. By 1880 wine exports had also overtaken sherry.

In 1851, Alexis Soyer opened an 'American bar' as part of a restaurant complex in South Kensington designed to cater for visitors to the Great Exhibition. Drinks advertised including 'mint julep', 'sherry cobbler', 'egg-nog' and 'brandy swash'. A few years later a selection of recipes for 'American Summer Drinks' included the new 'gin sling'. This was possibly the first time that a recipe for a gin-based drink intended for the upper classes had been published in Britain. These recipes were followed by a cookery book in 1862 – *The Cook's Guide and Housekeeper's and Butler's Assistant*, aimed at the middle-classes by the 'chief cook to Her Majesty the Queen', Charles Elmé Francatelli; in it he included a chapter on serving wine, others on cups and on 'English and Foreign Summer Drinks' – mostly soft drinks, but also a recipe for 'gin punch' – and a fourth on 'American Drinks' – slings, sours, egg-nogs, juleps and cocktails.

Encouraged by the temperance societies, tea-drinking increased dramatically during the 19th century; the alleged thirst of temperance reformers being the butt of many jokes. A 'young ooman' at a temperance meeting in Dickens's *Pickwick Papers* had drunk 'nine breakfast cups and a half [of tea]; and she's a swellin' wisibly before my wery eyes'! Until now, tea had been imported solely – and at considerable cost – from China. But with the discovery of tea growing wild in Assam by Major Robert Bruce in 1826, a committee was set up in 1834 to plan its cultivation in India on a large scale. The new varieties of Indian tea were soon available in abundance, and prices tumbled. As a result, by the 1840s tea was being drunk by all working people and often comprised the only hot item in their diet. A quite deceptive feeling of warmth and satisfaction could be enjoyed after a pot of tea, although it had minimal food value, whereas in reality, a glass of cold beer would have given more true value. Between 1840 and 1890, the national average consumption of tea rose from 1.6 lb per head annually, to 5.7 lb (about four cups a day per person) taken at breakfast, at work with dinner, with supper and at social gatherings ranging from family parties to church and chapel functions. Two well-known addicts were William Ewart Gladstone, who was reputed to put tea into his hot-water bottle in order to have a supply ready during the night, and Thomas Carlyle, who was so fond of black tea that when invited out he made his own pot before going, in case his hostess should offer him green instead.

The poor probably had to drink tea black, or with skimmed milk and brown sugar, but the correct way was to serve it with cream and very small lumps of sugar.

Pure coffee ready-ground was almost impossible to obtain before 1852; it was invariably adulterated with chicory. In fact, the introduction of chicory was allowed by law and preferred by a large proportion of customers because its strength made the coffee more economical. A book of household hints belonging to Mary Ann Disraeli was found on the study shelves at Hughenden. She had been brought up in a modest household and no doubt her mother instructed her in the ways of careful housekeeping, for the book, which includes several 'substitute' recipes, has one for coffee:

The roots of succory [chicory] and Dandelion form one of the best substitutes for coffee. Some there are who prefer Dandelion Coffee to Mecca [mocha] and many on the Continent prefer a mixture of succory and coffee to coffee alone. Wash well the roots of Dandelion but not scrape them dry then cut them in bits the size of peas and then roast them in a earthen pot or coffee roaster grind them in a coffee mill. The great secret of good coffee is to have it fresh burnt and fresh ground.

The cocoa and chocolate manufactured in Britain was still used for drinking rather than eating. Nearly all eating chocolate was imported from France and therefore treated as a luxury to be eaten only at dessert. The pioneer of English eating chocolate was John Cadbury, who started a factory at Bournville near Birmingham, and was selling 'French' eating chocolate in 1842; a rival product from Fry followed five years later.

Sugar consumption was still closely related to tea-drinking in the 19th century; the only people who refused to take sugar with their tea were Quakers and Methodists, abstaining as a protest against the slave trade. In 1840 the slave trade in the British Empire was abolished and West Indian plantation owners were faced with acute labour shortages. As a result, the price of sugar doubled to 9d or 10d per pound for white and 7d or 8d for brown, but 20 years later, both had stabilised at 5d or 6d with the reduction of duties. For the majority, sugar remained a luxury item, too expensive to be used in cakes, puddings and preserves, so they had to do without or buy cheap, manufactured products. As the century progressed, an increasing amount was sold in the form of dark treacle, which was cheap enough for the poor to spread on their bread as a substitute for butter. Towards the end of the century, cheap jam made from coloured, sweetened vegetable or fruit pulp gave them a sweeter, if less nourishing alternative.

White sugar was still sold in conical loaves to be cut into lumps as required in the kitchen. This was probably the main reason why desserts and cakes bought from professionals were so popular, saving the cook a great deal of time. With no prepared icing sugar, even people who made their own cakes seldom attempted their decoration. Ready-made sugar decorations, often very elaborate, could be bought from confectioners, but even these sugary delights often held hidden dangers. Especially in early Victorian times, many of the confectioners' colourings were poisonous, based on minerals like arsenic, copper, lead and zinc.

In 1820 a German chemist, Frederick Accum, published a 'Treatise on the Adulteration of Food and Culinary Poisons' which carried the appropriate biblical quotation 'There is death in the pot' as its subtitle. At the time his work aroused resentment amongst traders and he was discredited, but by the 1850s, further investigations were confirming his findings. This cartoon in *Punch* in 1855 vividly makes the point.

II

By Victorian times, the kitchen had acquired, according to the architect Robert Kerr in *The Gentleman's House* of 1864, 'the character of a complicated laboratory surrounded by numerous accessories specially contrived in respect of disposition, arrangement and fittings, for the administration of the culinary art in all its professional details'. The accessories might include a scullery, a pantry, meat, fish and game larders, a dairy and dairy scullery. 'Laboratory' was a good word to describe the Victorian kitchen with all its gadgets and labour-saving appliances designed to cope with four or five meals a day plus separate dishes for the nursery and servants.

The Edwardians developed further this scientific theme. Briggs in *The Essential of a Country House*, 1911, wrote: 'The centre point of interest in a house is the kitchen with the adjacent Pantry, and round those apartments must range the other rooms.' In the same year, the architect C. H. B. Quennell compared the kitchen offices of a large house to 'a modern factory'.

Mrs Beeton had firm ideas of how 'the great laboratory of the household' should be organised and equipped. She drew up five important points to be considered in its design: that is should be large and the position of the facilities should be convenient and easy to use; that the room be well lit, lofty and well ventilated; that it be sited away from the rest of the house to contain cooking odours and noise; that access to it be easy and not require passing through the house; that there should be easy access to plenty of fuel and water, with the scullery, pantry and storerooms sited nearby.

At Lanhydrock House in Cornwall there is a magnificent late Victorian kitchen with every possible convenience. When the house was rebuilt in 1883, after virtual destruction by a fire which actually started in the old kitchen, Lord Clifden and his architect, Richard Coad, provided adequate, up-to-date service rooms suitable for the high culinary standards of the time. In fact, the service quarters occupy rather more space than that allotted to family use, modelled almost exactly on Kerr's principles. The kitchen itself certainly fulfilled all Isabella Beeton's requirements.

Kitchens in houses like Lanhydrock had to be large to house the number of servants employed as well as the latest technology, particularly at the height of the Victorian period when a large number of guests could not be entertained without a great deal of support from below stairs. The size of the main household remained as it had been in the early part of the century, from about 50 in very large houses to less than 10. A strict hierarchy operated in the servants' hall, reflecting life in the family apartments and principal rooms. If the house was a really grand one, then at the head was the steward, usually with an under-butler. In most large houses the chief servants were the housekeeper and butler. The 'upper servants' ate separately in the steward or housekeeper's room and were waited on, while the 'lower servants' ate at a refectory table in the servants' hall.

By 1851, nearly 90 per cent of the indoor servants employed in England and Wales were female, mainly because of the stiff tax that had been imposed on male domestic servants in 1777. This had originally been set at one guinea per servant to help finance the War of American Independence and to encourage men to join the navy.

By the end of the century, the butler was the senior, sometimes the only, male servant

The kitchen at Lanhydrock, Cornwall, was built in 1883 in the style of a college hall with great wooden roof trusses supporting a high-gabled roof over clerestory windows; these were opened by a system of shafts and gearings connected to handwheels in the end dresser. A serving hatch in the far corner allowed food to be passed through to the serving room.

Opposite: The butler's domain was his pantry, where the silver was cleaned, the dining-room china and glass washed and the day's wines assembled. The butler's pantry at Cragside, Northumberland, was equipped with an internal telephone, an example of Lord Armstrong's many innovations at the house. The wicker hampers contained portable stoves for shooting parties on the grouse moors.

left in the house. Often a very grand figure in his black dress coat and white tie, he could be afforded only by wealthy households. At Clandon Park, where the Onslows employed around 17 indoor servants, the butler was paid £70 in 1876 plus 2s 6d a week beer money. He was responsible for the wine and beer, serving them and any special dishes at table, and supervising the footmen. The butler's domain was his pantry. At Lanhydrock, this was situated opposite the servery. Here, the butler would oversee the cleaning of all the silverware including the cutlery. Any valuable silver was kept in the strongroom next door to the butler's bedroom that led directly off his pantry. All the dining-room china and glass was washed in the two lead-lined sinks and the day's wines were assembled on the large table. A series of bells to summon him to the various principal rooms remains above the door at Lanhydrock. The butler's pantry at Cragside goes one better, with an internal telephone, an example of Lord Armstrong's many innovations at the house.

Footmen were still impressive figures in their full-dress livery. At Clandon in 1876 the footmen were provided with silk stockings, gloves and pumps and one guinea per annum to pay for the powder to dress their hair. Besides waiting at table, footmen looked after the fires and the lamps. Cleaning, filling and lighting the 194 oil lamps required every day in winter at Penrhyn was work for at least one footman and a special lamp room was provided. Gas mains were being laid in cities as early as the 1820s to light factories, business premises, public buildings and streets but it was some time before it was installed in private homes. When it did arrive, Sydney Smith declared it revolutionised dinner parties: 'better to eat dry bread by the splendour of gas than to dine on wild beef with wax candles'. By the 1860s gas lighting was widespread in middle-class urban homes, illuminating basement kitchens and heating water by means of geysers. But gas remained messy, smelly and noisy, until the industry was forced to improve by the challenge of electricity in the 1880s.

Cragside was the earliest house in the world to be lit by electricity derived from water power: arc light was first installed in 1878, followed two years later by a more extensive scheme using Joseph Swan's newly invented incandescent lamps. The house was described by a contemporary as 'the palace of a modern magician'. The 1st Lord Armstrong, one of Britain's greatest scientific geniuses, ensured that Cragside was full of inventions that were to revolutionise domestic life in the next half century.

The housekeeper managed the affairs of the household for her mistress, her authority being second only to the steward's. H. G. Wells's mother, Sarah, was the housekeeper at Uppark from 1880. He recalled in his autobiography that: 'She knew at best how a housekeeper should look, and assumed a lace cap, lace apron, black silk dress and all the rest of it'. But he added: 'Except that she was thoroughly honest, my mother was perhaps the worst housekeeper that was ever thought of. She did not know how to plan work, control servants, buy stores or economise in any way.' The housekeeper was responsible for cleaning the house, looking after the linen and the best china, often stored in locked cupboards in her own room if there was no separate china closet. She also ruled over the storeroom or 'dry store', containing all the groceries and bulk supplies for the house. At Wimpole, the dry store is only accessible from the housekeeper's room and although the present large cupboards were introduced later, the room gives a very good idea of how it would have looked.

The housekeeper had her own maids and together they worked in the still-room, making preserves and cordials from garden produce and baking cakes and biscuits. At

Above: All the groceries, including tea and spices and bulk supplies for the house, were kept in the storeroom or 'dry store', ruled over by the housekeeper. At Wimpole Hall, Cambridgeshire, the dry store is only accessible from the housekeeper's room.

Two photographs of 1910 showing kitchen staff. At Lyme Park, Cheshire, the chef, Oscar Peres, is shown with William Truelove, the head steward, presiding over the Christmas fare (*left*).
The acquisition of a French chef was essential for the family with serious social aspirations. The Rothschilds of Waddesdon Manor, Buckinghamshire, were even more sophisticated, with a pastry chef in his own kitchen, supported by his own team (*right*).

Springhill in Northern Ireland in the 1830s and '40s, it was customary for the young Conyngham daughters to help with the preserving. In 1946 Mina Lenox-Conyngham recalled in *An Old Ulster House* 'these charming girls, in their thin muslin gowns and sandalled shoes, fluttering from garden to still-room, like bees depositing their loads of sweets . . . . There still remains jars of pot-pourri and a few bottles of elderflower-water, over a hundred years old, and the story lingers that once, after the making of blackcurrant whiskey, the squeezed currants were thrown out to be eaten by the fowl, which promptly became intoxicated and reeled unsteadily about the yards.' At Lanhydrock the old still-room has continued to fulfil part of its original use: drinks and afternoon tea are produced from here for the visitors to the restaurant.

The acquisition of a French chef, or at the very least, a cook 'professed' in French practice, was essential for the family with serious social aspirations. A master chef would have his own retinue and was provided with a day-room near the kitchen, described by Kerr as 'his official retreat where alone he can reflect upon the mysteries of his art and consult his authorities'. The cook's sitting-room at Penrhyn is an example of such a temple of meditation.

These chefs could expect a good salary, higher than that of any other servant including the steward: in 1872 the chef at Petworth was paid £120, while the steward earned £105. Confectioners were often seen as a luxury, yet the spendthrift Duke of Portland, faced with ruin unless he cut down on his expenses, refused to part with his Italian confectioner. 'Good God', the Duke protested, 'mayn't a man have a biscuit with his glass of sherry?'

'Professed cooks' were employed in large houses where there was no chef. These were women who had worked their way up through the kitchen ranks to reach the top of their profession. They were much admired and feared. In 1824 Mary Elizabeth Lucy wrote from Charlecote: 'We have a most accomplished artist, Sharp, as cook, equal to any man'. According to *The Servants' Practical Guide* of 1880, a professed cook was expected to do only the 'proper cooking'. The plain cooking, required for the dining-room, and meals for the children and the servants, was done by the first kitchen-maid.

In smaller households, the cook generally described herself as a 'good plain cook', although 'good' was not always an accurate description. She earned £14 to £30 a year, had fewer kitchen staff and did more cooking than a professed cook, but was often untrained. She was obliged to resort to the new cookbooks that were written specifically for servants, assuming that they were now able to read. As the lady of the house was not expected to set foot in the kitchen, instruction books, particularly Mrs Beeton's, became indispensable.

Despite the lure of other employment opportunities, until 1914 there were still more than enough servants to run efficiently these spacious and labour-demanding 'modern factories'. The absolute minimum of servants was thought to be a butler, a cook, a governess and a nanny for the children, two maids and a boy to act as a general dogsbody. For example, George Bernard Shaw and his wife Charlotte lived in a relatively modest Edwardian villa, the New Rectory at Ayot St Lawrence in Hertfordshire, later renamed Shaw's Corner. They employed a married couple, Henry and Clara Higgs to be butler, gardener and housekeeper, as well as two maids, a cook, chauffeur and assistant gardener.

The writer Henry James had an indoor staff of four at Lamb House in Rye, Sussex, where he lived from 1898 to 1916: a man-servant, cook, parlourmaid and housemaid, who all lived in. Occasionally he had trouble with the servants. His first butler-valet's fondness for drink led to the man's dismissal after 16 years' service. Unfortunately his wife was Henry James's cook. As his distressed employer recalls 'I sit amid the ruins of a once happy household, clutching a charwoman in one hand and a knife-boy – from Lilliput – in the other.' Luckily, the charwoman, or cook-housekeeper, Mrs Paddington, turned out to be a great success. Some years later James wrote enthusiastically of her, 'a pearl of price; being an extremely good cook, an absolutely brilliant economist . . . and gets on beautifully with her fellow-servants, a thing that all "good" cooks don't do'. Henry James saw her each morning in the dining-room after breakfast to discuss menus and look at the tradesmen's books. The 'knife-boy', Burgess Noakes, was destined to graduate from houseboy to butler-valet and to serve his master with touching devotion until James's death.

But there were still large households. A sizeable establishment was kept by Waldorf and Nancy Astor at their London house in St James's Square and at Cliveden in Buckinghamshire, although most servants travelled between the two. In a description of life with the Astors before the First World War, their butler, Edwin Lee, recalls:

> At that particular time we had a very fine French chef who was considered one of the best in the country and a very nice man to work with. He had five girls working with him. We also had a stillroom where all the bread and cakes were made. Baking was done at Cliveden twice a week. The head stillroom maid used to travel between London and Cliveden. One under-stillroom maid was kept in either place . . . .
> In the house at Cliveden there was a housekeeper, 6 housemaids, 6 laundry maids and always one or two left in the kitchen apart from the travelling staff, also an Odd Man who used to look after the boilers, carry coal, answer the telephone – a most useful man in every way.

Mrs Beeton worried not only about the food for a household, but also concerned herself with the decoration of the kitchen. She advocated glazed tiles or bricks for the walls to make them easier to clean and more hygienic, although limewash, often with a touch of

Large kitchens, such as Wallington, Northumberland, had two closed ranges, set side by side. One was run at a low heat for heating water, simmering soups and stews, and for slow cooking. The other could be fired up to roast or bake.

blue to discourage flies was more usual in the average house and certainly more economical. Instead of cold, stone-flagged floors, tiles were recommended, or cement, covered with linoleum by the end of the century. For the cook's comfort a wooden duck-board was placed under the central table. Whatever the floor covering, floors were scrubbed at least twice a week and sanded with very fine silver sand, or covered with sawdust, to absorb splashes of grease and dropped debris, which was swept up twice a day.

The kitchen at Lanhydrock has a slate-flagged floor with walls hygienically covered to dado height with glazed white, simply patterned tiles and distempered upper walls making the room appear light and clean. In contrast, the dark green and cream glazed tiles lining the stone-flagged kitchen at Wallington in Northumberland make the room rather dark. Another forward-looking and functional kitchen can be seen at Wightwick Manor in the West Midlands, one of the National Trust's smaller Victorian country houses. It has survived virtually unaltered since the house was built between 1887–9, with walls of cream and red glazed bricks, and a floor of red quarry tiles.

Edwin Lutyens' high-ceilinged kitchen at 20th-century Castle Drogo, with its remarkable domed roof and granite walls, is a fine example of one of the last great kitchens. The only source of light is from a circular skylight, which Mrs Drewe thought insufficient, complaining that the room never received 'a glint of sun'. Lutyens, however, disagreed, saying that the skylight plus the white distemper on the ceiling would provide enough light for working.

All the kitchen fittings show the attention to detail and commonsense that is the hallmark of Lutyens' domestic work. A simple, circular beech table beneath the skylight was specially designed to reflect the dome above, while pastry- and chopping-boards were given rounded outer edges to fit the edges of the table itself. Drawings for the simple oak dressers, side-tables and even the pastry boards were sent down from Lutyens' London office in Queen Anne's Gate.

Although cooking facilities began to improve by leaps and bounds in the Victorian era, the basic design of the kitchen with its 'hearth' and simple furniture remained little changed. One or two great open or glass-fronted dressers of natural, stained or painted wood with shelves, cupboards and drawers held kitchen crockery, utensils like moulds, and kitchen linen. The essential pestle and mortar usually stood near the dresser, as at Lanhydrock. Often, the mortar was made out of part of a tree-trunk with a marble or stoneware basin, made by famous factories such as Minton, inserted into the top. The pestle was a stout wooden pole with its bulbous base resting in the bowl and its top secured to the kitchen wall by a metal ring. When gripped with both hands, the pestle could be moved up and down to break up ice or sugar or to pound meat until fine enough to go through the sieve.

A 'massive', firm and 'strongly made' wooden table, as recommended by Mrs Beeton, would occupy the centre of the room, and here most of the food preparation was done. Another type of Victorian table had a large slab of marble set into the top for making pastry and preparing sweetmeats if there was no separate pastry room, as at Cragside. Penrhyn Castle has a superb pastry room leading from the kitchen, where slate slabs from the family's quarry run the length of the room, providing a cool working surface for the pastry cooks.

A couple of wooden armchairs, usually Windsor, by the fire for the cook, and a clock on the wall completed the furniture of a typical Victorian kitchen. In an attempt to avoid late meals Dr William Kitchiner in *The Cook's Oracle*, 1817, recommended that a clock in the dining-room vibrate 'in unison' with a clock over the kitchen fireplace. Anne Cobbett, writing in *The English Housekeeper* in 1851, also recommended a clock, but with the provision that 'the lady should see to its being regulated, or this piece of furniture may do more harm than good. That good understanding which sometimes subsists between the clock and the cook, and which is brought about by the instrumentality of a broom-handle, or some such magic, should be noted by every provident housekeeper as one of the things to be guarded against.'

The central point of the Victorian kitchen was still the hearth, now fitted with a cast-iron range. *The English Housekeeper* stated: 'I know of no apparatus so desirable as the common kitchen range . . . .' The speed with which they were adopted was remarkable:

The kitchen at Wightwick Manor, West Midlands, has survived virtually unaltered since 1888, with its walls of cream and red glazed bricks for ease of cleaning, and floor of red quarry tiles. The original cooking range made by the Eagle Range & Gas Co, of Birmingham, is still in working order and is lit regularly.

few town houses had anything more than an open fire for cooking during the first half of the century, but by 1850 even working-class homes of very modest pretensions were being fitted with ranges. The very poor, especially in the countryside, still cooked on a small open grate, or over an open hearth.

The 'open range', developed from late 18th-century prototypes, was in use from about 1800 until well into the 1920s. In general, this range was more popular in the north of Britain where the climate was colder, because it warmed the kitchen at the same time as cooking the food. John Farey, writing in 1813 about Derbyshire, recorded that 'there is scarce a house without them'. The oven was a great improvement on 18th-century designs because it was equipped with a damper-controller flue which provided a passage for warm air round the side, away from the fire and over the top, giving a more even heat. The greatest drawback to the open range was its extravagant use of fuel.

The 'closed range', based on the principle suggested by George Bodley, was both more efficient and more economical than the open type, but did not come widely into use until the middle of the century. However, it soon became the most common type of Victorian cooking apparatus, especially in affluent households in the south and the Midlands. Towards the end of the century, closed ranges were being fitted in 90 per cent of all newly built houses.

The most successful early maker of closed ranges was William Flavel of Leamington Spa in Warwickshire. So many firms manufactured iron ranges in the town that the name 'Leamington' became almost synonymous with that of 'kitchener', the name used by Flavel to indicate the competence of his invention. The kitchener was expensive to buy and very hard work to keep clean, but the cook could boil, fry and bake at the same time. There is a particularly splendid free-standing Leamington kitchener in the centre of the kitchen at Saltram. It has two very large ovens for roasting and baking and a capacious hotplate, useable from both sides. Although free-standing ranges were preferred on the Continent, they were unusual in England. Most were set into the hearth with a neatly tiled, easily washable surround, like the range at Wightwick, which is still lit regularly and occasionally used for heating up food for functions in the house.

Large kitchens, such as those at Shugborough and Wallington, had two closed ranges, set side by side. One was run at a low heat and used for heating water, simmering soups and stews and slow cooking, while the other could be fired up to roast or bake. At Shugborough, a closed range dating from the 1870s is still in full working order and an accomplished cook bakes scones, biscuits and cakes for the visitors.

Looking after any kitchen range was a filthy job. Every day the fire box had to be cleaned out and ashes removed. The flues had to be brushed down and once a week swept more thoroughly with a long narrow brush; the ovens then had to be scraped, washed and dried before the whole iron case was blackleaded. Blacklead was a stick of carbon and iron mixed with a little drop of turpentine, which was brushed on and then brush-polished to bring up a shine. Any steel parts or brass fittings were then cleaned with emery paper and polished with leather. Finally, the fire box was relaid with paper and sticks and lit.

After centuries of only the clumsy flint and tinder-box to light a fire, the invention of matches in the late 18th century must have been a boon. Early 19th-century 'bottle matches', tipped with a mixture of chlorate of potash, sugar and gum arabic were popular but very dangerous. The matches were lit by dipping them into a bottle

At Erddig the roasting range was replaced in the Edwardian period by a range set into the hearth with an easy clean surround of glazed tiles. Joints of meat were hung in the half-cylindrical hastener or roasting screen from a bottle-jack in front of the fire. Batter pudding could be cooked in the dripping-pan in the bottom of the hastener.

containing asbestos soaked in sulphuric acid. The first friction matches were made in 1827 and many versions followed, the best known called 'lucifer' after Satan, all far from safe. The development of the safety match is credited to Johan Lundstrom of Sweden in 1855, but all 19th-century matches would be contained in strong boxes, often of metal, to prevent accidents. Cleaning and lighting the range was the first job of the day for the second kitchen-maid, who normally rose at 6am, but an hour earlier when the flues of the range needed sweeping. According to *The Servants' Practical Guide*, 1880, she could earn between £14 and £22 a year, compared with the £20–28 of a first kitchen-maid.

The kitchen range was a temperamental monster to control. Cooks had to be skilful to be able to handle the damper controls and to obtain good results in cooking; most were not. If the wrong dampers were left out the fire box might melt and the boiler crack. The temperature inside the ovens of early ranges was an unknown quantity, kitchen staff generally having their own methods of testing the heat either with flour or paper.

The following instructions come from Mrs Black's *Household Cookery and Laundry Work* of 1882:

1. If a sheet of paper burns when thrown in, the oven is too hot.
2. When the paper becomes dark brown, it is suitable for pastry.
3. When light brown, it does pies.
4. When dark yellow, for cakes.
5. When light yellow, for puddings, biscuits and small pastry.

Open ranges continued to be used for roasting because of complaints that meat could not be properly roasted in a closed range. The main feature of the kitchen at Lanhydrock is its spectacular open roasting range made by the famous domestic equipment suppliers, Clement Jeakes & Co., of Great Russell Street, London, which held Queen Victoria's Royal Warrant. All the roasting was done here; the smoke-jack has gearing that can drive several horizontal spits at once, as well as turn chains from which small joints, fowl or game can be hung. There is also a rail for clockwork bottle-jacks. Boiling and simmering took place on the comparatively modest closed range, which has ovens below for soufflés and fine baking. Plainer baking such as bread, scones, cakes and biscuits was done in the bakehouse next door in the elaborate coal-fired oven, also made by Jeakes which supplied equipment to houses as far apart as

The main feature of the kitchen at Lanhydrock, Cornwall is its spectacular open coal-fired roasting range, made by the famous domestic equipment suppliers, Clement Jeakes & Co. of Great Russell Street, London. The smoke-jack has gearing that can drive several horizontal spits at once, as well as turn chains from which small joints, fowl or game can be hung. There is also a rail for clockwork bottle-jacks. To lessen the hot air and fumes, louvres in the peak of the gable are connected by a flue to the chimney stack.

A photograph taken in the kitchen at Dunham Massey, Cheshire in 1883, showing the large closed range flanked by hot closets and an auxiliary gas cooker. The charcoal range on the other side of the kitchen had been converted to gas after the 7th Earl of Stamford installed a private gas-making system in the 1880s.

Cragside, Uppark and Dunham Massey. The oven took four days to heat up to a steady temperature, but once heated it was quite economical. Below the great central oven was the proving-oven where kneaded dough was put to rise before baking.

The everyday baking of bread, cakes and biscuits at Penrhyn was done in the bakehouse, next to the brew-house in the outer court. It was felt to be an essential office in isolated houses such as Penrhyn and Lanhydrock, where large quantities of bread were still baked every day. Many other large houses closed down their independent bakehouse, but reserved a place for a baking oven in the scullery, as at Charlecote. All the Lucy family's bread, cakes, pies, puddings and 'Charlecote biscuits' – given to the Prince Regent as mentioned in Mary Elizabeth's memoirs – were baked in this large oven, until the sophisticated New Gold Medal Eagle Range, now standing beside it, was installed about 1900. It is tunnel-shaped and brick-vaulted with a floor of clay tiles and a close-fitting ventilating iron door. Just in front of the door there is a convenient gap in the brick shelf, where cinders from the firing could be raked out so that they fell directly into an ash tray fitted underneath. Finer baking was done in the splendid 'Prize Kitchen' that replaced one of the earlier open grates in the kitchen, probably in the 1860s. This sophisticated closed range was made in Leamington by George William Groves and has a double roasting oven large enough for the biggest turkey and two single ovens for baking, with hot plates above. The central fire was normally shielded, but could be left open in order to roast small joints. Large joints were roasted in front of the surviving open range which is fitted with cast-iron side cheeks to give a smaller or larger fire and an iron ring that could be swung across the fire to support a large pot. A smoke-jack in the chimney operated the spit and a large dripping-tray stood underneath to catch the fat and juices from the meat.

At other houses, baking was done in the ovens of their ranges, although they were acknowledged to be less efficient at baking than the old brick-lined ovens. The decline in home-baking that had been occurring throughout the 18th century continued into

Alexis Soyer's famous kitchens at the Reform Club in London's Pall Mall were a Victorian tourist attraction. In 1841 Soyer introduced gas stoves which he believed to be clean and efficient. In this engraving can be seen the hot cupboard and the roasting range through the back of the open roasting screen or 'baffle'.

the next. 'Not only are there no ovens in vast numbers of our cottages, but many a small village is entirely without one' wrote Eliza Acton in her *Bread Book*, 1857.

Experiments to use gas for domestic cooking were made, but the problems proved enormous: the cost was much greater than coal; there were no meters; and most important of all, there was a general reluctance to use gas for cooking. It was believed that gas was dangerously explosive and that any food roasted or baked over gas jets would become impregnated with noxious fumes. Early designers of gas cookers and grills had a staunch ally in the famous French chef, Alexis Soyer, however. He believed it to be 'the greatest comfort ever introduced into any culinary arrangement', and in 1841 introduced gas stoves into the new kitchens of the Reform Club in London where he was chef. These were the most famous of all Victorian kitchens and proved to be a great tourist attraction.

Despite this enthusiasm, it was to be another 30 years before gas cookers began to replace coal ranges in domestic kitchens. The breakthrough came when the gas companies offered two important incentives. The first was the hiring out of gas cookers at a small rent. Then in the 1890s came the penny-in-the-slot meter system, bringing gas within the reach of even the poorer members of the population. By 1898, one home in four that had a gas supply had a cooker as well and cookery books began to include recipes tailored to suit gas stoves.

Since then, gas cooking has never looked back, although in large houses, particularly in the country, coal ranges continued to dominate the kitchens, often with a gas stove as a back-up. The Earl of Stamford installed a private gas-making system at Dunham Massey in the 1880s: a photograph of the kitchen in 1883 shows a large closed range flanked by hot closets and an auxiliary gas cooker. The charcoal range on the other side

By 1898, encouraged by the gas companies hiring out cookers at a small rent, one home in four with a gas supply also had a cooker. Meat was roasted by hanging it from hooks in the oven.

An advertisement from Mr Straw's grocery shop in Worksop, Nottinghamshire. Mrs Beeton worried not only about the food for a household but also the hygiene and cleanliness of the kitchen.

of the kitchen was converted to gas by Jeakes & Co. which also installed the gas-heated hot cupboards in the servery, built in 1905. The kitchen still has two smallish gas stoves: a cast-iron 'Black Beauty' dating from the 1900s, which had to be blackleaded, and another from the 1930s, enamelled in grey and white for easy wipe-down cleaning.

The gas cooker's rival, the electric cooker, came much later on the scene, for it was not until the 1880s that the possibilities were explored. The first electric cookers suitable for general use were demonstrated at the Electrical Fair held at the Crystal Palace in 1891. On the other side of the Atlantic a model electric kitchen, with a small electric range, broiler and kettles, was a feature of the Chicago World Fair in 1893. But probably the first viable cooker was made for sale by the Crompton Co. of Chelmsford in 1894. Like most early electric cookers, it resembled a safe and consisted of an oven and a number of separate appliances – grill, frying pan, kettle and hot plate – which were put on top of the oven or set on the floor beside it. Power was taken from the electric lighting mains and the oven and appliances were all wired separately. By 1900, the electric cooker had become a practical proposition, and a number of designs were put on the market. Ten years later, 10,000 electric ovens were in service.

The 'roast' remained, for every household that could afford it, an important symbol of wealth, status and national character even if it distorted the food budget for the rest of the week and meals had to be based on left-overs. The roasting of the meat was often the responsibility of the second kitchen-maid, if the household was not large enough to employ a separate roasting cook.

After roasting, boiling was the commonest and easiest method of cooking, although Mrs Beeton felt it necessary to warn that: 'Boiling . . . requires skilful management'. The main problem was controlling the heat of a range to achieve simmering rather than vigorous boiling, which toughened the meat. For gentle simmering, many large establishments had stewing pans, rows of hot plates heated by burning charcoal in alcoves beneath, like the stewing hearths of the 18th century. Advocates of French cookery like Alexis Soyer and Eliza Acton lamented that stewing and braising were not more widely used in Britain. Stewing, associated with inferior meat, had a low status and as Soyer said, 'Braising . . . like the sauté, belongs entirely to the French school'.

Victorian kitchens could be cluttered, especially if the full range of kitchen equipment recommended by Mrs Beeton was acquired. She modified her specifications according to the class of the household: mansion, good class house, middle-class house and very small house. But even for her middle-class household, she lists over 130 items as necessary for cooking, the preparation of food and cleaning the kitchen.

The development of the range had changed the shape of cooking pots and pans; they were now smaller, flat-bottomed and no longer had long handles. As French dishes became more popular, they became more specialised and middle-class kitchens were expected to have an impressive range of stewpans, saucepans, fish kettles, sauté pans, omelette pans, boilers, stock-pots and steamers. In well-to-do houses the *batterie de cuisine*, which included bowls and moulds, was of copper, with the initials of the owner of the house stamped prominently on them, and was used for 'best' cooking only.

Tin-plated, cast-iron pots and pans varnished black were used in more modest houses. Towards the end of the century, vitreous enamel began to be used as a finish and lightweight aluminium cookware first appeared.

The Victorian housewife was obsessed with running her kitchen economically – hence the old adage 'Waste not, want not' over many kitchen hearths. The 'digester', an

Left: Copper saucepans at Cragside, Northumberland. As French dishes grew in popularity, pots and pans became more specialised and the properly equipped kitchen was expected to have an impressive range including sauté pans, omelette pans, stock-pots and fish kettles.

Above: Copper bain-marie at Charlecote Park, Warwickshire. Every well-equipped Victorian kitchen had a bain-marie standing on the side of the range. It consisted of several lidded pans of different sizes, invariably of copper, standing – often on a trivet – in a shallow tin of warm water. A number of different sauces could thus be kept cooking gently without boiling.

early pressure cooker that gained a reputation for being the most economical of all cooking utensils, was used more often in small kitchens than large, for softening bones to make soup or broth. It was a heavy cast-iron pot with a looped handle and lid. The latter was fitted with a valve which could be raised to allow steam to escape when pressure exceeded 2 or 3 lb. As indispensable in large households were the two stock-pots – one for white soup and one for brown. These tall saucepans with well-fitting lids and taps at their base proved longer in their popularity than digesters.

Traditional implements like knives, choppers, ladles and sieves did not change, but hundreds of more specialised tools and gadgets were added to them. Mass-produced tinware, such as pastry and biscuit cutters, jelly moulds, meat presses and raised pie moulds, flooded middle-class kitchens. These smaller houses, with fewer servants, were the most likely to invest in the many labour-saving gadgets which began to arrive after 1850 from America, where there was already a servant shortage. There were devices to prepare apples, boil eggs, grind coffee, stone raisins and cherries, peel potatoes, scrape radishes and even shell peas. Several designs of mechanical cutters appeared for eggs, marmalade, bread, cucumbers and beans. There were invaluable mincing machines, sausage machines and rotary egg beaters and of course the essential

Above: Kitchen utensils on a side-table in the kitchen at Wightwick Manor, West Midlands: an earthenware water purifier; a wooden drum-type knife cleaner on its elegant cast-iron stand, originally shown at the 1851 Great Exhibition; and a wooden ice-cream churn.

Above right: Lanhydrock, Cornwall, has a model scullery, fitted with two slate-lined sinks for the preparation of vegetables and washing up of kitchen pots and pans. Roomy wooden plate racks near the sink stored kitchen utensils and crockery. Vegetables and puddings were cooked on the small closed range which also held the stock-pot. A central wooden table provided a working area for cleaning game and poultry.

tin-opener introduced during the 1860s. Even hand-operated food choppers for cutting up suet and vegetables, and food mixers became available.

Most kitchens had a scullery adjoining, which was 'the proper place for cleaning and preparing fish, vegetables etc, and generally for processes in connection with cooking which entail dirt or litter and should therefore be kept out of the kitchen' according to Murphy in *Our Homes*, as well as for washing up. In his *Encyclopaedia of Cottage, Farm and Villa Architecture and Furniture*, Loudon recommended at least two sinks, a board for dirty dishes and a plate-rack for drying. 'There might also be a fireplace, a small brick oven and a large oven if the bread be baked there; coppers for heating water for the use of the kitchen-maid, dressers and tables, shelves for saucepans, etc; and it should be well supplied with water.' This was the domain of the scullery maid, who had the lowliest job in the kitchen, earning between £12 and £18 a year in the 1880s.

Lanhydrock has a model scullery, fitted with two slate-lined sinks for the preparation of vegetables and, with the addition of a wooden tub, for washing up the kitchen and servants' crockery and pots and pans. Greasy pots could be scoured under steam jets over the iron draining board in the corner. Roomy wooden plate-racks attached to the walls near the sinks stored kitchen utensils and crockery. At Lanhydrock, as with some other big houses, vegetables and puddings for both the dining-room and the servants' hall were cooked on the small closed range in the corner, which also held the stock-pot. A central wooden table provided a working area for the scullery maid to skin, pluck and clean all the game, rabbits and poultry from the estate.

Dustbins were often banned from the scullery and the kitchen, because they encouraged smells. All organic waste in large houses was tipped down stone chutes into pig bins. At Chirk the bin was removed by farmhands daily and a clean one put in its place.

Although Cragside was adequately supplied with water pumped up to a tank above the house by means of a hydraulic ram, many houses still had a very irregular water

In the monumental scullery at Castle Drogo, Devon, Lutyens designed the teak draining boards and the long plate-rack that runs above the three large oak-framed sinks. The scullery was also used for the preparation of food, hence the enormous hexagonal pestle and mortar and matching chopping block.

The simple, circular beech table beneath the skylight of the kitchen at Castle Drogo. Lutyens designed it to reflect the dome above, while pastry- and chopping-boards were given rounded outer edges to fit the edges of the table (*see page 294*).

supply. Country cottages almost certainly had no running water and relied on wells, springs and rivers until late in the century. In London, around 1850, about 6 per cent of houses were entirely without water and a large number was supplied only by stand-pipes, which probably had to serve whole streets. Even in well-to-do areas, running water was available only three times a week. When there was water, it was notorious for its filth. The 2nd Lord Leconfield insisted that barrels of drinking water were delivered from Petworth when he and his family were in London, until 1895, when his son George died from typhoid fever contracted at Petworth. The establishment of a single, publicly owned Water Board in 1902, in place of private water companies, improved the water supply and the drainage system.

As estates produced less and less of their own food, relying instead on shops for provisions of all kinds, the need for large, specialised larders began to disappear. Small establishments simply had one larder near the kitchen, preferably on the north side of the house, where meat, fish, bread, cheese, fruit and vegetables were stored on shelves of thick slate and marble, embedded deep into the walls for coolness. In larger households, a wet larder was still used to store raw meat, fish and sometimes vegetables, while the dry larder accommodated cooked meat, dairy products and some dry stores. In remoter areas, however, estates continued to be more self-sufficient and needed specialist larders. The series of larders at Penrhyn was originally designed by Thomas Hopper, the architect, on the south side of the kitchen so that their windows faced north, but in the eventual arrangement, their south-facing windows had to be shaded by a pitched slate awning. They are all very cold with easily sluiced down, quarry-tiled floors and thick slate slabs set into the walls. All the raw meat was stored in the large wet larder, which has a safe for carcasses. In addition there were larders for dry stores, fish and game, and an extra larder in the housekeeper's domain on the ground floor.

A very good set of late Victorian larders can be seen at Lanhydrock, consisting of a dry larder, fish larder and meat larder. They are ideally positioned, close to the kitchen and yet isolated from the sometimes steamy atmosphere of the scullery. Sides and joints of meat were hung from the stout steel bars across the ceiling of the meat larder and prepared on the iron-bound chopping block and the dressing-tables. There are slate shelves and sloping slate sinks to allow the dressed meat to drain, after which it was kept in the insulated ice-chest. The fish larder next door also contains cold slate slabs, shelves and an ice-chest for storing both fresh and cooked fish.

Domestic ice-chests, the earliest form of refrigerators, were developed in the 1840s in Britain, when they were supplied by firms that sold ice. The early ice-chests were insulated wooden boxes, lined with zinc, tin or slate, and held a block of ice on which the food was placed. The ice for Lanhydrock was brought from a firm in Plymouth, travelling by train to Bodmin station, and then by cart. Another example of an ice-chest can be seen at Penrhyn; it was filled with ice from the castle ice tower.

By the 1850s, it had been realised that better use of the ice-chest could be made if the ice was at the top, with air circulating around it and the food was stored in the lower section. So successful were these ice-boxes that sophisticated models of chests and cupboards, known as refrigerators, were still shown in Harrods' 1929 catalogue, alongside gas and electric refrigerators. Large ice-cupboards survive in the larders of Dunham Massey and Shugborough.

The ability to store ice near the kitchen helped to popularise sorbets, ice-creams and iced puddings for fashionable dinners. Experiments in making artificial ice led to the

discovery that the addition of salt to ice made a colder, longer-lasting freezing mixture. Fancy pewter or copper moulds and copper bombes were plunged into a wooden freezing bucket, filled with layers of ice and coarse salt. Other fancy ice dishes like soufflés were frozen in an ice cave – a round or square box which was buried in freezing mixture. The drudgery of making large amounts led to the ice-cream making machine, which was one labour-saving gadget that did find its way into large kitchens.

At the end of the short corridor of larders at Lanhydrock, reasonably close to the kitchen, but as far away from the bakehouse as possible, is the dairy. This was for storage, preparation being done in the adjoining scullery. It faces north and is provided with ingenious cooling arrangements. Water piped into the house from a spring in the hillside above flows in a channel round a marble slab in the middle of the room and round slate slabs on its perimeter. The elaborate cold puddings of the period, which had to be prepared well in advance, were kept on the marble slab, while cream, butter and milk prepared in the scullery were stored on the slate shelves around the tiled walls.

The dairy scullery was one of the busiest rooms in the house. Twice a day, churns of milk were brought from the home farm by pony cart to be delivered to the exterior door. The churns were emptied into pans standing in cold water in the long slate trough against the wall. Whole milk was set aside for household use and the remainder went into the making of butter and clotted cream. For the latter, a scalding range was built on the inner wall of the house, heated to a gentle temperature by hot water pipes brought direct from the boiler house in the cellar below.

Because of the distance between kitchen and dining-room in Victorian houses, a serving-room was a necessity. At Lanhydrock, it is conveniently placed next door to the china closet and is fitted with a large iron hot-cupboard, heated by hot water pipes to keep food piping hot. At Wightwick the servery is combined with the china pantry, where the dinner services were washed up as well as stored. It has all the original fitted cupboards, drawers, glazed cabinets and deep sinks with wooden draining boards. Plate-warmers and heated serving dishes would be used as required and the food was passed through a serving hatch hidden by a screen into the dining-room.

Above left: The north-facing dairy at Lanhydrock, Cornwall, has a central marble table and around the tiled walls, slate shelves cooled by water channels. The elaborate cold puddings of the period were kept on the marble slab, while cream, butter and milk prepared in the adjoining scullery were stored on the slate shelves.

Above: The Victorian aversion to cooking smells percolating into the main rooms of the house dictated that the kitchen was placed at a distance from the dining-room, making a serving-room a necessity. At Lanhydrock, Cornwall, it is conveniently placed next door to the china closet and is fitted with a large iron hot-cupboard.

Rice à la Sœur Nightingale

'Fry the boiled rice with a little fresh butter, nutmeg, pepper and salt; and when quite hot, add the whites of three hard-boiled eggs shred fine, and the white parts of a dried haddock; pile all this up lightly in a hot dish; strew over the cone the yolks of the hard-boiled eggs previously rubbed through a wire sieve, and mixed with a little grated Parmesan cheese; garnish the rice round the base with fried croutons of bread, push in the oven for five minutes – just to slightly colour the surface of a golden hue, and serve immediately.'

From *The Cook's Guide*, Charles Elmé Francatelli, 1862

The practice of naming new dishes after well-known personalities was popular in Victorian times. The great chef Francatelli honoured Florence Nightingale when he named after her his new dish of Kedgeree (an English version of an Indian dish called *Khichiri*), for British-Indian cuisine was a chic novelty at London's dining-tables. It became a popular Victorian breakfast and supper dish.

Malecotony Soup

'To two Quarts of good Broth, add a little Ham, some Allspice, Mace, Cloves, Thyme, Marjoram, Basil and Onions. Boil all these together for one Hour adding two tablespoonfulls of Curry powder with a very little flour and butter. Pass it all thro' a Sieve and add to it a Chicken cut in small pieces with a *little* Garlic and Lemon (two cloves of Garlic and one good Lemon). Boil it half an Hour which will be sufficient to dress the chicken; Rice must be boiled very dry to eat with it – one pint of Patna Rice should be boiled in just one pint of Water. When it has just boiled up, it should be put at a distance from the fire (not to burn) and being covered close up, the steam will finish doing it.'

From a small book found on the shelves in Disraeli's study at Hughenden Manor, Buckinghamshire, alongside his wife Mary Anne's diaries/account books. The recipes, in either Mary Anne's or her housekeeper's hand, are mixed with household and gardening hints and remedies – even for distemper in dogs.

Malecotony or Mulligatawny Soup was a fashionable Victorian soup originating in southern India and deriving its name from the Tamil *milagutannir* meaning pepper-water.

Mulligatawny Soup

1 small fresh chicken
3 oz (75 g) butter
2 medium onions, chopped
1 tablespoon (15 ml) mild curry powder
1 garlic clove, crushed
1 tablespoon (15 ml) flour
3 pt (1.8 litres) cold water
8 oz (225 g) lean ham, chopped
4 whole cloves
2 large blades mace
sprig each of thyme, basil and marjoram
juice of 1 large lemon
salt and freshly milled black pepper
sour cream or yoghurt
boiled rice to serve

Cut the chicken into pieces and brown all over in the butter in a large flameproof casserole. Remove to a plate while you fry the onions. Stir in the curry powder and garlic and cook for a few minutes, then stir in the flour and continue to cook for another few seconds. Gradually stir in the water, then return the chicken to the casserole. Add the ham, cloves, mace, herbs, lemon juice and seasoning and bring to the boil. Simmer for 1–1½ hours or until the chicken is tender, then remove it and discard all the skin and bones. Return all the meat to the casserole, discarding the cloves, mace and herbs. Taste and adjust the seasoning as necessary, then reheat and pour into a tureen. Swirl in a little sour cream or yoghurt. Serve with a separate bowl of boiled rice. Serves 6–8.

A 19th-century grocer's bill heading.

Florence Nightingale's Kedgeree

1 lb (450 g) smoked haddock, cooked
3 eggs, hard-boiled
1 tablespoon (15 ml) Parmesan cheese, grated
3 oz (75 g) butter
6 oz (175 g) long grain rice, cooked
salt and freshly milled black pepper
freshly grated nutmeg
small triangles of fried bread to garnish
1 tablespoon (15 ml) fresh parsley, chopped

Remove the skin and bones from the fish and flake coarsely. Chop the whites of the hard-boiled eggs and add to the fish. Press the yolks through a sieve and mix with the cheese. Melt the butter in a saucepan and toss the rice in it over gentle heat until well coated and heated through. Mix in the fish and egg whites and gently continue to toss until the whole mixture is hot. Season with salt, pepper and nutmeg, then pile onto an ovenproof plate. Scatter the egg yolk and cheese mixture on top and place under a gentle grill for a few minutes until the cheese begins to colour. Arrange the triangles of fried bread around the rice and sprinkle with parsley. Serve immediately. Serves 4–6.

Crimped Salmon with Dutch sauce or Salmon Hollandaise

'To dress salmon or trout in perfection in this style, it is quite necessary that the fish be dressed a short time after being caught. If it be practicable to procure what is termed a *live salmon*, take out the gills, draw out the guts, &, wash the fish and crimp it on either side, by making deep incisions with a very sharp knife, and then throw it into a large tub containing clean, cold, spring-water, fresh from the pump; the water to be changed every half-hour, and the salmon to remain in it for about two hours. In crimping any sort of fish, the colder the water is the better; the coldness of the water petrifying the fish to a certain degree, gives it the firmness so much desired. Put the crimped salmon on to boil in hot water, with a good handful of salt; allow it to boil gently on the side of the stove, remembering that all crimped fish require considerably less time to boil than plain fish. As soon as the fish is done, it should be immediately drained from the water, dished up on a folded napkin; garnished round with picked parsley, and served with Dutch sauce.'

Dutch Sauce

'Four yolks of raw eggs, two ounces of fresh butter, half a gill of cream, a very small quantity of nutmeg, pepper, and salt, and a teaspoonful of elder vinegar:- having put the foregoing ingredients into a small stewpan, place it within another stewpan of rather larger size, containing half a pint of hot water, and then, after placing the sauce in its bath over the fire, proceed to work it swiftly, either with a wire whisk or small wooden spoon, until it begins to thicken and present a rich, smooth, creamy appearance. Great care must be taken to prevent this sauce from curdling and becoming decomposed, which may be prevented by not stirring it over too fierce a fire. If, however, this accident should occur, by adding either two more yolks, or a spoonful of white sauce, it will be remedied.'

From *The Cook's Guide*, Charles Elmé Francatelli, 1862

Crimped fish was a very popular English speciality in Victorian and Edwardian times. The method of preparation was applied particularly to salmon, cod, haddock and skate, but the fish had to be straight out of the water as it would have been at Penrhyn Castle. Lord Penrhyn had nets across the Menai Straits and the salmon was so abundant that his servants complained they had too much salmon to eat. Even if salmon could not be caught locally, by the middle of the 19th century it was being shipped regularly from Scotland packed in ice. Victorians and Edwardians would have used a whole salmon for this dish and used up the leftovers in hashes, rissoles and cutlets.

Poached Salmon Hollandaise

2½–3 lb (1.2–1.4 kg) piece of salmon
a little melted butter

FOR THE SAUCE

4 tablespoons (60 ml) white wine vinegar
6 black peppercorns
1 blade mace
1 slice of onion
1 small bayleaf
3 egg yolks
5 oz (150 g) unsalted butter, slightly soft
salt and freshly milled pepper
1 tablespoon (15 ml) single cream
squeeze of lemon juice (optional)
cucumber and fennel or dill to garnish

Brush a piece of foil large enough to wrap up the salmon with melted butter. Season the foil generously, then lay the fish on top and wrap into a parcel. Fill a fish kettle or large pan half full of water and bring it to the boil. Lower the parcel of salmon into the water, bring back to the boil, then simmer for about 15 minutes until cooked; bearing in mind that the thickness of the fish will vary the cooking time. Keep the fish warm in the foil while making the sauce.

To make the sauce, put the vinegar into a small saucepan with the spices, onion and bayleaf. Boil until reduced to a scant tablespoon, then set aside. Cream the eggs yolks in a bowl with a good knob of butter and a pinch of salt. Strain on the vinegar mixture, set the bowl over a pan of boiling water, turn off the heat and add the remaining butter in small pieces, stirring vigorously all the time. When all the butter has been added and the sauce is thick, taste and adjust the seasoning as necessary. Add the cream, and lemon juice if desired. The finished sauce should have the consistency of thick cream.

Serve the salmon decorated with cucumber slices and sprigs of fennel or dill and the sauce separately. Serves 6.

Homard à la Crème

'Cut up the live lobster and put these pieces into a sautépan containing ⅙ pint oil and 1 oz butter, both very hot. Fry them over an open fire until the pieces of lobster are stiffened and coloured, then clear them of all grease; swill the sautépan with 1 tablespoon burnt brandy, and add, immediately, 4 oz fresh, peeled truffles cut into slices.

Moisten, almost sufficiently to cover, with very fresh, thin cream; season with salt and cayenne, and cook the lobster. Then take the meat from the carapaces, and put it into a timbale [a metal dish]; reduce the cream to ⅓ pint, and mix therewith 3 tablespoonfuls melted, white meat-glaze and a few drops of lemon-juice. Strain this sauce through muslin, and pour it over the pieces of lobster.'

From *A Guide to Modern Cookery* by the famous French chef Escoffier, first published in 1907. His recipes were frequently inspired by those of the 14th-century French chef, Taillevent; so we have travelled the full circle.

This lobster dish epitomises the extravagance of the Edwardian era.

Lobster in Cream

1½–2 lb (750g–1 kg) lobster cooked in court
　bouillon and cut into neat pieces
1 oz (25g) butter
1 sherry glass of brandy
2 egg yolks
½ pt (300 ml) double cream
salt and freshly milled pepper
½ teaspoon paprika

Heat a frying or sauté pan and grease well with butter. Put in the lobster pieces, then season and heat gently for 2–3 minutes. Pour over the brandy and set alight. Draw aside. Beat the egg yolks, then add the cream and season well with salt, pepper and paprika. Stir quickly into the lobster and shake above the heat, stirring gently all the time until the sauce is thick and creamy. (Be very careful that it doesn't boil or it will curdle.) Serve lobster at once with boiled rice. Serves 3–4.

Haricot Mutton

'2 lb Neck or Loin of Mutton
1 pt water, 1 carrot, ½ turnip
1 onion, small tablespoonful of Flour,
　salt and pepper

Cut into chops & cut most of the fat from them, fry them in a little dripping, put them into a pan after they are browned nicely. Pour on the water slightly warm, cover closely, bring to a boil & let it cook gently. Clean & cut the vegatables into small pieces, fry them in the same dripping that the chops have been done in, add them to the chops. Let it cook gently 1½ to 2 hours. Mix the flour with a little cold water & stir into the haricot, season it, alow it to boil up then the dish is ready.'

From a hand-written recipe book belonging to Mrs Straw

The Straw family owned a grocer's shop in Worksop in Nottinghamshire. At first they lived 'above the shop' in Market Square, but as they prospered, moved into a semi-detached Edwardian villa, 7 Blyth Grove, in 1923. Mrs Straw started her recipe book in 1880 and must have used it all her married life until 1939, as the pages seem well-thumbed. She was a keen and good cook, who attended cookery lectures at one time. Her son William, who took over the housekeeping after her death, lists a number of recipes under this heading. Mutton was a very popular meat in Victorian times, although it is now almost unobtainable. It has a stronger taste than lamb, but lamb may be used instead.

Haricot of Lamb

2 lb (1.2 kg) middle neck of lamb or mutton
　divided into cutlets
2 onions, peeled and quartered
1 small piece swede or turnip
2 carrots
1 oz (25g) dripping or butter
1 tablespoon (15 ml) flour
¾ pt (450 ml) stock or water
salt and freshly milled black pepper
1 bouquet garni

Trim most of the fat from the cutlets, removing any superfluous bone and cut the onion, swede and carrots into short thick strips. Heat the dripping in a flameproof casserole until smoking, then brown the cutlets on both sides. Remove with a slotted spoon and reserve, then fry the vegetables until they are just coloured. Stir in the flour and cook for a minute or two, then stir in the stock or water. Bring gently to boiling point, replace the meat in the casserole and make sure that the liquid comes just level with the meat. Season well, add the bouquet garni, then cover with a lid. Simmer gently for about 1 hour, or until the meat is tender, turning the cutlets from time to time. Serve with creamed potatoes. Serves 4.

William Straw, grocer and seed merchant, stands outside his shop in the Market Square in Worksop, Nottinghamshire. The Straw family lived above the shop until 1923 when they moved to No.7 Blyth Grove.

Potatoes 'à la Maître d'Hôtel'

'Boil the potatoes in water, then peel them. Put some butter in a saucepan, with chopped parsley, pepper and salt. Toss in the potatoes; add a squeeze of lemon-juice, and serve at once. 1 pound of potatoes will require three-quarters of an ounce of butter.'

From *Wholesome Cookery*, Mary Beale, 6th edition, 1895

Mary was the sister-in-law of James Beale of Standen in Sussex. In the preface the author says that the menus and recipes have been carried out in a small household, with one cook and without the assistance of a kitchen maid. She advises the mistress of the house to provide her 'plain cook' with a *Mrs Beeton* or an *Eliza Acton*, the author of *Modern Cookery*, published in 1845, and the first English cookery writer to sum up the ingredients and method at the end of a recipe in a few lines. Mrs Beeton copied the idea, placing them at the head of each recipe as we do today.

Potatoes were served at all meals of a fashionable household and it was *de rigueur* to serve them in a different way each time. This recipe shows the influence of hotels and restaurants on domestic cooking.

Iced Oranges.

Trifle.

Compote of Peaches.

Strawberries.

Dessert Biscuits.

Blancmange à la Vanille.

Salad.

Nougat Almond Cake.

Compote of Pears.

Macedoine of Fruits with Jelly.

Savoury Jelly à la Bellevue.

Iced Pudding.

Apples à la Parisienne.

Puddings from Mrs Beeton's *Book of Household Management*.

Claret Jelly

'1 small bottle claret
1 cup of red currant jelly
¼ lb or less sugar
1 lemon, juice and rind, 1 oz isinglass
or a little more in Summer.

Simmer until the isinglass is dissolved. Strain through muslin into a mould. Stand until it is thoroughly cold and turn out carefully into a glass or silver dish.'

From a recipe book dated 1888 which once belonged to Parke near Bovey Tracey in Devon.

A sparkling wine-, liqueur- or fruit-flavoured jelly set with isinglass (made from the bladders of fish) or the newly introduced gelatine was a popular sweet entremet at the end of a Victorian dinner. Sometimes a variety of fruits was set in layers of jelly to make 'Macedoines'. As iced puddings became more and more fashionable, jellies were frozen for a short time before being turned out and sent to the table.

Cabinet Pudding

'Spread the inside of a mould with butter; ornament the bottom and sides with pieces of preserved fruits. Fill the mould with alternate slices of sponge cake, ratafias, and maccaroons, and some more pieces of dried fruits, or small lumps of guava jelly or apricot marmalade. Made a custard with 7 eggs, 1 pint of milk, 6 ounces of sugar, and a little vanilla or grated lemon-peel; add 1 wine-glassful of brandy. Let it get cold, and pour it by degrees into the mould so as to penetrate every corner; then cover the mould and steam it an hour. Serve cold with custard over it, into which mix another wine glassful of brandy.'

From *Wholesome Cookery*, Mary Beale, 1895

Also known as Chancellor's Pudding, this decorative dessert cream used up stale sponge cake. It was on the dinner menu with Charlotte Russe on 19 December 1914 at Erddig, for 'a very gay Party notwithstanding poor Philip's gout'.

Cabinet Pudding with Jam Sauce

a little unsalted butter
2 oz (50 g) glacé cherries, halved
1 oz (25 g) crystallised angelica
4 sponge cakes or 12 sponge fingers
1 oz (25 g) ratafias
4 eggs
1 tablespoon (15 ml) caster sugar
1 teaspoon (5 ml) cornflour
¾ pt (450 ml) single cream or milk
grated rind of ½ lemon
1 tablespoon (15 ml) brandy
2 oz (50 g) currants
2 oz (50 g) sultanas

JAM SAUCE

3 tablespoons (45 ml) apricot, strawberry or raspberry jam
6 tablespoons (90 ml) cold water
1 teaspoon (5 ml) lemon juice

Grease a straight-sided charlotte mould or soufflé dish with unsalted butter and line the bottom with buttered greaseproof paper or foil. Decorate with the halved glacé cherries and the angelica cut into diamond shapes. Cut the sponge cakes into small squares and arrange over the candied fruit in the mould, with the ratafias crumbled into pieces on top.

Cream the eggs, sugar and cornflour together in a basin. Bring the cream and lemon rind almost to the boil very slowly, then strain over the egg mixture, stirring vigorously. Add the brandy and dried fruit, then pour carefully over the cake in the mould. Leave to soak for about 15 minutes; then cover tightly with foil and tie down with string. Steam gently for about 1 hour or until the custard is set and firm. Allow to stand for a few minutes before turning out very carefully on to a warm serving dish. Remove the greaseproof paper or foil from what is now the top of the pudding.

To make jam sauce, melt the jam in a saucepan with the water and lemon juice. Push through a sieve to make it smooth.

Serve the pudding hot with a little jam sauce poured around the base of the pudding and extra sauce served separately. Serves 6.

Claret Jelly

1 pt (600 ml) claret
rind and juice of 1 lemon
1 oz (25 g) powdered gelatine
3–4 oz (75–125 g) granulated sugar
black grapes to decorate

Place 4 tablespoons (60 ml) of the claret and the lemon juice in a small basin and stir in the gelatine. If you wish to serve your wine jelly in a bowl, 1 oz (25 g) gelatine will be sufficient, but if you wish to turn it out of a fancy mould, add an extra ½ oz (12 g) to make certain, but do check quantities on the packet, because different makes can vary in strength. Leave for 5 minutes until swollen and soft, then stir this into half the remaining claret in a saucepan. Add the sugar and lemon rind, then bring slowly almost, but not quite, to the boil, stirring all the time. Strain into a bowl and gently stir in the remaining claret. Pour into a melted mould, or into a pretty bowl or stemmed glasses and leave to set in a cool place. Serve slightly chilled, decorated with small bunches of black grapes which have been frosted with egg white and caster sugar and offer whipped cream and ratafias with the jelly. Serves 6.

After-dinner Savouries

'Angels on Horseback

Prepare very thin slices of bacon, roll them round one large or two small oysters, secure them with string and fry, then serve very hot on little rounds of fried bread.

Anchovy Olives

Prepare anchovy butter and fill Spanish olives with it. Set each olive on end on a little round of fried bread. The olives must be carefully stoned and hollow.

Sardine Savoury

On little square pieces of fried bread lay a little finely chopped salad. Moisten at the last moment with mayonnaise sauce. On this lay little thin slices of sardines.'

From a hand-written book of recipes entitled 'Extracts Memoranda' of about 1890 belonging to July Lucy Hoare of Stourhead House in Wiltshire.

It was fashionable in Victorian and Edwardian times to conclude the main part of dinner with a savoury, although Escoffier felt 'they had no place on a good menu'.

Felbrigge Sponge Cake

'½ lb sugar, ¼ lb of flour, 7 eggs leaving out half the whites, the rind of half a lemon chopped fine, whisk it well and bake an hour and 10 minutes.'

From a small booklet of recipes, hints and remedies in various handwritings at Felbrigg Hall in Norfolk. Most of the recipes are anonymous dated about 1881.

This recipe is typical of the kind of light sponge or savoy cake popularly served for afternoon tea or among the sweet entremets or desserts for a grand dinner or banquet. The new wire egg-whisks introduced by the 1850s made beating eggs much easier and the cake would have been baked in a fancy tin mould.

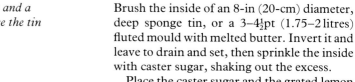

Felbrigg Sponge Cake

a little melted unsalted butter and a
    little caster sugar to prepare the tin
8 oz (225 g) caster sugar
finely grated rind ½ lemon
7 egg yolks
4 egg whites
4 oz (125 g) plain flour

Brush the inside of an 8-in (20-cm) diameter, deep sponge tin, or a 3–4½ pt (1.75–2 litres) fluted mould with melted butter. Invert it and leave to drain and set, then sprinkle the inside with caster sugar, shaking out the excess.

Place the caster sugar and the grated lemon rind in a large bowl with the egg yolks. Beat with an electric hand-whisk or by hand, until the mixture is thick and almost white. In a separate bowl, whisk the egg whites with a clean whisk until stiff but not dry. Sieve a little of the flour into the egg yolk mixture and fold in with a large metal spoon. Then fold in about half the egg whites, followed by about half the remaining flour mixture. Repeat, using all the ingredients, then spoon as gently as possible into the prepared tin or mould. Bake in a moderate oven (180°C, 350°F, gas mark 4) for 1–1¼ hours, or until the sponge feels firm and springy in the centre and has begun to shrink away slightly from the sides of the tin. Leave to cool in the tin for a few minutes, then turn out onto a wire rack to finish cooking. Sprinkle with caster sugar and eat as fresh as possible.

Kitchen still-life at Arlington Court, Devon.

III

Victorians regarded eating well almost a duty. Dr Kitchiner advised that the 'Stomach is the mainspring of our System – if it be not sufficiently wound up to warm the Heart and support the Circulation the whole business of Life will, in proportion, be ineffectively performed.'

This view continued unabated during Edward VII's reign. After racing, shooting and women, food was the King's greatest pleasure, earning him his nickname of Tum Tum. The King's day began with a breakfast of haddock, poached eggs, bacon, chicken and woodcock, prepared by his French chef, M. Menager; it ended after dinner with a plate of sandwiches, and sometimes even a quail or a cutlet. Members of his circle like Frank Green, the owner of Treasurer's House in York, enjoyed themselves with equal gusto. When asked by a royal visitor what was produced by the 'Green's Economiser', the machine that was the source of his wealth, he replied succinctly, 'Fox-hunting and champagne, Your Majesty!'

Entertaining, especially for the newly rich, upper middle-class host, was a necessary public relations exercise. For his wife and daughters it provided a unique opportunity to display their latest accomplishments. Diaries kept by Mrs John Ketton, wife of a self-made man who built up a prosperous business in cattle feedstuffs and purchased Felbrigg Hall in Norfolk from the Windhams, describe the daily happenings of country life between 1863 and 1870, when people seldom moved further from home than their horses could carry them. They met their few neighbours almost every week and enjoyed a modest range of social pleasures to the full. Summer brought cricket matches, dinner parties, croquet parties, and picnics on the cliffs. With autumn came 'the hateful shooting season' and riding parties. The hard winters brought long days of skating with great bonfires blazing at the lakeside, supper balls and yet more dinner and tea parties.

For the owners of large estates, weddings, christenings and comings of age were still occasions for great celebration to be shared with their tenants. After Emily Lucy's wedding at Charlecote on 21 October 1845, her mother, Mary Elizabeth, records in her memoirs: 'At three o'clock every cottage on the estate was regaled with beef, plum pudding and good ale in the new loft over the stables which holds about 300. At nine o'clock the tenantry, their wives and sons and daughters began to arrive for a ball. They danced in the large dinner room and supper was laid in the Great Hall.' A few years later, when Emily's brother Henry, who had inherited Charlecote in 1847, married Christina Cameron Campbell, Mary Elizabeth again describes the scene:

A booth 120 feet long was erected in the park at Charlecote, where dinner was laid for all the tenants who assembled at two o'clock to eat, drink and be merry. All the poor on the estate were feasted with as much as they could eat and drink. 600 lb weight of meat was consumed, 200 cwt of plum pudding, and upwards of 400 gallons of old ale, brewed at Charlecote, was drunk. There was a large tent for the wives and daughters of the tenants who met together to have tea and cake, and wine etc. All the women and village children had tea and plum cake, of which they cut 200 lb weight. Then followed all sorts of amusements and dancing till it grew dark when the revels were brought to a close by a grand display of fireworks.

A gouache by the Hon. Mrs Percy Wyndham, c.1865 showing the 1st Lord Leconfield breakfasting with Sir Reginald Graham in the Carved Room at Petworth, Sussex.

At the beginning of the 19th century, breakfast was taken between 9am and 11am, as in the previous century. But, in the country especially, it had become a more substantial meal of cold meats, game, grilled chops and steak, in addition to the chocolate, coffee or tea, toast, rolls and cakes of the earlier aristocratic breakfast. By the 1840s, as the pattern of 'going to the office' developed, in middle-class and well-to-do homes breakfast was eaten slightly earlier, from 8am onwards, and became less of a social meal. Disraeli, who retreated to Hughenden Manor almost every autumn when Parliament was in recess, seems to suggest that the virtues of the new breakfast should be credited to innkeepers rather than to housewives. In most people's minds, it has always had a rather masculine quality and was certainly more popular with the men of the household than the women. Accordingly, wives were advised in Mary Hooper's *Handbook for the Breakfast Table* of 1873, that 'men of business should leave their homes in the morning physically fortified against the fatigues of an anxious day.' Indeed, should they not be so fortified, they would eventually suffer 'a malady of incurable character'.

The journalist George Augustus Sala named some of the commonest middle-class breakfast dishes in an alleged consultation with a doctor about his liver:

> I used to eat a mutton-chop, or a rump-steak, or a good plateful from a cold joint, or a couple of eggs broiled on bacon, or a haddock, or a mackerel, or some pickled salmon, or some cold veal and ham pie or half a wild duck, or some devilled partridge, with plenty of bread and butter, or toast, or muffins and perhaps some anchovy sauce, or potted char, or preserved beef; the whole washed down by a couple of cups of tea or coffee.

In 1861, Mrs Beeton suggested any cold joint in the larder might be placed 'nicely garnished' on the sideboard beside the breakfast table, along with collared and potted meats or fish, cold game and poultry, veal and ham pies, game pies, cold ham and pressed tongue. These were to supplement a choice of dishes, which might include boiled or fried chicken or rabbit; steaks, chops, devilled turkey, kidneys, sausages, sheep's brains and tongues, sweetbreads, bacon, marrow toast, roast partridges, pigeons, woodcocks or quail.

The amount of meat served at breakfast depended on the wealth of the family. Large houses might have a choice of three cold dishes, such as a game pie, beef and ham, with perhaps kidneys, bacon and mutton cutlets as hot meats. For a family of moderate means, there might only be one meat dish, such as grilled bacon or broiled kidneys. If there were no guests present and for the less well-off, meat might appear on the breakfast table on only one or two days each week, in the form of rissoles or mince, made from left-over scraps, or the equally modest kidney or marrow toast. If fish was on offer, it was generally left over from dinner and served in the form of kedgeree, or dried or smoked, like kippers and haddock, or tinned. Mushrooms were popular.

Eggs, broiled, boiled, 'buttered' (scrambled with large amounts of butter – Soyer recommended two ounces per three eggs), or as omelettes, were thought more suitable for breakfast than any other dish. The popularity of boiled eggs encouraged a number of egg gadgets, like 'The Patent Signal Egg Boiler' to help boil them. The perennial problem of the perfectly timed egg was aggravated by the lack of grading of eggs at this time. Once boiled, 'The Lightning Egg Cutter' took the top off the egg.

Toast and marmalade followed the main courses, with fancy breads made fresh every morning by the kitchen maid, together with muffins, or crumb muffins made from stale white bread crumbs, oatcakes, crumpets, scones or bannocks.

All this food was washed down with coffee, chocolate or tea. Victorian mothers favoured chocolate or cocoa as a breakfast beverage, because it was thought to be more nourishing. Tea, which normally had a bad reputation, was generally felt to become more wholesome and less drug-like when taken with large quantities of bread and butter, or with toast and boiled eggs.

When the footman sounded the gong for breakfast, the entire family and all the staff assembled punctually in either the dining-room, or the breakfast or morning room if the house, like Lanhydrock, Penrhyn, Wightwick and Cragside, was large enough. Often the morning or breakfast room was next to the dining-room as at Penrhyn and Wightwick and was used for family dinners as well. Breakfast began with ten minutes of prayer conducted by the master of the house. The table had already been laid by the butler and footman, and the housekeeper had made sure that preserves, butter and bread were in place and that cold meats were on the sideboard.

After prayers, the servants were dismissed to get on with their work, and the family sat at table. The butler then carried in the kettle or urn, while the footman brought the tray of hot dishes which were kept warm by the fire in winter, or in one of the newly invented 'Universal' heaters. The butler enquired what each person wanted to eat, the footman handed it to the butler and he then served it. Attractive silver or silver-plated egg-cups, in stands complete with attached spoons, were very much the mode. Sometimes, to keep the eggs hot, they were wrapped in a napkin and the eggcups placed instead by people's plates. The mistress of the house served cups of tea if required and her eldest daughter, or the lady sitting on her right, served the coffee. Toast was

A postcard by L. C. Macbean featuring breakfast in the electric home, c.1915. Electric luxury items began to be produced by the Westinghouse Electric Corporation in America about 1911, with power taken from electric lighting mains.

Nicholas Condy's painting of workers on the Edgcumbe estates, *c*.1840. Agricultural workers, particularly in the early years of Victoria's reign, existed on a scanty and monotonous diet of bread, root vegetables, cabbage and salt pork or bacon. The estate workers depicted here were luckier, they have fresh fish and beer or wine to drink rather than weak tea.

brought in later; buttered toast was placed on a hot-water plate and dry toast in a rack. Rolls and muffins were kept warm on a trivet before the fire. When everyone present had been served, the servants withdrew.

In contrast to all this plenty, breakfast for those who were not well-off was a very simple meal. Porridge, which was given to children of all classes for health reasons, fulfilled a real need for the poor. This was eaten with cream, whole milk, or skimmed milk, and sugar, treacle or salt. Breakfast for the 90 children who lived in the Apprentice House at Quarry Bank Mill was porridge made with half milk and half water, served to them at the mill, where they started work at 6am.

Luncheon was the most informal of all Victorian meals and labelled 'an inconsequent meal' by Victorian gourmets. Mrs Beeton, however, felt it to be 'fully installed amongst our list of meals', although she continues '[it] should not be indulged in unless the hours between the breakfast and the dinner are many, or unless the former meal has been very slight.' For most of the population including children, domestic servants and agricultural labourers, their midday meal was the main one of the day, followed by a high tea or supper in the early evening. If they did not have midday dinner, labourers and factory workers took bread and cheese, bread and boiled bacon or a piece of pie to work, or bought a snack from the street food-stalls, while their wives and children were more likely to have only plain bread. Lunch for the children at Quarry Bank Mill was eaten in the schoolroom of the Apprentice House at midday and was again porridge, perhaps flavoured with an onion and a few vegetables, to fill them up and give them strength for the afternoon's work. Middle-class wives dutifully ate up left-overs from the dinner the night before, or from breakfast, while those husbands not able to travel home for lunch, patronised eating-houses, taverns and chop-houses. Simpson's in the Strand in London, for example, provided a plate of roast beef, pork or mutton with potatoes, a pie or pudding, bread, ale or porter, all for 1s, including 1d for the water. Not all men approved of the interruption to their day, and either ignored luncheon altogether, or just took a glass of wine and a biscuit in their offices.

Mrs Beeton has little to say about the luncheon menu, except that: 'The remains of cold joints, nicely garnished, a sweet, or a little hashed meat, poultry or game are the few articles placed on the table ... with bread and cheese, biscuits, butter, etc. If a substantial meal is desired, rump-steaks or mutton chops may be served, as also veal cutlets, kidneys or any dish of that kind .... In the summer, a few dishes of fresh fruit should be added ..., or instead of this a compote of fruit or fruit tart, or pudding.' All this was to be washed down with ale, porter and light wines; tea and coffee were never served at luncheon until the 1870s. Also, Lord Curzon of Kedleston advised 'No gentleman has soup at luncheon.'

Sometimes the mistress of the house took lunch with the children in the nursery. The food would be carried up on a tray by the nursery footman or, when the children were considered old enough, they joined the dining-room table at 1pm. They were served with a joint of meat, essential for its iron content, and vegetables, followed by milk puddings, boiled or baked suet puddings and fruit pies. To finish off came a 'luncheon cake' made with dried fruit, peel, nuts and caraway seeds.

Lunch as an occasion for entertaining was first introduced in the 1850s and became a feminine pastime, especially amongst ladies of leisure. It was a wonderful opportunity to show a considerable amount of hospitality at little expense to those whom you could not invite to dinner. Dishes would be dainty rather than filling and as visiting ladies ate luncheon without removing their bonnets or jackets, it was important that food was easy to handle. The meal was eaten in the dining-room with the table laid simply – a white cloth or just table mats, small cruets dotted about, or a large cruet and a pickle stand in the centre, and small vases of flowers. A water jug, or water decanter, and tumblers were placed at each corner of the table with two tablespoons, either crossed or side by side. Each place setting was laid with a large and small fork and knife, two plates – one for meat, one for cheese or butter – a dessertspoon, an ale or porter glass and a folded napkin, with a slice of bread placed in it.

Towards the end of the Victorian period, the style of the table depended on the fashionability of the hostess. For the ultra-fashionable, the only dishes on the table would be fruit. All food dishes would be on a side-table and served by the butler when the guests were seated. At less modish houses, joints of meat would be on the sideboard, cold sweets such as jellies, creams and pastry arranged down the centre of the table and hot and cold entrées placed by the butler before the host, if he was present, and hostess to serve. After the meal, the fashionable Victorian luncheon guests withdrew to the drawing-room, stayed for not longer than 20 minutes, then asked for their carriages to be summoned and took their leave.

At this time, it became fashionable to celebrate special occasions by giving a luncheon. On 16 January 1894 the opening of the Higher Grade School in Wolverhampton was celebrated with a luncheon at nearby Wightwick Manor, given by the owner Theodore Mander, who had made his fortune as a partner in a paint and varnish manufacturing company. Mander was a high-minded and paternalistic squire. His benefactions included a rest home for retired governesses and a village hall, and regular Sunday cricket matches were held between his firm and the village followed by supper at the Manor. Luncheon was served in the new dining-room, part of a wing added to the house in 1893 to provide extra accommodation for guests attending the cricket weeks that Mander wanted to organise. Food for the luncheon would probably have been brought in by outside caterers from Wolverhampton; the menu was as follows:

Consommé

Saumon en Mayonnaise

Soufflés de Homard à l'Adeline

Petites bouchées à la Montglas

Dindonneau froid à la Grande Duchesse

Soufflé à la Marguérite

Aloyau de boeuf rôti

Cotelettes de mouton en aspic

Galantine de volaille

Pâté de Gibier

Jambon Glacé, Langues

Dindon Rôti

Pièce de boeuf braisée à la Napolitaine

Faisans, Perdreaux

Gâteau d'Abricots

Gelée à la Russe, Gelée à la Française

Charlotte à l'Alexandra

Pommes à la Princesse Maud

Créme à la Munich

Fruits

The fashion for country-house parties during autumn and winter led to the 'shooting luncheon' taken at midday. The shots, firing the guns, their ladies, the gun-loaders and the beaters all had to be catered for. If the weather was fine the meal was eaten outside at trestle tables resplendent with white cloths; otherwise a table would be laid in the gamekeeper's cottage. Casseroles, stews, meat puddings, game pies and hams were served to the gentry by the butler and footman, with suet puddings, plum puddings, apple pies and dumplings to follow. For drinks, there would be wine, beer and cider, and sloe gin and cherry brandy to accompany the plum cake and cheese. The loaders preferred big hot joints of meat and jacket potatoes, and for the beaters bread and cheese, both served with beer.

The usual hour for luncheon in Edwardian times was 1.30 to 2pm, but as breakfast became lighter, the time was brought forward to 1pm. Lunch could be a very simple meal: Edwin Lutyens' ideal was 'cold meats, a salad, quaintly dressed in coloured bowl,

The table laid out for the wedding breakfast following the marriage of William Straw to Florence in the 1880s in Worksop, Nottinghamshire.

and refreshing coffee brewed by host and hostess – Mocha fresh ground, cream and golden candy – placed upon its own green linen cloth'.

Even if lunch was not always as simple as this, it was much less complicated than the Edwardian dinner. Soup and fish were generally omitted, and dishes were plainer, though often substantial. In the 1900s, Francis, a young nephew of Sir Charles and Lady Acland, found the atmosphere at Killerton stifling with its huge meals. Macaroni cheese followed by venison pie and apple tart with Devonshire cream was a typical luncheon.

The tables were laid more simply than at dinner, with either a tablecloth or luncheon mats. Sometimes an open-work or lace cloth was thrown over a coloured slip, which harmonised with the other decorations. Table napkins were either folded flat and placed on the side-plate, or in some simple shape such as 'Mitre', 'Lunch' or 'Slipper'.

For more modest Edwardian households, like the Straws of Worksop, lunch was the main meal of the day. Mr Straw would have shut up shop and come upstairs to eat a meal of soup, followed by a stew (see recipe on p.309) or meat-pie with vegetables, a simple pudding or a fruit pie, and a cup of tea.

By the 1840s, when the dinner hour had advanced to 7.30pm or 8pm, the gap between it and lunch became uncomfortably long. Ladies began to take a meal of tea and cakes in the afternoon, at first surreptitiously in their boudoirs or bedrooms, led it is said by Anna, Duchess of Bedford, and then openly in the drawing-room. By 1850 tea had become customary in all fashionable houses. 'There are few hours in life more agreeable than the hour dedicated to the ceremony known as afternoon tea,' wrote Henry James in *Portrait of a Lady*; although most men thought 'Five o'Clock Teas', or 'At Homes', 'a mild form of dissipation'. Ladies, however, enjoyed them immensely and such was their desire not to miss out on any five o'clock events that, according to *Manners and Tone of Good Society*, 1890, written by 'A Member of the Aristocracy', 'even the most pressed lady socialist looked in for a quarter of an hour or so,' between 4.15pm and 5.30pm.

Hostesses tried to outdo each other by a display of their finest bone-china tea-services, pretty table linen and cake stands, with an array of small cakes, biscuits and at least one large cake, either fruit, caraway seed or madeira, as well as hot teacakes and thin sandwiches, laid out in the drawing-room by the fire. Grand 'five o'clock teas' were served in the dining-room and ladies had to be escorted on a gentleman's right arm from the drawing-room where they had assembled to chat, sing and play musical instruments. As the usual ratio of men to women was about five to thirty, the male escorts could be busy people! The main sideboard in the dining-room was spread with a delightful choice of cakes, thin bread and butter, fancy biscuits, ices, fruits and dainty ham, tongue, beef and cucumber sandwiches. Tea and coffee were served from big silver urns and wine, claret, champagne-cups and sherry might also be offered. The cook, dressed in her best, dispensed the ice-creams and water ices, dropping them into a paper cup placed on a small ice plate, together with a small spoon. Ladies had to remove their gloves to eat ices, fruit and sandwiches, but their hats remained firmly on their heads.

An Edwardian afternoon tea in large houses was a formal affair with wooden cake-stands, hot dishes and small trays carried round by the butler or footmen who remained in attendance throughout the meal. The fashionable hour was now 5pm or even later. In *Down the Kitchen Sink*, 1975, Beverley Nichols recalled the scene at tea-time during

one of the weekend parties given by the society hostess, the Hon. Mrs Ronald Greville at her country house, Polesden Lacey in Surrey:

> Tea is at 5 o'clock . . . and not 5 minutes past . . . which means that the Spanish ambassador, who has gone for a walk down the yew avenue hastily retraces his steps, and that the Chancellor of the Exchequer . . . hurries down the great staircase, and the various gentlemen rise from their chaises-longues . . . and join the procession to the tea-room. The tea-pots, the cream-jugs, the milk-pots and the sugar basins are of Queen Anne silver; the tea-service is Meissen; and the doyleys, heavily monogrammed, are of Chantilly lace.

By this time afternoon tea was being adopted by lower and middle-class homes. A 'family' or high tea could consist of crusty bread and butter, muffins and crumpets, cheese, potted spreads of meat and fish and various cakes. A small tea was likely to consist of thin bread and butter, jam or honey, and cake in the drawing-room. Middle-class ladies might also appear at nursery tea, the last meal of the day for children. It was carried up by the footman on a tray at 4pm, and usually consisted of bread and butter and jam and a sponge cake. Tea was eaten by the servants in the kitchen at 5pm. As more women took work in offices, tea shops were introduced where they could meet and not be classed as prostitutes. The first were the ABC (Aerated Bread Company) shops which opened around 1880, to be followed by those run by Express Dairy Co., and Lyons. The last became a national institution overnight with 250 Corner Houses staffed by uniformed waitresses called 'nippies'.

In the early days of Victoria's reign, dinner for the middle and lower classes was taken in the early evening anytime between 5pm and 7pm. In 1855 Dickens asked Wilkie Collins to dine with him at his normal hour of 5.30pm, yet, ten years later, a similar invitation to Browning begs him to be punctual at 6.30pm. Professional families tended to dine as soon as work was over. In upper-class circles, where lateness had long been fashionable, dinner was served between 7.30pm and 9pm. But as the century progressed, the fashionable hour for dining for the middle-classes, particularly in towns,

Above left: The tea-table as advocated by Mrs Beeton. Victorian hostesses sought to outdo each other by a display of their finest bone china tea services, pretty table linen and cake stands. Mrs Beeton recommended the tea table be decorated with a few fresh flowers.

Above: The central hall at Wallington, Northumberland, created in the 1850s, was used by the Trevelyans for afternoon tea. This tea party was photographed in 1899.

also moved later, to 8–8.30pm, and as late as 9–10pm if entertaining. Amongst the causes were longer journeys home from the office to the suburbs and long office hours followed by visits to gentlemen's club for businessmen, the lengthening of parliamentary sittings for politicians, and the invention of gaslighting which extended the day.

Dinner parties ranked 'first amongst all entertainments, ... having more social significance and being more appreciated by society, than any other form ...' according to *Manners and Tone of Good Society*. A society hostess gave a dinner party once or perhaps twice a week; a middle-class family probably once a month, at considerable cost. It was a wonderful opportunity to show off the material possessions of the host: the solid furniture, the ornate silver tableware, the beautiful china; and to demonstrate his good taste in the selection of expensive wines and food dressed according to fashionable *haute cuisine*. Giving dinner parties was a direct route to obtaining a 'footing in society' and there was no surer or better passport than having a reputation for giving 'good dinners', which involved not only the food, but observing the minutest details of etiquette towards one's guests. The etiquette began with the invitations which for a large dinner party had to be ornate, embossed printed cards sent out within 21 days of the date of the dinner, or certainly within 14 days. For small dinner parties, 10 days' notice, or even less was sufficient and written notes would take the place of printed cards. They were all issued in the names of both host and hostess unlike invitations to all other social gatherings, which were in the name of the hostess only. Acceptances or refusals were expected within a day or two, to give the hostess time to find 'an eligible substitute', if necessary. Once accepted, there was no turning back, save for a death.

Guests were expected to arrive in full evening dress (white ties and white gloves for the men, low-cut long dresses and gloves for the ladies), within fifteen minutes of the appointed hour. If 8pm was the hour stated on the card, the intended dinner hour would be 8.15pm, and although the host would wait perhaps half an hour for a lady if necessary, he would not extend the same courtesy to a gentleman, unless that gentleman was of high rank and a particularly desirable guest. On arrival, guests would leave their cloaks and hats with a servant in the hall; gentlemen also left their gloves, but ladies did not remove theirs until seated at dinner. They were then led upstairs to the drawing-room by the butler where they were announced. According to *Manners and Tone of Good Society* it was considered 'very vulgar' for a lady and gentleman, on being announced, to enter the drawing-room 'arm-in-arm, or side by side', especially the former: the lady, or ladies, would enter the room in advance of the gentleman. Formal greetings were offered by the host and hostess; the ladies might at once seat themselves, while the gentlemen would stand about the room in groups for the ordeal of the '*mauvais quart d'heure*' without any comforting cigarettes or aperitifs to break the ice. In Edwardian times it became fashionable to have a drink before dinner to whet the appetite and stimulate the gastric juices. *Manner and Tone of Good Society* advised the hostess at small dinner-parties to introduce the persons of highest rank to each other, but not at large parties. People who were acquainted would acknowledge each other with a nod, a smile or a bow, but conversation was stiff and formal, until the welcome announcement of dinner by the butler, who would throw open the drawing-room door, saying 'in a loud and distinct voice, "dinner is served"'.

Then began the formal procession, often down the stairs, into dinner. Precedence was as important as ever, so it was invariably the host, escorting the lady of highest rank on his right arm, who led the way, followed by the lady second in rank with a gentleman second in rank and so on. The gentleman of highest rank would follow last with the hostess. A host and hostess would be most careful to invite an equal number of ladies and gentlemen and the host quietly informed each gentleman, shortly after his arrival, which lady he was to take into or 'hand into' dinner and he had no choice in the matter.

Formal dinners were always served in the dining-room, still a solid, masculine and rather sombre room in Victorian times, while the drawing-room remained essentially feminine. The dining-room at Cragside is a wonderful example of architect Norman Shaw's 'Old English' style, which was so popular in the late 19th century. The room is dominated by a huge stone, mock-medieval inglenook fireplace symbolising the hospitality and good cheer of the 'olden tymes'. The cosiness of hearth and home was very important to Lord Armstrong, who chose to have his portrait painted sitting on one of the oak settles in the inglenook with his dogs underneath the massive stone lintel with its suitably quaint North Country proverb 'East or West Hame's Best'.

Dining-tables, large and heavy, usually of walnut, mahogany or rosewood, with sturdy central pillars and ornate claw feet, were now left standing permanently in the centre of the room with the chairs arranged around. They had to be large for entertaining and for family meals, so were mostly capable of expanding. Cragside has an unusual expanding 'Capstan' dining-table, whose ingenuity must have appealed to Lord Armstrong, the engineer. Around it are 21 green leather dining-chairs. Across one end of the room is a built-in buffet or sideboard, designed by Shaw, who kept a close hand over the contents as well as the fittings of the room. The shelves of the sideboard were designed to display the family's blue and white Oriental porcelain, so fashionable in the 1870s, and the family plate on special occasions. Food was served from the sideboard itself and from additional serving tables, bought in from the kitchen at Cragside through a door to the left of the sideboard.

Cragside had to be extended considerably when the Armstrongs decided to make it their permanent home. They needed to entertain large numbers of guests attending state visits by potential purchasers of arms from the Tyneside works, among them the King of Siam, the Shah of Persia and the Crown Prince of Afghanistan, or the frequent weekend house parties. Shaw's last and grandest addition was the drawing-room, begun in 1883 and completed just before the visit of the Prince and Princess of Wales in August 1884. The position of the room provided a long processional route to the dining-room guaranteed to impress guests. The electric 'dressing gongs' in the two floors of bedrooms above the dining-room must also have impressed the house guests; they were operated from the butler's pantry to warn of approaching meal-times.

The Douglas-Pennants also entertained a great deal at Penrhyn Castle, where dinner was served in the large dining-room with the full complement of footmen in black and gold striped waistcoats, tail-coats and gloves. When only the family was in residence, meals would be taken in the smaller breakfast room next door. Guests processed from the drawing-room on the first floor with its dazzling silk hangings, curtains and upholstery, down the impressive grand staircase across the grand hall and into the sumptuous dining-room. The ceiling is decorated with ornate moulded plasterwork of Norman-style motifs and plants and flowers of West Indian origin, as the Pennant family made their first fortune in the Jamaican sugar trade. As it was a very long way from the dining-room to the 'necessary offices', at one end of the elaborately carved dado a secret cupboard was fitted to hold chamberpots for use by the gentlemen after the ladies had withdrawn to the drawing-room and the butler had escaped to his pantry.

The dining-room at Charlecote Park, Warwickshire. Victorian dining-rooms were primarily the gentlemen's territory, so their decoration was emphatically masculine with panelling, heavy plaster ceilings and furniture.

1st Lord Armstrong (1810–1900) of Cragside, Northumberland, a portrait by Henry Emmerson. The cosiness of hearth and home was very important to William Armstrong, who chose to have his portrait painted in the inglenook of the dining-room, beside the massive stone fireplace with its quaint North Country proverb, 'East or West Hame's Best'.

The large central oak-veneered table with its 20 ebony chairs dates from the 1830s, and there are four elaborately carved, oak buffets for displaying porcelain and serving food.

Double doors lead into the dining-room at Lanhydrock, rebuilt by Lord Clifden after the disastrous fire of 1881. The plaster ceiling and oak overmantel are decorated with designs of grapes and vine leaves, which are echoed above the carved panelling in the blue and gilt wallpaper, a modern reproduction from the original blocks of William Morris's 'Sunflower' design. Lord Clifden installed a central-heating system and an electric-lighting plant when he rebuilt the house, so the new dining-room was warm and comfortable; the long low radiators fit inconspicuously below the windows and

The dining-room at Wightwick Manor, West Midlands faces east, providing sunlight at breakfast but keeping it cool for the rest of the day. Most important of all, it is as far away as possible from the kitchen and 'obnoxious kitchen odours'. Dishes were carried to the serving-room and china pantry behind the hatch, always screened during meals.

opposite them is a fine steel grate. Lord Clifden, MP for East Cornwall, tended to concentrate his formal entertaining in his London house in South Audley Street during the 'Season', while at Lanhydrock he lived a quiet family life with his wife and nine children, and there must have been many happy informal dinner parties in this room.

On reaching the dining-room, the host would remain standing in his place at the bottom of the table until the guests had taken their seats, motioning the various couples to the places he wished them to occupy at the table: the custom of place names was never followed in good society. The ladies always sat at the right hand of the gentleman who had escorted them, the hostess at the top of the table with her gentleman escort at her left hand.

The rules about how a genteel dining-table should look were completely changed during Victoria's reign. 'Fashions are continually changing even at the best tables; and what is considered the height of good taste one year, is declared vulgar the next' complained Charles William Day in *Etiquette and the Wages of Society*. At the beginning of the period, service was still *à la française* – basically, as it had been since the Middle Ages, with a large number of substantial dishes placed on the table at the same time, in a sequence of two main courses consisting of a mixture of roasts, game, poultry and sweets, preceded by soup and fish and followed by dessert. Taking pride of place in the centre of the early Victorian table was a grand food dish, a plateau (a silver or glass oblong tray on small feet), or an ornate, massive épergne (a tall, silver or silver-gilt ornament with branches) holding a variety of pickles and sauces or sweetmeats. The dishes of food were arranged around these ornaments.

By the 1860s, however, a new style of service had become the fashion which was to revolutionise the art of dining. The custom in Russian society, introduced to Paris by the Russian ambassador in 1810, was to have the table laid with complete place-settings, to have all the courses handed round in silver dishes by a retinue of servants, and not to put dishes on the table for people to serve themselves. All the dishes on their arrival from the kitchen were placed on a massive mahogany sideboard or side-table, from where they were served by the butler and footmen. The old system had made it convenient to have a servant for every guest, whereas meals *à la russe* could be served by one person to every three or even four guests. Nevertheless *service à la russe* took longer to become fashionable in middle-class homes because of the additional tableware required. Most cookery writers sat on the fence by giving menus for both methods of service, but by the end of the century, *à la russe* had won the day.

Guests were no longer greeted, on entering the dining-room, by a table covered with an impressive array of different dishes. Now they encountered a profusion of cutlery and a veritable jungle of palms, ferns, flowers and fruit, tastefully arranged in a new range of glass and china vases, épergnes and tazze (stemmed shallow bowls, or plates, like cake stands). The edible centrepiece was replaced by a creation of china, glass or metal for holding flowers or candles, or both. The first models of these new table centres were on view at the Great Exhibition of 1851, described in *Cassell's Household Guide* as 'Pyramids of exquisitely chased crystal-light, airy, sparkling and fragrant with blossom.'

Fine porcelain centres were often made to match the dessert service. At intervals along the table could be placed small glass or china baskets filled with flowers or fruit for dessert. They were named Alexandra or Denmark baskets, in honour of the Princess of Wales who used them when entertaining at Marlborough House.

Flower arranging for the table became the subject of books: probably one of the first was *Flowers And How to Arrange Them* by Miss Maling, published in 1862, who declared: 'How important the arrangement of what Florists call "Cut Flowers" has become since the universal adoption of the "dîner russe", which requires so very many flowers.' Mrs Beeton recommended that 'In decorating a table, whether for luncheon, dessert, or supper, a vase or two of flowers should never be forgotten,' and that 'The table for a dinner à la Russe should be laid with flowers and plants in fancy flower-pots down the middle.'

Lamps or silver candelabra with wax candles were used for lighting the dinner table, often with coloured shades to 'produce a pretty effect', according to the author of *Manners and Tone of Good Society*. The shades would also prevent the guests being incommoded, 'by too close a proximity to the glare, occasioned by some dozens of candles, or by brilliant lamps.' She recommended that 'Wax candles should be lighted 10 or 15 minutes before the dinner is announced, that the lights may be steady and equal before the guests appear in the dining-room.'

The table was covered, 'without a wrinkle,' with a large white damask cloth reaching the floor by the footmen, and two slips or 'accident cloths' of the same damask were laid at the bottom and top of the table, which could be 'drawn away' after the first course to reveal the clean cloth underneath. In early Victorian times, the 'great cloth' was still removed before the dessert to show the beautifully polished table underneath; its removal requiring 'a deal of care and dexterity, especially where there were some eighteen to twenty guests', explains Eleanor Ormerod, the noted entomologist, in her autobiography. 'The operation was performed thus . . . . The great heavy central épergne had to be lifted a little way up by a strong manservant or two, while the cloth was slipped from beneath it, and the cloth travelled down the table till it came into the hands of the butler, who gathered it up.' With the influence of service *à la russe*, the tablecloth was retained throughout the meal and only the two accident cloths were removed before dessert. Alternatively, two large cloths could be laid and the upper one removed before dessert. The footmen used crumb-brushes in between courses to remove any debris. It was considered extremely vulgar to use table-mats, but a thick green baize table-cover could be placed beneath the cloth to protect the table.

The Edwardian dinner table was usually still covered with a white damask cloth, although owners of polished oak or mahogany tables sometimes preferred to replace it with small asbestos mats, covered by dainty lace doyleys for each place setting and beneath the various dishes to protect the tables from heat. Sometimes linen slips were laid along the sides of the table where the diners sat, again to protect the polished surface. When using a table-cloth, the 'silence cloth' was laid first: an old cloth or piece of serge or felt deadened sound, protected the surface of the table and improved the appearance of the cloth. To keep this silence cloth in place, it was lightly tacked round the under surface of the table, or drawn up beneath the edges of the table with a running string. The top cloth had to be large enough to hang down half a yard all round, and was either plain or embellished with lace insertions and borders, and embroidered with monograms. Lace table-cloths, placed over an under-slip that harmonised with the colour of the floral decorations, were sometimes used.

The Victorian table-napkin, a 28–30 inch square of starched, crisply ironed linen damask, was folded into elaborate forms for dinner parties. Mrs Beeton recommended that an inch thick slice of bread or a dinner-roll should be placed in those forms that

The table set for dinner at Castle Drogo, Devon. The Edwardian dinner table was far less elaborate than its Victorian predecessor. Tablecloths could be 'electrified', as at Castle Drogo, so that electric candelabra placed anywhere on the table might be illuminated. The leather screen hid the serving tables and the door to the kitchen.

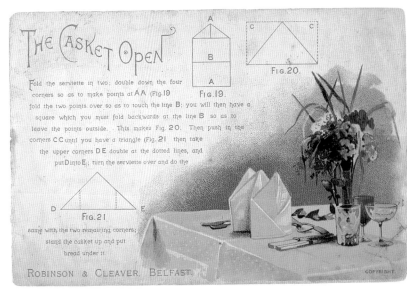

Above: A linen press was kept either outside the dining-room, as at Castle Drogo, or in the butler's pantry, to ensure that table linen was immaculate.

Above right: The Victorian table-napkin or serviette (the fashionable name towards the end of the century) was folded into elaborate forms for dinner parties.

were suitable, such as the 'Rose', 'Mitre', 'Neapolitan' and 'Star', and wherever possible a flower, or small posy of flowers, should also be slipped in.

The folded napkin was set beside each place setting or inserted in a wine glass or tumbler if it took the form of the 'Fan' or 'Flirt'. From the 1880s it was put in the centre of the place setting, to be unfolded by the diner and laid across his or her knee to make room for the soup-plate. *Manners and Tone of Good Society* warns that 'If a lady were aware that she would be some time occupied in removing her gloves, she would make room for the soup-plate before taking them off, otherwise the servant would be at her elbow offering her soup, before she had made room for the soup-plate by removing the serviette.'

Instead of cutlery being brought to the dinner as necessary, the Victorians dictated that it was now laid out on the table at each place-setting before the meal began. Two large knives, a silver knife for fish, and a tablespoon for soup were placed on the right of a place setting, while three large forks and a silver fork for fish were on the left. Dessertspoons for fruit-tarts and custards and small forks for other puddings were placed in front of the guest on an empty plate before the sweet entremets were handed round. Cutlery grew more and more elaborate as the century progressed, and wealthy households purchased large sets of silver cutlery for entertaining. The development in mid-century of electro-plated nickel silver (EPNS) cutlery, providing an alternative to the labour-intensive steel for more modest homes, helped to standardise the shapes particularly of the knife-blades and the forks.

By 1850 dining-table manners had become so circumscribed and there were so many constantly changing rules about what cutlery to use when eating various dishes that it must often have been difficult to keep up with fashion. By mid-century, fish should be eaten with just a fork and a crust of bread, but 30 years later *Manners and Tone of Good Society* regarded this as 'an unheard-of way in polite society and it should be eaten with a silver fish knife and fork. All made dishes should be eaten with a fork only and so should jellies, blancmanges and iced puddings, while a knife and fork should be used for eating asparagus and salad.' It was extremely vulgar to use your knife for conveying peas to the mouth; indeed, putting the knife into the mouth at any time during dinner 'would be an unpardonable offence against good breeding'. Also, 'the mouth should not be kept open in expectation of the well-laden fork's arrival,' but should be opened only 'at the moment when it has reached the lips'. Fingers should no longer touch any type of food, except small fruit like grapes and strawberries. Even cheese had to be cut into 'small morsels' and conveyed to the mouth on small pieces of bread.

Menus or dinner cards were warmly approved of at large dinner-parties served *à la russe*, allowing guests to pace themselves through the meal. Unless an establishment was very large, the mistress of the house usually wrote out the menu, preferably in French. This continued to be the custom at Lanhydrock right up to 1969 when the last Robartes left the house, where the daily menu books provide a mine of information. Menus would be placed in porcelain holders and examples of these survive at Erddig.

Different wines now called for different types of glasses. At the beginning of the Victorian period, glasses were still placed on the sideboard until called for, and washed as required, but by the middle of the century they were arranged on the table for the first time, to the right of each place setting. Three wine glasses were provided for each guest at dinner as well as a water-bottle and tumbler. Women were not expected to take drink seriously and many Victorian ladies mixed water with their sherry and claret and drank from a tumbler. With the lifting of the glass tax in 1845, cut glass became the rage. As a result, later Victorian glass was immensely heavy, with deeply cut decoration.

A variety of wines was now served with dinner but not appreciated by everyone: Francatelli was of the opinion that 'the palate is confused and made indiscriminating by a greater number'. He advised that decanted 'genuine old Madeira, or East India Sherry, or Amontillado, prove welcome stomachics after soup of any kind.' Decanted hock and chablis were served only with oysters before the soup, or with the fish afterwards. Champagne, carried round by the butler with a white napkin around the neck of the bottle, was drunk immediately after the first entrée had been served, and continued to be offered three or four times during the remainder of dinner until dessert. Since a lady might not ask for wine herself – at least until the middle of the century – the gentlemen had to make sure that their companions were served with the wine they preferred, both during and after dinner and call for the same wine themselves. When the glasses were brought, it was considered polite for the gentleman to bow to his companion and drink with her. It was not done, either, to gulp down a glass of wine. Even gentlemen drank slowly of the different wines served with each course, until the ladies left the room and they could settle to their port. Even then, they were expected to appear in the drawing-room quite soon after the ladies' coffee-tray had been removed, as the custom of separation was already being vigorously resented by women.

A dinner served *à la française* was divided into three courses plus dessert, followed by a drinking interval for the men, and coffee. The first course consisted of soup and/or fish – always both for parties of six or more. Sometimes oysters were served as an appetiser before the soup. The second course was made up solely of meat dishes, except in less sophisticated circles when the English custom of serving green vegetables with the meat was retained. These meat dishes were divided into 'removes', or '*relevés*', which were placed at the ends of the table where they 'removed' the soup and fish, and 'entrées' or side-dishes. The removes were the larger, plainer items such as roasts, and the entrées the smaller more complicated dishes such as fricassées, rissoles, patties and ragoûts, which were supposed to show, according to Mrs Marshall, a renowned cookery

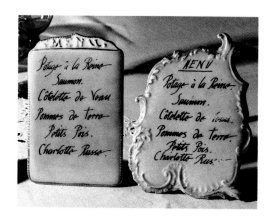

Porcelain menus from Wightwick Manor, West Midlands. Menus, preferably in French, were used at large dinner parties served *à la russe*, allowing guests to pace themselves through the meal.

Above: 'A State Party' by Richard Doyle, from *Birds Eye View of Society*, 1864. At a state banquet there would be at least one servant per guest for service *à la française*, where guests helped themselves to dishes close by, but had to rely on footmen to bring other dishes and wine, and to change plates and cutlery. The host was expected to carve, sometimes with great difficulty when the table was crammed with food and ornaments.

Right: Table setting *à la française* by Mrs Beeton. When guests entered the room, they were still greeted by a table covered with an impressive array of dishes for the first course. The soup tureen and plates stand at one end of the table, the fish at the other, a mixture of dishes in between. There is a profusion of cutlery, glasses and cruet stands.

writer and owner of a famous cookery school, 'the skill of the cook or the taste of the dinner giver, but more often were 'very abortive attempts at Continental cooking'.

The third course consisted of items classed as delicacies, which included game, poultry or shellfish, and if the French custom was followed, vegetables, as well as a savoury and the puddings and sweets. Ices, fruit, fancy biscuits, light cakes, bonbons and other confectionery formed dessert. Variety in dishes was scaled roughly according to numbers of guests: the minimum for six was two or three for the first course and four or five for both the second and third; for twelve, it was usual to provide three to four for the first course, six to eight for the second, and eight to ten for the third, usually with a further eight to a dozen for dessert. A menu *à la française* for six compiled by Mrs Beeton reads as follows:

DINNER FOR 6 PERSONS (October)

FIRST COURSE

Mock-turtle Soup
Brill and Lobster Sauce. Fried Whitings

ENTRÉES

Fowl à la Béchamel. Oyster Patties

SECOND COURSE

Roast sucking-Pig. Stewed Rump of Beef à la Jardinière.
Vegetables

THIRD COURSE

Grouse.

Charlotte aux Pommes. Coffee Cream. Sweet Omelet.
Apricot Tart. Iced Pudding

DESSERT

Visually, service *à la française* was more exciting: diners could see the elaborately decorated dishes on offer before deciding which to choose, but its chief disadvantage was that the food was cold by the time it came to be eaten. Plates were heated up and dishes were covered with huge silver dish covers for their long journey from the kitchen to the dining-room, but even if they arrived on the table hot, carving and serving precedence made sure that they seldom remained so. The soups and fish were served by the host and hostess; then it was the host, helped by the most important male guest, who had to grapple with the roasts. Soyer, after observing the Reform Club members, was particularly sympathetic towards the inept carver:

> you are all aware ... of the continual tribulation in carving at table, for appetites more or less colossal, and when all eyes are fixed upon you with anxious avidity. Very few persons are perfect in this useful art ... it certainly often happens that the greatest gourmet is the worst carver, and complains sadly during that very long process, saying to himself, 'I am last to be served; my dinner will be cold.'

Although servants were at hand, standing behind their master or mistress to change the plates and cutlery and bring wine, gentlemen were expected to serve their lady companions before themselves from the dishes close by. It was thought impolite to stretch or demand a dish at the other end of the table.

Dinner *à la russe* not only shortened the length of the meal, but also increased the chances of the food staying hot. Carving and apportioning were carried out by the servants, hopefully more swiftly and skilfully, and the dishes were handed round in pairs or sets of alternatives. Although dishes no longer had to be so elaborately decorated as they were not displayed on the table, service *à la russe* focused more attention on individual dishes so that the standard of cooking had to be more sophisticated. There was usually a choice of two soups (one thick, one clear), two or three fish dishes, three or four entrées, several roasts with vegetables, a salad made by the butler, often a sorbet served between the roasts, four or five entremets, one or two entrées and finally dessert. The butler stood behind his master's chair and kept a careful eye on the table. As each course progressed, he judged the moment to ring the dining-room bell for the next course. It was vital that he should coordinate with the cook; having to wait between courses was regarded as bad form.

In the 1870s the 4th Earl of Onslow and his young wife Florence set about reviving the estate of their country house at Clandon Park, Surrey. Soon they had established a reputation for lavish hospitality. Lady Onslow recorded their guests and menus for formal lunches, dinners and suppers in her Dinner Book, which she kept intermittently until 1910, the year before the death of her husband. The dinners were usually for 16 or 18 and followed the pattern of a set menu with small seasonal changes. It seems unlikely that Sarah Rogers, the cook-housekeeper at Clandon, would have been able to produce the sophisticated dinners expected from this family in the highest circle of English society when entertaining, so probably a professional chef was brought in. Most entertaining at Clandon tended to be in the summer and the dinner was served in the Speakers' Parlour, the splendid ground-floor room which takes its name from the portraits of the three Onslow Speakers of the House of Commons that hang there. It became the dining-room at the beginning of the 19th century and still retains the decoration and furniture of that period; the large mahogany dining-table with its four extra leaves can seat up to 22. Food was carried upstairs from the basement kitchen immediately below and served from the large sideboard by liveried footmen under the watchful eye of Thomas Pick, the Onslows' butler.

The first menu in the Countess's Dinner Book was for dinner served *à la russe* to 16 guests on a chilly evening in June 1875:

The Speakers' Parlour, Clandon Park, Surrey. For the dinners given in the late 19th century by the 4th Earl and Lady Onslow, food was served from the large sideboard.

POTAGES

Julienne. Purée de Petits Pois.

POISSONS

Saumon, Sauce Tartar. Blanchaille.

ENTRÉES

Côtelettes de Riz de Veau à la Tina.
Côtelettes d'Agneau aux Petits Pois.
Foie Gras en Aspic.

RÔTIS

Selle de Mouton.
Chapons Jambon d'York.
Leverets. Cailles.

ENTREMETS

Creppes Froides. Gelée aux Fraises.
Boudin Glacé aux Abricots.
Pailles de Parmesan.
Glacés.

After the savoury, a dessert plate would have been placed before each guest, superimposed by an ice plate, a doyley and a finger-glass, half-filled with perfumed water (cold in summer and tepid in winter). An ice spoon and a dessert knife and fork were also on the dessert plate. Dinner glasses were replaced by two glasses for sherry and claret to drink with the dessert. The guests would have placed their finger-glass and doyley to their left and, once the ices had been eaten, the ice plates were removed leaving the dessert plates. Preserved ginger was frequently passed round to prepare the palate for the small glasses of liqueur, which might be handed to the guests on a salver.

Although the fruit for dessert had probably been on the table throughout the meal, guests had to wait for it to be served to them in the correct order of precedence. There were many rules about eating fruit, according to *Manners and Tone of Good Society*: 'When eating grapes, the half-closed hand should be placed to the lips, and the stones and skins adroitly allowed to fall into the fingers and quickly placed on the side of the plate, the back of the hand concealing the manoeuvres from view.' Cherries and other

Table setting *à la russe* by Mrs Beeton. All the dishes in the various courses were handed round by a retinue of servants, so that the table was filled with a veritable jungle of flowers, ferns and fruit, tastefully arranged.

fruit with stones would be eaten in the same way. Apples, pears and 'pines' had to be eaten with a dessert knife and fork, while peaches and melons required the aid of a spoon as well as a fork.

After the guests' glasses had been filled and before leaving the dining-room, the butler would place a claret-jug and two decanters of sherry in front of the host. He would then pass it round, commencing with the gentleman nearest to him. It was no longer the fashion for gentlemen to toast each other at dinner or dessert and they filled their glasses when they wished as the decanter did the rounds. A lady was not supposed to require a second glass of wine at dessert. If she did, the gentleman seated next to her would fill her glass; she would not help herself.

After the wine had been passed once around the table, or about ten minutes after the servants had left the dining-room, the hostess would give the signal for the ladies to leave, by bowing to the lady of highest rank present. She would then rise from her seat, as would all the ladies who, after finishing their dessert, had commenced putting on their gloves. The gentlemen would remain standing by their chairs until the ladies had left. The gentlemen now turned to their claret, port and coffee. The ladies meanwhile made their way back upstairs to the drawing-room, where their coffee was served. It was no longer fashionable for the gentlemen to sit over their wine for more than 15 or 20 minutes, so once they had drunk their coffee, they joined the ladies and tea was served. There would be more polite conversation, or perhaps a guest would sing or play if the dinner was not too formal. At a country-house dinner-party a round of cards might be played. At about 10.30 pm, guests would make formal departures. The host would see the principal ladies to their carriages, helped by a gentleman friend or relation. Guests were expected to call on the host and hostess within a week to thank them.

By Edwardian times the fashionable dinner, like the table on which it was served, was becoming lighter and less elaborate. The number of dishes set before the diner had been reduced, and the dishes themselves were not so heavily decorated. As the great chef Escoffier said in *A Guide to Modern Cookery*, first published in 1907, 'dishes, therefore must be faultless to make up for this; they must be savoury and light'. Lady Jeune, a well-known society hostess, but also a 'modern woman' in revolt against extravagance and outdated customs, believed that 'No dinner should consist of more than eight dishes: soup, fish, entrée, joint, game, sweet, hors d'oeuvre and perhaps an ice, but each dish should be perfect of its kind.'

The hors d'oeuvre course became fashionable in Edwardian times. The idea of eating tasty trifles as an appetiser seems to have started in Russia, where guests helped themselves to caviare, salt herring, anchovies and other highly flavoured items, followed by Kummel and brandy from a sideboard in an ante-room before the announcement of dinner. In Britain, hors d'oeuvres in the form of sardines, anchovies, salamis, radishes, olives, smoked salmon and canapés had been introduced first by hotels and restaurants at the end of the 19th century as a convenient way of amusing the customer while his dinner was being prepared. Because of their popularity, they were adopted as a separate course in private households, although not generally written on the menu. Caviare, served very cold, oysters served with thin brown bread and butter, lemon mignonette (coarsely ground pepper) and horseradish powder were offered as alternatives. Iced melon served with caster sugar and powdered ginger appeared before 1914.

Service remained *à la russe*, so that as soon as diners were seated, the hors d'oeuvre was brought in by the footman or maid, while the butler served chablis or Sauterne. The courses that followed were very similar to their Victorian counterparts, though great importance was now attached to the entrée, termed the 'Cook's highwater mark' because it gave scope to the cook's talent in preparing and decorating 'made dishes'. 'Entrées', wrote C. Herman Senn in 1907, 'are generally looked upon as the most essential part of a dinner .... There may be dinners without Hors d'oeuvre, even without Soup, and without a Remove or Relevé, but there can be no well-balanced dinner without an Entrée course.' An entrée dish could be of vegetables, fish, meat, poultry (the most popular), and game, but its essence was that it was composed of more than one ingredient as distinct from solid meats with a garnish, and was served in decorated shapes and moulds. The entrée might consist of such tempting items as *Soufflé de Volaille à la Hollandaise*, *Huitres au Jambon Dubarry*, and *Escalopes de Venaison à la Polonaise*. At Erddig dinner-parties the dishes were simpler, such as Vol au Vent of Chicken, Chicken Shape and Oyster Patties. The entrée required no carving and was served as sent in from the kitchen, with claret or Burgundy.

The remove or *relevé* usually consisted of a substantial joint, served with two or three green vegetables and potatoes. Contemporary cookery books devoted increasing space to the preparation and service of vegetable dishes. Viola Bankes in her reminiscences, *A Kingston Lacy Childhood*, recalls some of the fresh vegetables brought from the garden to the kitchen door in the early years of this century: 'Basketfuls of old fashioned, black winter spinach were finely puréed through wire sieves, tender young runner beans sliced paper thin and potatoes made to look like rice, all served up when our mother was in residence, in magnificently polished silver dishes with silver compartments and silver lids.'

Favourite Edwardian sweets for dinner were pancackes, soufflés, charlottes, fruit flans and compotes, blancmanges, mousses, creams and bavarois. Savouries followed, although they were frequently omitted or served instead of a sweet at small dinners. Escoffier did not approve of savouries, feeling they had no place on a good menu, but cheese savouries were thought to act as a digestive or corrective to the previous courses. At a dinner of many courses, cheese on its own was seldom offered, but at a short or informal meal it was often substituted for the savoury. Two kinds were usually offered, as well as biscuits, pulled bread (pieces of crumb baked until crisp), small pats of butter, and sometimes celery.

When not entertaining, the dinners of even the wealthiest were relatively plain, consisting usually of one soup or fish, one remove – either poultry or a joint, one entrée, two vegetables, a pudding or a tart and a little dessert. At a middle-class dinner, if there was a choice of meats, one was probably yesterday's remains, either cold or made into a hash. Cold meat was accompanied only by boiled or mashed potatoes and bottled sauce with no salad.

For labourers in towns the diet could be very limited as few houses had anything more than an open fire for cooking. Food for them, therefore, needed to be easy to prepare but tasty and, if possible, hot: potatoes, boiled or roasted in their jackets, bacon which could be fried over the fire and eaten with bread spread with a little butter, and tea to give warmth and comfort. Roasts, broths, stews and puddings became for many town dwellers the Sunday feast, when they had the time to prepare and cook them. One of the advantages of urban life was the ready-made food from street stalls – hot peas, pies, chips, baked potatoes and muffins.

The pauper apprentices at Quarry Bank Mill had their dinner at 7pm after a full day working in the mill. Tables and benches were set out in the schoolroom, where the children were also taught to read and write. Dinner on weekdays was mainly boiled potatoes with a vegetable-based stew once or twice a week. Boiled pork was served as a treat on Sundays.

The agricultural worker in the south of England, particularly at the beginning of Victoria's reign, existed on a scanty and monotonous diet of bread, dumplings, boiled potatoes, root vegetables and weak tea for dinner. 'Meat' would be salt pork or bacon; fresh meat was scarcely ever seen unless it was a poached hare or rabbit. In the north, conditions were better because milk and butter as well as eggs were available to the labourer to make his diet a little less monotonous.

For the wealthy, as the fashion for giving late dinners became established, so substantial hot suppers declined. The ideal supper was now light, wholesome and attractive to look at: cold meats, pies, potted meats and sandwiches, sausage rolls, galantine, patties and salads, particularly of salmon, crab or lobster. Hot soup might begin the meal. Creams, custards and jellies, followed by ices, fresh fruit, sweetmeats, light sponge cakes and biscuits would complete it. For a large number of guests, standing suppers with the food arranged on a buffet, were popular. A fancy dress supper ball for at least 200 guests was held at Lanhydrock in January 1893. Dancing began at 10pm, continuing into the early hours of the morning. A report in the local paper read:

Great credit is due to the following who took an important part in making a large entertainment such as this a success. Mrs Condy, the housekeeper for providing a most *recherché* supper, everything in season that could possibly be found, adorning

The Buffet by Jean Louis Forain. Supper balls with food arranged as a buffet became very much the fashion in late Victorian times.

the table and everything turned out with her own hands; Mr Richards, the butler, who has been in the family for upwards of forty years, for superintending the waiting with great tact and forethought; Mr Hawkin, the head gardener, for carrying out with exquisite taste all the decorations both in the ballroom and on the supper table. . . .

There is no record of the actual dishes that were served that January evening at Lanhydrock, but no doubt Mrs Beeton's advice would have been heeded on the choice and appearance of food: 'The colours and flavours of the various dishes should contrast nicely . . . . The garnishing of the dishes has also much to do with the appearance of a supper table . . . .' They should all be 'garnished sufficiently to be in good taste without looking absurd. The eye, in fact, should be as much gratified as the palate.'

As had been the custom over the centuries, the evening could be rounded off with music and games. At Erddig, Mrs Yorke recorded the amusements for supper given on 24 October 1911: 'Letter Game, Bridge in Saloon, Music in Hall. A very successful party: all went well.' On another occasion, 13 February 1913, the amusements provided were 'Philip [Yorke]'s Sketch Books, and Music in the Hall.'

Finally, the household could retire for the night. Mrs Beeton, ever-mindful of good regulation, warns, 'it is well to remember that early rising is almost impossible, if late going to bed be the order, or rather, disorder of the house'.

When the Yorkes were enjoying their musical evenings at Erddig, the outbreak of the First World War was barely eighteen months away. Life was never to be quite the same.

As with the South African War of 1899, the First World War pointed up the very poor nutritional state of the nation. Recruiters were horrified to discover how large a proportion of the population was seriously undernourished: 66 per cent of men called up were found to be of inferior health, including 11 per cent declared permanent invalids. All kinds of reforms were put in train as a result: it was no longer possible to dismiss nutrition and vitamins as interesting curiosities.

The First World War was without precedent for the British in terms of the carnage wrought. There was scarcely a family who did not lose a son, a father or a husband in the years between 1914 and 1918, and war proved no respecter of rank. Many of the National Trust houses mentioned in this book lost their sons and heirs: indeed, this often proved a factor in the estate passing to the National Trust following the establishment of the Country Houses Scheme in 1937. Adrian, eldest son of Julius and Frances Drewe, was killed in Flanders in 1917, serving in the Royal Field Artillery. His devastated parents established a Memorial Room in his honour at Castle Drogo which can be visited still. The heir to Lanhydrock, Tommy Agar-Robartes, died at the Battle of Loos in 1915. A pall of grief descended upon his eight brothers and sisters that coloured the rest of their lives. With the death in 1969 of Tommy's twin sister, Miss Eva, the last of the Robartes had gone from the lovely house and estate.

With the outbreak of the war in 1914, the immense army of servants that had run the great country houses began to melt away, as women as well as men were drawn into the war effort. And this army did not return. By the 1920s only well-to-do houses could afford the new kind of servants who demanded better wages and conditions. This had a tremendous effect on the development of kitchens and service quarters. At Kedleston, for instance, the Scarsdales abandoned the great kitchen pavilion built by Robert Adam in the 18th century, eventually converting bedrooms in the family pavilion into a small kitchen, next to a new, small dining-room.

James Lees-Milne poignantly illustrates this social change in his diaries. Appointed the National Trust's Secretary to the Country Houses Committee in 1936, he was responsible for the transfer of many historic houses and estates to the National Trust. In *Ancestral Voices*, he describes a visit in October 1942 (in the midst of the Second World War), to Stourhead, the great 18th-century house and garden in Wiltshire. Sir Henry and Lady Hoare had lost their only child, Harry, killed in action in Palestine, in 1917. Now they were considering giving their estate to the National Trust:

> Sir Henry is an astonishing nineteenth-century John Bull, hobbling on two sticks .... Lady Hoare is an absolute treasure, and unique ...: dressed in a long black skirt, belled from a wasp waist and trailing over her ankles.
>
> For dinner we had soup, whiting, pheasant, apple pie, dessert, a white Rhine wine and port. Lady Hoare has no housemaid, and only a cook and butler. But she said with satisfaction, 'The Duchess of Somerset at Maiden Bradley has to do all her own cooking'.

SELECT BIBLIOGRAPHY

General

Aylett, Mary and Ordish, Olive, *First Catch your Hare*, 1965
Ayrton, Elisabeth, *The Cookery of England*, 1974
Brett, Gerard, *Dinner is Served*, 1968
Black, Maggie, *A Heritage of British Cookery*, 1977
Brooke, Sheena, *Hearts and Home*, 1973
Burnett, John, *Plenty and Want*, 1966
Clair, Colin, *Kitchen and Table*, 1964
Cooper, Charles, *The English Table in History and Literature*, 1931
Davidson, Caroline, *A Woman's Work is Never Done*, 1982
Drummond, J.C., and Wilbraham, Anne, *The Englishman's Food*, 1939
Fussell, G.E, and K.R., *The Englishman Countryman from Tudor Times to the Victorian Age*, 1955
Girouard, Mark, *Life in the English Country House*, 1978
Hardyment, Christina, *From Mangle to Microwave*, 1988
Hardyment, Christina, *Home Comfort: A History of Domestic Arrangements*, 1992
Harrison, Molly, *The Kitchen In History*, 1972
Hartley, Dorothy, *Food in England*, 1954
Hole, Christina, *English Home Life, 1500–1800*, 2nd ed., 1949
Hutchins, Sheila, *English Recipes and Others*, 1967
Ketcham Wheaton, Barbara, *Savouring the Past*, 1983
McKendrey, Maxime, *Seven Hundred Years of English Cookery*, 1983
Mennell, Stephen, *All Manners of Food*, 1985
Moss, Peter, *Meals through the Ages*, 1958
Norwak, Mary, *Kitchen Antiques*, 1979
Palmer, Arnold, *Movable Feasts*, 1984
Price, Rebecca, *The Compleat Cook*, intro. Madeleine Masson, 1974
Price, Bernard, *The Story of English Furniture*, 1978
Pullar, Philippa, *Consuming Passions*, 1970
Stewart, Katie, *Cooking and Eating*, 1975
Tannahill, Reay, *Food in History*, 1973
Wilson, C. Anne, *Food and Drink in Britain*, 1973
Wilson, C. Anne (ed.), *The Appetites and the Eye*, 1990
Yarwood, Doreen, *The British Kitchen*, 1981

Good Lordship and Feasting
MEDIEVAL AND EARLY TUDOR FOOD

Ashley, Sir William, *The Bread of our Forefathers*, 1928
Austin, Thomas (ed.), *Two Fifteenth Century Cookery Books* (Harleian Mss 279 and 4016, *c*.1450), 1888
Berners, Dame Juliana (attrib.), *Treatyse of Fysshynge with an Angle*, 15th century
Biblesworth, Walter de, *Treatise* ed. T. Wright, *A Volume of Vocabularies*, 1857
Boorde, Dr Andrew, *A Compendyous Regiment, or A Dyettary of Helth*, 1542, ed. Frederick J. Furnivall, 1870
Brome, John, Accounts for Baddesley Clinton, 1442–58, Shakespeare Birthplace Trust
Bryene, Dame Alice de, *The Household Book of Dame Alice de Bryene of Acton Hall, Suffolk, Sept.1412–Sept.1413*, trans. M.K. Dale and ed. V.B. Redstone, 1931
Buxton, Moira, *Medieval Cooking Today*, 1983
Caxton, William, *The Noble Boke of Curtasye* (including *The Babees Book of Manners*), 1475 (see also Furnivall, Frederick J.)
Cogan, Thomas, *The Haven of Health ... Augmented*, 1612
Coppack, Glyn, *Abbeys and Priories*, 1990
Dyer, Christopher, *Standards of Living in the later Middle Ages*, 1989
Elyot, Sir Thomas, *The Castel of Helth ... Augmented*, 1539
Fastolf, Sir John, Accounts for Caister Castle, Shakespeare Birthplace Trust
Fitzstephen, William, *Description of London*, *c*.1183
Forme of Cury, *c*.1390 (see also Warner, R.)
Furnivall, Frederick J. (ed.), *Early English Meals and Manners* (including Caxton, *The Noble Boke of Curtasye*, Wynkyn de Worde, *Boke of Kervynge* and John Russell, *Boke of Nurture*), 1868
Goodwin, Gillian, *Manchet and Trencher*, 1983
Heiatt and Butler, *Curye on Inglysch*, 1985
Jeaffreson, J.C., *A Book about the Table*, 1875
Knowles, D., *The Monastic Orders in England, 914–1216*, 1949

Langland, William, *Vision of Piers Plowman*, 1367–70, ed. A.V.C. Schmidt and D.A. Pearsall, 1978
Luttrell Papers, Dunster Castle, Somerset Record Office, Taunton, 1420
Mayster Ion Gardener, 'The feate of gardening', ed. Hon. A.M.T. Amherst, *Archaeologia*, 1894
Mead, William Edward, *The English Medieval Feast*, 1931
Myddelton Papers, Chirk Castle, 14th century, National Library of Wales, Aberystwyth
Neckham, Alexander, *De Utensilibus*, 12th century, ed. T. Wright in *A Volume of Vocabularies*, 1857
Northumberland, Henry Percy, 5th Earl of, *The Regulations and Establishment of the Household of Henry Algernon Percy ... 1512*, new ed. 1905
Paston Family, *The Paston Letters 1422–1509*, ed. Norman Davis, 1st edition., 1971
Riley, H.T., *Memorials of London, 1276–1419*, 1868
Russell, John, *Boke of Nurture*, *c*.1450 (see also Furnivall, Frederick J.)
Tannhaüser, *Höfzucht*, 14th-century poem of manners
Thurley, Simon, *The 16th-century Kitchens at Hampton Court*, reprinted 1990
Tusser, Thomas, *A Hundredth Good Pointes of Husbandrie*, 1557, new ed. 1810
Warner, Richard, *Antiquitates Culinariae: Tracts on Culinary Affairs of the Old English* (including *Forme of Cury*), 1791
Worde, Wynkyn de, *Boke of Kervynge*, 1508 (see also Furnivall, Frederick J.)
Wood, Margaret, *The English Medieval House*, 1965

Suckets and Marchpane
ELIZABETHAN FOOD

Aikin, Lucy, *Memoirs of the Court of Queen Elizabeth*, 1819
Amherst, Hon. Alicia M.T., *A History of Gardening in England*, 1896
Anon., *A Proper Newe Book of Cokerye*, *c*.1540, ed. C.F. Frere, 1913
Anon., *The Good Huswives Handmaid, for Cookerie in her Kitchin*, 1597
Anon., *The Good Hous-wives Treasurie*, 1588
Anon., *The Newe Jewell of Health*, 1576

Anon., *The Profittable Arte of Gardening*, 1563
Anon., *A Booke of Cookery very Necessary to all such as Delight Therein*, 1584
Boorde, Dr Andrew, *A Compendyous Regyment, or A Dyettary of Helth*, 1542, ed. Frederick J. Furnivall, 1870
Boynton, Lindsay, and Thornton, Peter (ed.), *The Hardwick Hall Inventories of 1601*, Journal of the Furniture History Society, Vol.VII, 1971
Braithwaite, Richard, *Some Rules & Orders for the Government of the House of an Earl*, early 17th century
Carew, Richard, *Survey of Cornwall*, 1602
Cogan, Thomas, *The Haven of Health*, 1584
Dawson, Thomas, *The Good Huswifes Jewell ... with Additions*, 1596
Durant, David N., *Bess of Hardwick*, 1977
Elyot, Sir Thomas, *The Castel of Helth ... Augmented*, 1539
Emmison, F.G., *Tudor Secretary: Sir William Petre at Court and Home*, 1961
Emmison, F.G., *Tudor Food and Pastimes*, 1964
Gerard, John, *The Herball or Generall Historie of Plantes*, 1597
Girouard, Mark, *Robert Smythson and the Elizabethan Country House*, 1983
Hakluyt, Richard, *Principal Navigations, Voiages, and Discoveries of the English Nation*, 1589; enlarged ed. 3 vols, 1598–1600
Harrison, William, *An Historical Description of the Island of Britayne, etc.*, 1577, ed. Frederick J. Furnivall and Withington, L., *Description of England in Shakespeare's Youth*, 1902
Hentzner, Paul, *A Journey into England in the Year 1598*
Markham, Gervase, *The English Huswife*, 1615
Nichols, John, *The Progresses and Public Processions of Queen Elizabeth*, 3 vols, 1823
Northumberland, Henry Algernon Percy, 9th Earl of, *The Household Papers*, ed. G.R. Bath, 1962
Partridge, John, *The Treasurie of Commodious Conceits and Hidden Secrets*, 1584
Platt, Sir Hugh, *Delightes for Ladies*, 1605
Puttenham, George, *Art of English Poesie*, 1589

Rawson, Maud Stepney, *Bess of Hardwick*, 1910
St John Hope, W. H., *Cowdray and Easebourne Priory*, 1919
Salzman, L. F., *England in Tudor Times*, 1926
Sass, Lorna, *The Queen's Taste*, 1977
Scot, Reginald, *Perfite Platforme of a Hoppe Garden*, 1574
Seager, Francis, *Schoole of Vertue and Booke of Goode Nourture for Chyldren*, 1557, ed. Frederick J. Furnivall, 1868
Spurling, Hilary (ed.), *Elinor Fettiplace's Receipt Book*, 1604
Symonds, R. W., 'The Dyning Parlor and its Furniture', *The Connoisseur*, 1944
Turbevile, George, *The Noble Art of Venerie of Hunting*, 1575
Tusser, Thomas, *Five Hundredth Pointes of Good Husbandrie*, 1559
Vaughan, Dr William, *Directions for Health*, 1600
Wilson, C. Anne, (ed.), 'Banquetting Stuffe', 1991
Woodward, Marcus (ed.), *Leaves from Gerard's Herball*, 1972

Sweet Herbs and Strong Bitter Brews
STUART FOOD

à Wood, Anthony, *Diaries*, 1650
Aubrey, John, *Brief Lives*, c.1680
Bankes Family Archives, Dorset County Record Office, Dorchester
Berry, Elizabeth K., (ed.), *Henry Ferrers, an early Warwickshire Antiquary, 1550–1633*, Dugdale Society Occasional Papers, No. 16
Birkett, Elizabeth, *A Commonplace Book*, 1699
Bradley, Richard, *The Country Housewife and Lady's Director*, 6th edition., 1727–32
Browne Papers, Townend, Cumbria Record Office, Kendal
Clifford, Lady Anne, *Diaries*, ed. D. J. H. Clifford, 1990
Cogan, Thomas, *The Haven of Health*, 1584
Cromwell, Elizabeth, *The Court and Kitchin of Elizabeth*, 1664
Digby, Sir Kenelm, *The Closet of the Eminently Learned Sir Kenelme Digbie, Kt. Opened*, 1699, ed. A. Macdonnell, 1910
Evelyn, John, *Diary*, ed. E. S. de Beer, 6 vols, 1955
Evelyn, John, *Acetaria*, 1699
Henry Ferrers, an early Warwickshire Antiquary, 1550–1633, Dugdale Society Occasional Papers, No. 16, ed. E. K. Berry
Harrison, William, *Descriptions of England*, 1577
Hinton, R. W. K., *The Eastland Trade*, 1959

Hole, Christina, *The English Housewife in the Seventeenth Century*, 1953
Holme, Randle, *Academy of Armory*, 1688
Jackson-Stops, Gervase, *The English Country House in Perspective*, 1990
Ketton-Cremer, R. W., *Felbrigg: The Story of a House*, 1962
Lamb, Patrick, *Royal Cookery*, 1710
Markham, Gervase, *Farewell to Husbandry*, 1620
Markham, Gervase, *The English Huswife*, 1615
May, Robert, *The Accomplisht Cook*, 1660
Misson, F. M., *Memoirs and Observations on his Travels over England in 1696*, trans. J. Ozell, 1719
Murrell, John, *A New Booke of Cookerie*, 1st ed., 1614
Murrell, John, *A Delightfull Daily Exercise For Ladies and Gentlewomen*, 1st ed., 1617
Myddelton, W. M. (ed.), *Chirk Castle Accounts, Vol.I 1605–66*, 1908 *Vol.II 1666–1753*, 1931
North, Roger, *Treatise on Houseplanning*, end of 17th century
Northumberland, Henry Algernon Percy, 9th Earl of, household accounts in *The Petworth Archives, Vols I and II*, ed. Alison McCann, 1979
Parkinson, John, *Herball*, 1630
Parkinson, John, *Paradisi in Sole, Paradisus Terrestris*, 1629
Pepys, Samuel, *Diary*, ed. R. Latham and W. Matthews, 11 vols, 1970–83
Pratt, James Norwood, *The Tea Lovers' Treasury*, 1982
Rose, Giles, *A Perfect School of Instructions for the Officers of the Mouth* (Escole parfaite des officers de bouche), 1682
Sackville-West, Vita, *Knole and the Sackvilles*, 1922
Thompson, Gladys Scott, *Life in a Noble Household 1641–1700*, 1937
Woolley, Hannah, *The Accomplisht Lady's Delight*, 1685
Woolley, Hannah, *The Queen-Like Closet*, 1670
Worlidge, John, *Vinetum Britannicus*, 1676

An Elegant Repast
GEORGIAN FOOD

Anson Papers, Shugborough Estate, County Record Office, Stafford
Baillie, Lady Grisell, *The Household Book, 1692–1733*, ed. R. Scott-Moncrieff, 1911
Bayne-Powell, Rosamund, *Housekeeping in the Eighteenth Century*, 1956
Boswell, James, *London Journal*, ed. F. A. Pottle, 1763
Bradley, Richard, *The Country Housewife and Lady's Director*, 6th ed., 1736

Burney, Fanny, *Letters and Journals*, 10 vols, ed. Joyce Hemlow, 1972–81
Byng, John, *The Torrington Diaries*, ed. C. Bruyn Andrews, 1954
Campbell, Robert, *The London Tradesman*, 1969
Carter, Charles, *Complete Practical Cook*, 1730
Carter, Charles, *Complete City and Country Cook*, 1732
Creevey, Thomas, *The Creevey Papers*, ed. Sir H. Maxwell, 2 vols, 1903
Cruickshank, Dan, and Burton, Neil, *Life in the Georgian City*, 1990
Rochefoucauld, François De La, *A Frenchman In England, 1784*, ed. J. Marchand, 1933
Defoe, Daniel, *Tour through the Whole Island of Great Britain 1724–6*, 3 vols, 1927
Eales, Mary, *Receipts*, 1718
Ellis, William, *The Country Housewife's Family Companion*, 1750
Fletcher, Ronald, *The Parkers at Saltram 1769–89*, 1970
Glasse, Hannah, *The Art of Cookery made Plain and Easy*, 1747
Hanway, Jonas, *An Essay on Tea*, 1757
Hickman, Peggy, *A Jane Austen Household Book with Martha Lloyd's Recipes*, 1978
Hussey, Christopher, *English Country Houses: Mid-Georgian 1760–1800*, 1956
Kalm, Per, *Account of his Visit to England … in 1748*, trans. J. Lucas, 1892
Lybbe Powys, Mrs Philip, *Passages from the Diaries of Mrs Lybbe Powys, 1756–1808*, ed. E. J. Climenson, 1899
Mandeville, Bernard, *The Fable of the Bees*, 1724
Mavor, William Fordyce, *British Tourists (including Moritz, Travels through Various parts of England in 1782)*, 4 vols, 1798
Meade-Fetherstonhaugh, Margaret, and Warner, Oliver, *Uppark and Its People*, 1964
Ozell (trans.), *Misson's Memoirs and Observations on his Travels over England*, 1696
Porter, Roy, *English Society in the Eighteenth Century*, 1982
Powell, Rosamund Bayne, *Housekeeping in the Eighteenth Century*, 1956
Pückler-Muskau, Prince Herman von, *Tour in England, Ireland and France in the years 1826–1829*, 4 vols, 1832
Raffald, Elizabeth, *The Experienced English Housekeeper*, 1769
Rundell, Maria, *A New System of Domestic Cookery; … adapted to the Use of Private Families*, 1807
Saltram Household Accounts, Plymouth Record Office
Smith, Eliza, *The Compleat Housewife or Accomplished Gentlewoman's Companion*, 1727

Smith, Mary, *The Complete Housekeeper and Professed Cook*, 1772
Smollett, Tobias, *The Expedition of Humphry Clinker*, 1771
Smollett, Tobias, *Travels through France and Italy*, 1766
Swift, Jonathan, *Directions to the Servants*, 1745
Swift, Jonathan, *Journal of Stella*, 1711
Trusler, Rev. John, *The Honours of the Table*, 1788
Verney, Lady Margaret, (ed.), *The Verney Letters of the Eighteenth Century*, 2 vols, 1930
Walpole, Horace, *Diary*, 42 vols, 1937–81
Walpole, Horace, *Journal of Visits to Country Seats, etc.*, Walpole Society, 1928
Waterson, Merlin, *The Servants' Hall: a domestic history of Erddig*, 1980
Whatman, Susanna, *The Housekeeping Book of 1776*, ed. C. Hardyment, 1987
Woodforde, Rev. James, *The Diary of a Country Parson*, ed. John Beresford, 1924–31
Yorke Papers, Erddig, Clwyd Record Office
Young, Arthur, *Annals of Agriculture*, 47 vols, 1784–1809

The Well-Ordered Table
VICTORIAN AND EDWARDIAN FOOD

Acland, Anne, *A Devon Family – The Story of the Aclands*, 1981
Acton, Eliza, *Modern Cookery in all its Branches*, 1845
Acton, Eliza, *The English Bread Book*, 1857
Anon., *The Servant's Practical Guide*, 1880
Anon. ['A member of the aristocracy'], *Manners and Tone of Good Society*, n.d. [10th ed., c.1882]
Aslett, Clive, *The Last Country Houses*, 1982
Astor, Michael, *Tribal Feelings*, 1963
Bankes, Viola, *A Kingston Lacy Childhood*, 1986
Beale, Mary, *Wholesome Cookery*, 6th ed., 1895
Beeton, Isabella, *The Book of Household Management*, 1861
Berriedale-Johnson, Michelle, *The Victorian Cook Book*, 1989
Black, Mrs, *Household Cookery and Laundry Work*, 1882
Blake, Robert, *Disraeli*, 1966
Brillat-Savarin, Anthelme, *A Handbook of Gastronomy* (trans.), 1884
Brotherton, Martha, *Vegetarian Cookery Book*, 1866
Cobbett, Anne, *The English Housekeeper*, 1851
Cobbett, William, *Rural Rides*, 1830
Collis, Maurice, *Nancy Astor*, 1960

Davies, Jennifer, *The Victorian Kitchen*, 1989

Day, Charles William, *Etiquette and the Usages of Society*, 1824

Dolby, Richard, *Dictionary of Cookery*, 1830

Escoffier, Auguste, *Guide Culinaire*, 1903, trans. as *A Guide to Modern Cookery*, 1907

Fairfax-Lucy, Alice, *Charlecote and the Lucys*, 1958

Fairfax-Lucy, Alice, *Mistress of Charlecote: the Memoirs of Mary Elizabeth Lucy*, 1983

Francatelli, Charles Elmé, *The Cook's Guide and the Housekeeper's and Butler's Assistant*, 1862

Francatelli, Charles Elmé, *A Plain Cookery Book for the Working Classes*, 1852

Franklin, Jill, *The Gentleman's Country House and its Plan 1835–1914*, 1981

Freeman, Sarah, *Mutton and Oysters*, 1989

Girouard, Mark, *The Victorian Country House*, rev. ed. 1979

Hartcup, Adeline, *Below Stairs in Great Country Houses*, 1980

Hare, Augustus, *The Story of my Life*, 6 vols, 1896–1900

Hayward, Abraham, *The Art of Dining*, 1851

Hooper, Mary, *Handbook for the Breakfast Table*, 1873

Horne, Pamela, *The Rise and Fall of the Victorian Servant*, 1986

Keith, Edward, *Memories of Wallington*, 1939

Kerr, Robert, *The Gentleman's House*, 1864

Kettner, E. S. Dallas, *Book of the Table*, 1877

Kitchiner, Dr William, *The Cook's Oracle*, 1817

Lankester, Edwin, *Vegetable Substances Used for the Food of Man*, 1846

Lees-Milne, James, *Ancestral Voices*, 1975

Lenox-Conyngham, Mina, *An Old Ulster House*, 1946

Loftie, Mrs, *The Dining-room*, 1878

Loudon, John Claudius, *Encyclopaedia of Cottage, Farm and Villa Architecture and Furniture*, 1833

Maling, Miss, *Flowers And How to Arrange Them*, 1862

Mayhew, Henry, *Selections from London Labour and London Poor*, 1851

Montgomery Hyde, H., *Henry James at Home*, 1969

Nichols, Beverley, *Down the Kitchen Sink*, 1975

Rundell, Mrs, *A New System of Domestic Cookery*, 1807

Sinclair, Sir John, *The Code of Health and Longevity*, 1807

Soyer, Alexis, *The Gastronomic Regenerator*, 1845

Soyer, Alexis, *The Modern Housewife*, 1849

Soyer, Alexis, *A Shilling Cookery for the People*, 1855

Sykes, Christopher, *Nancy – The Life of Lady Astor*, 1972

Thompson, F. M. L., *English Landed Society in the Nineteenth Century*, 1963

Trevelyan, Sir Charles, *Wallington: its history and treasures*, 1939

Walsh, J. H., *A Manual of Domestic Economy*, 1879

LIST OF PLATES

The author and publishers would like to acknowledge the many institutions and individuals who have granted permission to reproduce their material in these pages.

Please note that figures in **bold** refer to page numbers.

NTPL – National Trust Photographic Library
NT – National Trust Regional Libraries and Archives

US CONVERSION TABLE

Information very kindly provided by the Good Housekeeping Institute

Dry Measures

1 US cup	=	50 g	=	2 oz of:	breadcrumbs; fresh cake crumbs
1 US cup	=	75 g	=	3 oz of:	rolled oats
1 US cup	=	90 g	=	$3\frac{1}{2}$ oz of:	desiccated coconut; ground almonds
1 US cup	=	100 g	=	4 oz of:	suet; grated hard cheese; walnut pieces; drinking chocolate; icing sugar; cocoa; flaked almonds; pasta; frozen peas
1 US cup	=	125 g	=	5 oz of:	white flour; self-raising flour; currants; muesli; chopped dates; ground roasted almonds
1 US cup	=	150 g	=	$5\frac{1}{2}$ oz of:	wholemeal flour; raisins; cornflour
1 US cup	=	175 g	=	6 oz of:	apricots; mixed peel; sultanas
1 US cup	=	200 g	=	7 oz of:	caster sugar; soft brown sugar; demerara sugar; glacé cherries; lentils; long grain and brown rice; flaked and drained tuna fish
1 US cup	=	225 g	=	$\frac{1}{2}$ lb of:	cream cheese; cottage cheese
1 US cup	=	300 g	=	11 oz of:	mincemeat; marmalade
1 US cup	=	350 g	=	12 oz of:	syrup; treacle; jam

Liquid Measures

$\frac{1}{4}$ US cup	=	60 ml	=	2 fluid oz
1 US cup	=	240 ml	=	8 fluid oz
2 US cups (1 US pint)	=	480 ml	=	16 fluid oz

Butter, Lard and Margarine Measures

$\frac{1}{4}$ stick	=	25 g	=	2 level tablespoons	=	1 oz
1 stick ($\frac{1}{2}$ US cup)	=	100 g	=	8 level tablespoons	=	4 oz

INDEX